VW
Owners
Workshop
Manual

by J H Haynes
Member of the Guild of Motoring Writers
and K F Kinchin

Models covered:

UK: VW Golf 1093 & 1471 cc
            VW Scirocco 1471 cc
USA: VW Rabbit 89.7 cu in (1471 cc)
            VW Scirocco 89.7 cu in (1471 cc)

Covers all versions of above.
Does not cover 1588 cc (97 cu in) models.

ISBN 0 85696 284 8

Printed in England

J H Haynes and Company Limited
Sparkford Yeovil Somerset England
distributed in the USA by
Haynes Publications Inc
9421 Winnetka Avenue
Chatsworth Los Angeles
California 91311 USA

Acknowledgements

Special thanks are due to the VW Organization for their assistance with technical information and the supply of certain illustrations. Castrol Limited provided the lubrication details.

Car Mechanics magazine kindly provided many of the photographs used in the bodywork repair sequence of Chapter 13.

Lastly thanks to all of those at Sparkford who helped in the production of this manual. To Brian Horsfall who took the vehicle to pieces and offered much valued advice on how best to assemble it again. To Les Brazier, who photographed the operations and to Rod Grainger, the editor, who gave much good advice and help in producing the manuscript.

About this manual

Introduction

The Volkswagen Golf and its other close relatives, the Scirocco and the Rabbit, have a design based on scientific research. The bodywork layout is the result of experimental construction and testing on the E.S.V. (experimental safety vehicle) which has produced a very strong and safe bodyshell having most attractive lines.

Although the vehicle has been in production for a relatively short period the number of modifications has passed the hundred mark, so improvement is going along all the while. We have incorporated details of these modifications in the text. Most of them deal with minor improvements to components and revised tolerances and limits. One or two emphasise the importance of disconnecting the battery before working on the electrical circuits.

We took all the major components of one of these cars to pieces and rebuilt them. No special tools were used, although some time and exasperation could have been saved if we had had access to them, so we have pointed out where special tools are invaluable.

There are some jobs which cannot be done by the D-I-Y owner because they involve jigs and measuring instruments which are not available outside the VW/Audi organization. In these cases we have pointed out why the job should not be undertaken.

The vehicle is a fine piece of engineering which needs looking after if it is to give of its best. We hope that the owner may be helped by getting out the *Haynes* manual.

Its use

The book is divided into thirteen Chapters. Each Chapter is divided into numbered Sections which are headed in **bold** type between horizontal lines. Each Section consists of serially numbered paragraphs.

Procedures, once described in the text, are not normally repeated. If it is necessary to refer to a particular paragraph in another Chapter the reference is self-explanatory (eg; 'Chapter 1/5:5'). Cross-references given without the use of the word 'Chapter' apply to a Section in the same Chapter (eg; 'See Section 8' means also 'in this Chapter').

All illustrations carry a caption. Where the illustration is designated as a Figure the reference is merely a sequence number for the Chapter. Where the illustration is not designated as a Figure (ie; photographs) the reference number pinpoints the relevant Section and paragraph of the Chapter in which the photograph appears.

When the left or right side of the vehicle is mentioned it is as if looking forward from the rear of the car.

Whilst every care is taken to ensure that the information in this manual is correct no liability can be accepted by the authors or publishers for loss, damage or injury caused by any errors in, or omissions from, the information given.

Special tools and meters

1   This car has been made to metric sizes. All the threads are metric, except on the air-conditioner, which is the one unit you cannot service. You will therefore require spanners to fit metric sizes. We also recommend the acquisition of Allen keys in the following sizes: 6, 8, 10, 11 and 12 mm.

2   A torque wrench must be used (0 to 60 lb ft/0 to 8 kg m), if serious work is contemplated.

3   Although we have tried to produce workable limits in Imperial measure the fact remains that the makers tolerances are all in metric measure so a set of metric feeler gauges will help to set tolerances really accurately.

4   The extractor for the gearbox bearings is almost essential if the gearbox is to be dismantled. In every official agents workshop there is a special tool board on which all these 'goodies' are mounted. It is just possible that they might let a good customer look at the board to see what these tools are like.

5   Finally, the question of meters. We have referred in various places to strobe lights, dwell meters, pressure gauges with adapters, internal micrometers, voltmeters, ammeters, ohmmeters and tachometers. These cost a lot of money. Without them some jobs cannot be done properly. Possibly a VW/Audi owners club would be prepared to invest in them. If you are going to buy them yourself, start with a voltmeter and tachometer. Then a strobe light and dwell meter. It opens up a whole new range of Christmas presents for the man, or woman, who has everything! And intelligently used, they will pay for themselves in terms of fuel consumption and servicing bills.

Contents

Volkswagen Golf (UK)

Volkswagen Scirocco TS (UK)

Volkswagen Rabbit (USA)

Buying spare parts
and vehicle identification numbers

Buying spare parts

Spare parts are available from many sources, for example: VW garages, other garages and accessory shops, and motor factors. Our advice regarding spare part sources is as follows:

Officially appointed VW garages - This is the best source of parts which are peculiar to your vehicle and are otherwise not generally available (eg; complete cylinder heads, internal gearbox components, badges, interior trim etc). It is also the only place at which you should buy parts if your car is still under warranty - non-VW components may invalidate the warranty. To be sure of obtaining the correct parts it will always be necessary to give the storeman your car's engine and chassis number, and if possible, to take the 'old' part along for positive identification. Remember that many parts are available on a factory exchange scheme - any parts returned should always be clean! It obviously makes good sense to go straight to the specialists on your car for this type of part for they are best equipped to supply you.

Other garages and accessory shops - These are often very good places to buy materials and components needed for the maintenance of your car (eg; oil filters, spark plugs, bulbs, fan belts, oils and greases, touch-up paint, filler paste etc). They also sell general accessories, usually have convenient opening hours, charge lower prices and can often be found not far from home.

Motor factors - Good factors will stock all of the more important components which wear out relatively quickly (eg; clutch components, pistons, valves, exhaust system, brake cylinders/pipes/hoses/seals/shoes and pads etc). Motor factors will often provide new or reconditioned components on a part exchange basis - this can save a considerable amount of money.

Vehicle identification numbers

It is most important to identify the vehicle accurately when ordering spare parts or asking for information. There have been over one hundred modifications to this range already.

The vehicle identification plate is on the top of the frame by the radiator (photo). *The chassis number is* on the top of the right-hand front suspension strut housing (photo). *The engine number* on the 1.5 litre is on the cylinder block just above the distributor. On the 1.1 litre it is below the distributor on the end of the cylinder block. *The transmission code* is stamped on the top of the flange where the transmission joins the engine.

These numbers should be identified and recorded by the owner, they are required when ordering spares, going through the customs, and regrettably, by the police, if the vehicle is stolen.

When ordering spares remember that VW output is such that inevitably spares vary, are duplicated, and are held on a usage basis. If the storeman does not have the correct identification, he cannot produce the correct item. It is a good idea to take the old part if possible to compare it with a new one. The storeman has many customers to satisfy, so be accurate and patient. In some cases, particularly in the brake system, more than one manufacturer supplies an assembly eg; both Teves and Girling supply front calipers. The assemblies are interchangeable but the integral parts are not, although both use the same brake pads. This is only one of the pitfalls in the buying of spares, so be careful to make an ally of the storeman. When fitting accessories it is best to fit VW recommended ones. They are designed specifically for the vehicle.

The vehicle identification plate is just above the radiator

The chassis number is on top of the right-hand front suspension strut

The engine number on the 1.5 litre is just above the distributor on the cylinder block. On the 1.1 litre it is just below the distributor on the end of the block

Routine maintenance

This is a subject on which much is written but often little done. The amount of maintenance required depends on the life the car leads. A vehicle which is in use everyday in all weathers needs regular attention. One which goes out on Sundays only will get along better if it is left alone for considerable periods. There is such a thing as over-maintenance. The following schedule is for a hard driven workhorse. If regular use is made of official agents' computerised diagnosis service, only daily and weekly maintenance is necessary.

1 Daily maintenance

1 Check engine oil level
2 Check coolant level
3 Check tyre pressures
4 Check that all lights work

2 Weekly maintenance

1 Check the brake fluid level
2 Examine the tyres for cuts and uneven wear
3 Check the fluid level in the washer tank
4 Check the battery electrolyte
5 Check the alternator drivebelt tension
6 Check the air pump drivebelt (if fitted)
7 Inspect the engine compartment for oil or coolant leaks, loose nuts and bolts and fraying hoses
8 Clean out the interior of the car
9 Wash all mud off the body and dry with a chamois leather
10 Clean all the windows

3 Monthly maintenance

As for weekly maintenance plus the following (place the vehicle on a hoist or over a pit):

1 Examine the underside of the vehicle for, rusting, damage from stones and oil leaks
2 Check brake hydraulic hoses for chafing and hydraulic pipes for damage or leakage
3 Inspect the rear brake lining for thickness
4 Check the front disc pads for wear
5 Check the steering joints for wear
6 Check the front wheel bearings for wear
7 Examine the engine and gearbox mountings
8 Measure the clutch free-play
9 Inspect silencers and silencer fastenings
10 Inspect contact breaker points and adjust as necessary

4 Every 5,000 miles (7500 km)

1 Change engine oil and fit new filter
2 Check the level of the oil in the gearbox
3 Examine air cleaner and service it
4 Examine spark plugs and service them
5 Check fuel filters

6 Check valve clearance
7 Lubricate door hinges, locks and catches

5 Every 20,000 miles (30,000 km)

1 Have the steering geometry checked
2 Have the compression checked
3 Have the dwell angle checked
4 Have the headlamp beams checked for alignment and intensity
5 Have the ignition timing checked and check operation of the advance and retard mechanism

6 Maintenance of bodywork and fittings

The ultimate trade-in value of the vehicle will depend on the condition of the bodywork. Regular washing and application of wax at three month intervals will take care of the paintwork and chrome. Clean out the interior weekly and remove the mats for cleaning. Check that the interior of the car is dry. Brush the seats and clean with a vacuum cleaner. Deal with all minor bodywork damage right away (see Chapter 12) and remove tar or other soiling before it attacks the paintwork. The vehicle should be kept in an unheated garage. Try not to leave ot covered with rainwater. Sponge the water off and wipe dry if possible before locking the garage.

Filling the engine with oil

Filling the gearbox

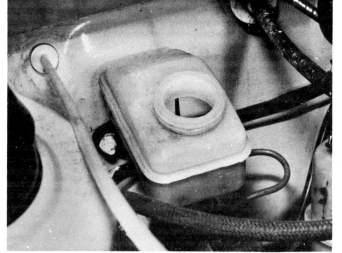

Top-up the brake fluid reservoir

Check the pressure in the spare tyre

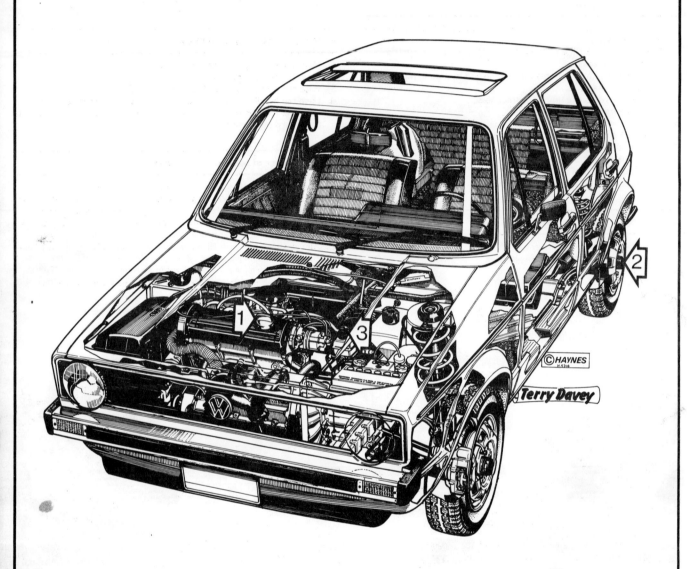

Recommended lubricants and fluids

Engine (1)	Castrol GTX
Gearbox:	
Manual	Castrol Hypoy Light (80 EP)
Automatic	Castrol TQ Dexron ®
Final drive (automatic models only)	Castrol Hypoy B (90 EP)
Rack and pinion unit	Obtain special lubricant from VW/Audi agent
Rear wheel bearings (2)	Castrol LM Grease
Parking brake compensator	Castrol LM Grease
Clutch cable	Castrol LM Grease
Hinges, locks, pivots, distributor etc	Castrol GTX
Brake fluid (3)	Castrol Girling Universal Brake and Clutch Fluid

Note: the above are general recommendations. Lubrication requirements vary from territory-to-territory and also depend on vehicle usage.
Consult the operators handbook supplied with your car

Use of English

As this book has been written in England, it uses the appropriate English component names, phrases, and spelling. Some of these differ from those used in America. Normally, these cause no difficulty, but to make sure, a glossary is printed below. In ordering spare parts remember the parts list will probably use these words:

Glossary

English	American	English	American
Aerial	Antenna	Interior light	Dome lamp
Accelerator	Gas pedal	Layshaft (of gearbox)	Counter shaft
Alternator	Generator (AC)	Leading shoe (of brake)	Primary shoe
Anti-roll bar	Stabiliser or sway bar	Locks	Latches
Battery	Energizer	Motorway	Freeway, turnpike etc.
Bodywork	Sheet metal	Number plate	Licence plate
Bonnet (engine cover)	Hood	Paraffin	Kerosene
Boot lid	Trunk lid	Petrol	Gasoline
Boot (luggage compartment)	Trunk	Petrol tank	Gas tank
Bottom gear	1st gear	'Pinking'	'Pinging'
Bulkhead	Firewall	Quarter light	Quarter window
Camfollower or tappet	Valve lifter or tappet	Retread	Recap
Carburettor	Carburetor	Reverse	Back-up
Catch	Latch	Rocker cover	Valve cover
Choke/venturi	Barrel	Roof rack	Car-top carrier
Circlip	Snap ring	Saloon	Sedan
Clearance	Lash	Seized	Frozen
Crownwheel	Ring gear (of differential)	Side indicator lights	Side marker lights
Disc (brake)	Rotor/disk	Side light	Parking light
Propeller shaft	Driveshaft	Silencer	Muffler
Drop arm	Pitman arm	Spanner	Wrench
Drop head coupe	Convertible	Sill panel (beneath doors)	Rocker panel
Dynamo	Generator (DC)	Split cotter (for valve spring cap)	Lock (for valve spring retainer)
Earth (electrical)	Ground	Split pin	Cotter pin
Engineer's blue	Prussion blue	Steering arm	Spindle arm
Estate car	Station wagon	Sump	Oil pan
Exhaust manifold	Header	Tab washer	Tang; lock
Fast back (Coupe)	Hard top	Tailgate	Liftgate
Fault finding/diagnosis	Trouble shooting	Tappet	Valve lifter
Float chamber	Float bowl	Thrust bearing	Throw-out bearing
Free-play	Lash	Top gear	High
Freewheel	Coast	Trackrod (of steering)	Tie-rod (or connecting rod)
Gudgeon pin	Piston pin or wrist pin	Trailing shoe (of brake)	Secondary shoe
Gearchange	Shift	Transmission	Whole drive line
Gearbox	Transmission	Tyre	Tire
Halfshaft	Axle-shaft	Van	Panel wagon/van
Handbrake	Parking brake	Vice	Vise
Hood	Soft top	Wheel nut	Lug nut
Hot spot	Heat riser	Windscreen	Windshield
Indicator	Turn signal	Wing/mudguard	Fender
Interior light	Dome lamp		

Miscellaneous points

An "Oil seal" is fitted to components lubricated by grease!

A "Damper" is a "Shock absorber", it damps out bouncing, and absorbs shocks of bump impact. Both names are correct, and both are used haphazardly.

Note that British drum brakes are different from the Bendix type that is common in America, so different descriptive names result. The shoe end furthest from the hydraulic wheel cylinder is on a pivot; interconnection between the shoes as on Bendix brakes is most uncommon. Therefore the phrase "Primary" or "Secondary" shoe does not apply. A shoe is said to be Leading or Trailing. A "Leading" shoe is one on which a point on the drum, as it rotates forward, reaches the shoe at the end worked by the hydraulic cylinder before the anchor end. The opposite is a trailing shoe, and this one has no self servo from the wrapping effect of the rotating drum.

Chapter 1 Engine

Contents

Specifications

Type ... ... 4 cylinder, in-line, water-cooled with overhead valves. 5 bearing crankshaft. Camshaft driven by a toothed plastic belt. The 1.1 litre differs from the 1.5 litre having a different type of cylinder block and layout of water and oil pumps. The distributor and fuel pumps are driven by the camshaft, no intermediate shaft being fitted.

Engine codes

F.A.   50HP (DIN), 1093 cc fitted to Golf/Scirocco.

F.B.   75HP (DIN) 1471 cc fitted to very early Scirocco models only. This engine has flat crown pistons and uses W200 T 3 spark plugs. May be used with 98 RON grade fuel. In other respects as for F.H. engine.

F.C.   70HP (SAE) 1471 cc fitted to Rabbit and Scirocco (USA) with manual gearbox 020.

F.D.   85HP (DIN) 1471 cc fitted to Scirocco LS and TS

F.G.   70HP (SAE) 1471 cc fitted to Rabbit and Scirocco (USA) with automatic gearbox 010.

F.H.   70HP (DIN) 1471 cc fitted to Golf and Scirocco. Small recess in piston crown. Uses W175 T 30 spark plugs.

F.J.   52HP (DIN) 1093 cc fitted to Golf/Scirocco.

Engine (general)

Code	F.A.	F.J.	F.H.	F.D.	F.C.	F.G.
Output kilowatts at rpm.	37 6000	38 6000	51 5800	63 5800	- -	- -
Output HP (DIN) at rpm.	50 6000	52 6000	70 5800	85 5800	74 5800	74 5800

Code	F.A.	F.J.	F.H.	F.D.	F.C.	F.G.
Torque mkg at	8.0	8.0	11.4	12.3	11.7	11.7
rpm	3000	3000	3000	3200	3500	3500
Torque lbs ft at	57.8	57.8	82.5	89	81	81
rpm	3000	3000	3000	3200	3500	3500
Capacity cc	1093	1093	1471	1471	1471	1471
cu ins	67	67	97.0	97.0	97.0	97.0
Stroke mm	72	72	80	80	80	80
ins	2.83	2.83	3.15	3.15	3.15	3.15
Bore mm	69.5	69.5	76.5	76.5	76.5	76.5
ins	2.736	2.736	3.01	3.01	3.01	3.01
Compression ratio	8.0:1	8.0:1	8.2:1	9.7:1	8.2:1	8.2:1
Mean piston speed m.s	14.4	14.4	15.5	15.5	15.5	15.5
at rpm	6000	6000	5800	5800	5800	5800
Mean piston speed ft/sec	47.24	47.24	50.8	50.8	50.8	50.8
at rpm	6000	6000	5800	5800	5800	5800
Octane requirement RON	91	91	91	98	91	91

Valve timing at 1 mm valve lift, clearance 0

	1.1 litre F.A. F.J.	1.5 litre F.H. F.D.	1.5 litre USA F.C. F.G.
Inlet opens	2° BTDC	9° BTDC	4° BTDC
Inlet closes	38° ABDC	41° ABDC	47° ABDC
Exhaust opens	48.5 BBDC	49° BBDC	43° BBDC
Exhaust closes	3° ATDC	1° ATDC	7° ATDC

Valve tappet clearance (warm), set with oil temperature 35°C (95°F)

		1.1 litre	1.5 litre
Inlet:			
mm	... ...	0.20	0.25 ± 0.05
ins	... ...	0.008	0.010
Exhaust:			
mm	... ...	0.30	0.45 ± 0.05
ins	... ...	0.012	0.018

Order of valves starting at the sprocket end

1.1 litre	... ...	Inlet, exhaust, inlet, exhaust, inlet, exhaust, inlet, exhaust.
1.5 litre	... ...	Exhaust, inlet, exhaust, inlet, inlet, exhaust, inlet, exhaust.

Lubrication

		litres	U.S. pints	Imp. pints
1.1 litre refill capacity:				
without filter change	... ...	2.8	5.8	4.9
with filter change	... ...	3.25	6.8	5.7
1.5 litre refill capacity:				
without filter change	... ...	3.0	6.35	5.3
with filter change	... ...	3.5	7.4	6.2

Oil pressure at temp. 80°C (172°F):

		kg sq. cm	psi
1.1 litre:			
max	... ...	2	28.5
min	... ...	0.30 to 0.6	4.5 to 9
1.5 litre:			
max (2000 rpm)	... ...	2	28.5
min	... ...	0.3 to 0.6	4.5 to 9.0

Oil pump:

1.1 litre	... ...	Eccentric gear type driven by crankshaft.
1.5 litre	... ...	Straight gear type driven by intermediate shaft.

Limits and fits

Pistons with connecting rods

	1.1 litre and 1.5 litre	
	mm	in

Piston/cylinder clearance:

max	0.07	0.0028
standard	0.03	0.0012
Maximum allowable wear on piston diameter from standard size measured 5/8 in (16 mm) from bottom of skirt at 90° to piston pin ...	0.04	0.0016
Maximum difference of piston weight in one engine	17g	0.6 oz
Maximum difference of connecting rod weight in one engine	15g	0.53 oz
Piston pin diameter	22.02	0.867
Small end bush/piston pin clearance	0.03	0.0012

For piston sizes and cylinder measurements see Section 7

Piston rings

	mm	in
Side clearance all rings (max).	0.15	0.006
Ring thickness:		
Top pressure ring	2.0	0.079
Middle pressure ring	2.5	0.098
Scraper ring	4.0	0.158
Ring gaps:		
Top and middle standard	0.45	0.018
Top and middle max	1.00	0.04
Scraper ring	0.25 to 0.40	0.010 to 0.016

	1.1 litre		1.5 litre	
	mm	in	mm	in
Big-end bearings				
Radial clearance:				
std	0.02 to 0.076	0.0008 to 0.003	0.02 to 0.076	0.0008 to 0.076
max	0.095	0.0037	0.12	0.0047
Axial clearance:				
std	0.05 to 0.31	0.002 to 0.012	0.05 to 0.31	0.002 to 0.012
max	0.40	0.016	0.37	0.015
Main bearings				
Radial clearance:				
std	0.036 to 0.095	0.0014 to 0.0037	0.03 to 0.083	0.0012 to 0.0032
max	0.15	0.006	0.17	0.007
Crankshaft end clearance:				
measured at No 3 bearing:				
std	0.07 to 0.18	0.0028 to 0.007	0.07 to 0.17	0.0028 to 0.007
max	0.20	0.008	0.37	0.0146
Crankshaft run-out max	0.06	0.0024	0.06	0.0024
Main journals:				
Standard	54.00	2.126		
Undersize 1	53.75	2.116		
Undersize 2	53.50	2.106		
Undersize 3	53.25	2.097		
Max ovality	0.03	0.0012		As for 1.1 litre.
Big-end journals:				
Standard	46.00	1.811		
Undersize 1	45.75	1.801		
Undersize 2	45.50	1.791		
Undersize 3	45.25	1.781		
Max ovality	0.03	0.0012		
Cylinder bores				
Max ovality	0.04	0.0016	0.04	0.0016

Flywheel

Lateral run-out max at centre of clutch surface   0.08   0.0032   0.08   0.0032

Camshaft

	mm	in
Endfloat max (1.1 litre and 1.5 litre)	0.15	0.06

Valve guides

Maximum rock at the end of rear valve stems, valve fully inserted:

	1.1 litre	**1.5 litre**
Inlet	0.7 mm (0.027 in)	0.4 mm (0.015 in)
Exhaust	0.9 mm (0.035 in)	0.8 mm (0.031 in)

Valves

	1.1 litre		**1.5 litre**	
	in	mm	in	mm
Inlet:				
Head diameter	1.244	31.6	1.338	34
Stem diameter	0.314	7.97	0.314	7.97
Seat width	0.078	2.0	0.078	2
Seat angle		45°		45°
Exhaust:				
Head diameter	1.106	28.1	1.221	31
Stem diameter	0.314	7.97	0.314	7.97
Seat width	0.094	2.4	0.094	2.4
Seat angle		45°		45°

Torque wrench settings

	1.1 litre		**1.5 litre**	
	lbs ft	mkg	lbs ft	mkg
Ball socket stud for rocker arms	50	7	—	—
Camshaft bearing caps	—	—	15	2
Camshaft sprocket	58	8	58	8
Carburettor to manifold	14.5	2	14.5	2
Clutch to flywheel	18	2.5	15	2
Clutch pressure plate bolts	—	—	54	7.5
Connecting rod caps	22	3	25	3.5
Crankshaft bearing caps	47	6.5	47	6.5
Crankshaft pulley to shaft	58	8	58	8
Crankshaft pulley to sprocket	15	2	15	2
Cylinder head (hot)	43	6	61	8.5
Cylinder head (cold)	43	6	54	7.5
Cylinder head cover	6	1	6	1
Driveshafts to flanges	32	4.5	32	4.5
Engine to transmission	40	5.5	40	5.5
Engine mount to engine	29	4	29	4
Engine support to block	29	4	29	4
Exhaust manifold to head	18	2.5	18	2.5
Exhaust pipe to silencer	15	2.1	—	—
Flywheel bolts to crankshaft	54	7.5	—	—
Inlet manifold to head	18	2.5	18	2.5
Intermediate plate to engine	7	1	—	—
Intermediate shaft flange	—	—	18	2.5
Intermediate shaft sprocket	—	—	58	8
Oil drain plug	22	3	22	3
Oil filter	15	2	15	2
Oil pump to engine	6	0.8	15	2
Oil pressure relief valve	18	2.5	—	—
Oil pressure switch	7	1	7	1
Spark plugs	22	3	22	3
Sump pan to block	6	1	7	1
Temperature sender unit	5	0.7	5	0.7
Tensioner nut for timing belt	—	—	32	4.5
Timing belt guard	7	1	7	1
Water flange and heater flange to head	—	—	7	1
Water pump to block	7	1	15	2
Distributor flange	—	—	15	2

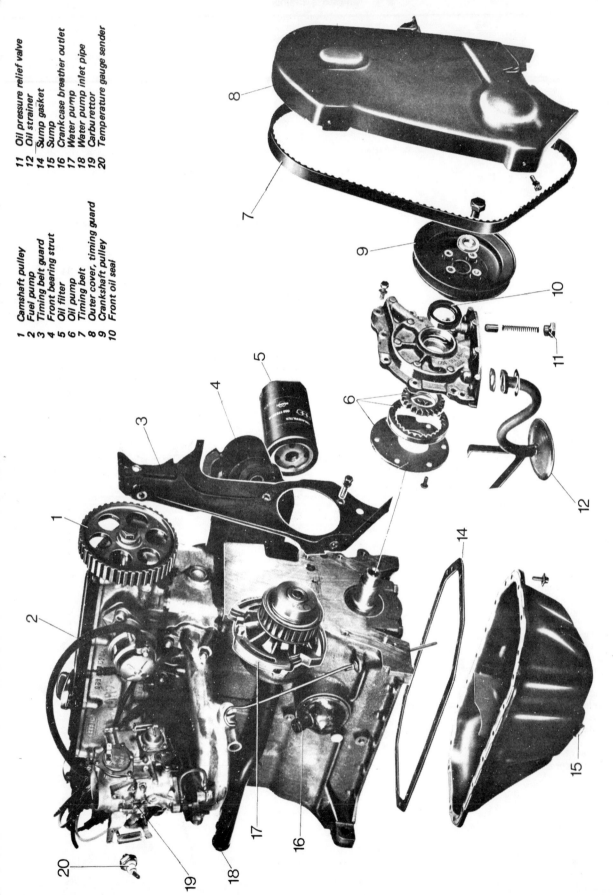

1 Camshaft pulley
2 Fuel pump
3 Timing belt guard
4 Front bearing strut
5 Oil filter
6 Oil pump
7 Timing belt
8 Outer cover, timing guard
9 Crankshaft pulley
10 Front oil seal

11 Oil pressure relief valve
12 Oil strainer
14 Sump gasket
15 Sump
16 Crankcase breather outlet
17 Water pump
18 Water pump inlet pipe
19 Carburettor
20 Temperature gauge sender

Fig. 1.1. 1.1 litre engine - general layout

1 General description - 1.1 and 1.5 litre engines

1 The two engines are similar in design but different in layout. Both are mounted transversely, the 1.1 litre block sloping forward at 15° and the 1.5 litre sloping backwards at 20° to the vertical.

2 The 1.1 litre cylinder head has an overhead camshaft driven by a toothed belt. Motion to the valves is transferred via rocker fingers. The camshaft drives the distrubutor which is bolted to the end of the cylinder head and by means of an extra cam the fuel pump which is bolted to the side of the head. The water pump is situated on the right-hand side of the engine driven by the timing belt. Moving the pump body round in its eccentric mounting provides the tension adjustment for the timing belt. The oil pump is driven directly from the crankshaft and is fitted at the front end of the block concentric with the crankshaft.

3 The 1.5 litre engine also has an overhead camshaft driven by a timing belt but in this case the belt has a separate tensioning device. The camshaft passes directly on the tappet buckets there being no rocker arms. An extra shaft called the intermediate shaft, driven by the timing belt runs parallel to the crankshaft, on the right-hand side of the engine. This shaft drives by means of a screw gear the driveshaft for the distributor and the oil pump. It also drives, by means of a cam, the fuel pump. The water pump is bolted to the left-hand side of the block and is driven by a Vee-belt from the crankshaft pulley. This belt also drives the alternator.

4 Both engines are cooled by a crossflow radiator, but due to the different arrangement of water pumps the 1.1 litre radiator header tank is on the right, whereas the 1.5 litre one has its header tank on the left. This necessitates a much different arrangement of coolant hoses.

5 The arrangements for supporting the engine and transmission are much the same, Brackets at the front of the engine and rear of the gearbox, a side support to the frame behind the engine (or on the right-hand side) and a torwue reaction damper from the left side of the engine to the frame below the radiator.

6 Both of the engines used in the Golf are fitted with a Solex single barrel downdraught carburettor but the 1.5 litre engine for the higher powered Scirocco and for the Rabbit are fitted with twin barrel down-draft carburettors, the European version has a Solex and the USA version a Zenith.

7 The gearboxes are different and so too are the clutches. These details are discussed in Chapters 5 and 6. The layout of the rear oil seal and fly-wheel details are shown in Fig. 1.2

8 One fundamental difference not easily observed is in the design of the

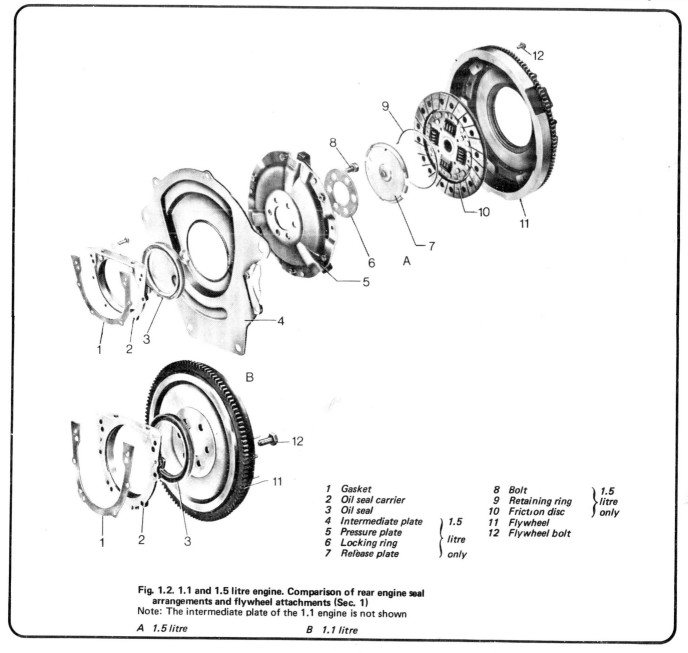

1	Gasket
2	Oil seal carrier
3	Oil seal
4	Intermediate plate	} 1.5
5	Pressure plate	
6	Locking ring	} litre
7	Release plate	} only

8	Bolt	} 1.5
9	Retaining ring	} litre
10	Friction disc	} only
11	Flywheel	
12	Flywheel bolt	

Fig. 1.2. 1.1 and 1.5 litre engine. Comparison of rear engine seal arrangements and flywheel attachments (Sec. 1)
Note: The intermediate plate of the 1.1 engine is not shown

A   1.5 litre   B   1.1 litre

cylinder head. On the original 1.5 litre engine fitted to the Passat/Dasher and converted for the Golf/Scirocco/Rabbit the one side of the engine is clear of pipe work and has all the ancillaries. Thus the exhaust and inlet manifolds are fitted to the same side of the head. On the 1.1 litre engine the head has been designed for crossflow of the combustible gases so that the inlet and exhaust manifolds are on opposite sides of the engine which has led to the different layout of the distributor and pumps, making the 1.1 litre engine a less complicated engine but not so accessible.

2 Engine overhaul - repairs possible with the engine in the car

1 Before you commence dismantling the engine disconnect the battery earth strap. Accidental short circuits can damage the alternator diodes, and that will be expensive.
2 The question as to whether to remove the bonnet (hood) is a personal one. It takes five minutes. Mark the hinge strips for easy replacement and remove four bolts. An extra person to hold it is needed, and then you can see what you are doing. It is possible to work with it in position but it does tend to get in the way, and the number of times you bump your head on it can spoil the day for you.
3 If you are going to get underneath the car then it must be supported firmly. It is not enough to lift it on a jack and leave it there. One safe method is to raise the front wheels on firm blocks, but remember that if the axle driveshafts are to be undone for any reason the front wheels must be turnable so that you can get at all the flange bolts. The ideal is to work over a pit; if that is not possible then support the body on axle stands.
4 The removal of the ancillaries, distributor, water pump, fuel pump, alternator and thermostat may be done without disturbing other parts.
5 The cylinder head can be removed for decarbonizing but care must be taken not to bend the timing belt too much or it will crack.
6 The clutch and rear oil seal may be serviced only after the gearbox has been removed (Chapter 6). It is necessary to remove the engine to service the front crankshaft oil seal.
7 If a long Allen key (5 mm) is available the sump may be removed from underneath. On the 1.5 litre engine this permits removal of the oil pump. On the 1.1 litre the oil pump may not be removed until the crankshaft pulley and front seal are taken off.
8 If the head and sump are removed it is possible to remove the connecting rod bearing caps and withdraw the pistons and connecting rods upwards.

3 Engine and manual gearbox removal - method and tools required

1 If extensive repairs are contemplated it is better to remove the engine and gearbox from the car and do the job properly. Allow an hour and a half to get it out if it is the first time you have done it. About the same time is required to install it and reconnect the various pieces. Two people will be needed for some of the time.
2 A hoist, capacity 3 cwt (150 kg), will be needed and the engine must be lifted approximately three feet (1 metre). If the hoist is not portable then sufficient room must be left behind the car to push the car back out of the way so that the power unit may be lowered. Blocks will be needed to support the engine after removal.
3 Ideally the car should be over a pit. If this is not possible then the body must be supported on axle stands so that the front wheels may be turned to undo the driveshaft nuts. The left one is accessible from above but the right-hand shaft must be undone from underneath. There are other jobs best done from below. Removal of the shift linkage can only be done from underneath, as can the removal of the exhaust pipe bracket. When all the jobs are done under the car, lower the car back to its wheels.
4 Draining of oil and coolant is best done away from the working area if possible. This saves the mess made by spilled oil in the place where you must work.
5 No special tools are required. A good set of metric Allen keys is essential. Spanners, ring and open-ended, plus a set of socket spanners, all metric, for sizes 5,6,7,8,9,10,11 and 12 mm plus a plug spanner and a 14 mm ring for the oil drain plug. Screwdrivers, knife edge and crosshead, pliers and a mole wrench, plus a set of feeler gauges (preferably metric), and a straight-edge.
6 Once the engine is out of the vehicle take it from the working area and clean it thoroughly externally. Then take the opportunity to clean

and, if necessary, repair the engine compartment.
7 A good strong bench and a vice, plus room to lay out the parts in order as they are dismantled will help a lot.
8 Containers for nuts and bolts, and containers for oil and coolant, grease, jointing compound, and valve grinding paste plus a valve grinding suction lifter, should be obtained before starting the overhaul.
9 A complete set of gaskets and seals for the engine is needed.
10 It is possible to hire a hoist in most places. It all sounds expensive, but then so is having an engine overhaul done at a garage.
11 Take your time. Have a notebook and pencil to note down the tricky bits, some means of fastening tags to wires, some plastic bags to keep things in, and some method of cleaning your hands without being hounded out of the kitchen. We use a proprietary hand cleanser and clean rag.
12 There are many more aids, forceps (which you can buy at most fishing tackle shops), a small magnet, and some lengths of stiff wire, for picking up things which have fallen into awkward places, and finally a good torch to see in the dark places.

4 Engine and manual gearbox - removal and replacement

1 The procedure for both the 1.1 litre and the 1.5 litre is almost identical. The operation described here is for the 1.1 litre with notations where the 1.5 litre differs.
2 Disconnect the battery earth strap and remove the bonnet hood (photo). This is not essential but if it is out of the way it cannot get knocked and the supporting arm is a nuisance when lifting.
3 Undo the four clips and remove the air cleaner complete with hoses On later models the air cleaner is on top of the carburettor but it should be removed for safety reasons.
4 Put a flat container under the radiator and remove the bottom hose. About 9.7 Imp. pints (5.5 litres) of expensive coolant will come out, this should be then stored away. Use a 2 gallon (10 litre) container. Now remove the plug from under the exhaust manifold if there is one, (our vehicle did not have one), and a further 2 Imp. pints (1 litre) will) will drain away. The heater control valve must be set to open and the top taken off the coolant overflow tank.
5 The radiator hoses may now be disconnected and the wires to the thermo-switch and the fan motor unplugged. Tag the leads for ease of assembly.
6 Opinions differ about the necessity to remove the radiator. On the 1.1 litre it must be removed as the engine slopes towards it.
On the 1.5 litre where the engine slopes away from the radiator there is certainly more room but we still followed the official VW schedule which is to remove the radiator before proceeding further. Undo the hose on the 1.5 litre engine radiator which goes to the overflow tank. On the Rabbit and Scirocco USA version remove the clamp holding the control valve for afterburn. This leaves the radiator isolated. Note that the header tank is on the left for the 1.1 litre and the right for the 1.5 litre. The two nuts may be removed from the bottom mountings (photo) and then the radiator may be lifted and the wire clips at the top disengaged (photo). The radiator complete with fan and cowling may now be lifted out. (photo).
7 It is now convenient to remove the various pieces of wiring which connect the engine to the body. Begin with the starter motor. There is one heavy lead with a securing nut and two push on clips. Remove the wiring from the choke heater and the magnetic cut off valve of the carburettor and tag the wires. The coil will remain on the bulkhead but the LT and HT leads to the distributor must be disconnected. Pull off the leads to the oil pressure sender unit and the coolant temperature sender. Remove the leads from the TDC sensor. Finally remove the gearbox earth strap and the lead to the reversing light, if fitted.
8 Disconnect the fuel hoses from the carburettor and undo the accelerator cable and tie it out of the way. (Chapter 3).
9 Slacken off the clutch cable adjuster (Chapter 5) and remove the cable from the operating lever. Tie it out of the way.
10 On the 1.5 litre engine, unscrew the exhaust pipe from the exhaust manifold and remove the support bracket. On the 1.1 litre remove the clamp which holds the exhaust pipe to the manifold, and then remove the clamp holding the pipe to the engine block. On 1.5 engines the exhaust and inlet are on the same side, on the 1.1 on opposite sides.
11 On 1.5 litre engined vehicles with twin headlamps the headlamp protecting cover must now be taken off.
12 Remove the bolts from the driveshaft flanges (photo) and fasten the driveshafts out of the way. Cover the CVJ s in polythene bags. Undo

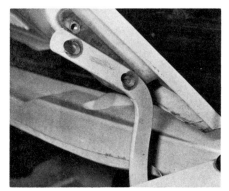

4.2 Undo the bonnet hinge bolts

4.6a Undo the nuts holding the bottom of the radiator to the frame and ...

4.6b ... lift the radiator and slide the clip out of its housing

4.6c Lift the radiator out of the car

4.12a Undo the bolts securing the driveshaft

4.12b Undo the speedometer drive

4.13 Disconnect the gearchange linkage (1.1 litre)

4.14a Remove the torque absorber bracket from the frame and ...

4.14b ... the bracket from the cylinder block

the speedo drive (photo) from the gearbox and plug the hole left in the gearbox to stop grit or dirt entering the gearbox.

13 Disconnect the gearchange linkage from the gearbox. For the 1.1 litre remove the square-headed bolt connecting the gearchange and the bracket (photo). On the 1.5 litre the relay lever and the gearchange rod must be disconnected.

14 The front engine mounting is next. This is really a torque absorber. Take the bracket off the frame and the bracket off the cylinder block (photos).

15 From underneath the vehicle remove the large bracket which holds the unit to the body. There are three nuts (photo). This may seem undue work. We thought so and removed the nut from the mounting stud only. As a result when we came to remove the engine it would not slide out of the gearbox bracket mounting and we had to stop and remove the whole of the bracket holding the right-hand side of the engine to the car.

16 Position the lifting gear, fit the slings and take the weight of the engine. The engine is now supported at either end. Undo the nuts holding the engine carrier to the body and those holding the gearbox carrier

at the rear. Remove the nuts holding the bracket to the gearbox as well (photos). Lift slightly on the hoist, check that all is clear and then lift the engine and gearbox up slightly, then remove the bracket holding the gearbox completely away and lift the engine up turning it slightly as necessary (photo).

17 Lay the engine and transmission down on blocks ready for cleaning.

18 Replacement is the reverse of removal, but these are some points to remember. When refitting the engine to the transmission the recess in the flywheel must be level with the driveshaft flange. The TDC marker must be fitted after the gearbox is joined to the engine.

19 When lifting the engine remember the angle at which it will finally set. Lower it into the frame and ease the front engine bearer into place and fit the securing bolt and nut.

20 We found a little difficulty lining up the rear bracket but by lowering the engine down it was possible to put the rear bracket over the gearbox studs and then raise the engine, pivoting about the front bracket bolt until it was possible to fit the securing bolt in the rear bracket. The nuts were then fitted to the top of the gearbox and the whole assembly carefully lined up. We then fitted the torque control arm

4.15 Remove the bracket holding the engine to the frame

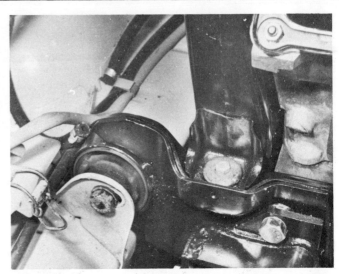

4.16a Undo the nut and remove the bolt holding the engine carrier to the frame

4.16b Undo the nuts holding the gearbox carrier to the gearbox and the nut and bolt holding the carrier to the frame

4.16c Lift the engine out of the frame turning it as necessary

and bracket, and finally the rear mounting. The whole operation took ten minutes, but perhaps we were lucky. **Do not** use exessive force, if it won't go, lift it up and try again.

21 Connecting up is easy if you remember to tag all the wires and hoses. If you did not, this might help. It is for a 1.1 litre Golf.

　　Brown cable - carburettor earth.
　　Black cable - automatic choke.
　　Blue/white cable - temperature sender.
　　Blue/black cable - oil pressure switch.

　　There is a wire to the carburettor magnetic cut-off valve and two to the radiator thermo-switch. The fan motor and the TDC marker have small plugs. The alternator connector plug fits only one way and is held in with a clamp. The green wire goes from the distributor LT to the coil LT terminal. Do not forget the gearbox earth strap.

22 After installing the radiator and hoses fill the radiator via the over-flow tank. Open the heater valve. Fill the tank to the mark and then bleed the system by opening the small valve at the top of the radiator header tank. Carry on with this until no more air comes out of the bleed valve, filling the overflow tank as necessary.

23 Refit the accelerator cable, (Chapter 3), and the clutch cable (Chapter 5), and adjust them carefully.

24 The starter must be securely bolted. Smear it with a little petroleum jelly. Fit the starter solenoid cables and then reconnect the gear selector and adjust it (Chapter 6).

25 Refit the drive shafts (Chapter 8) and the wire to the reverse light. Reconnect the exhaust to the manifold and fit the bracket holding the

pipe to the block.

26 Install the air cleaner (Chapter 3) and connect the air inlet hoses.

27 Reconnect the fuel hoses. This may give trouble. The hose was originally crimped on and it may be necessary to pull off the clip, open it out and then refit it on the hose, push the hose on and tighten the clip with pliers. Refit the distributor cap and connect the HT leads to the coil and plug.

28 Install the battery, clamp it in place and reconnect the leads. The braided copper one is the negative. This should be the big moment. Work around to see that no ends are dangling loose and if all is in order turn the ignition key. Remember that the carburettor is empty so the engine will turn for some time before the petrol is pumped through to the cylinders. Ours started first time. We hope yours does too.

5　Engine and automatic transmission - removal and replacement

1　The procedure is generally the same as for Section 4, but there are some extra tasks.

2　Remove the accelerator control wire and bracket from the carburettor. Move the selector to 'P' and disconnect the selector cable (Chapter 7). Detach the accelerator cable bracket from the carburettor: **do not** alter the cable adjustment.

3　Remove the rear transmission mounting and then remove the torque converter cover plate. Through this aperture undo the bolts holding the torque converter to the driveplate.

4 Remove the engine as in Section **4**.
5 Installation is the reverse of removal. Torque the converter to drive-plate bolts to 40 lbs ft. Install the engine and transmission, reconnect as in Section 4 and adjust the control cable and accelerator cable as in Chapter 7.

Fig. 1.3. Remove the compressor (B) (Sec. 6)

6 Engine and gearbox (vehicles with air-conditioning equipment) - removal

1 The air-conditioner is discussed in Chapter 2. It is sufficient here to say that **on no account** must the refrigerant hoses be disconnected.
2 The compressor is driven by a belt. Remove the belt and remove the compressor holding bolts. Suspend it out of the way (Fig. 1.3.).
3 Remove the radiator, shroud and fan and then remove the condenser (Fig. 1.4). Suspend the condenser out of the way (Fig. 1.5). Do not put any strain on the refrigerant hoses.
4 The normal dismantling and reassembly drill may now be carried out taking care not to strain the hose connections to the compressor and condenser.
5 After the engine and transmission have been reassembled to the vehicle the condenser may be refitted to the radiator assembly and the compressor bolted in place on its mounting. The belt may then be adjusted correctly.
6 We recommend that before attempting to remove the compressor and condenser that the owner should visit an accredited agent and seek advice on the matter. The task is not difficult but there are several versions of the equipment, notably one for USA, one for Canada and one for elsewhere. VW have published a 25 page instruction on the subject and insist that only trained personnel adjust the equipment. In view of its dangerous potential in unskilled hands we recommend extreme caution.

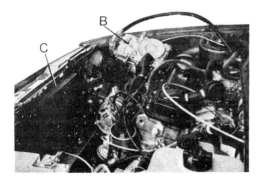

Fig. 1.4. Remove the radiator and fan and take the condenser (C) away (Sec. 6)

7 Separating the engine from the gearbox (1.1 litre and 1.5 litre)

1 The procedure is slightly different. The 1.1 litre engine is dealt with first. The engine must be supported so that the gearbox can be eased away from it. Either support the engine on blocks so that the gearbox overhangs the bench, or do the job while the engine and gearbox are on the hoist.
2 Because the rear bearing of the starter armature is in the bellhousing it is necessary to remove the starter before separating the engine and gearbox. Remove the bolts holding the starter flange to the bellhousing and remove the starter. One of the bolts is hidden in the flange.
3 Now remove the TDC marker (photo) VW recommend a sawn off plug spanner for this task if the engine is still in the vehicle, otherwise use a 14 mm ring spanner. On the 1.5 litre turn the crankshaft until the

Fig. 1.5. Lay the compressor (B) and the condenser to one side. Do not disconnect the hoses (Sec. 6)

7.3 Removing the TDC sensor plug

lug on the flywheel (33° BTDC) is visible through the TDC marker hole (see Fig. 1.6). If this is not done on the 1.5 litre the housing will foul the flywheel when separated.

4   At the bottom of the bellhousing a small casting is bolted to the housing to shield the flywheel. Remove the three bolts holding it and take it away.

5   There are five bolts holding the gearbox to the engine. Remove these and ease the transmission complete from the cylinder block.

6   **Do not** insert wedges or you will damage the facing, tap the gearbox gently and wriggle it off the two dowels which locate it (photo). The intermediate plate will remain in position.

7   The 1.5 litre engine procedure is slightly different. Proceed as for the 1.1 litre but before removing the bolts securing the engine to the transmission remove the cover plate over the driveshaft flange. The connecting bolts may now be removed but in this case ease the transmission away carefully in a straight line until the transaxle driveshaft and the clutch pushrod clear the clutch and flywheel. It is essential

that no stress is put on the driveshaft or pushrod or they may be bent and may also damage other clutch parts.

8   Engine dismantling (1.5 litre engine) - removal of parts bolted to the exterior of the head and block

1   Take off the camshaft cover, noting where the packing pieces fit under the bolts, and then remove the cover from the timing belt. Note where the two tee-headed bolts go and put them back in the cover.

2   It is now possible to save a lot of trouble when assembling the engine by studying the timing marks. On the intermediate pulley for the timing belt one tooth has a centre-punch mark. Turn the engine until this mates with a notch on the V-belt pulley bolted to the crankshaft drive pulley (photo). The easier way to turn the engine is to remove the plugs and turn it with a socket spanner on the crankshaft pulley nut.

3   When these match look at the drivebelt sprocket on the camshaft.

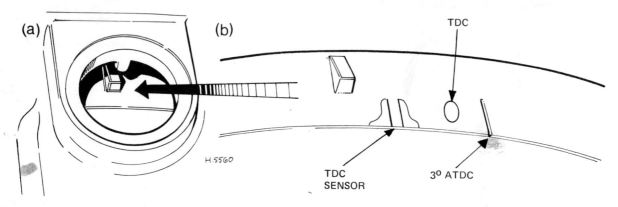

Fig. 1.6. 1.5 litre engine - **TDC sensor hole and timing marks (Sec. 7)**

a)   *View through TDC hole (note lug)*   b)   *Marking on flywheel (Rabbit)*

7.6 Removing the gearbox

8.2 The punch mark 'A' on the geartooth of the intermediate shaft pulley must line up with the Vee-notch in the Vee-belt pulley on the crankshaft. This ensures correct timing

8.3a The centre punch mark on the camshaft sprocket 'A' must be in line with the shoulder of the head. This lines up the valves with the pistons

8.3b The cams of no 1 cylinder both in the valve closed position

8.3c Note the position of the rotor arm. It should point to the no 1 cylinder mark on the rim of the distributor body

One tooth of this has a centre-punch mark. This should be level with the camshaft cover flange (photo). Having turned the engine until these marks agree now look at the cams for No 1 cylinder, the one nearest the timing belt. They will both be in the 'valve closed' position (photo). Now look through the hole in which the TDC sensor goes where the timing marks show on the periphery of the flywheel and note the reading. Check where the rotor arm points on the distributor, it should point to No 1 plug lead and a mark on the edge of the rim of the base of the distributor (photo). The distributor body is held in position by a bolt and clamp. Using a centre-punch move the distributor body and the cylinder block in such a way that the marks are adjacent and may be used to set the distributor body at the right position on reassembly of the engine.

4   Remove the clamp, and holding the crankshaft to prevent it turning, lift the distributor body slowly out of the cylinder block. This will cause the distributor shaft to rotate slightly as its skew drive gear moves over the one on the intermediate shaft. Do not allow the distributor body to rotate. Note the amount the shaft has rotated and replace the distributor. The rotor should rotate to the mark on the rim for No 1 cylinder. When you are satisfied that you understand the method of resetting the timing remove the distributor. If you look down the hole left in the cylinder block you will see the top of the oil pump driveshaft. This has a slot in it. Note the angle of the slot carefully so that it can be set for easy reassembly. It is quite easy to reach and turn with a finger or a screwdriver. It should be parallel to the crankshaft.

5   Remove the oil filter be careful there is still oil inside it, and then remove the bracket holding it to the block. This requires an Allen key, the same key being used for the fuel pump which is next to the filter. Set the pump aside for overhaul (Chapter 3). Remove the oil pressure transmitter unit.

6   Slacken the bolts holding the alternator strap to the alternator and the block and then slacken the socket headed bolt which acts as a hinge pin for the alternator tensioning system. If you cannot slacken this bolt, do not shear off the serrations in the bolt socket but undo the two bolts holding the alternator bracket to the block, remove the tensioning strap and ease the V-belt off the pulley taking the alternator away. The socket headed bolt may now be held in a vice and the bracket with alternator turned to loosen it.

However, if you can slacken the bolt then remove the tensioning strap, move the alternator to slacken the V-belt and remove the V-belt. Then take the long hinge bolt right out and remove the alternator. Remove the V-belt, inspect it for wear, cracks or fraying and replace with a new one if necessary.

7   Undo the clip holding the water hose to the flange on the side of the cylinder block and ease the hose clear. Remove the four bolts holding the water pump to the cylinder block (2 long, 2 short) and lever the pump away from the block. It may have stuck but be gentle and do not push wedges in between machined surfaces. Note where the O-ring fits. Set the water pump with hoses and pulley on one side for overhaul (Chapter 2).

8   Before removing the timing drivebelt check it for correct tension. If held between the finger and thumb halfway between the intermediate shaft and the camshaft it should be possible to twist it through 90°. If it is too slack, adjust it by slackening the bolt holding the eccentric cam on the tensioner wheel. If you are satisfied it can be adjusted to the correct tension remove it and examine it for wear. Now is the time to order a new one if necessary, not when the engine is almost assembled.

Remove the crankshaft pulley by taking out the centre bolt and drawing off the two pulleys together. Do not separate them unless necessary, and if you do, the angular relationship between the pulley keyway and the timing notch on the V-belt pulley must be maintained, on reassembly. Remove the centre bolt from the camshaft driving sprocket and pull it off the camshaft. Do not lose the Woodruff key.

9   Remove the exhaust manifold first. There is a small bracket connecting the two manifolds, remove this and then undo the nuts from the studs holding the exhaust manifold to the block. Remove the manifold to one side. The inlet manifold and carburettor may be removed together. There are 8 socket headed bolts, four short and four long, note where each kind goes and then set the manifold on one side for examination (Chapter 3).

10 It will be seen that the clutch of the 1.5 litre engine is different from the usual design. The pressure plate is bolted to the crankshaft flange and flywheel is bolted to the pressure plate. This is explained more fully in Chapter 5. Holding the flywheel from rotating by use of a clamp undo the bolts holding the flywheel to the pressure plate. Work on a diagonal pattern slackening each one two or three turns until the tension is relieved and then remove the bolts and take the flywheel off the pressure plate (see Fig. 1.2). The clutch disc will be loose inside the flywheel so take this away at the same time noting which way round it goes. Facing you now is the clutch pressure plate bolted to the crankshaft flange. In the centre of this is the clutch release plate held in place by an oversize circlip or retaining ring. Note that the ends of the clip are opposite a slot in the pressure plate. Lever the clip out with a screwdriver and holding the pressure plate with a suitable lever undo the five bolts holding the plate to the flange. These are tight (54 lbs ft/7.5 mkg) and inserted with Loctite. The engine is now ready for cylinder head removal (Section 10).

9   Engine dismantling (1.1 litre engine) - removal of parts bolted to the exterior of the head and block

1   The engine must be supported firmly with wooden blocks. Refer to Fig. 1.1.

2   Remove the two self-tapping screws and one 10 mm bolt holding the timing bolt outer cover to the cover body and pull the outer cover away upwards (photo).

3   Remove the alternator. Slacken off the nut on the clamp bolt of the tensioning clamp. The bolt has a square head held in lugs on the clamp. Now remove the belt and then undo and remove the hinge bolt lifting the alternator away at the same time. This operation is described fully in Chapter 10.

4   At this point it is a good thing to line up the valve timing marks to become familiar with the set up and gain confidence for the rebuilding operation. Remove the valve cover plate from the cylinder head to expose the camshaft. Using a 19 mm spanner on the crankshaft pulley nut turn the crankshaft until the Vee-notch in the pulley is level with the 'O' mark on the timing bracket indicator (photo). Now look to see whether both valves of No 1 cylinder (the one nearest the timing belt) are closed. If not rotate the crankshaft 360° and look again. They snould be and if you look at the camshaft drive pulley right at the bottom a tooth should have a mark opposite a blade on the timing belt casing (photo).

9.2 Pull the outer cover of the belt guard upwards to remove it

9.4a The timing mark bracket with the notch in the Vee-belt pulley. 'O' is TDC, 'Z' is the dynamic timing mark

9.4b The mark on the crankshaft sprocket lined up with the edge of the belt guard

9.6a Testing the tension of the timing belt

9.6b Slacken off the clamp screws of the water pump and rotate the body with a lever to adjust the tension of the timing belt

9.10 Removing the distributor

5   Go to the other end of the cylinder head. The rotor of the distributor should point to a mark on the rim of the distributor casing. Scribe a line across the distributor casing and the adaptor onto the cylinder head and mark the junctions with a centre-punch. This will make the reassembly of the ignition timing simple.

6   Now check the tension of the timing belt. Hold it between your forefinger and thumb and twist it (photo). It should be possible to twist it through 90° when held in the middle. If it turns more or less then slacken off the water pump bolts, put a screwdriver in the slot and turn the water pump body in its housing. This will tighten the belt. (photo). Check that the belt can be adjusted correctly. If it cannot then now is the time to order a new one, not when you are already to re-assemble the engine.

7   Slacken the bolt adjustment and remove the belt. **Do not** twist it too much, it is plastic and will crack if handled roughly.

8   At the back of the water pump is a flange and a metal pipe. Remove the two nuts from the flange. Undo the clips holding the hose from this pipe to the inlet manifold and those to the coolant exit at the rear of the cylinder block. Remove the pipe but watch out, there may be coolant in it. Undo the four bolts holding the water pump to the block and remove the water pump. Note where the 'O' ring fits. Again watch for coolant, it doesn't do any harm but it can go up your sleeve! The timing belt casing will also come away at this point. Note where the spacer washer goes.

9   Remove the screws holding fuel pump to the head, pull off the hose if it is still there and lay the fuel pump to one side.

10   Undo the three bolts holding the distributor and remove it. Note that the key on the end of the shaft is offset (photo).

11   Remove the five 12 mm bolts from the exhaust manifold and take off the manifold.

12   Remove the eight 12 mm bolts holding the inlet manifold and remove the manifold and carburettor together.

13   The clutch on this engine is conventional. Remove the bolts holding the pressure plate to the flywheel. Turn each bolt two or three turns at a time working diagonally until the spring tension is eased and then extract the bolts and remove the pressure plate and clutch disc. Note which way the disc goes, there is a long boss.

14   Clamp the flywheel, and remove the six bolts holding the flywheel to the crankshaft flange. Remove the flywheel.

15   The next job is to remove the cylinder head. Turn to Section 12.

10 Cylinder head (1.5 litre) - removal and overhaul

1   The engine supports should be checked and re-aligned if necessary. It is best to carry right through with the overhaul of the cylinder head as it is dismantled.

2   Refer to Fig. 1.7. Remove the camshaft bearing caps. These have to go back the same way in the same place. They are numbered (photo), but put a centre-punch on the side nearest the front of the head (where the sprocket was). No 1 is the one with a small oil seal on it.

Remove bearing caps 5, 1, and 3 in that order. Now undo the nuts holding 2 and 4 in a diagonal pattern and the camshaft will lift them up as the pressure of the valve springs is exerted. When they are free lift the caps off and the camshaft may be lifted out as well. The oil seal on the front end will come with it.

3   The tappet buckets are now exposed and may be lifted out (photo).

Take each one out in turn, prise the little disc out of the bucket by inserting a small screwdriver either side and lift the disc away. On the reverse the disc is engraved with a size (eg; 3.75). This is its thickness number. Note the number and then clean the disc and replace it number side down.

There are eight of these and they must not be mixed. On assembly they must go back into the bore from which they came. This problem exists also for the valves so a container for each valve assembly and tappet is indicated. Label them 1 to 8, 1 and 2 will be No 1 cylinder exhaust and inlet respectively. No. 3 will be No 2 cylinder exhaust and No 4 its inlet valve. No 5 will be the inlet valve for No 3 cylinder and No 6 its exhaust valve. No 7 will be the inlet valve for No 4 cylinder and No 8 its exhaust valve. Note down the thickness of all the tappet clearance discs from No 1 valve to No 8 valve and keep it for use on reassembly.

4   The next job is to remove the cylinder head bolts. These are hidden away down in the well of the head and to make life easier are socket headed bolts. If you do not have VW/Audi tool 157 which is a 10 mm socket bolt hexagonal key with a ½ in square socket at the other end then a 10 mm Allen key is sufficient used the wrong way round, that is with the long arm fitted to the nut. Fit a suitable socket over the short arm and a socket extension bar into the socket (see Fig. 1.8 and proceed to undo the cylinder head bolts according to the sequence shown in Fig. 1.9).

5   When all ten bolts have been removed lift the head from the cylinder block. It may need a little tapping to loosen it but do not try to prise it loose by hammering in wedges. The one we took off was not stuck hard. Lift off the gasket and cover the top of the cylinder block with a clean cloth.

6   Take the cylinder head away from the clean area and with a wire brush, blunt screwdriver and steel wool clean off all the carbon from inside the cylinder head combustion chambers, valve faces and exhaust ports. When the head is clean and shining wash your hands and take it back to the work area. Remove the spark plugs for servicing.(Chapter 4).

7   The valves are not easy to get out unless a suitable extractor is available. Because the cotters and spring caps are set so far down in the head a long claw is necessary on the extractor, and it must be split sufficiently to enable the collets to be removed and inserted. If such a tool is not to hand then find a piece of steel tube about 1 inch (25.4 mm) inside diameter which will fit over the valve stem and press down the spring cover (see Fig. 1.10). The length will depend on the size of the extractor so fit the extractor over the head fully extended, measure the distance between the claw and the valve spring seat and cut the tube to a suitable length.

8   The next step is to cut two windows of suitable size, say one inch (25.4 mm) long and 5/8 in (15.9 mm) wide in opposite sides of the tube. The tube may then be used with the compressor to extract the collets from each valve stem in turn and the valve, springs collets and seats may joint the tappet in the appropriate receptacle, keeping them strictly together for replacement in the same valve guide from which they were taken.

9   The valve springs may easily be checked. It is unlikely that you have a calibrated valve spring compressor, so arrange the spring on the top of a vice with the upper seat in position. Pass a piece of stout wire through the seat and the spring, tie a big knot in the end above the seat so that it will not pull through the hole and hang 100 lbs (45.4 kg) on the

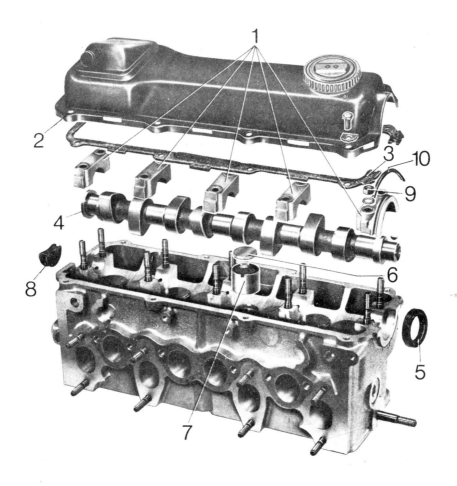

Fig. 1.7. 1.5 litre engine - cylinder head - exploded view (Secs. 10 and 29)

1	Bearing caps 2, 3, 4, 5	4	Camshaft	7	Tappet bucket
2	Valve cover	5	Seal	8	Plug
3	Valve cover packing strips	6	Tappet disc		

9 No. 1 bearing cup
10 Oil seal

10.2 The camshaft bearing caps are numbered. This one is number 4. Note which way it goes round before removing it

10.3 The tappet bucket with the disc

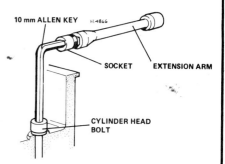

Fig. 1.8. 1.5 litre and 1.1 litre. Method of undoing cylinder head bolts (Secs. 10 and 12)

	O10	O4	O2	O6	O8
	O7	O5	O1	O3	O9

Fig. 1.9. 1.5 litre and 1.1 litre. Diagram showing the sequence of tightening the cylinder head bolts (Secs. 10, 12, 29 & 30)

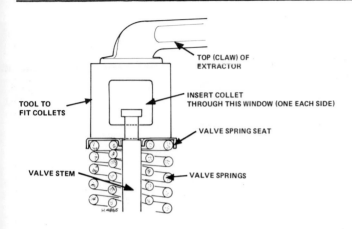

Fig. 1.10. 1.5 litre. Improvised tool used to remove and refit collets to valve stems (Sec. 10)

other end (for the outer spring). The measurement of the length of the spring under this load should be 0.916 inches (23.266 mm). If it is less than 0.900 inches (22.86 mm) then it needs replacing. Check all the outer springs first and then repeat for the inners 48 lbs (21.8 kg) and a limit of 0.17 inches (17.78 mm).

10 The valves should be cleaned and checked for signs of wear or burring. Where this has occured the inlet valves may be reground on a machine at the agents, but exhaust valves must not be reground in the machine but ground in by hand. Dimensions are shown in Fig.1.11 There is also the question of wear in the valve guides. This may be detected by fitting a new valve in the guide and checking the amount that the rim of the valve will move sideways, when the top of the valve stem is flush with the top of valve guide. The rock limit for the inlet valve guide is 0.04 inches (1 mm) and 0.05 inches (1.3 mm) for the exhaust valve. This can be measured with feeler gauges if you use a clamp as a datum but it must be with a new valve. If the rock is at this limit with your own valve, or less than this then there is nothing to worry about. If the rock exceeds the limit with a new valve then this will probably mean a new cylinder head so consult an agent before going any further.

11 Do not labour away too long grinding in the valves. If the valve

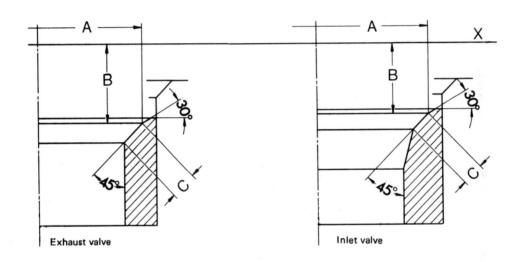

Exhaust valve   Inlet valve

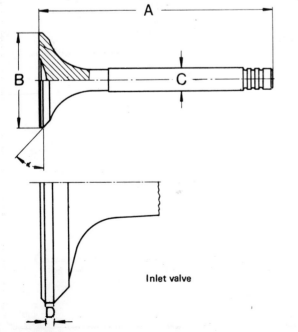

Inlet valve

Fig. 1.11. 1.5 litre and 1.1 litre - Valve and valve seat rework measurements (Sec. 10)

Note: The exhaust valve must **not** be machined. The seat face angles must be retained

VALVE SEAT - dimensions

Dimension	Symbol	INLET VALVE				EXHAUST VALVE			
		1.1 litre		1.5 litre		1.1 litre		1.5 litre	
		mm	ins	mm	ins	mm	ins	mm	ins
Valve seat dia.	a	30	1.181	33.2	1.307	26.5	1.043	30.8	1.213
Depth below cylinder head	b	8.85	0.348	9.00	0.354	9.15	0.360	9.60	0.387
Width of seat	c	2.0	0.079	2.00	0.079	2.40	0.094	2.40	0.094

INLET VALVE - dimensions

		1.1 litre engine	1.5 litre engine
Length	a	104 mm (4.094 in)	98.7 mm (3.885 in)
Diameter of head	b	31.6 mm (1.244 in)	34 mm (1.339 in)
Diameter of stem	c	7.97 mm (0.314 in)	7.97 mm (0.314 in)
Depth of head (minimum)	d	0.5 mm (0.02 in)	0.5 mm (0.02 in)

seat and valve are not satisfactory after fifteen minutes hard work then you will probably do more harm than good by going on. Make sure both surfaces are clean, smear the grinding paste onto the valve evenly and using a suction type cup work the valve with an oscillating motion lifting the valve away from the seat occasionally to stop ridging. Clean the seat and valve frequently and carry on until there is an even band, grey in colour on both seat and valve (about 1/16 in/1.58 mm wide). Wipe off all the paste and leave well alone.

12 The surface of the head must be checked with a straight-edge and feeler gauge. Lay the straight-edge along the centre of the machined face of the head. Make sure there are no ridges at the extreme ends and measure the clearance with feelers between each combustion chamber head. This is the area where the narrowest part of the cylinder head gasket comes - and where the gasket is most likely to fail. If the straight-edge is firmly in place and feelers in excess of 0.004 in (0.1 mm) can be put between the head and the straight-edge then the head should be taken to the agent for servicing or, more probably, a new one.

13 Finally, there is the question of valve stem seals. It is best to replace them if there is any appreciable amount of oil carbon (the soft greasy sort) on the valve head (not the valve face) for this means oil has been finding its way down the guides. If there is no such carbon then leave well alone, but if it is necessary to replace the seal there may be snags. Pulling off the old seal is simple with pliers. With a packet of new oil seals is a small plastic sleeve. This is fitted over the valve stem and lubricated and then the seal should be pushed on over the plastic sleeve until it seats on the guide. This must be done with a special tool VW 10 204 which fits snugly round the outside of the seal and pushes it on squarely. If the seal is assembled without the plastic sleeve the seal will be damaged and oil consumption will become excessive. If you cannot put them on properly then ask the agent to do it for you.

14 The camshaft should be tested if possible for 'run-out' by mounting it between centres in a lathe and checking the bearing surfaces with a dial gauge. Examine the cam lobes for wear and burrs. Small blemishes may be removed with a fine oil stone but do not attempt to remove grooves or ridges. If it is necessary to replace the camshaft be careful that you get the right one, there are several kinds which will fit but give entirely the wrong valve timing. Refit the camshaft and its bearings without the valves in the head and check the endplay. The limit for this is 0.005 in (0.015 mm). Radial play must be negligible 0.0015 to 0.0024 in (0.04 to 0.06 mm). The limits are tight in all cases, and measurement is difficult, but fortunately the camshaft bearings do not seem to wear and the valves keep the shaft in the upper half of the bearing.

15 When all the parts, head, valves, seats, springs, guides, seals and camshaft have been pronounced satisfactory (photo) then assembly of the head may commence. Insert the valve in the correct guide (photo), fit the inner seat, valve springs and outer seat (photo), assemble the valve spring compressor and possibly the small tube and compress the valve spring until the collets may be assembled to the valve stem (photo). If your fingers are too big, as mine are, put a blob of grease on the collet and pick it up with a small screwdriver, then insert it into the slot on the valve stem, assemble the second collet and holding them carefully together in place ease off the compressor until the spring seats the collets home. Remove the compressor, put a rag over the valve stem and compress the spring by pushing down on the valve stem. Let the valve close sharply. This is to ensure that the collets are seated correctly. If they are they will not come out. If they are not then they will and you will find them in the rag. If you did not have a rag, you may never find them again, for if they do come out they fly a considerable distance if allowed so to do. Repeat until all eight valves are in position in the cylinder head.

16 Replace the tappets in the bores from which they came (photo) and install the camshaft (photo). Fit a new oil seal at the sprocket end, lubricate the bearings set the shaft in position and install bearing caps (photo) nos 2 and 4 tightening the nuts in a diagonal pattern until the shaft is in place. Now install the other bearing caps making sure they are the right way round (centre-punch marks toward the drive pulley) and torque the caps down using a diagonal pattern to the specified torque. Install a new plug at the opposite end to the sprocket. The head is now ready for assembly except that valve clearances have not been adjusted.

This is done in the next Section.

10.15a The valves, springs, cap and collets ready for assembly

10.15b Insert the valve into the correct guide

10.15c Fit the springs and cap

10.15d Fit the compressor and assemble the collets

10.16a The tappet bucket and disc ready for assembly

10.16b Fit the camshaft ...

10.16c ... and the bearing caps

11.4 Measuring the tolerance between the cam and the tappet

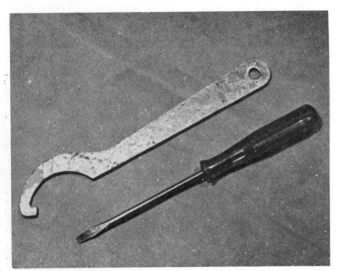

11.7a Ideally use VW/Audi tools 10.209 and 10.208 but the C-spanner and screwdriver shown do the job adequately

11.7b Press the tappet bucket rim down against the spring and lever the disc away

11 Cylinder head (1.5 litre engine) - adjustment of valve clearances

1   A special Section is devoted to this task to make reference in other parts of the book more simple.

2   Briefly the adjustment consists of measuring the clearance, calculating the error and replacing the disc with one of the correct thickness. The 26 different thicknesses of tappet clearance disc progress from 3.00 mm to 4.25 mm in stages of 0.05 of a millimetre which seems to indicate that the first thoughts of a sensible man comtemplating adjustment of the tappet clearance will be to buy a set of feeler gauges graduated in metric measure. Otherwise, a lot of calculation will be necessary and a set of conversion tables to transpose 0.05 mm steps into thousandths of an inch. However, it is not too difficult referring to the table in paragraph 7, the thinnest disc is 3.00 mm (0.1181 inches). The thickness progresses at the rate of 0.05 mm (0.001969 inch) and since feeler gauges measure only to the nearest thousandth, 0.001969 inches may be taken for practical purposes as 0.002 inches. By calculating 25 size increases at this rate the thickest disc 4.25 mm becomes 0.1681 inches whereas its true value is 0.1673 and the error over the total range is 0.0008 inches which is acceptable.

3   If routine adjustment is to be done with the engine in the car first remove the valve cover (cylinder cover). The procedure is the same except that during an engine overhaul the adjustment disc will already have been removed and cleaned. Further, the size etched on the back

of the disc will be known.

4   If the job is done with the engine in the car the discs must be removed and identified if the tolerance is outside the Specifications given. The engine will rotate more easily if the plugs are removed. **Do not** rotate the engine by turning the camshaft sprocket, this will stretch the timing belt. Use either the alternator drivebelt or jack up one front wheel and with the engine in gear rotate the roadwheel. Using feeler gauges measure the clearance between the tappet bucket and the cam when the high point of the cam is at the top (photo).

5   Repeat this measurement for all the valves in turn and then compare the measurements with the Specifications. This presents a further complication because in December 1974 VW decided that all 1.5 litre engine valve tolerances should be set at 35ºC (95ºF) and that the clearances should be:

Inlet valve	0.25 ± 0.05 mm	0.010 ± 0.002 in
Exhaust valve	0.45 ± 0.05 mm	0.017 ± 0.002 in

6   This is a reasonable temperature if the engine is in the car and can be run up to the right temperature before checking the tolerances but if not then the valves must be correctly set cold and checked again after warming up (The old 'cold' tolerance was inlet 0.15 to 0.25 mm, exhaust 0.4 to 0.5 mm).

7   Make a table of the actual tolerances and then calculate the error from the correct tolerances. Suppose on No 1 exhaust valve the measured tolerance is 0.15 mm, due say to grinding in a valve. It is

0.3 mm too small so it must be adjusted and a disc 0.3 mm thinner fitted instead of the present disc. As the discs are in steps of 0.05 mm variation the required disc can be selected once the size of the disc at present installed is known. If you have dismantled and reassembled the head then you know the size etched on the back of the disc but if you do not then the disc must be removed to find out. Ideally VW/Audi tools 10.209 and 10.208 should be used but we managed quite well within the tools shown in the photograph. They were a small electricians screwdriver and a 'C' spanner which was just the right size to push the tappet down without pushing the tappet disc (ie; push the rim down). With the cam turned to give maximum clearance the tappet is pushed down with VW/Audi 10.209 or its counterpart against the valve springs while the tappet disc is levered out and removed by the VW/Audi 10208 or a screwdriver. Be careful, if the spanner slips when the disc is halfway out the disc will fly out sharply (photo).

Once all the disc sizes are known a table may be constructed and the sizes of the new discs required may be calculated. Going back to the example, if the present disc is marked 3.60 then one marked 3.30 is required. A table of sizes and part numbers is given below:

Part No.	Thickness (mm)	Part No.	Thickness (mm)
056 109 555	3.00	056 109 568	3.65
056 109 556	3.05	056 109 569	3.70
056 109 557	3.10	056 109 570	3.75
056 109 558	3.15	056 109 571	3.80
056 109 559	3.20	056 109 572	3.85
056 109 560	3.25	056 109 573	3.90
056 109 561	3.30	056 109 574	3.95
056 109 562	3.35	056 109 575	4.00
056 109 563	3.40	056 109 576	4.05
056 109 564	3.45	056 109 577	4.10
056 109 565	3.50	056 109 578	4.15
056 109 566	3.55	056 109 579	4.20
056 109 567	3.60	056 109 580	4.25

8   As it is unlikely that you will have the spares it will be necessary to wait until they have been obtained until the tappets can be adjusted. If the adjustment was done cold then it must be checked again when the engine is hot, and if the cylinder head has been overhauled it should be checked again, hot, after 500 km (300 miles). The recommended mileage for checking is at 1000 km (600 miles) from new and then every 30000 km (18000 miles). Once the correct clearances have been achieved the cylinder head may be put on one side until required for reassembly. Replace the spark plugs. If the engine is in the car the valve cover should be replaced and the air cleaner reassembled.

9   One final suggestion. If you have done the job and know the sizes of all the discs this information should be kept in a safe place. It will save a lot of time during the next overhaul.

12 Cylinder head (1.1 litre engine) - removal and overhaul

1   The coverplate, distributor, inlet and exhaust manifolds, and the fuel pump have already been removed (Section 9) and the cylinder head is left on the block. Refer to Figs. 1.12 and 1.13.

2   Remove the springs from the tappet adjusters. This looks difficult but is suprisingly easy. Insert a screwdriver between the spring and the ball stud and lever the lower position of the spring away from the stud. When it is clear you can lift the circular part which fits into a slot in the ball stud head away from the stud and ease the spring away completely. The small diagram shows the idea.

3   According to the VW 'official' manual the next thing to do is to screw in the ball stud until the rocker finger may be removed. Along with several other people who have worked on this engine we found that the screwing in of the ball stud difficult. At this stage it must be done with a 7 mm Allen key. We could not move the ball stud this way at this juncture and when we learned that other people had actually broken a key we went cautiously. Push down on the valve spring and sufficient clearance can be gained to remove the rocker finger without struggling with the ball stud, (photo). Freeing the ball stud is discussed in paragraph 16 of this Section. Remove all of the rocker fingers, noting which valve they came from for correct replacement.

4   Next remove the camshaft sprocket (photos). Collect the key and store it safely.

5   At the other end of the camshaft is more trouble. A flange holds the shaft in place and this must be removed (photo). Three bolts hold it in place. The heads of the bolts have shallow inserts for a 6 mm key. Unless care is taken this shallow insert can be distorted. On the engine

we dismantled, which had been misused, the bolts were difficult. However, after a little persuasion two of them came out and the reason for the third one being difficult became obvious. The flange was slightly warped and after two bolts had been taken out a gap appeared between the flange and the head. The third bolt then came out easily. If one or more of these bolts is damaged during removal they should be replaced by new ones preferably with an easier type of tightening arrangement.

6   The camshaft may now be withdrawn out of the end of the head (photo).

7   The cylinder head bolts should now be removed. These are also difficult to start. The arrangement shown in Fig. 1.8 may help. Undo the bolts in the reverse order to the tightening sequences given in Fig. 1.9.

8   The cylinder head may now be lifted away from the block. The first thing to do is to take it away from the working area and clean off all carbon from the combustion spaces and valve heads. When it is clean turn it upside down and with a straight-edge and feeler gauges check that the head has not warped. Lay the straight-edge on the longitudinal centre line and insert the feelers, if possible, between the straight-edge and the cylinder head face particularly at the edges of the cylinders. A maximum distortion of 0.1 mm (0.004 in) is acceptable. If the distortion is greater the head should be taken to the agent or a reputable machine shop for correction. Do not attempt to correct this distortion yourself, it is a highly skilled job.

9   There is a special tool for valve removal, VW 2001, but you can make one at home from a piece of flat steel, bent and cut to suit the head (photo). The tool is fitted over the valve stem and under the ball socket, which is the opposite way to VW 2001 (photo). The tool may be pulled back, pushing the valve springs down. Hold the spring down, push the valve up from underneath and remove the collets. Remove the springs and push the valve out. Valves and springs should be kept together and identified with the same valve seat. The easiest way to do this is to make eight ½ inch holes in a piece of cardboard, label them with the same sequence as the head and as the valves are removed poke the valve through the appropriate hole and put the springs and caps on the stem.

10 When the valves have been removed take the spring seats off and clean all the deposit in the recess away (photo). The question of refitting oil seals is discussed in Section 10, paragraph 13. VW recommend fitting new ones every time. This is easy to do if you have tool VW 10204 but not so easy without it.

11 The wear in the valve stems is discussed in Section 10, paragraph 10. Rock limit for the 1.1 litre is quoted (with a new valve) as inlet guide 1 mm (0.04 in); exhaust guide 1.3 mm (0.5 ins). It is often hard to decide, but if there are no signs of oil carbon on the valve head fit the same valve back. The important thing is that the seal is fitted correctly. So far, VW have not indicated that guides may be replaced so a new head may be necessary.

12 Overhaul of valves and valve seats is discussed in Section 10, paragraph 10. The inlet valve may be trued on a valve grinding machine but the exhaust valve must not be corrected by machining.

13 Limits for valve springs have not been given. So the only method is to compare them all against one another, or better still against a new one. If they are all the same free-length there is no reason to scrap any of them.

14 If the camshaft bearings show signs of wear have the camshaft tested in a lathe for run-out. There must not be more than 0.01 mm (0.0004 in) run-out.

15 Camshaft endfloat must be checked with the camshaft installed properly in the head after the distributor flange and oil seal have been fitted. A maximum of 0.15 mm (0.006 ins) is allowed. Again this is hard to check unless a clock gauge is available with VW tool 387, but it can be done with feelers. Unless the shaft shows signs of wear it is reasonable to think the adjustment is correct. If it does then consult the VW agent for there is nothing you can do about it.

Finally examine the cam faces for wear, burrs, and burr marks. Very slight marks may be polished off with fine emery but extensive marks regretfully indicate a new shaft. Once the case hardening is broken down wear will become rapid interfering with the valve timing.

16 Before commencing assembly of the head there is the question of seized up ball studs. Unless the stud will turn in its adaptor plug the adjustment of valve clearances is impossible. The stud has two sections of thread separated by a 'waist'. They screw down into a Helicoil insert in the adaptor plug. (photo). The adaptor may be removed from the head using a 24 mm socket (on a 15/16 in socket) as a last resort (photo) and the adaptor held in a vice. We found that all those in our engine

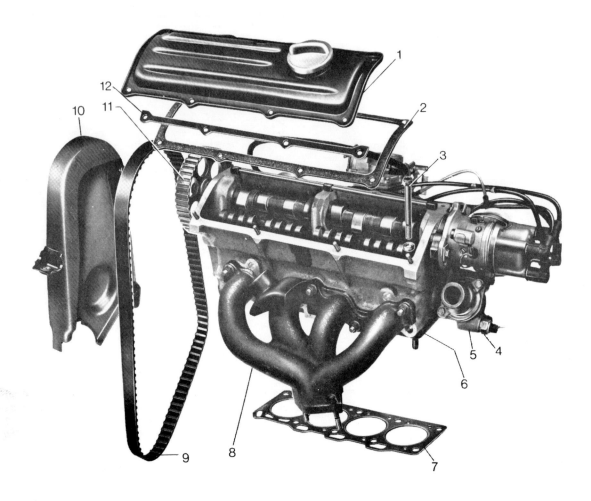

Fig. 1.12. 1.1 litre engine - cylinder head assembly - general layout (Sec. 12)

1	Valve cover	4	Temperature sender
2	Gasket	5	Coolant flange
3	Cylinder head bolt	6	Cylinder head
7	Cylinder head gasket	10	Belt cover
8	Exhaust.manifold	11	Camshaft pulley
9	Timing belt	12	Valve cover lock plate

12.3 Press down the valve spring and wriggle away the rocker fingers

12.4a Undo the sprocket nut (note the guard securing bolt can be seen through the sprocket) ...

12.4b ... and take off the sprocket and key

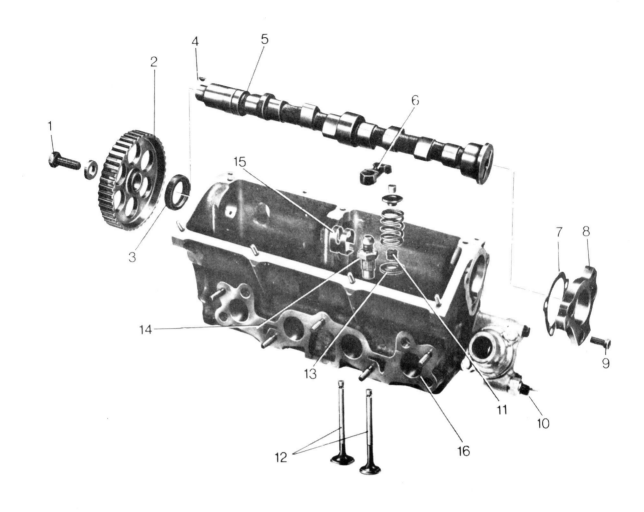

Fig. 1.13. 1.1 litre engine - cylinder head - exploded view (Sec. 12)

1	Bolt	6	Rocker finger	11	Valve stem seal
2	Camshaft pulley	7	Gasket	12	Valves
3	Oil seal	8	Distributor flange	13	Lower spring seat
4	Woodruff key	9	Socket head bolt	14	Ball stud
5	Camshaft	10	Temperature sender unit	15	Retaining clip
				16	Cylinder head

12.5 Remove the flange from the distributor end and ...

12.6 ... withdraw the camshaft

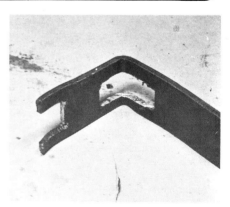

12.9a The home made valve spring compressor

12.9b Compressor in action

12.10 Valve spring seat removed for cleaning

12.16a The ball stud and its adaptor ...

12.16b ... removed from the cylinder head

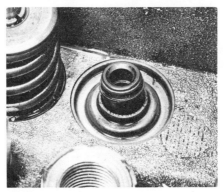

12.18a Valve spring seat and valve guide seal in position

12.18b Fitting the valve

12.19 Fit a new oil seal at the sprocket end of the camshaft

12.20 Fitting the spring clip to the ball stud and finger

12.21 Checking the valve clearance

seem to have seized up but once we had turned the ball socket a few times then the stud moved easily. It will help if you grip the Allen key with a mole wrench close to the ball and turn the key and the wrench together. However, they must be made to turn reasonably easily, not loosely, even if you have to dismantle them all.

17 When all the overhaul work has been completed clean up and lay the parts out for assembly.

18 Refit the spring seat and seal (photo) and then insert the valve (photo). Fit the valve spring and cap and then using a suitable block of wood under the head to hold the valve up, press down on the valve spring cap with the compressor (photo 12.9b) and insert the collets Cover the collets with a duster and press the valve down sharply and let it spring back to place to check that the collets are sealed. Work right down the head until all the valves are installed.

19 Press out the oil seal at the sprocket end of the head and press in a new one, if required (photo). Lightly oil the camshaft bearing surfaces and insert the camshaft from the distributor end. When the camshaft is correctly seated fit a new gasket to the distributor flange and bolt it to

the head torquing the bolts correctly (2 mkg, 15 lb ft). Check the end-float of the crankshaft (paragraph 15). Install the camshaft bearing oil pipe (if removed) and then refit the camshaft pulley and key.

20 Install the rocker fingers on the same valves that they were on before. To do this either use the valve compressor VW 2001 or push down on the valve cap but be careful the collets are not displaced (photo 12.3). Seat the fingers carefully and then install the springs. Push the lower part of the spring into place and lift the top part over the finger to fit in the slot (photo).

21 Using an Allen key in the ball socket and the correct feeler gauge between the lower surface of the cam (the round piece not the pointed end) and the top of the finger (photo) set the correct tolerance for each valve (see Specifications).

Again starting from the sprocket end the valves are: *No 1 cylinder inlet, no 1 cylinder exhaust, no 2 cylinder inlet, no 2 cylinder exhaust, no 3 cylinder inlet, no 3 cylinder exhaust, no 4 cylinder inlet, no 4 cylinder exhaust.*

22 When this operation is complete loosely fit the valve cover and set the head on one side for assembly to the block in due course.

13 Cylinder head (1.1 litre engine) - adjustment of valve clearances

1   The method is described in Section 12 but for owners requiring only to adjust the valve clearance a simpler procedure is tabulated.
2   Run the engine until the engine coolant is 35°C (95°F).
3   Remove the valve cover from the cylinder head and adjust the tappet sin the following manner.
4   Using a 19 mm socket turn the crankshaft pulley nut until the two cams for hot cylinder, nearest to the camshaft sprocket, are at equal angles from the valves. Check the exhaust valve (nearest to sprocket) clearance. If it is incorrect turn the ball socket under the rocker finger spring using an Allen key (7 mm). Repeat the operation for the inlet valve. If the ball socket will not move read Section 12.
5   Turn the crankshaft pulley nut so that no 3 cylinder cams are equally spaced and repeat the operation. Repeat for no 4 cylinder and then no 2.
6   The sequence of valves starting at the camshaft sprocket is different from the 1.5 litre. In this case, starting at the sprocket end, the order is: *no 1 cylinder inlet then exhaust, no 2 cylinder inlet then exhaust, no 3 cylinder inlet then exhaust and no 4 cylinder inlet then exhaust.*
7   Do not turn the engine by turning the camshaft sprocket or you will stretch the timing belt.
8   Replace the cylinder head valve cover using a new gasket.

14 Engine dismantling (1.5 litre engine) - removal of crankshaft connecting rods, pistons and intermediate shaft

1   Turn the engine on its side and remove the sump (oil pan). There may be more oil to run out so be ready to catch it. The oil pump complete with strainer may now be removed after undoing the two socket headed bolts. Lay it on one side for inspection and overhaul.
2   At the flywheel end remove the six bolts holding the oil seal flange and the gasket to the cylinder block and take off the flange.

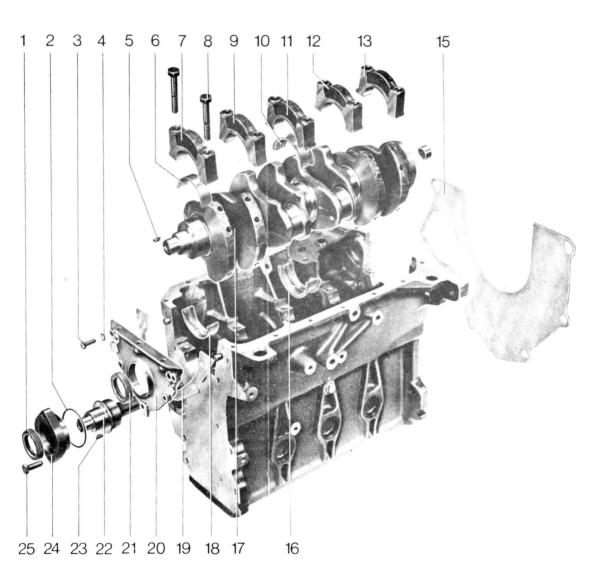

Fig. 1.14. 1.5 litre engine - crankshaft and cylinder block (Sec. 14)

1 Oil seal	7 Bearing cap hole	13 Bearing cap No. 5	19 Gasket
2 'O' ring	8 Bolt	15 Intermediate plate	20 Oil seal flange
3 Bolt	9 Bearing cap No. 2	16 Upper shell bearing	21 Oil seal
4 Washer	10 Shell bearing lower	No. 3	22 Intermediate shaft
5 Woodruff key	No. 3	17 Crankshaft	23 Key
6 Shell bearing lower	11 Bearing cap No. 3	18 Upper shell bearing	24 Flange
Nos. 1,2,4 & 5	12 Bearing cap No. 4	Nos. 1,2,4 & 5	25 Bolt

14.3a The two bolts holding the intermediate shaft are marked 'A'

14.3b Removing the intermedaite shaft

14.6 The top of the piston has an arrow

14.7 Measuring the axial play of the crankshaft at no 3 bearing

3   Remove the intermediate pulley and then undo the two bolts hold-ing the intermediate shaft oil seal flange after which the intermediate shaft may be drawn out (photos).
4   Undo the five bolts holding the oil seal flange to the front of the block and remove the flange and seal.
5   Refer to Fig. 1.14. It is important that all the bearing caps are replaced in exactly the way they are fitted before dismantling. This applies also to the shell bearings and pistons. Using a centre-punch mark the connecting rod bearing caps on the edge nearest the front (timing wheel end) using one dot for number 1, two for number 2, and so on.
6   Undo the nuts or bolts from no 1 connecting rod bearing and remove the bearing cap. It would appear that some connecting rods have bolts fitting through the caps into the rods. Whichever are fitted VW recommend that they be replaced by new ones on overhaul, so add them to the order list. Gently push the connecting rod and piston out of the block through the top. Do not force it, if there is difficulty then draw the piston back and you will probably find a ridge of carbon at the top of the bore. Remove this with a scraper and if there is a metal ridge reduce this as well but do not score the bore. The piston and connect-ing rod will now come out. On the top of the piston there is an arrow which should point towards the front of the engine (photo). Replace the connecting rod bearing cap the right way round and mark the connecting rod and bearing cap with a centre punch so that they may be easily assembled correctly. All this takes time but the effect on assembly more than saves any time spent now on marking parts. Set the

connecting rod and piston on one side labelled No 1 and proceed to remove 2,3 and 4 labelling them likewise.
7   Now examine the main bearing caps. It will be seen that the caps are numbered one to five and that the number is on the side of the engine opposite the oil pump housing. Identify these numbers. If any are obscured then mark the caps as in the same way as the connecting rod caps. Before removing the caps push the crankshaft to the rear and measure the axial play at no 3 main bearing (photo). It should not be more than 0.010 in (0.25 mm). Remove the bearing caps retaining nuts, remove the bearing caps and lift out the crankshaft. If the main bearings are not being renewed make sure the shells are identified so that they go back into the same housing the same way round. The engine is now completely dismantled. Clean the carbon off the pistons and tidy up all round. It is now time to start measuring and sorting out what needs to be done to bring the engine back to standard.

---

15 Engine dismantling (1.1 litre engine) - removal of crankshaft, connecting rods and pistons

---

1   Turn the engine onto the side and remove the sump (oil pan). There will be sludge and a little oil so try to catch this as the sump is detached. Set the sump aside for cleaning. Refer to Figs. 1.15 and 1.16
2   Now set the engine to stand on the cylinder head face. Remove the oil strainer and then the crankshaft pulley (photos). Collect the key

and store it with the pulley.

3   Seven bolts hold the oil pump to the cylinder block, remove these and pull the oil pump off the crankshaft. The oil seal is in the oil pump housing (photo). There are two dowels, do not put wedges in the joint, tap the pump away.

4   At the other end of the block the oil seal is held in a housing. Undo the bolts holding it and draw it away from the block.

5   Refer to Section 14, paragraph 5 and carry on from there. The procedure is exactly the same except that the axial play of the shaft (paragraph 7) should not be more than 0.2 mm (0.009 inch).

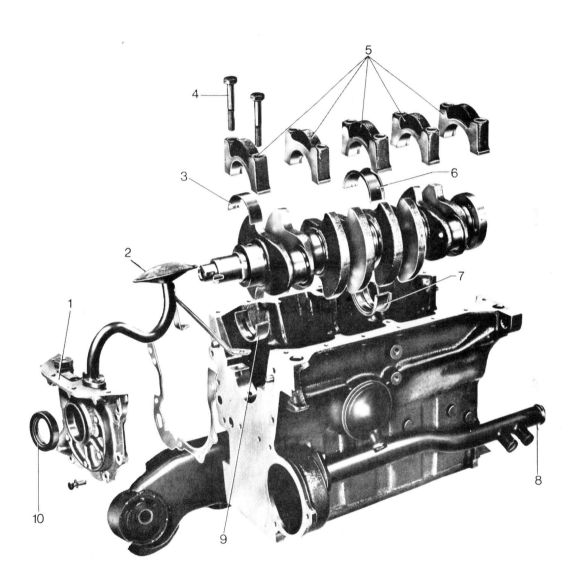

Fig. 1.15. 1.1 litre engine - crankshaft and cylinder block (Sec. 15)

1	Oil pump casing	6	Bearing shell 3, flange, no groove
2	Oil strainer	7	Bearing shell 3, flange, with groove
3	Bearing shell 1,2,4,5 (no groove)	8	Water pump inlet pipe
4	Bearing cap bolts	9	Bearing shell 1,2,4,5 (with groove)
5	Bearing caps	10	Oil seal

Fig. 1.16. 1.1 litre engine - piston and connecting rods (Sec. 15)

1 Rings	4 Connecting rod	7 Bearing cap	9 Piston pin
2 Piston pin circlip	5 Lower bearing shell	8 High tension connecting bolts	10 Upper bearing shell
3 Piston	6 Cap nuts		

15.2a Remove the oil strainer, two bolts to the stays and a flange to the pump

15.2b Remove the crankshaft pulley. Do not separate the Vee-belt pulley from the sprocket - watch out for the key

15.3 Remove the oil pump. Note the dowels

16 Measurement of crankshaft journals and shell bearings (1.1 litre and 1.5 litre)

1 The method is the same for both engines but the limits are different.
2 The easiest way to measure the radial clearance is by using 'Plastigage' strip. This is obtainable in three grades.

Marking	Packet colour	Size mm.
PG 1	Green	0.025 to 0.075
PG 2	Red	0.05 to 0.15
PG 3	Blue	0.10 to 0.23

Clean the shaft and shell bearing, carefully, lay the plastigage strip along the journal replace the bearing and tighten the cap. The torque varies according to the bearing. The table below will help.

Bearing	Maximum clearance mm	in	Torque reqd mkg	lb ft	Plastigage colour
Main (1.1 litre)	0.15	0.006	6.5	47	Blue
Main (1.5 litre)	0.17	0.007	6.5	47	Blue
Big-end (1.1 litre)	0.095	0.004	3.0	22	Red
Big-end (1.5 litre)	0.12	0.005	3.5	24	Red

3 Fig. 1.17 shows the way to locate the strip. Remove the bearing cap extract the flattened strip and measure the width at each end. This will indicate the extent of radial play and whether there is any taper or not. Be careful not to rotate the shaft in the bearing while doing the job or the Plastigage will be rendered useless.
4 The ovality or out-of-roundness of the journal is also important. This can be checked with vernier calipers and must not exceed 0.03 mm (0.0012 inches). This limit also applies to the taper of the journal. If no suitable vernier is available use another strip of plastigage at a line parallel to the first one but 90° round the circumference of the journal.
5 If the shaft and shell bearings come within the limits laid down then all is well. If not then there is the problem of whether the shaft or the bearings, or both are at fault. This can only be determined by the use of micrometers. We suggest you consult your VW agent or a reputable engineering company who specialize in regrind operations and take their advice. In the event that the shaft must be reground the workshop doing the work should be asked to fit the bearings.

It is early days to expect undersize II and III to be arriving but these represent further standard regrind sizes for which shell bearings are available. The dimensions are given in the Specifications.
6 If you do not use 'Plastigage' and measure the journals and bearings with a micrometer there are a number of things to consider. Are the micrometers correctly zeroed, and are you experienced in measuring with a precision instrument? Do not accept a marginal decision but get it checked. The grinding of shafts is an expensive business.
7 When you are satisfied that the main and big-end bearings are servicable remove the shaft and clean it very carefully. Clean out the oilways and be sure no bits of rag get into them. Set the crankshaft aside and proceed to examine the state of the pistons and bores.

17 Measurement of cylinder bores and pistons (1.1 litre and 1.5 litre)

1 The procedure is the same for both engines. First determine the 'Honing group' of your engine. On the 1.5 litre this is stamped on the block just above the alternator, it will be a three figure number between 651 and 753 (see table below) On the 1.1 litre engine the data is next to the engine number below the exhaust manifold. It will be 'O', 'I', or 'II'. These figures indicate the group in which the engine was included during selective assembly. Study of the tables in paragraph 3 will show

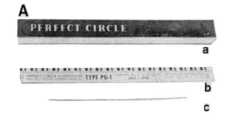

Fig. 1.17. Measurement of bearing clearance using plastigauge strip (Sec. 16)

A   The plastigauge packet (a) packaging (b) scale in mm and ins (c) the plastigauge wire
B   The gauge wire should be set along the journal as shown at 'a'

that pistons are selected to fit the various groups. If you do not understand this system consult someone who does, for if the wrong piston is fitted, engine seizure could happen.

2   The wear on the cylinder bores is uneven. Maximum wear may be expected on the diameter at 90° to the piston pin. There is no short cut to measuring the bore. It must be done with an internal micrometer. Measure the diameter, parallel to the piston pin and at right-angles to the pin, at 10 mm (0.04 in) from the top of the bore, midway, and 10 mm (0.04 in) from the bottom of the bore. This will give six readings and if any of them vary more than 0.04 mm (0.0016 in) from the bore diameter given by the honing code then the block must be machined and new pistons fitted. Should the difference be much more than 0.04 mm then the lubrication system is suspect. Scores due to broken rings or other misfortunes are even worse and the block should be taken to the agent should these be present for his advice.

Ovality must not be more than 0.03 mm (0.0011 in), measurement in excess of this also requires machining.

3   Table of cylinder bore and piston sizes.

Engine	Hone state	Code No	Cylinder diameter mm	in	Piston diameter mm	in
	Basic	651	76.51	3.0122	76.48	3.0110
	Basic	652	76.52	3.0126	76.49	3.0114
	Basic	653	76.53	3.0130	76.50	3.0118
	1st O/s	676	76.76	3.0220	76.73	3.0209
	1st O/s	677	76.77	3.0224	76.74	3.0213
	1st O/s	678	76.78	3.0228	76.75	3.0217
1.5 litre	2nd O/s	701	77.01	3.0319	76.98	3.0307
	2nd O/s	702	77.02	3.0323	76.99	3.0311
	2nd O/s	703	77.03	3.0327	77.00	3.0315
	3rd O/s	751	77.51	3.0516	77.48	3.0504
	3rd O/s	752	77.52	3.0520	77.49	3.0508
	3rd O/s	753	77.53	3.0524	77.50	3.0512
	Basic	0	69.51	2.7366	69.48	2.7355
1.1 litre	Basic	1	69.52	2.7370	69.49	2.7359
	Basic	11	69.53	2.7374	69.50	2.7363

So far regrind sizes for the 1.1 litre have not been published, nor would one expect them on an engine issued as recently as this.

4   It is no use considering the pistons until the cylinder bore problem has been settled, but once that has been done the required piston size may be read from the table in paragraph 3. If the bore has not worn enough to warrant rework the next thing is to see whether the pistons are in limit. On the piston crown are two pieces of information: an arrow which points, when the engine is assembled to the front of the engine and the piston nominal diameter in millimetres. The piston diameter should be measured 16 mm (5/8 in) from the bottom edge of the piston at right-angles to the piston pin. If the measured diameter varies from the nominal diameter by more than 0.04 mm (0.0016 in) then the piston should be replaced. If the bores show no wear and the pistons are in limit then they may be put back in the engine. If only the pistons are worn then new pistons to fit the bores may be fitted but care must be taken to see that the difference in weight between any of the pistons in one engine does not exceed 17 grams.

5   There are more measurements to be taken concerning the rings. These are dealt with in Section 14.

6   When buying new pistons care should be taken not only to obtain the correct weight and diameter but also the correct shape. There are several different shapes, flat crowns, dished crowns and so on. You will want the shape identical with the pistons taken out of the engine. Pistons are supplied for the 1.5 engine by either Mahle or K.S. and must not vary in weight more than 17 grams. Consult the VW agent, he has the latest information.

7   This all sounds very alarming but unless the engine is badly neglected it is hardly likely to require regrinding, and if it does the firm who do the job will fit the pistons for you. Even if the bore is worn the worst that can happen is excessive oil consumption, the engine will not collapse or stop as in the case of a worn big-end. Even high oil consumption can be overcome by fitting new piston rings.

18 Measurement and servicing of piston pins and piston rings (1.1 and 1.5 litre)

1   As yet the pistons have not been removed from the connecting rods. If the piston has passed inspection so far then it must be removed from the connecting rod, the piston pin checked and the rings removed. checked and possibly replaced. It is suggested that each piston is removed serviced and replaced in turn, this avoids confusion.

2   If the piston failed its inspection then remove the piston pin and fit a new piston assembly with new rings as supplied from the VW store. The old piston will make a good ashtray!

3   From the outset it must be clear that rings come in sets, if you break one then the minimum purchase is three, so be careful.

4   To remove the piston pin first remove the circlips from each end and then push the pin out. If it is tight, then raise the temperature of the piston to 60°C (140°F), hold it by a light bulb and the pin will come out easily. Check the play in the connecting rod bush, if the pin seems loose the running clearance limits are 0.011 to 0.025 mm (0.0004 to 0.0009 in) which means if you can rock it at all then either the bush or the pin are worn. New bushes can be obtained and pressed into the connecting rod if necessary, but they must then be reamed to size to fit the pin. It is felt that this job should be left to the agent, not because it is difficult, but because it requires an expensive reamer. However, this is rarely necessary.

5   It is almost certain that the rings will require attention. There are three, the top two are compression rings, the lowest one is the oil scraper ring. The compression rings will probably be free in the grooves but the scraper ring may be seized in the groove. This presents a problem, soak the ring in paraffin or some suitable solvent and ease it gently until it will rotate round the piston. The rings must now be removed from the piston. This is done only with care. There are special tools which are called piston ring pliers which can be bought and will break rings just as easily as any other tool if not used carefully, but do make the job simpler, if used with care. Once the rings are eased out of the grooves and off the piston make sure that the top compression ring is marked so that it can go back into the groove the right way up. The middle ring has 'TOP' marked on it as does the scraper ring. Gently remove all carbon from the rings and grooves. Now insert the ring in its groove and roll it round the piston to see that the groove is clear (photo).

6   Clean the cylinder bore and using the piston as a fixture push the ring down the bore until it is 15 mm (5/8 in) from the top. Now measure the gap with a feeler gauge (photo). This should be not more than

18.5 Checking the piston ring and groove for burrs

18.6 Insert the ring in the bore and check with a feeler gauge

18.7 Checking the ring to groove clearance

1.0 mm (0.039 in) for compression and scraper rings.

7 Refit the rings to the piston spacing the gaps at 120 degree intervals and making sure the top is the right way up. With a feeler gauge measure the clearance between the ring and the piston groove (photo). This must not exceed 0.15 mm (0.006 in).

8 If new rings are to be fitted the gap must be measured in the cylinder and adjusted if necessary with a fine file to the limits shown in the Specifications.

9 If the rings are correct then refit the piston to the connecting rod, making sure the arrow on the piston points to the front, (you marked the bearing cap), refit the circlips and proceed to check the rings on the other three pistons.

10 On 1.5 litre engines a different type of scraper ring may be used. It may be easily recognized by a spiral spring in the ring across the gap. This is where things become difficult. Two types of piston are used in production (Mahle and KS) and there are different diameters for the oil scraper grooves. If you find your vehicle has these rings it would be best to go to the agent, and ask how to refit them according to the latest instructions. The modification is to overcome excessive oil consumption, so if you have this problem and the old pattern rings, a visit to the agent is also required, for this may be cure for your trouble.

19 Connecting rods - inspection and renewal

1 It is most unusual to have to renew a connecting rod but if this has

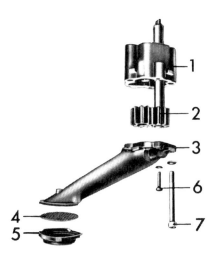

Fig. 1.18. 1.5 litre engine - oil pump - exploded view (Sec. 20)

1 Body	3 Cover	5 Cap	7 Bolt (2)
2 Gears	4 Strainer	6 Bolt (2)	

to be done then a complete set of four must be installed.

20 Oil pump (1.5 litre) - inspection and overhaul

1 Refer to Fig. 1.18. The strainer gauze may be removed when the cap is levered off with a screwdriver. Clean the gauze, replace it and refit the cap.

2 Remove the two small bolts and take the cover away from the body. Examine the face of the cover (photo). As will be seen in the photograph the gears have marked the cover. If the depth of this marking is significant then the face of the cover must be machined flat again.

3 Remove the gears and wash the body and gears in clean paraffin. Dry them and reassemble the gears, lubricating them with clean engine oil. Measure the backlash between the gears with a feeler gauge (photo). This should be 0.05 to 0.20 mm (0.002 to 0.008 in).

4 Now place a straight-edge over the pump body along the line joining the centre of the two gears and measure with a feeler gauge the axial clearance between the gears and the straight-edge (photo). This must not be more than 0.15 mm (0.006 in).

5 If all is well, check that the shaft is not slack in its bearings, and reassemble the pump for fitting to the engine.

6 If there is any doubt about the pump it is recommended strongly that a replacement be obtained. Once wear starts in a pump it progresses rapidly. In view of the damage that may follow a loss of oil pressure skimping the oil pump repair is a false economy.

21 Oil pump (1.1 litre) - inspection and overhaul

1 The oil pump for the 1.1 litre engine is very different from the 1.5 litre. Having removed it from the shaft (photo 15.3) lay it down on its back and remove the three crosshead screws holding the cover to the body. It may be necessary to remove these with an impact screwdriver.

2 Turn the cover plate over, wipe it clean and examine the surface for scoring or scuffing (photo). The one illustrated has marks where the gears have been bearing, but no significant wear. If there is, this may be machined away, but the surface must be flat.

3 Examine the gears for signs of wear. There should be no significant backlash or wear between the gears and the case. Remove the gears and examine the teeth for damage of any sort. There should be no wear on the interior of the casing (photos).

4 Remove the pressure valve (photo) and check the spring and plunger.

5 Clean all the parts carefully. If gears are to be renewed, both gears must be renewed together. They are obtainable in pairs only. The inner gear goes in only one way but the outer gear may be inadvertently put in upside down. There is a centre-punch mark on the top surface and this **must** be visible after assembly.

6 Clean out the valve plunger recess carefully and check that the seating is not ridged on the plunger. When replacing the spring and plunger torque the base plug to 2.5 mkg (18 lb ft).

7 The oil seal for the crankshaft should be pressed out and a new one fitted. Be careful not to damage the seal when installing it.

8 If there is the slightest doubt about the condition of the pump consult the VW agent. If this item does not work properly the engine will soon wear out.

20.2 Examine the face of the cover of the oil pump for scoring

20.3 Checking the backlash of the oil pump gears

20.4 Checking the endfloat of the oil pump gears

21.2 The inside surface of the oil pump cover (1.1 litre). The shiny surfaces show where the gears have rubbed

21.3a View of the pump, cover removed

21.3b View of the pump, gears removed

21.4 Oil pump pressure valve

22 Intermediate shaft (1.5 litre) - inspection and overhaul

1   Check the fit of the intermediate shaft in its bearings. If there is excessive play the shaft must be compared with a new one. If the shaft is in good order and the bearings in the block are worn this job is beyond your scope, you may even need a new block so seek expert advice.
2   Check the surface of the cam which drives the fuel pump. If serious ridging is present a new shaft is indicated.
3   Check the teeth of the distributor drive gear for scuffing or chipping. Check the condition of the timing belt pulley.
4   It is unlikely that damage to this shaft has happened but if it has seek advice from the VW agent.
5   There is an oil seal in the flange for the intermediate shaft. This may need renewal if there are signs of leakage. To do this remove the timing belt pulley and withdraw the flange from the shaft. The oil seal may now be prised out and a new one pressed in. Always fit a new 'O' ring on the flange before assembling it to the cylinder block.

23 Flywheel (1.1 and 1.5 litre engine) - inspection and repair

1   There is not much you can do about the flywheel if it is damaged.
2   Inspect the starter ring teeth. If these are chipped or worn it is possible to replace the starter ring. This means heating the ring until it

may be withdrawn from the flywheel, or alternatively splitting it. A new one must then be shrunk on. If you know how to do this and you can get a new ring then the job can be done but it is beyond the capacity of most owners.
3   Serious pitting on the flywheel clutch facing again requires a new flywheel. Do not attempt to clean the pitting off with a scraper or emery. The face must be machined. The maximum allowed run-out is 0.0032 ins (see Specifications).
4   If it is necessary to fit a new flywheel to the 1.5 litre engine the ignition timing mark must be made by the owner. The new flywheel has only the TDC mark. For engines requiring a mark at 7.5° before TDC measure along the rim from the TDC mark 16 mm (0.63 in) to the left and make a notch with a three cornered file. For the USA version with 3° ATDC measure 6 mm (0.24 in) to the right of the TDC mark and make the notch.

24 Crankshaft oil seals (1.5 litre engine) - refitting

1   This task has been left until the assembly of the engine is ready to commence because the seals are easily damaged and once placed in the flanges should be assembled to the engine.
2   The rear (flywheel) oil seal is contained in an aluminium frame (photo). Ease out the old seal, clean the housing and press in the new seal. Official agents have two special tools to do this: 10.205 and 10.220

24.2 The rear oil seal in its mounting

24.3a The rear oil seal in its casing installed over the crankshaft flange

24.3b The front oil seal of the 1.5 litre engine

27.1a Fit the upper bearing shells to the block. This is no 3 with the flanges

27.1b Lightly oil the bearing shell and ...

27.1c ... lower the crankshaft into its bearing

so it is evident that the seating of this seal needs care. In August 1974 a modification to the crankshaft changed the diameter of the flange to which the flywheel in fitted from 82 mm to 85 mm. The inner diameter of the oil seal has been altered to suit. The outer diameter remains the same. Tools VW 10.205 and 10.220 are no longer of use to remove and fit the new seal and tool 2003 must be used. This seems all the more reason why the flange should be removed before refitting the oil seal. Ease it in very gently and press it in the last bit either with a plate in a large vice or a mandrel press. Alternatively use the flywheel bolts and make up a suitable disc. Do not hammer it in, if the lips of the seal are damaged oil will seep through to the clutch eventually and you will be in the repair business again.

3   The front seal is also delicate, although if this one does not work at the worst you will only lose oil. Ease the seal out of the flange, clean the flange and press the seal into position. VW say this seal may be replaced with the engine in position in the car and so it may if you have VW tools 10.219 and 10.203 to remove and replace it and you have practiced the job with the engine out of the chassis. We did not think this was a job for the DIY owner. Tool 10.219 is a piece of steel rod shaped to extract the seal. 10.203 is a collar placed over the crankshaft in place of the pulley and pushes the seal into position when the pulley nut is tightened. A modification introduced in August 1974 requires this seal to be pressed in until it is 2 mm (0.08 in) below the outer face of the flange. Tool 10.219 is no use for removing this seal and tool 10.203 must be modified to allow the tool to enter the flange to a depth of 2 mm (0.08 in). If the rear and front seals are to be replaced with the engine in position we believe that it is better to remove the oil seal flanges, replace the seals and fit new gaskets using a sealing compound. This will permit proper examination of the shaft for scoring or wear (photos).

25 Crankshaft oil seals (1.1 litre engine) - refitting

1   The fitting of the front oil seal is described in Section 21 (oil pump).
2   The rear seal is fitted in exactly the same way as the 1.5 litre engine, Section 24.

26 Engine assembly - general instructions

If the work has been carried out carefully all of the components of the engine have been overhauled, or new ones obtained, and the engine is ready for assembly. This is the most pleasant part of the job.

Clear away any dirty rags, old parts, dirty paraffin and with clean hands and clean overalls, lay out the clean tools on a clean bench.

Plenty of clean non-fluffy rag will be needed, an oil can full of clean engine oil and a set of engine overhaul gaskets. This is a standard pack. Undo the pack and identify each of its contents.

A further tool is required. This is a torque wrench capable of measuring up to 60 lb ft (8.5 kg m). It will also be necessary to have an extension bar and socket spanners for metric sizes (mm) 6,8,10,12 and 14.

From now on nuts and bolts must be tightened to specified torques. These are not quoted in the text but are listed in the Specifications. Use the open end or ring spanner to do up the nuts and bolts but use the torque wrench to tighten the last bit.

We have tried to divide the job so far into tasks without being dogmatic. The assembly problem will follow the same pattern and we suggest you complete the tasks without interruption. Put the crankshaft in place and fit all the main bearings and then think about the next job. This way you will not forget things. Finally, take your time, if you are not sure then go over it again.

27 Engine assembly (1.1 and 1.5 litre engine) - assembly of connecting rods, pistons, crankshaft and intermediate shaft

1   Place the cylinder block upside down on the bench. Wipe carefully the main journal seatings and fit the main bearing top halves into place. Nos 1, 2, 4 and 5 are plain shells with grooves in them. No 3 has small flanges (photo). If the old bearings are being refitted it is essential that they go back in the same housing the same way round. Lightly oil the shells (photo) and lift in the crankshaft (photo).
2   Fit the lower shells to the bearing caps and install them over the studs (photo). These are plain shells. Once again if the old ones are being

27.2 Fit the lower main bearing caps and ...

27.3 ... tighten the nuts to the correct torque

27.7a Fit a ring compressor to the piston and install the piston and connecting rod

27.7b Fit the bearing cap to the connecting rod

28.1 Install the oil pump (1.5 litre)

28.2a Install the oil pump strainer (1.1 litre) and fit the sump

28.2b Trim the oil pump gasket (1.1 litre)

28.3 Fit the sump pan (1.5 litre)

29.2 Clean the cylinder head and fit a new gasket (1.5 litre)

29.3 Fit the cylinder head (1.5 litre)

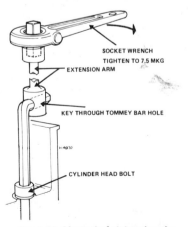

Fig. 1.19. Method of tightening the cylinder head bolts if the special Allen key is not available (Sec. 29)

SOCKET WRENCH TIGHTEN TO 7.5 MKG

EXTENSION ARM

KEY THROUGH TOMMEY BAR HOLE

CYLINDER HEAD BOLT

29.7 Refit the distributor (1.5 litre) remember the centre punch marks. Refit the oil filter flange to the block

used they must go back in the same place the same way round. This applies anyway to the bearing caps. They are numbered, one goes next to the timing gears and the numbers are on the side opposite to the oil pump.

3 Tighten the bearing cap nuts to 12 ft lb (1.8 kg m) and then tap the shaft to the rear to seat the bearings. Now using a diagonal pattern torque the cap nuts to 47 lb ft (6.5 kg m) (photo). Lever the shaft to the rear as far as it will go and check the clearance between No 3 main bearing and the crankshaft with a feeler gauge to determine crankshaft endfloat. it should be between 0.07 to 0.17 mm (0.0028 to 0.0067 in) for new bearings and not more than 0.25 mm (0.010 in) maximum for the 1.5 litre or 0.20 mm (0.009 in) for the 1.1 litre. If the maximum is exceeded then No 3 bearing must be replaced by a new one.

4 Lubricate the rear of the crankshaft and using a new gasket install the rear oil seal and flange. Tighten the six bolts to the correct torque 7 ft lb (1 kg m).

5 On the 1.5 litre engine lubricate the front of the crankshaft and fit the front oil seal and flange. Torque the nuts to the correct amount.

6 On the 1.5 litre engine install the intermediate shaft. Remember to fit a new 'O' ring and torque the flange bolts correctly.

7 Lay the block on one side. Fit a ring compressor to No 1 piston (see next paragraph) and insert the connecting rod (minus bearing cap) and piston into No 1 cylinder (photo). Check that the arrow on the piston points to the front of the block and gradually ease the piston and rings into the block removing the ring compressor as the rings go into the bore. When all the rings are safely in, pull the big-end bearing to one side of the crankshaft, check that the shell bearing is seated correctly in the connecting rod, lubricate the shell, and fit the connecting rod to the crankshaft journal. Check that the other half of the shell bearing is seated in the bearing cap, lubricate the bearing and fit the cap to the connecting rod (photo). Check that all the markings (installed on dismantling) agree and having fitted new bolts or nuts, torque the nuts to the correct torque. Repeat the process for pistons 2,3 and 4.

8 The use of a ring compressor is strongly recommended. It is cheap enough to buy, but if you cannot get one then make one. A piece of 1/16 in (1.58 mm) thick sheet metal about 2 in (50.8 mm) wide wrapped round the piston to compress the rings into the grooves is all that is required. It may be held in position with a large Jubilee clip or some similar device. This way the rings go in safely. It is very difficult to coax the rings in one at a time and a broken ring will not only hold up the job for even a week, but a new set of rings must be bought. That will cost more than a ring compressor.

9 Once all the big-end bearings are installed check the axial play of each bearing. Push the connecting rod against the crankshaft web and measure the gap on the other side with a feeler gauge. It should not be more than 0.40 mm (0.015 in). If it is then consult the agent. Either the bearings are faulty or there has been a possible fault introduced when regrinding the journal. Turn the cylinder block back onto the face to which the cylinder head fits.

28 Engine assembly (1.1 and 1.5 litre) - oil pump, strainer, sump and pulley

1 On the 1.5 litre engine the strainer is fitted to the pump and both parts of the lubrication system are bolted in together. (photo). If you have not dismantled the gauze from the strainer check that it is clean. Lever it out and wash it if necessary. Two bolts hold the pump in place.

2 On the 1.1 litre engine the oil pump has been overhauled and is ready for bolting to the block. Install a new gasket. Lightly oil the shaft and ease it into the oil seal. Position the pump on the dowels and insert the holding bolts. Torque to the correct amount. Fit a new gasket to the strainer flange and refit the strainer to the oil pump, bolting the support stays at the same time (photo). Carefully trim the top of the gasket where it protrudes from the sump flange (photo).

3 Fit a new sump gasket using a good cold non-set joint compound and assemble the sump to the cylinder block. The procedure is the same for both engines. Fit all the bolts loosely and then tighten progressively starting in the middle of the long side (photo).

4 Assemble the intermediate shaft pulley on the 1.5 litre engine and tighten the bolt correctly.

5 On both engines assemble the combined Vee-belt and timing belt pulley to the crankshaft.

29 Engine assembly (1.5 litre) - cylinder head, timing belt and distributor

1 Turn the engine over and support it on the sump with wooden blocks. Clean the top face of the block. Make a final inspection of the bores and lubricate them.

2 If you look at the edge of the block between No 3 and No 4 cylinders on the side above the distributors, the engine number is stamped on an inclined surface. Using this as a datum, install a new cylinder head gasket so that the word 'OBEN' engraved on the gasket is over this datum point and on the top side of the gasket (photo).

3 The cylinder head was overhauled in Section 10 and the camshaft assembled with the correct clearances for the valves in Section 11. Refer to Fig. 1.7 replace the head on the block (photo) and refit No 7 and No 8 holding down bolts. Do not use jointing compound. Check that the gasket is seating correctly and fit the remainder of the holding down bolts. Now following the sequence in Fig. 1.9 tighten up the bolts until the head is firmly held. Now using the torque wrench (see Fig. 1.19) tighten the bolts to 54 lb ft (7.5 kg m) in the sequence shown. That is all there is to it.

4 Fit the pulley to the camshaft and torque to Specifications.

5 Turn the camshaft pulley so that both cams for No 1 cylinder are in the open position and the dot on the camshaft gear tooth is in line with the valve cover (photo 8.3a). The photo shows it in line with the edge of the head, allow for the thickness of the cover flange and gasket.

6 Rotate the crankshaft pulley and the intermediate shaft pulley until the dot on the intermediate shaft pulley and the mark on the V-belt pulley coincide (photo 8.2). Install the timing belt tensioner loosely and then the timing belt. Making sure the marks are still in place put a spanner on the adjuster and tighten the belt until it will twist only 90 degrees when held between the finger and thumb halfway between the camshaft pulley and the intermediate shaft pulley. Tighten the eccentric adjuster fixing nut to 32 lb ft (4.5 kg m). Recheck the timing marks, repeat the operation if they do not agree with Specification (ie; one shaft has moved).

7 Refer back to Section 8, paragraph 2, and read paragraphs 2,3 and 4. The timing marks are all set ready to install the distributor so install it (photo). If you have lost the place turn to Chapter 4. Tighten the clamp. Make sure the distributor shaft is in mesh with the oil pump shaft; the distributor will not seat correctly if it is not. The points should be set correctly, see Chapter 4.

30 Engine assembly (1.1 litre) - cylinder head, timing belt, fuel pump, water pump and distributor

1 Turn the engine over and support it on the sump with wooden blocks. It must be secure for the head bolts are tight fitting. Clean top of the cylinder head carefully and lubricate the bores.

2 Fit a new cylinder head gasket. It has been found that the gasket leaks sometimes at the left-hand front corner (No 1 cylinder) so smear a little compound round the water hole and the stud hole (photo).

3 Now refit the cylinder head to the block. Make sure the head clean before putting it in place. Then insert the bolts and tighten to the correct torque in the sequence given in Fig. 1.9 (photos). The head was overhauled and partially assembled in Section 12, with the camshaft, valves and springs. The oil seal at the sprocket and of the camshaft was renewed, and the sprocket and key fitted. The distributor flange is also in place.

4 Fit the timing indicator bracket to the block.

5 Fit the timing belt guard and the water pump, but do not tighten the pump securing bolts. Remember to fit a new 'O' ring to the pump. Now turn to Section 9, read paragraphs 4, 5 and 6 and study the photos.

6 Turn the distributor motor so that the blade points to No 1 cylinder firing mark. Line up the mark on the camshaft sprocket with the blade of the belt guard (photo 9.4b), line-up the Vee-notch in the crankshaft pulley with the 'O' mark on the timing indicator bracket (photo 9.4a), check that both valves of No 1 cylinder are closed and install the timing belt. Using a lever on the water pump adjust the tension on the belt (photo 9.6a) and tighten the water pump holding bolts (photo 9.6b). Check that the marks still agree and install the distributor (photo 9.10). Set it so that the marks you made in paragraph 5, Section 9, line up and then tighten the distributor clamp bolts. If you did not mark the distributor then read Chapter 4, Section 8. If you have carried out all the instructions in this paragraph then the engine is

30.2 The front left-hand corner of the gasket. Smear some jointing compound round the water and bolt holes (1.1 litre)

30.3a Refit the cylinder head (1.1 litre)

30.3b Torque the cylinder head bolts to the correct value in the correct sequence

30.12 Refit the valve cover (1.1 litre). Do not forget the locking strips

31.2 Fit a new oil filter

31.3 Fit the water pump pulley

31.5 Refit the inlet manifold

31.6 Refit the exhaust manifold

31.8 Fit a new oil seal over the no 1 camshaft bearing

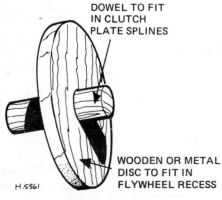

DOWEL TO FIT IN CLUTCH PLATE SPLINES

WOODEN OR METAL DISC TO FIT IN FLYWHEEL RECESS

H.5561

Fig. 1.20. Homemade tool for centreing the clutch plate on the 1.5 litre engine (Sec. 31)

32.6 Fit the exhaust manifold complete with shield

32.7 Fit the inlet manifold

timed sufficiently correctly to start when installed in the frame.

7   Refit the petrol pump to its flange, check that the plunger is resting squarely on the cam and tighten the bolts.

8   Install a new valve cover gasket and fit the valve cover with the supports strips the correct way round (photo).

31 Engine assembly (1.5 litre) - assembly of ancillaries

1   The remainder of the assembly consists of bolting on the various components to the exterior of the engine.

2   Install the oil pressure sender switch. Torque to the correct amount. Using a new gasket and jointing compound refit the oil filter to the cylinder block (photo 29.7). Do not fit the filter yet. Assemble the distance piece and the fuel pump to the block (photo, Chapter 3, 4.4). Use a new flange ring. If a new pump is to be fitted it may be different from the old one and will require different holding bolts (8 x 30 mm instead of 8 x 22 mm). Refer to Chapter 3 for details. Make sure the lever is correctly seated on the cam. Now install the new oil filter (photo).

3   Refit the water pump using a new O-ring. Refit the water pump pulley to the water pump coupling (photo). Refit the water hose from the pump to the flange on the cylinder block. The flange should not have been dismantled but if for some reason it has then a new gasket will be needed and jointing compound.

4   If the alternator bracket was removed refit it and then refit the alternator. Install the V-belt and adjust the tension (Chapter 10).

5   Wipe the face of the block and fit a new inlet manifold gasket. Position the four exhaust manifold gaskets at the same time. Carefully fit the inlet manifold (photo) and tighten it squarely, there are eight socket head screws, four short and four long. Tighten these to the correct torque. Install the carburettor if not already fitted and the fuel hose from the carburettor to the fuel pump.

6   Fit the exhaust manifold over the studs, fit the washers and nuts and tighten the nuts to the correct torque (photo).

7   Check that the coolant drain plug is in place and correctly tightened.

8   Fit the small oil seal to No 1 camshaft bearing cap (photo), and check that the valve is in place at the end of the cylinder head. Fit a new gasket to the valve cover and bolt it to the cylinder head. Do not forget the packing pieces. Tighten down methodically to 6 lb ft (1 kg m).

9   Refit the timing belt guard. Rotate the engine and check that the belts do not foul it, adjust if necessary.

10 Fit the spark plugs to the correct torque. They should have been serviced and refitted finger-tight before the head was assembled.

11 It now remains to fit the clutch and gearbox. At the back end of the engine is the crankshaft oil seal surrounding the crankshaft flange. Make sure the clutch components and flywheel are free from grease, wash your hands and keep the whole operation clean. It is necessary to fit the intermediate plate in position over the dowels and secure it temporarily. It is then in position when refitting the gearbox.

12 Fit the pressure plate to the flange. The bolts should be installed with Loctite and tightened in a diagonal fashion to the correct torque. Refit the release plate and install the retaining ring (large circlip). The ring ends must come together opposite a slot in the pressure plate as they did before you dismantled them (Section 8, paragraph 10). Now fit the

clutch disc, boss side outwards, and install the flywheel over the pressure plate. Install the bolts and tighten them until hand-tight.

13 The next bit is very important. If the clutch disc is not centred correctly the gearbox will not fit, so this job must be done accurately. The best thing is tool VW 547 which fits in the flywheel and has a spiggot which fits exactly in the centre of the clutch plate splines. If you cannot borrow tool VW 547 then we suggest you make up a tool as suggested in the sketch (Fig. 1.20). Once the clutch plate is centred tighten the bolts in a diagonal fashion to the correct torque.

14 Turn the flywheel until the recess in the rim of flywheel is opposite the driveshaft flange. Fit the gearbox to the engine flange and install the top mounting bolts and then the lower ones. The TDC sender unit must be removed from the casing while this is done. Tighten all the bolts to the correct torque. Be careful as the splines on the driveshaft engage the clutch disc. Keep everything level and do not force matters or you will bend something. Fit the cover plate to the driveshaft flange, and refit the cover plate to the driveshaft flange.

15 Install the TDC sender unit and refit the starter torquing all bolts to the specified amount.

16 The engine is now ready to go back into the vehicle. Turn to Section 4, paragraph 18 and carry on from there.

32 Engine assembly (1.1 litre) - assembly of ancillaries

1   This Section carries on from Section 30.

2   Refit the alternator to the engine but leave the bolts slack.

3   Now position the timing belt casing cover and tighten the holding bolts. Make sure the belt does not foul the guard.

4   At the rear of the engine fit a new gasket to the coolant flange and refit the flange. Fit a new 'O' ring in the thermostat cover and refit the thermostat and cover.

5   Next fit the alternator belt and adjust the tension correctly (see Chapter 10).

6   The exhaust manifold gasket is in two pieces. Clean the face and install the manifold and gasket (photo).

7   Fit a new inlet manifold gasket and install the manifold (photo). Install the carburettor in place on the manifold.

8   Check that the oil pressure sender unit (photo) and the coolant temperature sender units are in position.

9   Fit a new oil filter. Use a new washer under the joint (photo).

10 Refit the intermediate plate on the dowels. Make sure the TDC sender unit is taken out of the casing.

11 Install the flywheel. The bolts must be fitted with Loctite and torqued correctly (photo).

12 Fit the clutch disc and the pressure plate. Fit the bolts loosely and centre the clutch disc carefully. Tighten the holding bolts to the correct torque. Note that the disc goes in one way only, boss to flywheel (photo).

13 Gently ease the gearbox into place and install the engine transmission bolts. It is necessary to have the engine overhang the bench to get the gearbox in place. The long bolts go in from the gearbox side and the short one from the engine side. Torque them to the correct amount. (photo).

14 Refit the starter and tighten the bolts. Finally fit the long water

32.8 Fit the oil pressure sender unit

32.9 Fit a new oil filter. Don't forget the washer underneath

32.11 Fit the flywheel. Use Loctite on the bolts

32.12 Fit the clutch disc (note boss) and pressure plate

32.13 Refit the gearbox to the engine and install the starter

32.14 Fit the pipe to the back of the water pump and the small hose to the inlet manifold

pipe to the water pump flange. Use a new gasket. It will be in the way if you fit it before and it may have to be removed to fit the gearbox. Connect the small hose from this pipe to the inlet manifold and tighten the clips (photo).

15 Fit the crankcase breather tube and attach the top end temporarily to the manifold. It is difficult to fit this when the engine is in place.
16 The engine and gearbox are now ready to go back into the vehicle, turn to Section 4, paragraph 18 and carry on from there.

33 Fault diagnosis - Engine

Note: When investigating faults do not be tempted into making snap decisions. Start from the beginning of the check procedure and follow it through There may be more than one fault.

Symptom	Reason/s	Remedy
Engine will not turn over when the starter switch is operated	Flat battery Bad battery connections Bad connections at solenoid switch and/or starter motor	Check that battery is fully charged and that all connections are clean and tight.
	Starter motor jammed Solenoid defective Starter motor defective	Remove starter and check (Chapter 10).
Engine turns over normally but will not fire	No spark at plugs No fuel reaching engine Too much fuel reaching engine (flooding)	Check ignition (Chapter 4). Check fuel system (Chapter 3). Check fuel system (Chapter 3).
Engine runs unevenly and misfires or lack of power	Ignition fault Fuel system fault Valve clearances wrong Engine badly worn	Check ignition, plug leads faulty or loose (Chapter 4). Dirt in carburettor, faulty fuel pump (Chapter 3). Check valve clearances. Overhaul engine.
Excessive oil consumption or smoky exhaust	Wear in engine cylinders Wear in valve stems	Overhaul engine.
Oil on engine and garage floor	Leaking gaskets/seals	Locate leak and fit new seal or gasket.
Excessive mechanical noise	Wrong tappet setting Worn bearings Piston slap when cold (disappears when hot)	Adjust tappet clearance. Overhaul engine. Pistons/bores approaching rebore stage.
Engine vibrates excessively	Side or front engine bearers require adjustment Ignition not adjusted correctly. Plugs dirty.	Refit or replace Check ignition (Chapter 4).
Engine runs on when ignition switched off	Carburettor electro magnetic valve faulty	Check valve (Chapter 3).
Engine cuts out after less than 100 yards journey	Automatic choke not correctly adjusted	Adjust (Chapter 3).
Engine cuts out after 4 or 5 mins.	Carburettor icing	Fit radiator blind. Adjust idle speed.

Chapter 2 Cooling, heating and exhaust systems

Contents

Specifications

Radiator ... ...   Alloy construction with crossflow. 1.1 litre engine header tank on left. 1.5 litre engine header tank on right.

Cooling fan ... ...   Electric drive controlled by a thermoswitch in radiator tank. Switches on 90°C (194°F); switches off 85°C (185°F).

Inlet manifold ... ...   Heated by coolant on both systems.

Thermostat

Type	Bellows operated. In 1.5 engine situated in water pump casing, in 1.1 engine situated in rear flange.
Opens (1.5 litre)	80°C (176°F).
Fully open (1.5 litre)	94°C (200°F).
Minimum stroke (1.5 litre)	7 mm (0.27 ins).
Opens (1.1 litre)	80°C (176°F).
Fully open (1.1 litre)	100°C (212°F).
Minimum stroke (1.1 litre)	7 mm (0.27 ins).

Pump

1.5 litre	Left-hand side of the engine below the alternator. Driven by Vee-belt which drives the alternator from the crankshaft pulley.
1.1 litre	Right-hand side of the engine. Driven by the camshaft toothed drivebelt.

System test pressures (both systems)

Cooling system test	1.0 kg/cm^2 (14 lbs/sq.in)
Cooling system cap	0.9 to 1.15 kg/cm^2 (8.5 to 16.3 lbs/sq.in)

Cooling system capacity (both systems) ... ...   6.5 litres; 1.8 U.S galls; 1.4 Imp. gallons.

Antifreeze

Frost protection to °C	°F	%	G.10. Litres	U S pints	Imp. pints	Water Litres	U S pints	Imp. pints
* −25	−13	40/60	2.6	5.0	4.5	3.9	7.6	6.8
−35	−31	50/50	3.25	6.3	5.8	3.25	6.3	5.8

* Vehicle issued for temperáte climates are factory filled with a 40/60 mixture of G.10 and water.

Torque wrench settings

1.5 litre engine

	mkg	lb ft
Pulley to water pump	2	15
Water pump impeller unit to casing	1	7
Side delivery flange to block	1	7
Water pump to block	2	15
Temperature sender unit to delivery flange	0.7	5
Thermostat cover to pump housing	1	7

1.1 litre engine

	mkg	lb ft
Water pump to block	1	7
Temperature sender to delivery flange	0.7	5
Thermostat cover to flange	1	7

1 Cooling system - general description

1 Although the systems are basically the same, the 1.5 litre and 1.1 litre engine cooling systems differ considerably in detail. Both use cross-flow radiators, but where the 1.5 system flows from right to left the reverse is true of the 1.1 system.

2 On the 1.5 litre engine the coolant pump is on the left side of the engine, driven by a Vee-belt from the crankshaft pulley. This belt also drives the alternator. On the 1.1 litre engine the coolant pump is driven by the camshaft drivebelt and is mounted in such a way as to provide the tension arrangement for the drivebelt. The pumps are different in construction. The impeller unit for the 1.5 litre engine may be replaced but no repairs are possible to the pump fitted to the 1.1 litre engine.

3 On the 1.5 litre engine the thermostat is situated in the water pump housing and diverts the flow of coolant back to the cylinder block until the coolant temperature is 80°C, thereafter it diverts the flow to the radiator.

4 The 1.1 litre engine works on a different system. The thermostat is in the flange at the rear of the block and coolant is diverted back to the block through the inlet manifold until the thermostat opens and allows it to go to the radiator.

5 In both systems the inlet manifold is heated by the coolant.

6 The fan is driven by an electric motor which is switched on and off by a temperature operated switch screwed into the transfer tank at the opposite end of the radiator to the header tank. This switch may be removed and tested and replaced by a new one if necessary.

7 Thus the warm-up period is shortened as much as possible, first by the thermostat which does not bring the radiator into the circuit until the coolant has reached 80°C and is only fully open at 94°C, then the radiator must warm-up from cold to 90°C before the fan operates. On the other hand on hot days when the engine is idling in a traffic jam, the fan which would by revolving slowly if driven by a belt from the crankshaft pulley is operating at maximum speed and helping to reduce overheating.

8 Both systems are fitted with an expansion tank through which the system is filled. This tank is fitted with a pressure cap and the system must be kept topped-up to the lower mark on the tank when the engine is cold (photo).

2 Antifreeze

1 The coolant should not need to be topped-up. It is installed at the factory and is a mixture of a glycol ethelene type of inhibitor and water, This mixture not only renders the system frost proof but raises the boiling point and acts as an anti-corrosion agent. A table of mixture by volume is given in the Specifications. When first taking delivery of the car it is recommended that the composition of the coolant be determined and a quantity of the same consentration be purchased and kept to replace any spillage or accidental waste. It is too late to start worrying about this after the coolant level has fallen as you cannot buy G.10 at the corner shop.

2 It is recommended that the system be drained and refilled with fresh antifreeze every two years.

3 Draining, flushing and refilling the system

1 According to the oracles there should be a drain plug in the cylinder block. We found one on the 1.5 litre engine, by the starter under the exhaust manifold; which is in a very awkward place, but although we were told there was a similar plug on the 1.1 litre we could not find it! It certainly wasn't on the cylinder block.

1.8 The expansion tank has a large hose to its base and a pressure cap

3.3 The air bleed screw on the top of the radiator. This is on the 1.1 litre. On the 1.5 litre it is at the other end (right-hand) of the radiator

2   Unless you can drain the block there is not much point in trying to flush the system, as about 1 litre of coolant remains in the block after the radiator has been removed. We do not therefore recommend trying to flush out the system by pumping water through it in the reverse direction to normal flow. This only moves sludge from one place to another. Wait until the whole system is dismantled and then clean it thoroughly.

3   Refitting after overhaul needs care. When everything is connected up, make sure the heater valve is open, and fill the system through the overflow tank. It will take time as the coolant has to filter down. There will be air locks, and to deal with these a bleeder screw (photo) is fitted

to the top of the radiator. Leave this undone and let liquid seep out of it until you are sure that no more air remains in the system, then close it. If after the vehicle has run a few miles, it makes rude noises in the cooling system after switching off then there is still air in the system, which must be removed via the bleeder screw.

4   Coolant hoses - maintenance and emergency repairs

1   Probably the most neglected part of the car is the coolant hose and yet negligent owners always seem surprised when a hose bursts, or

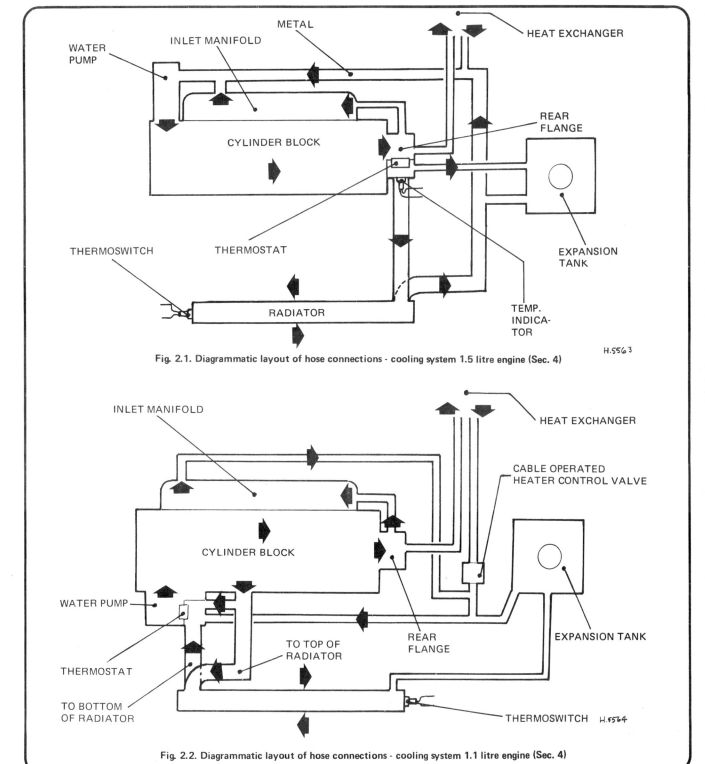

Fig. 2.1. Diagrammatic layout of hose connections - cooling system 1.5 litre engine (Sec. 4)

H.5563

Fig. 2.2. Diagrammatic layout of hose connections - cooling system 1.1 litre engine (Sec. 4)

H.5564

collapses.

2　Hoses age and become hard, crack, split and decay generally over a period of time. They are subject to high temperatures and up to 15 psi (1.1 kg/s.cm) pressure during normal running. Their worst enemy is oil, which, if spilt on hose should be wiped off straight away. Hoses will chafe if not correctly supported, and then pin-hole punctures will release a stream of hot coolant.

3　Examine the hoses when checking oil and battery levels. Check the tightness of clips every three months, or after a long fast run. If the clips are digging in to the hose too deeply move the clip, or if this is not practical, replace the hose. If a hose is becoming stiff, shows signs of cracks developing, then renew it right away. When a hose bursts the hose must be renewed and the antifreeze - which is expensive.

4　If the hose does burst stop the engine as soon as possible. Open the bonnet (hood) cautiously, there may be a jet of hot coolant spraying about. As soon as possible drop a substantial cloth over the actual puncture. Put another cloth over the radiator cap and turn it to release the pressure. The jet spray will subside and the fault may be located. If the problem is with the smaller hoses it may be possible to short circuit the burst. It may be that the heater circuit can be isolated and the hose for that used as an emergency repair. If one of the larger hoses has fractured, insulation tape may be used as a temporary repair. A more substantial temporary repair may be made by cutting the hose right through and inserting a short length of metal or similar tubing with two Jubilee clips. This will hold well until the correct part can be fitted.

5　**Never** pour cold water into a hot engine while it is not running, that is the easiest way to crack the cylinder head. If sufficient coolant remains to circulate then cold coolant may be added to **hot coolant,** but **not** to hot metal.

6　Finally, if a burst does happen the cause must be located before proceeding. It may be neglect or old age, in which case no further action other than renewal, is necessary, but if a new hose bursts then the cause must be located right away.

5　Cooling system - fault diagnosis (general)

1　If the coolant level in the overflow/pressure tank falls, first check the hose clips and hoses for leaks or signs of perishing. Tighten or replace as necessary.

2　If there are no signs of leakage at the hose joints then the radiator must be checked for leaks which may be caused by electrolysis. No repair is possible; the radiator must be exchanged.

3　However, overheating may also be due to incorrect operation of the thermoswitch and fan motor. Remove one wire from the thermoswitch and check the voltage between the fan motor housing and the battery negative terminal. If there is a voltage reading then the fan motor is faulty and must be replaced. If there is no reading on the voltmeter, then the coolant must be drained off and the thermoswitch removed for inspection. Green or blue deposits on the bottom of the switch indicates electrolysis and coating of the switch and probably the radiator with verdigris. This will appreciably affect cooling and will eventually cause leaks through corrosion. There are a number of patent solutions to descale radiators, but they will not deal satisfactory with verdigris. Flush out the radiator with clean water and try again. If it still overheats then consult the agent. It will probably mean a new radiator.

4　Before doing this, check that the pump drive is operating correctly, there are no kinks in hoses and check the operating temperatures of the thermostat and the thermoswitch (Sections 11 and 7). There is a fault diagnosis chart at the end of the Chapter.

6　Radiator - removal, testing and replacement

1　Remove the bottom hose, catching the coolant in a clean container of sufficient capacity. Undo the overflow tank filler cap and open the vehicle heater valve. When no further coolant runs out remove the top hose and wait for more coolant to run out. Disconnect the battery earth strap.

2　Pull off the rubber cap from the thermoswitch and disconnect the leads. Unplug the fan motor. Remove the two bolts holding the radiator to the frame (photo 4.5a, Chapter 1). This will need a 10 mm socket spanner, and then lift the radiator up and move it sideways to disconnect the top clip (photo 4.5b, Chapter 1).

3　Lay the radiator down and remove the nuts holding the cowling and fan with motor to the radiator. The radiator may now be examined for leaks. It should be pressure tested in a tank of hot water, blocking one outlet and fitting the other with a bung through which compressed air at 14 lbs/square inch is applied. Leaks will be seen as streams of bubbles.

4　It is not possible to repair this radiator without special equipment, so an exchange radiator will be necessary. These are several brands of chemical which poured into the system may effect a temporary repair, but seldom effect a permenant repair. We recommend their use only in emergencies.

5　Replacement is the reverse of removal.

7　Fan and thermo-switch - testing and replacement

1　The fan and cowling may be removed from the radiator or more easily the fan can be removed from the cowling and eased out through the struts. Disconnect the battery earth strap before commencing work, undo the plug connecting the fan to the electric wiring harness, remove the three nuts holding the fan in position and remove motor and assembly together.

2　The fan blades are removed from the motor by undoing the bolt in the centre of the fan hub and levering the plastic blade assembly off the motor shaft.

3　The motor is dismantled by undoing the through bolts and pulling off the end caps, but there is no point in doing this as spares are not available, the unit is replaced in one piece.

4　To satisfy the curious we removed the through bolts. Pulling off the end cap was difficult and unfortunately the bearing came off with the shaft (photo). This presented difficulties on reassembly as the cage for the spherical part of the shaft may only be installed when the bearing has been removed from the housing. The shaft and bearing may then be re-installed. The commutator and brush gear may be cleaned and then reassembled (photos). Be careful of the two thin washers at the end of the commutator. If one of these is damaged replacements are not available. It is recommended that this unit be renewed if faulty.

5　The fan motor either works or it does not. Supply 12 volts to the

7.4a The fan motor housing. The bearing has come out of the cage - this is not the way to do it!

7.4b Fan motor brush gear. Be careful of the thin washers

7.4c Fan motor armature. Note the suppressor

plug momentarily. If the motor runs it is satisfactory. **Do not** allow it to run for more than a few seconds with the fan removed.

6   The thermo-switch is located in the back tank of the radiator. It is covered with a rubber sleeve. Remove the sleeve and disconnect the wires. The switch may be tested by connecting a simple bulb circuit or an ohmmeter across the tags of the switch and observing the point at which the switch closes. The temperature of the coolant in the header tank may then be checked. This will be in excess of the specified 90°C (194°F) but will give a good idea of the temperature in the lower tank. If the fan does not work shortly after the thermostat has opened and the engine has reached normal running temperature then stop the engine right away. Pull off the leads from the thermo-switch and with a suitable instrument, check whether the switch has closed or not. If it has, then check the fan circuit and do not proceed until this has been sorted out or the engine will overheat. If the switch has not closed, and you are sure the coolant temperature is in excess of 90°C (194°F) then the switch is faulty and must be renewed. To get you home connect the two switch leads together (short out the switch). The fan will then run when the ignition is switched on.

7   Removal of the thermo-switch involves draining the radiator. Once the bottom tank is empty (there is no need to take out the plug from the cylinder block) using a socket spanner remove the thermo-switch. It may be tested then in a beaker of water in the same way as the thermostat (Section 11), but using a meter to determine the opening point. However, more practically, the switch either works or it does not. If it does not fit a new one.

8   Coolant pump and thermostat (1.5 litre) - removal and replacement

1   The alternator must first be removed before the coolant pump may be taken off the block.

2   Drain the coolant from the circuit by removing the bottom hose from the radiator. Slacken the bolt holding the alternator hinge to the block and slacken the tie strap at the top of the alternator. Push the alternator towards the block and remove the V-belt. Remove the timing drivebelt guard, disconnect the alternator plug and remove the alternator.

3   Disconnect the three coolant hoses from the pump then remove the four bolts holding the pump to the cylinder block (photo). The pump will probably be stuck to the block but will come off if tapped gently. Remove the O-ring with the pump.

4   Remove the pulley and then take out the eight bolts which secure the bearing housing and impeller to water pump housing. The two halves may now be separated (photo). **Do not** drive a wedge in to break the joint. Clean off the old gasket. Remove the two bolts holding the thermostat housing and remove the housing with the thermostat (photo). Set the thermostat aside for testing if suspect (photo).

5   Examine the thermostat valve seating in the housing and remove any sludge or scale.

6   The impeller housing and impeller complete with bearing are serviced as one part, so that if the coolant is leaking through the bearing or the impeller is damaged the housing must be replaced with a complete new assembly.

7   Fit a new gasket using a waterproof jointing compound such as

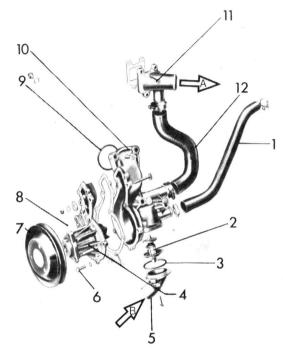

Fig. 2.3. Water pump and hoses - exploded view - 1.5 litre engine (Sec. 8)

1	Return hose from heater valve	8	Pump impeller housing
2	Thermostat	9	'O' ring
3	'O' ring	10	Pump body
4	Gasket	11	Outlet from cylinder block
5	Thermostat housing	12	Return hose (cut-out when thermostat opens)
6	Bolt		
7	Water pump pulley		

Arrows: A to radiator header tank
            B from radiator bottom tank

8.3 The water pump ready for removal - it may be removed with the engine in the car (1.5 litre)

8.4a Water pump, impeller removed from housing (1.5 litre)

8.4b Thermostat housing removed (1.5 litre)

8.4c Thermostat removal (1.5 litre)

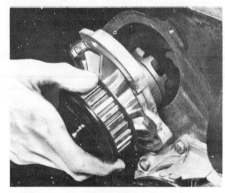

9.6 Remove the water pump (1.1 litre)

9.7 Examine the impeller. Fit a new 'O' ring

10.2 The thermostat (1.1 litre)

10.3 The thermostat housing, and the temperature sender (1.1 litre)

Golden Hermatite. Set the halves together and tighten the bolts to 7.2 lb ft (1 kg m). Reassemble the thermostat and housing using a new O-ring. Refit the pulley and tighten to 7.2 lb ft (1 kg m). Again using a new O-ring fit the pump to the block and tighten to 14.4 lb ft (2 kg m). Replace the alternator and fit the drive belt guard. Refit the V-belt and tension it correctly. Reconnect the hoses and tighten the clips. Refill the cooling system.

9 Coolant pump (1.1 litre) - removal, overhaul and replacement

1   It is possible to remove the water pump without taking the engine out of the car but care must be taken not to upset the valve timing. The thermostat is not an integral part of the pump as in the 1.5 litre.
2   No repairs are possible to the pump; if it is not working correctly, then a replacement must be fitted.
3   Remove the bottom hose from the radiator and catch the coolant in a container of suitable size.
4   Undo the bolts holding the timing belt cover and remove the cover upwards. Turn the camshaft sprocket until the top bolt of the timing belt case can be seen through the sprocket and remove this bolt. (photo 12.4a, Chapter 1). Using a ring spanner on the crankshaft pulley nut turn the engine until the mark on the camshaft lines up with the blade of the belt guard (photo 9.4b, Chapter 1), and the notch in the Vee-belt pulley lines up with 'O' on the timing bracket (photo 9.4a, Chapter 1).
5   Undo the bolts holding the guard and coolant pump and slacken the timing belt by rotating the coolant pump (photo 9.6 b, Chapter 1).
6   Gently ease the timing belt off the coolant pump and push it towards the centre of the block. Now remove the belt guard and water pump (photo). If you have to remove the belt, do not twist it too much or it will crack.
7   Examine the pump impeller and the bearing, if faulty the pump must be renewed (photo).
8   When refitting be sure to fit a new 'O' ring to the pump.
9   Replacement is the reverse of removal. When checking the tension of the timing belt consult photo 9.6a of Chapter 1. Be quite sure the

timing marks line up correctly.
10 After refilling the system, remember to bleed the air out of it.

10 Thermostat (1.1 litre) - removal and replacement

1   The thermostat is fitted to the coolant flange at the rear of the block just under the distributor.
2   To remove it, first disconnect the bottom radiator hose and drain off the coolant. Now remove the two bolts holding the flange to the housing and draw the thermostat cover away. There is no need to remove the hose. The thermostat may now be lifted out (photo) and tested.
3   Clean out the housing before refitting (photo) the thermostat and always fit a new 'O' ring.

11 Thermostat - testing

1   Refer to Fig. 2.4. Measure the dimension 'a' while the thermostat is cold. Immerse it in water in a container and heat the water to 80°C 176°F). The thermostat should now commence to expand. At temperature 94°C (200°F) for the 1.5 litre or 100°C (212°F) for the 1.1 litre the thermostat should have opened 7 mm to dimension 'b'. This is the full stroke.
2   Consult the following table:

Temperature	'a' 1.1 litre & 1.5 litre	'b' 1.1 litre	'b' 1.5 litre
Room temperature	31 mm (1.22 in)	—	—
94°C (200°F)	—	—	37 mm (1.46 in)
100°C (212°F)	—	37 mm (1.46 in)	—

3   If the measurements are different, a new thermostat is required.

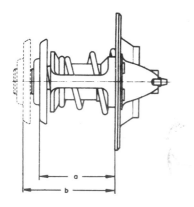

Fig. 2.4. Thermostat dimensions (Sec. 11)

'a'   cold, 1.1 and 1.5 litre engine   31 mm (1.22 in)
'b'   94°C (194°F) 1.5 litre engine   37 mm (1.46 in)
'b'   100°C (212°F) 1.1 litre engine   37 mm (1.46 in)

12 Temperature indicator sender - checking and removal

1   On both engines this is screwed into the coolant flange at the rear of the cylinder block (photo 10.3 for 1.1 litre).
2   Before removing it drain the coolant from the radiator.
3   The resistance varies as the temperature increases. To check the sender disconnect the lead and using an ohmmeter, check the resistance cold and again with the engine hot. The cold resistance should be 270 ohms ± 5% and the normal working temperature resistance 150 ohms ± 5%. If it is not within these limits it should be renewed. It will be noted that the resistance decreases with rise in temperature. (see also Chapter 11, Section 21).

13 Heating system - general description

1   The system consists of an heat-exchanger, blower motor and fan, a control box behind the dashboard, a control valve in the engine compartment and an extensive ducting system. Refer to Figs. 2.16 and 2.15.

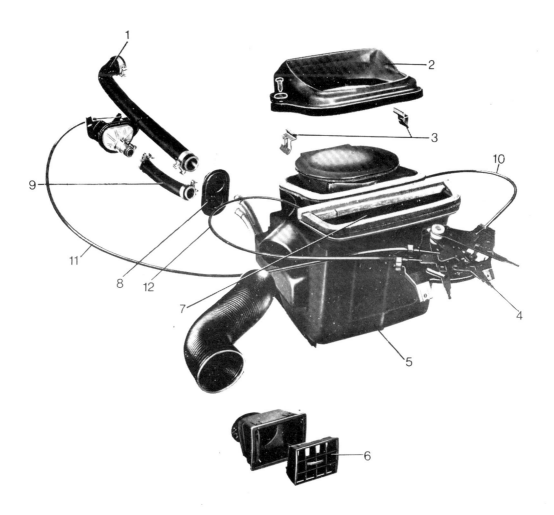

Fig. 2.5. Heater and hoses - exploded view (Secs. 13 and 15)

1 Hose to cylinder head	*4 Fresh air controls*	*7 Air outlet to dashboard*	*10 Cable to air direction flap*
2 Heater cover	*5 Heater body*	*8 Grommet*	*11 Cable to control valve*
3 Clips	*6 Air outlet and flap*	*9 Hose to valve*	*12 Cable to cut-off flap*

2   Coolant is fed to the heat-exchanger from the Tee-piece at the back of the cylinder block. It does not circulate until the valve in the engine compartment is opened moving the lever 'C' on the fascia board. This operates a bowden cable which rotates a lever on the valve. Coolant is then drawn through the heat-exchanger and back to the water pump. The temperature of the coolant is in excess of 90°C when it leaves the cylinder block. The quantity of coolant circulating depends upon how much the valve is opened, so that the heat available to the car interior is governed this way.

3   The heater cover sits in the engine compartment behind the windscreen wiper motor. Under the cover, operated by a bowden cable from the control box, is a circular dished flap. This controls the amount of air admitted to the system, and can close the system completely if so wished. Directly under the flap is the fan motor and fan. The flap control also operates the switch for the blower motor. When the flap is fully open the last bit of movement of lever 'B' switches on the blower motor. On the Golf L and LS the Scirocco and the Rabbit there is a two speed blower motor and the high speed is switched on by a second contact by moving lever 'B' to the end of its travel.

4   The air is drawn through the heat exchanger into the fresh air housing and directed by an adjustable cut off flap which is operated by lever 'A' to direct air to the windscreen, footwell or side windows as the driver wishes.

14 Heater system controls - removal and replacement

1   The control unit is located in the centre of the dash board. It is accessible after the radio has been removed (Chapter 11) or on cars without a radio, the glovebox. Once the radio is extracted the control unit may be seen (photo). Disconnect the battery earth strap and undo the two crosshead screws holding the control unit and it may be eased forward.

2   The middle lever controls the heater valve. It is reasonably easy to unhook the bowden cable and extract it through the bulkhead, if care is exercised to fit a replacement.

3   The upper and lower cables control the airflow. Although the cable for the upper lever is visible at its far end, right at the bottom of the

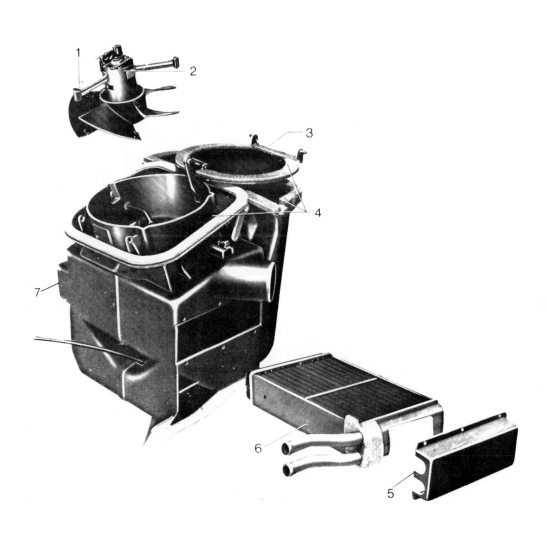

Fig. 2.6. Heater body and heat-exchanger - exploded view (Secs. 13 and 15)

1 *Wiring clip*	3 *Cut-off flap*	5 *Cover for heat-exchanger*	7 *Heater body*
2 *Fan motor and fan*	4 *Gaskets*	6 *Heat-exchanger*	

fresh air housing it is necessary to dismantle the housing to replace it. The outer end of the lever cable operates the flap under the heater cover. This may be got at by removing the heater cover but you will probably break the plastic dowels when extracting them, so get some new ones before tackling the job.

4   It is best to replace the heater cables completely if the inner cable snaps. In this way the exact length required is obtained. We found it a good thing to fit new cable clamps too, as the old ones seem to distort when removed.

15 Heating system components - removal and replacement

1   Refer to Figs. 2.5 and 2.6. The heater cover may be removed from the back of the engine compartment by extracting the two plastic pegs.

14.1 The heater control unit

We found these depressingly prone to break. This gives access to the cut-off flap and its actuating lever. Disconnect the cable and unhook one pivot of the cut-off flap. The flap may now be removed.

2   The fan motor is inside the throat of the inlet to the fresh air housing and may be lifted out. Disconnect the fan cable by pulling off the clip.

3   The housing is held to the body by two metal clips which are difficult to locate and even more difficult to operate. In the centre of the clip is a tongue or retaining spring. This must be pressed in and the clip will come undone. There is a clip on each side of the housing. Once these are free the housing *should* be drawn off the heat exchanger. The large air pipes to the dashboard outlets pull out of the housing.

4   The heat exchanger must be removed after the fresh air housing. Two pipes go through the double grommet and are connected to hoses. It will be necessary to drain the radiator before these hoses are disconnected.

5   To add to the confusion a new direct flow fresh heater box was introduced in March 1975. The fresh air is taken direct from the plenum chamber to the fresh air flaps on the dashboard and no longer goes through the fresh air box. Only this type of box is available and it does not have connections for the air hoses fitted to the pre-1975 vehicle. It is therefore necessary to cut the new fresh air box and install two connectors (part 171, 819, 741) before the new box may be connected.

6   Re-installation is the reverse of removal. Fitting the clips is a tricky business. The tab of the clip should be pushed into the retainer on the fresh air housing and the housing lifted squarely until the spring clicks into position.

7   The air outlet in the middle of the dashboard is rivetted on the Scirocco but kept in place by clips on other models.

8   Unless the heat-exchanger leaks, the control cables break or the fan decides not to work we suggest you leave well alone. The dismantling and reassembly is not a long job if you are good at that sort of thing, but you can get into trouble trying to get the housing clips off and on. It is not a job for the average D-I-Y enthusiast and unless the job is done carefully the housing may crack or split.

9   In an emergency if the heat exchanger is leaking close to the heater valve, this is on the return circuit, disconnect the hose from the engine to the heat exchanger when it is clipped to the heat exchanger and block the hose. If the engine is hot it would be best to wait until the system cools, but before pulling off the hose clip it with a mole wrench or some similar device and hold the end up above the level of the coolant in the

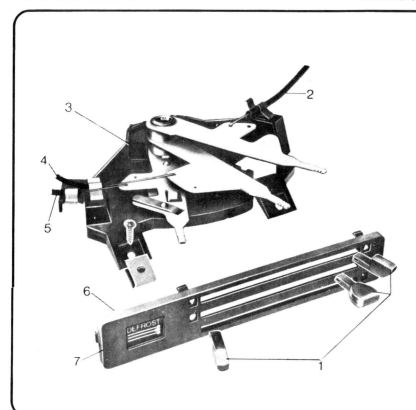

Fig. 2.7. Heater controls in dashboard
(Sec. 14)

1   *Pull off knobs*
2   *Cable for air direction*
3   *Body*
4   *Cable to control valve*
5   *Cable to cut-off flap*
6   *Light bulb 1.2 watt*
7   *Trim plate*

overflow tank. Remove the cap from the coolant overflow tank. You
will loose some coolant, but if the coolant is leaking into the interior of
the car the sooner the heat exchanger is empty the better.

Make sure the clip on the hose is firm and you may well be able to
proceed gently to somewhere where you can get the heater system
properly blocked off until the heat exchanger can be repaired or
replaced.

16 Exhaust system - removal and replacement

1   This sytem is simple and orthodox on the European version consisting of a downpipe from the exhaust manifold flange to an expansion
unit, corrugated to allow for temperature variations. The manifold on
the 1.1 litre is on the left side of the engine opposite to the inlet

16.1a The circular clamp and the bracket holding the exhaust pipe to
the engine on the 1.1 litre

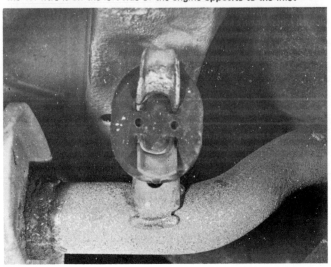

16.1b The doughnut support for the exhaust system

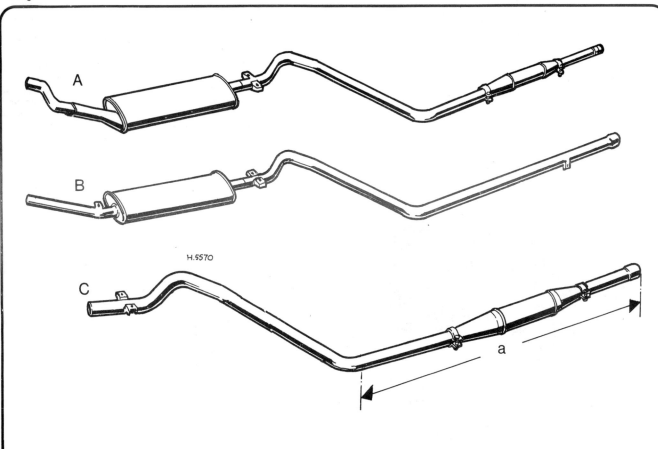

Fig. 2.8. Modification to exhaust pipes (Sec. 16)

A   Old pattern   B   New pattern
C   When fitting a new main silencer to early type vehicles the intermediate pipe must be shortened so that 'a' is 844 mm (33.25 in) for
    the 1.1 litre and 1107 mm (43.5 in) for the 1.5 litre

manifold. Thus the exhaust pipe runs down between the engine and the radiator. On the 1.5 litre the inlet and exhaust manifold are both on the same (right) side of the block and the double exhaust runs down behind the block, merging into one pipe as it bends to the rear. The pipe is attached to the manifold by a circular clamp on the 1.1 litre (photo) but the 1.5 litre has a square flange with bolts. The downpipe is held to the expansion unit by a clip. At the other end a long pipe is clipped to the expansion unit. This pipe is carried on two 'doughnut' rubber supports which fit over clips attached to the pipe and body (photo). Towards the rear, the pipe has a sharp bend to the left and an equally difficult bend where it climbs over the rear axle and enters the silencer. At the front and rear of the silencers are clips, and the tailpipe is hung on another 'doughnut' and bracket. A manifold system was introduced in April 1975 which is discussed in paragraph 6.

2   The 'doughnut' is a brave attempt to do away with the normal rusty seized up nuts and bolts that used to hold the exhaust pipe but reports from North America indicate that they have a short life and should be included in the first aid spares kit.

3   The system is also prone to rattle if not carefully positioned away from the floorpan. We also looked with mis-giving at the bend over the back axle. It is possible to wriggle the pipe clear but very difficult, unless the vehicle is on a hoist or over a pit. It is easy to saw the old pipe in half but there is still the problem of fitting the new one. The pipe is in a very exposed situation and will not last anything like the life of the vehicle. Various experts estimate that three systems at least are needed to outlast the vehicle. We suggest that the possibility of fitting a stainless steel version should be investigated on first replacement. Costs vary according to locality but it might prove to be a worthwhile investment.

4   The U.S.A. version is slightly complicated by the addition of a catalytic converter which must be replaced every 30000 miles. There is a warning light on the dashboard to warn you about this.

5   It is necessary to raise the car on a hoist or at least on axle stands to work underneath. Remove the shield protecting the converter, remove the flange bolts and take the converter away. When installing the new one always use a new gasket and retighten the bolts after the unit has been heated by a reasonably long drive.

6   In April 1975 the exhaust system was modified on all versions of the car. A double walled intermediate pipe is now fitted in place of the front silencer (the corrugated expansion unit). The front and tailpipes of the main silencer have also been modified. Refer to Fig. 2.8 for details. The old pattern of intermediate pipe and silencer may still be obtained but the old pattern of main silencer may not. To overcome this problem the intermediate pipe must be shortened as shown in the diagram.

17 Air conditioning system - general notes

1   The unit works on exactly the same principle as a domestic refrigerator, having a compressor, a condenser and an evaporator. The

Fig. 2.9. Adjusting the air compressor belt (Sec. 17)

A Bolt   C Bracket
B Bracket   D Lever
Support the lever on bracket 'B' and lift bracket 'C'.
Tighten the bolt.

condenser is attached to the car radiator system. The compressor, belt-driver from the crankshaft pulley, is installed on a bracket in the engine compartment. The evaporator is installed in a housing under the dashboard which takes the place of the normal fresh air housing. This housing also contains a normal heat exchanger unit for warming the intake air. The evaporator has a blower motor to circulate cold air as required.

2   The system is controlled by a unit on the dashboard similar to the normal heater control in appearance.

3   The refrigerant used is difluorodichloromethane (CF_2CL_2) more commonly known as Frigen F12 or Freon F12. It is a dangerous substance in unskilled hands. As a liquid it is very cold and if it touches the skin there will be cold burns and frostbite. As a gas it is colourless and has no odour. Heavier than air it displaces oxygen and can cause axphixiation if pockets of it collect in pits or similar workplaces. It does not burn, but even a lighted cigarette, causes it to breakdown into constituent gases, some of which are poisonous to the extent of being fatal. So if you have an air-conditioner and your car catches fire, you have an additional problem.

4   We strongly recommend that even trained refrigeration mechanics do not adjust the system unless they have had instruction by VW. The notes for V.W. personnel cover 25 pages. For the remainder we suggest that the system is left entirely alone, except for the adjustment of the compressor drivebelt, which should have 10 to 15 mm (0.4 to 0.6 inch) deflection in the centre when depressed by the thumb (see Fig. 2.9).

For 'Fault diagnosis - Cooling system' - see next page

10 Fault diagnosis - cooling system

Note: Check that the coolant level is correct. Check that the radiator is not obstructed by flies, leaves or other debris.

Symptom	Reason	Remedy
Engine apparently cool, gauge registers in the red sector	Engine temperature sensor or wiring defective	Replace sensor check wiring and ground connections (Chapter 11).
Engine overheating, gauge does not register in the red sector	Voltage stabilizer faulty Temperature gauge defective	Check stabilizer (Chapter 11). Replace gauge.
Engine and radiator overheating, gauge shows red. Fan operating	Coolant level too low Water pump belt slipping or broken (1.5 litre)	Check for leaks. Check cap valve overflow tank. Adjust or replace.
Engine overheats very quickly. Tank of radiator cool.	Thermostat not opening water not circulating through radiator	Replace thermostat.
Engine cool, gauge not in red despite hard driving in cold climates	Normal operation but if very cool then thermostat stuck open	Replace thermostat.
Engine overheating, pump and fan working, gauge in red.	Brakes binding Ignition retarded Mixture incorrect Cylinder head gasket blown	Adjust (Chapter 9). Check and adjust (Chapter 4). Adjust (Chapter 3). Replace (Chapter 1).
Engine overheating, gauge red, fan not working	Thermo switch not working Fuse blown Fan motor defective	Bridge terminals. Fan should run. Check fuse and replace if necessary. Trace fault. Replace fan motor.
Engine overheating all system working correctly	Wrong grade of fuel	Use correct grade RON. See operating handbook.

Chapter 3
Carburation, fuel and emission control systems

Contents

Specifications

Fuel pump	Diaphragm type mechanically operated. The drive on the 1.5 litre engine is from the intermediate shaft. On the 1.1 litre engine the pump is located on the cylinder head driven from the camshaft.

Carburettor

1.1 litre engine (table 1 below)	Solex downdraught 34 PICT 5 until June 1975. Thereafter, 31 PICT 5.
1.5 litre engine (tables 2, 3 and 4 below)	Solex 34 PICT 5 until May 1974. Thereafter, twin-barrel SOLEX 2B2. The Rabbit is fitted with a Zenith 32/32 2B2 twin-barrel downdraught.
Fuel tank capacity	45 litres; 12 U S gallons; 10 Imperial gallons.
Air cleaner	Paper element type mounted on the bodyframe inside the engine compartment. In June 1975 the 1.1 litre engine air cleaner was mounted on the carburettor.
Emission control	E.G.R. fitted to all Rabbit and Scirocco (USA) vehicles. Afterburn fitted to vehicles bound for California.

Carburettor Table 1: Golf/Scirocco 1.1 litre engine

Manual transmission only. Single barrel carburettor.

Type of engine	F.A. F.J.	F.A. F.J.	F.A.
Date introduced	August 1974	December 1974	May 1975
Engine number	F.A. 000 001 F.J. 000 001	F.A. 090907 F.J. 003 500	F.A. 173 708
Carburettor	SOLEX 34 PICT 5	SOLEX 34 PICT 5	SOLEX 31 PICT 5
Part number	036 129 015	036 129 015 B	036 129 015 A
Venturi dia (mm)	24.5	24.5	25.5
Main jet	X120	X120	X130
Air connection jet	145Z	145Z	100Z
Pilot jet/idling jet	g50	g50	52.5
Pilot air jet/idling air jet	90	85	100
Aux. fuel jet	35	35	35
Aux. air jet	160	160	150
Power fuel without ball	0.7 left	0.7 left	0.6 left/right
Injection amount (cm³ per stroke)...	1.05 to 1.35	1.05 to 1.35	0.95 to 1.25
Float needle valve dia (mm) ...	1.5	1.5	1.5

Needle valve washer thickness (mm)	0.5	0.5	2.0
Throttle valve gap (mm)	—	—	0.75
Choke valve gap (mm)	2.8 to 3.2	2.8 to 3.2	3.0 to 3.4
Octane requirement (RON) ...	91	91	91
Idling speed (rpm)	900 - 1000	900 - 1000	900 - 1000
C.O. valve (vol %)	1.0 to 2.0	1.0 to 2.0	1.0 to 2.0

Carburettor Table 2: Golf/Scirocco 1.5 litre engine type F.H. * (70HP)

Automatic and manual transmission. European version. *For Scirocco with F.D. engine see table 3*

Transmission	Manual		Automatic	
Date introduced	April 1974	January 1975	August 1974	January 1975
Engine number	F.H. 000 001	F.H. 081 804	F.H. 000 001	F.H. 081 804
Carburettor SOLEX	34 PICT 5	34 PICT 5	34 PICT 5	34 PICT 5
Part number	055 129 015D	055 129015K	055 129015E	055 129015L
Jets and settings:				
Venturi dia (mm)	27	27	27	27
Main jet	X135	X135	X135	X135
Air correction jet	115Z	115Z	115Z	115Z
Pilot/idling jet	52.5	52.5	52.5	52.5/60
Pilot/idling air jet	100	95	100	95
Aux. fuel jet	40	40	40	40
Aux. air jet	140	140	140	140
Power fuel with or without ball	0.7 without	0.7 without	0.7 without	0.7 without
Injection amount (cm^3 per stroke)	0.95 to 1.25	0.95 to 1.25	0.95 to 1.25	0.95 to 1.25
Float needle valve dia (mm)	1.5	1.5	1.5	1.5
Needle valve washer thickness (mm) ...	0.5	0.5	0.5	0.5
Throttle valve gap (mm) ...	—	—	—	—
Choke valve gap (mm) ...	2.7 to 3.7	2.7 to 3.7	2.7 to 3.7	2.7 to 3.7
Octane requirement (RON)...	91	91	91	91
Idling speed (rpm)	900 - 1000	900 - 1000	900 - 1000	900 - 1000
C.O. valve (vol %)	1.0 to 2.0	1.0 to 2.0	1.0 to 2.0	1.0 to 2.0

Carburettor Table 3: Scirocco 1.5 litre engine (85 HP) type F.D.

Automatic and manual transmission. European version.

Transmission	Manual				Automatic			
Date introduced	May 1974		April 1975		August 1974		May 1975	
Engine number	F.D. 000 001		F.D. 014 750		F.D. 000 001		F.D. 017 967	
Carburettor (SOLEX)	2B2		2B2		2B2		2B2	
Part number	055 129 017		055 129 017P		055 129 017A		055 129 017Q	
Jets and settings:	1st stage	2nd stage	1st stage	2nd stage	1st stage	2nd stage	1st stage	2nd stage
Venturi dia (mm)	24	27	24	27	24	27	24	27
Main jet	X115	X125	X117.5	X125	X115	X125	X117.5	X125
Air correction jet	140	92.5	140	92.5	140	92.5	140	92.5
Pilot/idling jet	52.5	70	52.5	70	52.5	70	52.5	70
Pilot/idling air jet	140	100	135	100	135	100	135	100
Aux. fuel jet	42.5	—	42.5	—	42.5	—	42.5	—
Aux. air jet	130	—	130	—	130	—	130	—
Power fuel with or without ball	—	1.3 without	—	1.3 without	—	1.3 without	—	1.3 without
Injection amount (cm^3 per stroke)	0.85 to 1.15		cold & warm 0.9 to 1.05		cold 1.35 to 1.65 warm 0.75 to 1.05		cold 1.35 to 1.65 warm 0.75 to 1.05	

Float needle valve diameter (mm)	2	—	2	—	—	2	—	2
Needle valve washer thickness (mm) ...	2	—	—	—	—	—	—	—
Throttle valve gap (mm) ...	0.45 to 0.5		0.45 to 0.5		0.45 to 0.5		0.45 to 0.5	
Choke valve gap (mm) ...	3.2 to 3.7		3.2 to 3.7		3.2 to 3.7		3.2 to 3.7	
Octane requirement (RON)...	98		98		98		98	
Idling speed (rpm)	900 - 1000		900 - 1000		900 - 1000		900 - 1000	
C.O. valve (vol %)	1.0 - 2.0		1.0 - 2.0		1.0 - 2.0		1.0 - 2.0	

Carburettor Table 4: Rabbit/Scirocco 1.5 litre engine (74 HP) type F.C. F.G.

U.S.A. version

	Manual		Automatic	
Engine code letter	F.C.		F.G	
Engine number	F.C. 000 001		F.G. 000 001	
Carburettor (Zenith)	2B2		2B2	
Part number	055 129 017B		055 129 017C	
	1st stage	**2nd stage**	**1st stage**	**2nd stage**
Jets and settings:				
Venturi dia (mm)	24	27	24	27
Main jet	115	115	115	115
Air correction jet	140	92.5	140	92.5
Pilot idle jet	52.5	70	52.5	70
Idle air jet	135	100	135	100
Aux. fuel jet	42.5		42.5	
Aux. air jet	127.5		127.5	
Power fuel with ball	1.0		1.0	
Injection quantity (cm^3 per stroke)	0.75 to 1.05		0.75 to 1.05	
Float adjustment (mm):				
1st stage	28$\pm$ 0.5		28$\pm$ 0.5	
2nd stage	30$\pm$ 0.5		30$\pm$ 0.5	
Float needle dia (mm)	2		2	
Choke valve gap (mm)	3.8 - 4.2		3.8 - 4.2	
Fuel requirement (RON)	91		91	
Idling speed (rpm)	850 - 1000		850 - 1000	
C.O. (vol %)*	2.0$\pm$ 0.5		2.0$\pm$ 0.5	

These are measured in front of the catalytic converter.

1 General description

1   The 45 litre (10 Imp. gallon) tank is situated at the rear of the car. Fuel is drawn from it through a strainer along a pipe on the right-hand side of the car by a mechanically driven diaphragm type pump. On cars built for the USA a special fuel evaporative control system is installed to prevent fumes from the petrol tank escaping to the atmosphere while the car is stationary.

2   The arrangement of the fuel pump is different on the 1.1 litre and 1.5 litre engines. On the former the pump is driven by a cam on the camshaft and is bolted to the cylinder head. On the 1.5 litre the pump is bolted to the side of the cylinder block and is driven by a cam on the intermediate shaft.

3   On earlier types the paper element air cleaner is situated in a rectangular box mounted on the wing inside the engine compartment. On the later types a circular case is fastened direct to the top of the carburettor and inlet manifold.

4   Early types of Golf and Scirocco were fitted with a single barrel Solex downdraught carburettor. It is labelled 35 PICT 5 but the part number and jet sizes vary according to the engine code. In April 1975 another version was introduced to the 1.1 litre engine, 31 PICT 5, which is similar but requires a modified inlet manifold.

5   The 85HP engine has always been fitted with a twin-barrel downdraught Solex labelled 2B2, to cope with the extra fuel problems of increased power.

6   The USA version of the Scirocco and the Rabbit are fitted with a double-barrelled carburettor of almost identical design, this time made by Zenith. This is labelled 2B2 also but is sometimes referred to as 32/ 32 - 2B2.

7   All carburettors are fitted with electrically heated automatic chokes and electro-magnetic cut-off valves. They also have mechanically operated acceleration pumps.

8   The USA version of the vehicle have complicated emission control equipment involving P.C.V. (positive crankcase ventilation), A.I.R. (Air injection reactor), T.A.C. (Thermostatic air cleaner), E.G.R. (Exhaust gas recirculation), C.A.T. (Catalytic converter) and the fuel evaporative control to the fuel tank mentioned in paragraph 1. It is a truly formidable list which is discussed later in the Chapter. In addition to all this the engine is fitted with a dual diaphragm distributor, which being translated, means two hoses to the vacuum advance and retard mechanism.

2 Air cleaner - removal, servicing and replacement

1   The air cleaner on early models is fixed to the right-hand wing inside the engine compartment. (photo). The inlet pipe may be fixed to a shield over the exhaust manifold in cold weather, or removed and fixed to the radiator grille in warm weather.

2   Remove the four clips holding the top to the body of the cleaner and remove the element (photo). This should be taken away from the vehicle

2.1 The air cleaner (B) is on the right-hand wing. The inlet hose is connected to the exhaust manifold shield (A). The hose (C) connects the cleaner to the carburettor cover (D)

2.2 Remove the paper element and tap out the dust

2.3a The carburettor top cover is held in place with a clip

2.3b The temperature controlled flap mechanism

3.1 Top cover and filter removed for cleaning

3.4 Removing the fuel pump (1.5 litre)

and tapped gently to remove the dust collected in it. Do not attempt to wash it or clean it with solvent. Opinions vary about the frequency at which cleaning should be done, but every 18000 miles or 2 years is the official interval. In dusty conditions we recommend weekly until you find out how much dust is collected each week. After finding out you can work out a sensible interval.

3   Inside the box is a spring loaded temperature controlled valve. Ease the box away from the wing, it rests on two rubber spiggots and is held by more clips. Undo the clips holding the air inlet cap to the carburettor (photo), undo the clip holding the crankcase ventilation pipe and pull off this clip. Pull the end of the inlet hose from the exhaust manifold guard and lift the box away from the vehicle. The temperature valve may be quickly checked by pouring hot water over the bulb (photo). The flap will open very quickly blocking off the warm air inlet and opening the inlet which allows cool air to enter the carburettor.

4   When replacing the box fit the rubber spiggots into the wing and settle the case carefully. If the clips seem very stiff stop and resettle the box. It is very easy to split the case.

5   On later models a circular air cleaner is mounted directly on top of the carburettor inlet. The method of dismantling and assembly remains the same, except that the clamp holding the cleaner to the barrel is different and, of course the cap over the carburettor intake no longer exists.

3   Fuel pump (1.5 litre engine) - testing, removal, repair and replacement

1   Refer to Fig. 3.1. Although it rarely goes wrong the fuel pump can be the unsuspected reason for poor starting and irregular running. If the filter is choked, the diaphragm damaged or the valves leaking, the pump may deliver enough petrol to keep the engine running, but not enough for a cold start or running under heavy load. It is easy to test the pump and to clean or replace the filter, but beyond that no repair may be done as the unit is sealed on manufacture and must be renewed if faulty

(photo).

2   Undo the small screw on the top cover and lift off the cover and filter, inspect the filter and clean it if necessary. Replace the filter and cover using a new sealing ring if necessary.

3   To test the quantity output of the pump first run the engine for a few minutes until the carburettor is full. Switch off and remove the hose from the carburettor intake. Be careful not to spill any fuel and arrange to catch the fuel in a measuring glass or similar container. There is plenty of hose so that the container may be held well away from the engine.

   Now get a helper to start the engine and run it at a fast tick-over for 30 seconds. There will be enough petrol in the carburettor bowl for this. Stop the engine and measure the amount of petrol in the container. There should be at least 200 cc (½ US pint). There is not much point in pressure testing the pump for it cannot be repaired, but if it is wished to confirm the quantity test it is possible to fit a Tee-piece in the supply hose to the carburettor and fit a pressure gauge. The pressure at 3500 rpm should be between 2.5 and 3.5 lbs per sq. in. (0.2 to 0.25 kg/s.cm.). Outside these limits the pump should be renewed.

4   To remove the pump clip the hoses and remove them, then remove the two socket headed bolts holding the pump and insulating flange to the block (photo). The right-hand one may be difficult as it is near to the oil filter and the filter may have to be removed to get at it if you do not have a suitable key.

5   Replacement pumps may be a new pattern with a heat insulating flange of different thickness from the old pump. The new type pump measures 1.8 inches (47 mm) from the tip of the operating lever to the body flange. The old one is 0.2 in (5 mm) shorter. The insulating flange is thicker for the new pump and longer screws, 8 mm x 30 instead of 8 mm x 22, are required. The new pump is said to give better hot starting.

6   When replacing the pump always secure the hoses to the pump with clips. It is best to fit the hose to the inlet side first and then turn the engine (not run it, turn it), to check that the pump is working. Catch the ejected fuel in a rag. Then connect the output hose. Tighten the holding bolts to 14 ft lbs (2 kg m).

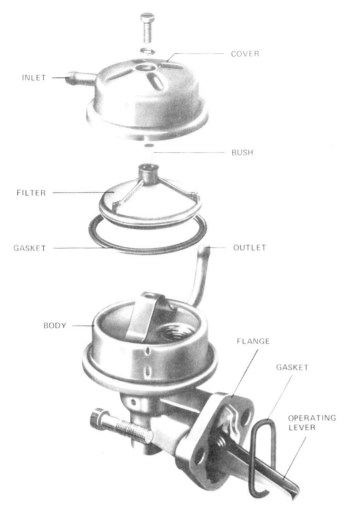

Fig. 3.1. Fuel pump (1.5 litre engine) - exploded view (Sec. 3)

Labels: COVER, INLET, BUSH, FILTER, GASKET, OUTLET, BODY, FLANGE, GASKET, OPERATING LEVER

4 Fuel pump (1.1 litre engine) - removal, repair and replacement

1   The pump on the 1.1 litre engine is identical to the 1.5 litre (Section 3) until the method of actuating the pump is observed.

2   The 1.5 litre pump has an arm resting on a cam. The 1.1 litre pump actuating rod rests firmly on the cam without the linkage, to transfer the motion through 90° (photo). As can be seen the actuating rod is spring loaded.

3   To remove the pump from the head remove the two screws and having pulled off the hoses, lift the pump away (photo). Tie the hoses out of the way keeping them upright to prevent loss of fuel.

4   Dismantling for filter cleaning, and testing is as for the pump in Section 3. But the remarks in paragraph 4 and 5 do not apply.

5 Inlet manifold (1.1 litre engine) - general description

A standard manifold is fitted to all models except thoses fitted with the 31 PICT carburettor. The new manifold may be recognised by the studs which hold the air cleaner. The cross-section of the manifold is smaller and the rubber connection from the carburettor to the manifold has been left out. The joint is now a rigid one.

6 Carburettor (Solex 34 PICT 5) - general description

The carburettor is basically a tube through which air is drawn into the engine by the action of the pistons and en route fuel is introduced into the air stream in the tube due to the fact that the air pressure is lowered when drawn through the 'tube'.

The main fuel discharge point is situated in the 'tube' - choke is the proper name for the tube to be used from now on - between two flaps - operated by the accelerator pedal and positioned at the engine end of the choke tube. The other is the strangler - which is operated by an automatic device.

When the engine is warm and running normally the strangler is wide open and the throttle open partially or fully - the amount of fuel/air mixture being controlled according to the required speed.

When cold the strangler is closed - partially or fully and the suction therefore draws more fuel and less air, ie; a richer mixture to aid starting a cold engine.

At idling speeds the throttle flap is shut so that no air and fuel can get to the engine in the regular way. For this there are separate routes leading to small holes in the side of the choke tube, on the engine side of the throttle flap. These 'bleed' the requisite amounts of fuel and air to the engine for slow speeds only.

The fuel is held in a separate chamber alongside the choke tube and its level is governed by a float so that it is not too high or low. If too high, it would pass into the choke tube without suction. If too low, it would only be drawn in at a higher suction than required for proper operation.

The main jet which is simply an orifice of a particular size through which the fuel passes, is designed to let so much fuel flow at particular conditions of suction (properly called depression) in the choke tube. At idling speed the depression draws fuel from orifices below the throttle

4.2 The spring loaded actuating rod

4.3 Removing the fuel pump (1.1 litre)

which has passed through the main jet and after that a pilot jet to reduce the quantity further.

Both main and pilot jets have air bleed jets also which let in air to assist emulsification of the eventual fuel/air mixture.

The strangler flap is controlled by an electrically operated bi-metal strip. This consists of a coiled bi-metal strip connected to the choke flap spindle. When the ignition is switched off the coiled metal strip is cool and the flap is shut. When the ignition is switched on current flows through the strip which heats up and uncoils - opening the choke flap after some minutes. If anything should go wrong with this electrical arrangement the flap will return to the closed position.

The fuel in the float chamber is regulated at the correct height by a float which operates a needle valve. When the level drops the needle is lowered away from the entry orifice and fuel under pressure from the fuel pump enters. When the level rises the flow is shut off. The pump delivery potential is always greater than the maximum requirement from the carburettor.

Another device fitted is an electro-magnetic cut-off jet. This is a somewhat unhappy feature which is designed to positively stop the fuel flow when the engine is stopped. Otherwise the engine tends to run on - even with the ignition switched off - when the engine is hot.

7 Carburettor (Solex 34 PICT 5) - removal, overhaul and replacement

1   This Section does not deal with adjustments, these are explained in Section 8.

2   The carburettor should not be dismantled without a very good reason. Any alterations of the settings will alter the C.O. content of the exhaust gas and may cause the owner to offend the Emission Regulations. However the top may be separated from the body to check the level of fuel in the float chamber and the jets may be cleaned without altering any vital settings.

3   Remove the air cleaner from the top of the carburettor. Clean the carburettor as much as possible externally, remove the nuts from the bolts holding the carburettor to the inlet manifold. Remove the battery earth strap. This will stop any sparks when you remove the wires from

the electro-magnetic cut-off valve, the choke and the carburettor earth terminal. The latter is necessary because of the rubber mounting. Pull off the fuel hose and plug it. Tie it safely out of the way.

4   Disconnect the accelerator cable from the carburettor throttle lever. Undo the two screws holding the cable bracket to the top of the carburettor and move the cable out of the way. Do not alter the adjusting nuts which hold the outer cable. The device which holds the accelerator cable to the lever caused some muttering when we first met it. A metal locking tag is folded round the nut. The ends of the tag bear on the screw thread and must be levered away to free the nut. It is easy when you know how but with the carburettor still on the car, the connector is in an awkward place. The carburettor may now be removed from the engine (photo).

5   Examine the automatic choke. First remove the screws and plastic cover. The automatic choke is held to the carburettor body by a clamp ring. Examine the joint and a mark will be found on the body opposite a mark on the choke to ensure correct assembly (photo). If you cannot find such a mark make one. Undo the three screws from the clamp ring and take the cover away from the body (photo).

6   Note how the lever fits into the choke element. The spring was introduced in January 1975 to locate the lever more securely. Earlier models did not have this spring.

7   Refer to photo 7.5b. It will be seen that the choke lever is controlled also by a vacuum diaphragm rod which is spring loaded. This arrangement varies the angle of the choke according to the vacuum state in the venturi. When setting the choke gap, the diaphragm rod must be pushed fully in. This is discussed in the tests and adjustments.

8   Unhook the return spring and remove the five screws holding the top of the carburettor to the body. Lift the top away (photo). Be careful not to damage the gasket. The float may be removed from the float chamber (photo) and checked for leaks. A simple way to do this is to immerse it in warm, not hot, water. Any pin holes will be detected by bubbles as the air inside the float expands. Dry the float thoroughly. It may not be repaired, only replaced by a new one.

9   The needle valve may be unscrewed from the top of the carburettor and checked. Clean out the float chamber removing any sediment with a soft hair brush.

7.4 The carburettor with the cable, air cleaner, wiring and fuel hose removed ready to be taken off the engine

7.5a Note the marking 'A' on the cover and body

7.5b Choke cover removed. Choke lever fits in loop at end of expander element. Spring was fitted for 1975 to secure lever better

7.8a Take the top of the carburettor away

7.8b Remove the float

7.11 'A' main jet plug, 'B' main jet, 'C' air jet and emulsion tube, 'D' pilot air jet, 'E' auxillary air jet, 'G' main fuel/air delivery tube, 'F' injection pipe from accelerator pump

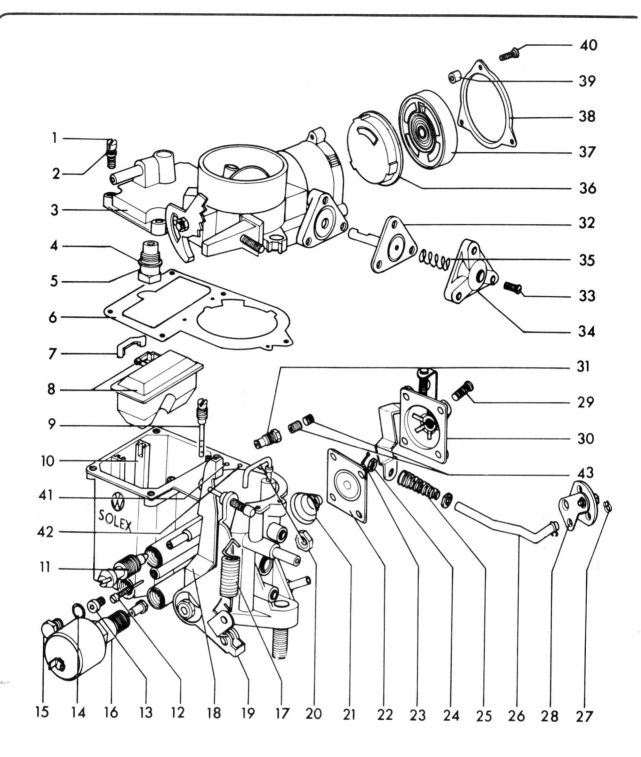

Fig. 3.2. Carburettor - Solex 34 PICT 5 - exploded view
Note: The accelerator cable clamp is not shown

1	Cover screw	12	Idle mixture control screw	23	Split pin	35	Spring
2	Spring washer	13	Main jet	24	Washer	36	Protection cap
3	Top cover	14	Washer	25	Spring	37	Heater coil and insert
4	Needle valve washer	15	Plug	26	Connecting link	38	Retaining ring
5	Needle valve	16	Electromagnetic cut-off valve	27	Circlip	39	Spacer
6	Gasket	17	Return spring	28	Bell crank lever (adjustable)	40	Screw
7	Float pin bracket	18	Fast idle lever	29	Countersunk screw	41	Pilot air jet
8	Float and pin	19	Throttle lever	30	Pump cover	42	Auxiliary air jet
9	Air correction jet and emulsion tube	20	Injection pipe from accelerator pump	31	Pilot jet	43	Auxiliary fuel jet and plug
10	Carburettor lower housing	21	Diaphragm spring	32	Vacuum diaphragm		
11	Bypass air screw	22	Accelerator pump diaphragm	33	Countersunk screw		
				34	Diaphragm cover		

7.14 The electro-magnetic cut-off valve removed for inspection

8.1 The choke flap adjusting screw is marked 'A'. The throttle adjusting screws are marked. 'B' is for basic adjustment 'C' is for cold idling adjustment

8.5 The fast idle cam is marked 'A'. The bypass air check screw is marked 'B'. The volume control screw is marked 'C'

8.6 The accelerator pump connecting rod is at the base of the carburettor. The adjusting nut is marked 'A'

Fig. 3.3. The early type of adjusting screw for the accelerator pump injection amount (Sec. 8)

(−) = Amount reduced
(+) = Amount increased

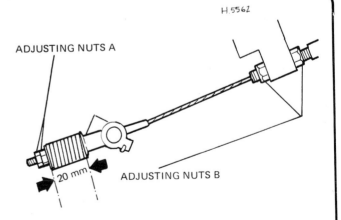

Fig. 3.4. Accelerator cable adjustment (Sec. 8)

*Turn adjusting nut 'A' until the measurement as shown is achieved.
Adjust the full throttle position by turning the nuts at 'B'*

10 Remove the plug from the outside at the base of the float chamber and then through this hole unscrew the main jet and check that it is clear. Jets **must not** be cleaned with wires or pins. Use compressed air to blow out any obstruction. If wire is pushed in the jet will be enlarged and the delicate balance of fuel mixture upset. If in doubt fit a new jet (see Specifications).

11 On the top rim of the body are two more jets and the air connection jet with the emulsion tube. Unscrew the air connection jet (photo) take it out and clean the emulsion tube. The jet next to it is the pilot air jet and the one on the outside is the auxiliary air jet. These may be removed and cleaned. They may be identified by Fig. 3.2 and the photo.

12 There are two more jets to find. The pilot jet and the auxiliary fuel jet. The pilot jet is alongside the accelerator pump cover; the auxiliary fuel jet is approached from the same side as the pilot jet but hides behind a plug, and is not easily accessible.

13 With all the removable jets taken out blow out all the drillings with compressed air.

14 The electro-magnetic cut-off valve may be removed (photo) and its action tested by supplying 12 volts to the tag terminal and earthing the case.

15 The accelerator pump may be dismantled and the diaphragm inspected for cracks or damage. **Do not** undo the screw on the end of the operating rod or the pump will have to be recalibrated. Take the rod off the lever at the other end. Undo the four screws holding the pump cover and extract the diaphragm. Watch out for the spring and fit it back the correct way. When refitting the cover tighten the screws with the diaphragm centre pushed in. This means holding the operating lever out while the screws are tightened.

16 The choke vacuum diaphragm may be inspected in a similar way. **Do not** alter the setting of the centre screw or the choke opening will need to be reset.

17 There is one other check to make. If the bushes of the throttle butterfly flap are worn and the spindle is loose in its bearings then air may leak past and affect the air fuel ratio. The remedy is, unfortunately a replacement carburettor.

18 Assemble all the parts methodically. Put a little jointing compound on the main jet plug. If the gasket is broken fit a new one, do not try to stick the old one in place. The carburettor should not need calibration as you have not moved any of the adjusting screw.

8 Carburettor (Solex 34 PICT 5) - tests and adjustments

1 The choke flap must be set so that in the closed position there is a gap of 2.8 to 3.2 mm between the choke and the carburettor bore. This may be taken as 0.12 inches and is almost exactly the size of a No. 31 drill. Remove the air cleaner. Read Section 7, paragraphs 5, 6 and 7. Dismantle the automatic choke. Insert a No. 31 drill between the choke flap and the bore on the lower side and turn the adjusting screw until the flap just grips the drill shank. The vacuum diaphragm rod must be pushed in against the adjusting screw during this test so you need a helper to hold the rod against the screw while you adjust the flap setting (photo).

2 There are two screws for adjusting the throttle on later models. On early models only the basic adjustment screw was fitted but problems with cold idling led to a second screw being installed. Refer to photo 8.1. The screw marked 'B' is for basic adjustment. This is set at the factory and should not be altered. If by mischance it is moved, then reset it in the following manner.

3 Turn the screw out until there is a gap between it and the fast idle cam (see photo 8.5). Now turn it back until it just touches the cam and then turn it one quarter of a turn more. It is advisable to check the drilling speed adjustment after doing this.

4 To set the cold idle stop screw, turn the screw until the engine idles satisfactorily when cold, Now run the engine until it is properly warm, there must be a gap of at least 0.2 mm (0.008 inch) between the end of the screw and the fast idle cam at idling speed when the engine is properly warm.

5 With the throttle stop screws correctly adjusted the slow running or idling speed should be adjusted to between 900-1000 rpm. For this job a revolution counter must be used and an exhaust gas analyser. The adjustment is simple. Make sure the choke valve is fully open. Turn the bypass air screw to obtain the right speed (photo). The C.O. content of the exhaust gas must now be checked, it should be 1.0 to 2.0 volume %. Correct if necessary, by adjusting the volume control screw (photo). As we said it is simple enough to do if you have the instruments and

know how to use them. If you do not, then it is a job for the VW agent.

6 The accelerator pump may be adjusted to give the correct quantity of fuel per stroke by turning the nut on the end of the correcting lever (photo). A piece of rubber or plastic tube must be clipped over the injection pipe in the carburettor bore (photo 7.11) and led out to a measuring cylinder. The VW agent has a small pipe for this job VW tool 119. With the tube in position operate the throttle until fuel comes out of the tube into the glass. Empty the glass and then operate the throttle five times catching the fuel in the measuring glass. Divide the amount in the glass by five. The answer should be between 1 cc and 1.35 ccs. To adjust the stroke alter the setting of the nut and repeat the test. Lengthen the rod (ie; screw out the nut to decrease the amount injected) On some early models a different arrangement may be met. This is shown at Fig. 3.3. Screw the screw out to increase the amount injected.

7 The adjustment of the throttle cable is important. Refer to Fig. 3.4. Adjust the nut 'A' until the measurements shown is 20 mm (0.79 in) at the idle setting. Now depress the accelerator to the full throttle position and adjust the nuts at 'B' so that the throttle valve is fully open. If this is not done carefully it is possible to put considerable strain on the butterfly spindle on the accelerator cable. Adjustment of the cable for the automatic gearbox is discussed in Chapter 7.

9 Accelerator cables - renewal

1 The renewal presents no problem. Disconnect the cable from the carburettor, then unhook it from the accelerator pedal. Withdraw the cable through the grommet and fit the new cable in its place.

2 There have been a considerable number of changes in the type of cable fitted. There are four types for use with manual gearbox, white, yellow, black and green according to the engine fitted and RH or LH drive. Consult the storeman for the correct part.(VW workshop Bulletin No. 38 of 20.12.74, refers).

10 Carburettor (Solex 31 PICT 5) - general description

1 This carburettor is fitted to the 1.1 litre engine after June 1975. It is introduced after engine F.A.173.708. The specification is given in the tables at the beginning of the Chapter.

2 It was introduced together with the circular type air cleaner.

3 The intake manifold has a smaller cross-section and has studs for securing the air cleaner.

4 The construction and the methods of test and adjustment are as for the 34 PICT 5. It cannot be fitted to the older type of car unless the modified manifold is also installed.

5 A diagram of its components is given at Fig. 3.5.

11 Carburettor (Solex/Zenith 2B2 - twin choke) - general description

1 The carburettor has two venturi tubes, two float chambers and two throttle valves. However, it is not, as would seem, two separate carburettors. The throttle valve of stage II remains firmly shut until released by the movement to full throttle of the butterfly valve of stage 1. Once the system of locking levers releases stage II throttle, it is then controlled by a vacuum capsule and opens according to the depression in the venturis of both stages. Fig. 3.6 shows the layout of the interlock and the diagrammatic layout of the vacuum capsule.

2 At idling speed most of the fuel is supplied by stage 1. The fuel flows through the main jet to the idling fuel jet and mixes with the idle air supply to form the idle mixture. It is then delivered via drillings in the carburettor body into the choke tube just below the throttle valve. The composition of this mixture is governed by the mixture regulating screw, which governs the C.O. value.

3 During the idling period, stage II also supplies fuel to its own venturi via a similar system of drilling and jets.

4 Further supply of fuel during the idle period is provided through the auxiliary fuel jet and auxiliary air jet of stage 1. These intermingle in the emulsion tube and enter the inlet via the same passage below the throttle flap of stage 1. The flow of this fuel is controlled by the bypass air control screw. The entire supply can be shut off by the magnetic cut-off valve which operates when the ignition is switched off.

5 Stage II does not have an auxiliary supply system, bypass control screw, mixture regulating screw or cut-off valve. All idle adjustments and mixture control adjustments are done on stage 1.

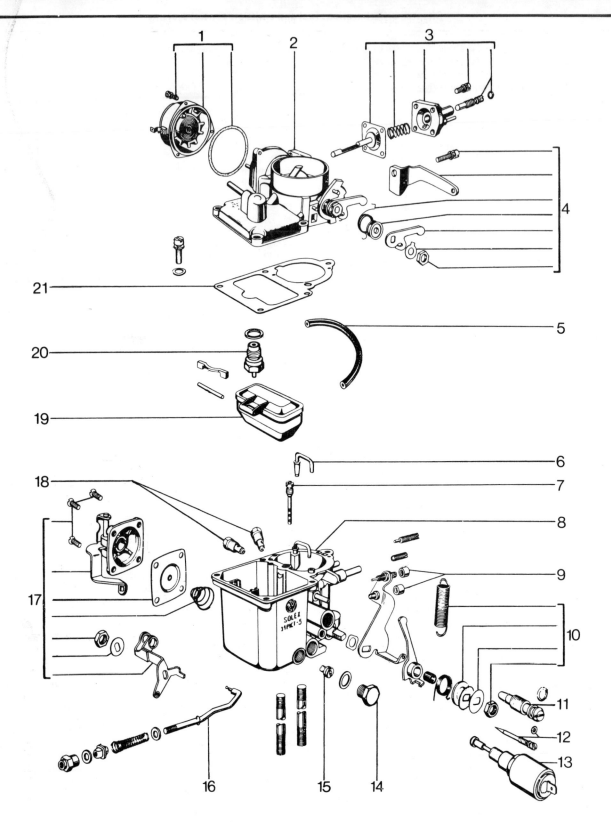

Fig. 3.5. Carburettor - Solex 31 PICT 5 - exploded view

1	Automatic choke assembly	7	Air correction jet and emulsion tube	11	Bypass air screw	17	Accelerator pump assembly
2	Carburettor top			12	Idle mixture control screw	18	Pilot and auxiliary fuel jets
3	Choke vacuum control assembly	8	Carburettor body	13	Electro-magnetic cut-off		
4	Fast idle cam and levers	9	Throttle stop screws	14	Plug	19	Float
5	Hose	10	Throttle levers and springs	15	Main jet	20	Needle valve
6	Accelerator pump inlet tube			16	Accelerator pump link	21	Gasket

6   As the throttle valve is opened the accelerator pump comes into action delivering fuel to the air stream and the bypass of stage 1 is further activated. Then the main jet system comes into action and delivers fuel to the atomiser in the venturi and as the throttle is now opening to the inlet manifold. The butterfly valve of stage II is still closed, and the only contribution from stage II is via the basic idle system.

7   As full load conditions are approached, the supply of fuel from stage 1 increases through the main jet system and the interlock mechanism of the throttle valve of stage II is released allowing the butterfly valve to open and fuel is supplied via the main jet of stage II to the atomiser in stage II venturi. The enrichment tube of stage II also supplies fuel to the stage II venturi.

8   The position of the butterfly valve of stage II is governed by a vacuum capsule which is operated by the increasing depression in the venturi of both stages 1 and 11.

9   Fig. 3.6 shows the diagrammatic arrangement of the throttle interlock. Fig. 3.7 shows the diagrammatic layout of stage 1 and Fig. 3.8 the layout of stage II under basic load conditions. Fig. 3.9 shows stages 1 and II under full load conditions.

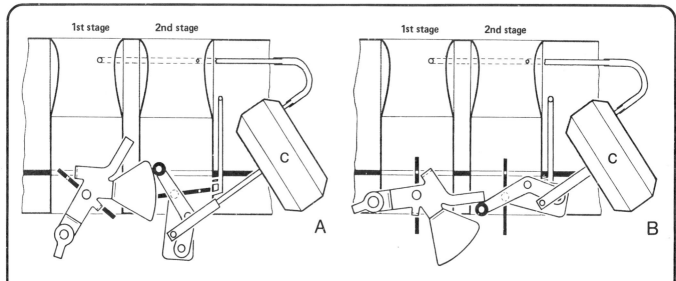

Fig. 3.6. Carburettor Solex/Zenith 2 B.2 arrangement of throttle interlock mechanism (Sec. 11)

A   The first stage throttle is opening during the transitional stage from idling to full throttle. The second stage throttle is locked shut by the lever mechanism

B   The interlock mechanism is non-operative at full throttle conditions and the 2nd stage throttle is now open and controlled by the vacuum capsule 'c'

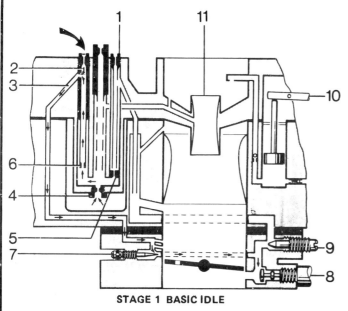

STAGE 1 BASIC IDLE

Fig. 3.7. Carburettor Solex/Zenith 2 B.2 diagrammatic cross-section of Stage 1 - basic idle layout (Sec. 11)

1 Auxiliary air jet	7 Mixture control screw (CO control)
2 Idle air jet	
3 Idle air drilling	8 Magnetic cut-off valve
4 Idle fuel jet	9 Slow running control screw (bypass air)
5 Auxiliary fuel jet	10 Accelerator pump
6 Main jet	11 Atomiser

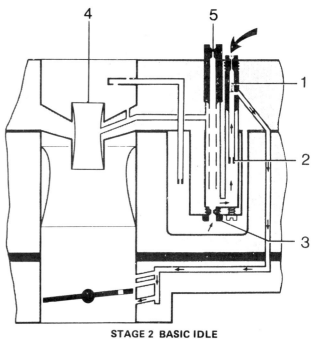

STAGE 2 BASIC IDLE

Fig. 3.8. Carburettor Solex/Zenith 2 B.2 diagrammatic cross-section of Stage II - basic idle layout (Sec. 11)

1 Idle air jet	4 Atomiser
2 Idle fuel jet	5 Air correction jet
3 Main jet	

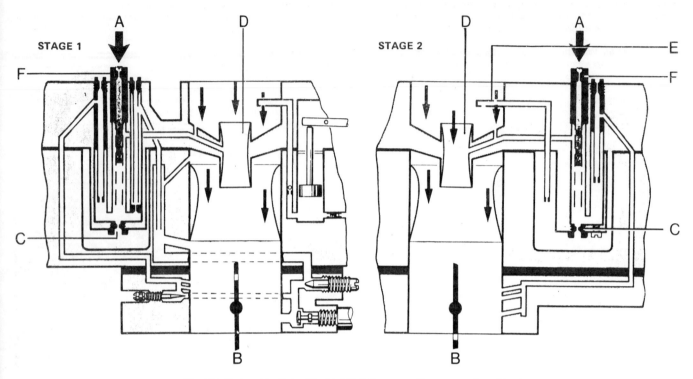

Fig. 3.9. Carburettor Solex/Zenith 2 B.2 diagrammatic cross-section of both stages at full load conditions (Sec. 11)

A Main air supply to air correction jet	B Throttle	D Atomiser	F Air correction jet
	C Main jet	E 2nd stage enrichment	

Note: heavy arrows show airflow

Fig. 3.10. Carburettor Solex/Zenith 2 B.2 jet locations 1 (Sec. 12)

1 Full load enrichment stage 2
2 Air correction jet stage 1
3 Air correction jet stage 2
4 Pilot air and fuel jet stage 1
5 Pilot air and fuel jet stage 2
6 Auxiliary air jet stage 1

Note: auxiliary fuel jet stage 1 is below 6

---

12 Carburettor (Solex/Zenith 2B2 - twin choke) - removal, overhaul, static adjustment and replacement

1   Apart from cleaning the jets, setting the choke and throttle flaps and checking the accelerator pump injection capacity, the only other repair possible is the adjustment of the float level. These tests are included in this paragraph because they must be done with the carburettor away from the car. Running tests are described in Section 13.

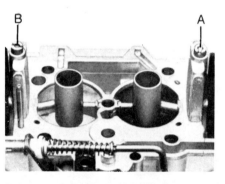

Fig. 3.11. Carburettor Solex/Zenith 2 B.2 jet locations 2 (Sec. 12)

When the top of the carburettor is removed and turned upside down the main jets are accessible
A Main jet 1st stage   B Main jet 2nd stage

2   To remove the carburettor, first take off the air cleaner. Disconnect the accelerator cable and take off the plug or clip the fuel hose. Remove the battery earth strap and then disconnect the wiring from the magnetic cut-off valve, the automatic choke and the microswitch (if fitted) on the accelerator linkage. Tag these wires for easy replacement Label the vacuum hoses and remove them. Undo the bolts holding the carburettor to the manifold and take the carburettor away.
3   Replacement is the reverse of removal. Be careful when refitting the accelerator cable to secure the outer cable in the clamp on the carburettor so that there is no stress on the butterfly valve of stage 1 when the accelerator is fully depressed. If the pedal is not fully depressed when the valve is exactly at full throttle position of the valve you will be pushing the pedal down and straining the throttle linkage of the carburettor.
4   Refer to Fig. 3.10. The carious jets, except the main jets may be

located, removed and blown out with compressed air. **Do not** clean them with wire or a pin. If they are so blocked that the compressed air will not remove the obstruction then fit a new jet.

5   Remove the screws holding the carburettor top to the carburettor body and turn the head upside down, The main jets are now accessible and may be serviced (Fig. 3.11 refers).

6   The automatic choke is identical with that of the PICT 34 carburettor (see Section 7, paragraphs 5, 6 and 7) except that the heater resistance element has a different value. The method of setting the gap is the same as described in Section 8, paragraph 1. This time use a No. 28 drill, the gap should be between 3.2 to 3.7 mm (0.130 to 0.147 in). Be careful to set the drill to measure the lower gap, ie; at the edge of the carburettor **not** in the centre adjacent to stage II bore.

7   On this carburettor the throttle gap for stage 1 must be set carefully. Turn the carburettor up-side-down. Refer to Fig. 3.12. The gap must be between 0.45 and 0.5 mm (0.018 and 0.020 in). Use a No. 77 or a No. 78 drill, inserted as shown in the Fig. 3.12. Turn the adjusting screw until the flap just holds the drill.

8   The measurement and adjustment of the accelerator pump output must be done with the carburettor assembled but not bolted to the manifold. Make sure the float chambers are full and that a supply of fuel to the carburettor is available. A piece of hose and a funnel connected to the carburettor inlet will do. Hold the carburettor over a large funnel and operate the throttle lever until fuel begins to run from the carburettor into the funnel. Now hold a measuring glass under the funnel and operate the throttle fully ten times. Allow the fuel to run into the glass and divide the quantity by ten. The correct amount varies

according to which engine the carburettor is fitted to, so look in the Specifications for the answer. Adjustment is shown in Fig. 3.13.

9   While the top is separated from the carburettor body the float position may be checked. Refer to Fig. 3.14 and measure the distance shown. The levels are correct if 'b' for the first stage is 28 mm (1.102 in) and for the 2nd stage 30 mm (1.118 in). If these are not correct the only adjustment is by bending the bracket.

13 Carburettor (Solex/Zenith 2 B.2 - twin choke) - running adjustments

1   The carburettor should have been checked as described in Section 12, and the ignition timing must be correct. Valve clearances and contact breaker dwell angles must be correct. If these adjustments are not in order it is unlikely that the required C.O. value will be attained.

2   Refer to Fig. 3.15. The bypass air control screw (sometimes called the idle speed screw) is at the side of the automatic choke. A revolution counter must be fitted and the screw turned to set the speed at 900-1000 rpm. The engine must be warm so that the oil temperature is approximately 60°C (140°F) and the choke valve be fully opened.

3   Having set the idle speed now use an exhaust gas analyser to check the C.O. content of the emission. This must be less than 2%. Turn the mixture regulating screw. Fig. 3.16, until the required value is obtained. This may alter the idle speed which must then be readjusted and the C.O. value checked again. Repeat the operation until both of the values required are achieved.

4   The throttle valve basic adjustment is controlled by a set screw (Fig.

Fig. 3.12. Carburettor Solex/Zenith 2 B.2 throttle valve gap setting Stage I (Sec. 12)

Insert a No. 78 drill as shown and adjust the gap by turning the screw 'A'

Fig. 3.14. Carburettor Solex/Zenith 2 B.2 float level check (Sec. 12)

Turn the carburettor top upside down and measure dimension b.
For 1st stage float   b = 1.18 in (28 mm)
For 2nd stage float   b = 1.12 in (30 mm)

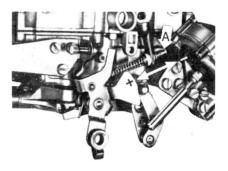

Fig. 3.13. Carburettor Solex/Zenith 2 B.2 accelerator pump adjustment (Sec. 12)

Turn screw 'A' to increase or decrease the injection quantity

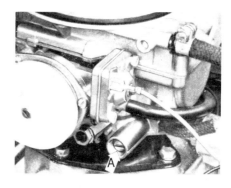

Fig. 3.15. Carburettor Solex/Zenith 2 B.2 idle speed adjustment (Sec. 13)

To vary idle speed turn the screw 'A'

Fig. 3.16. Carburettor Solex/Zenith 2 B.2 CO content check (Sec. 13)

To adjust mixture turn screw at 'A'

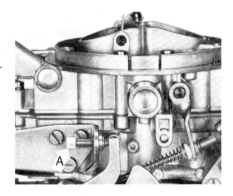

Fig. 3.17. Carburettor Solex/Zenith 2 B.2 throttle valve setting (Sec. 13)

Screw 'A' is the stop screw for basic adjustment

14.1 The crankcase ventilation hose, container and non-return valve

3.17). This is factory set and sealed with a plastic cap. In the event of the adjustment being altered for some reason, remove the cap, turn the screw out until there is a gap between the end of it and the fast idle cam. Now screw it in again until it just touches the cam and then a further one quarter turn. Check the idle speed and C.O. value and adjust if necessary.

14 Emission control - positive crankcase ventilation (P.C.V.)

1   A bulbous joint at the side of the cylinder block carries a rubber hose which is connected to a plastic container. (photo). This is connected to a plastic non-return valve which in turn is connected to the air cleaner elbow. Fumes are drawn into the inlet system via this method and burned. The non-return valve prevents a back fire going through to the crankcase. The filter unit should be replaced every 15000 miles.
2   On some models the hose is taken from the valve cover instead of the side of the cylinder block.

15 Emission control - catalytic converter (C.A.T.)

1   This item is fitted to vehicles for USA. It is situated in the exhaust pipe system at the front. A light on the dashboard is fitted to remind the driver that the converter must be changed every 30000 miles.
2   It helps to reduce the amount of hydrocarbons and C.O. by converting them into water and CO_2.
3   Raise the vehicle on a hoist, remove the shield, unbolt the flanges on each end of the converter and install a new one using new gaskets.

16 Emission control - exhaust gas recirculation (E.G.R.)

1   The principle of the system is to extract a portion of the hot burnt gas from the exhaust manifold and to inject it into the inlet manifold where it mixes with the fuel and air and enters the cylinders again. The result is to lower the flame peaks during combustion and so to lower the production of the oxides of nitrogen which are a small but important part of pollution. The exhaust gas passes through a filter which removes any carbon particles and then through a valve which is operated by the depression in the choke of the carburettor.
2   A very basic layout of the early system is shown at Fig. 3.18. To this have now been added several more refinements. A temperature valve and a micro-switch on the accelerator linkage, plus a thermostatic air cleaner.
3   We do not recommend that the owner tries to adjust this system, indeed no test data is as yet available outside the VW organisation and for this reason the adjustment of the system is a matter, at the time of writing, for the VW agent.
4   There are a few jobs which can be done. The filter, which is fixed to the exhaust manifold may be changed. This should be done at 15000 mile intervals. Other than this check that all hoses and wires are intact and then leave well alone.

17 Emission control - A.I.S. (afterburn)

1   This system is fitted in addition to E.G.R. Its purpose is to provide extra air so that Hydrocarbons and C.O. still in the emission stream may burn in the exhaust system. A basic layout is shown in Fig. 3.19.
2   An air pump belt-driven by the engine, sucks air through a filter and delivers it to the cylinder head by means of a pipe manifold so that the air is injected just behind the exhaust valve port into each cylinder. Inserted between the pump and the manifold is a non-return valve called the anti-backfire valve which prevents the gases blowing back into the pump, if a backfire occurs in the exhaust system.
3   When the driver lifts his foot from the accelerator suddenly the throttle closes and the mixture becomes over-rich. This can cause banging in the exhaust. To prevent this a branch pipe from the air filter supplies air via a control valve to the inlet manifold. The valve is vacuum operated by a line from the inlet manifold (Fig. 3.20).
4   The filter should be replaced every 20000 miles. Every 10000 miles the belt tension should be checked and adjusted if necessary and the hoses examined for leaks and chafing.
5   If banging does occur in the exhaust system it must be cured right away as otherwise damage to the silencers will occur. Banging of this sort is usually caused by a defective air control valve, or a leak in the

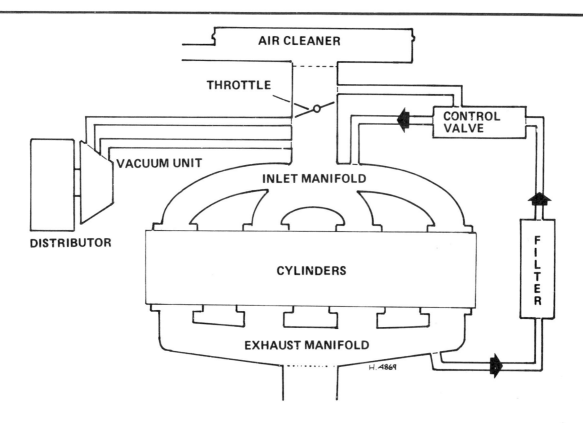

Fig. 3.18. Rabbit and Scirocco USA basic layout of E.G.R. (Sec. 17)

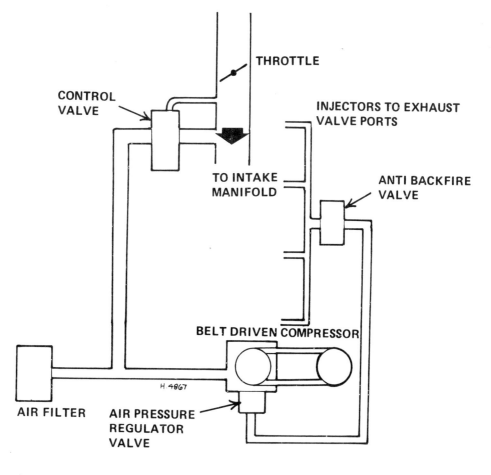

Fig. 3.19. Rabbit and Scirocco USA basic layout of A.I.S. (Sec. 17)

hose system, but it may be an engine defect. We suggest the car should be taken to the dealer right away and checked on the computor.

6   The anti-backfire valve is screwed to the air injection manifold. To remove it the manifold must be removed from the cylinder head. It is just below the spark plugs

7   The filter and the control valve are on the right-hand side of the engine compartment. If the wing nut on the bottom of the filter housing is removed the cover and the filter may be removed (Fig. 3.21).

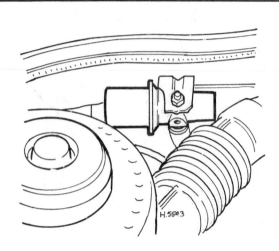

Fig. 3.20. Rabbit - anti-backfire valve in the A.I.S. located on the right side of the engine compartment (Sec. 17)

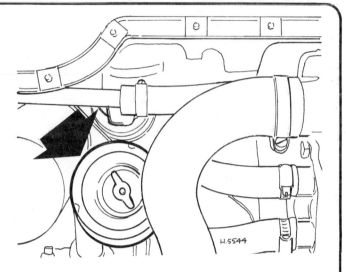

Fig. 3.21. Rabbit - air filter in A.I.S. located behind the radiator (Sec. 17)

18 Fault diagnosis - Carburation; fuel and emission control systems

Symptom	Probable reason	Remedy
1 No fuel at carburettor	Tank empty Fuel pump filter clogged Faulty fuel pump	Fill tank! Clean filter. Replace pump with a new one.
2 Engine will not start	Choke valve stuck or throttle stuck Auto choke not working Carburettor flooding	Dismantle and correct. Dismantle and correct. Punctured float or needle valve faulty. Replace.
3 Engine idles or junts, or stalls	Leak in brakes servo hose Leak in EGR hose Air leaks round inlet manifold Jets blocked	Replace. Replace. Replace gasket. Clean.
4 Engine will not stop when ignition switched off	Electro-magnetic cut-off valve not working	Check wiring. If wiring correct, replace valve.
5 Backfire in exhaust, vehicles fitted with afterburn	Faulty air control valve or leaking hoses	Tighten hoses, if this does not cure then replace valve.
6 'Flat spots' engine will not accelerate from idle evenly	Accelerator pump not working properly Partial or full load enrichment systems choked Fuel pump faulty	Test and adjust. Clean and adjust. Check delivery and replace if necessary.
7 Black smoke from exhaust, engine rough at low speeds. Plugs fouled	Too much fuel	Check pump outlet. Check needle valve. Check fuel level in float chamber.
8 Engine accelerates but lacks power at speed	Enrichment system not working Dirt in tank or pipe lines	Dismantle and clean. Flush and clean filters.
9 Miles per gallon too low	Wrong jets fitted Float punctured Leaks in fuel hose or petrol tank Automatic choke incorrect Brakes binding Ignition incorrectly set Engine overheating	Check and fit correct jets. Test and replace. Remove and service. Test and adjust. Adjust brakes (Chapter 9). Check and adjust (Chapter 4). Check cooling system (Chapter 2).
10 Flat spots (Scirocco 85 BHP)	2nd stage throttle valve sticking	Check valve for free movement. Check vacuum capsule for damaged diaphragm.
11 Flat spots and high fuel cunsumption	Broken spring in choke cover	Replace cover.
12 Engine cuts out after 100 yards	Automatic choke faulty	Dismantle and check automatic choke.
13 Engine cuts out (1.1 litre only)	Fuel blockage	Remove fuel gauge sender from tank and check strainer.

Chapter 4 Ignition system

Contents

Specifications

Distributor

Model	Golf/Scirocco 1.1 litre		Golf/Scirocco 1.5 litre		Rabbit/Scirocco 1.5 litre	
Engine code	F.A.	F.J.	F.H.	F.D.	F.C.	F.G.
HP (DIN)	50	52	70	85	74	74
Compression ratio	8	8	8.2	9.7	8.2	8.2
Distributor part no.	036/905/205	036/905/205B	055/905/205A	055/905/205C	055/905/205B	055/905/205B
Ignition timing	10° BTDC	10° BTDC	7.5° BTDC	7.5° BTDC	3° ATDC	3° ATDC
Engine speed rpm	900-1000	900-1000	900-1000	900-1000	900-1000	900-1000
Hoses	off	off	pff	pff	on	on

Firing order ... ... 1 − 3 − 4 − 2

CB points gap ... ... 0.3 to 0.4 mm (0.012 to 0.016 inches)

Dwell angle (all models):

Setting ... ... 44° to 50°
Wear limit ... ... 42° to 58°

Centrifugal advance

	F.A.	F.J.	F.H.	F.D.	F.C. & F.G.
	Golf/Scirocco		Golf/Scirocco	Scirocco	Rabbit/Scirocco
Begins:					
rpm	1050-1450	1050-1450	950-1250	950-1250	1100-1400
rpm	21000	2100	2200	2200	2200
degrees	10-14	10-14	15-20	15-20	15-19
rpm	3600	3600	4000	4000	3000
degrees	20-24	20-24	22-26	22-26	18-23
Ends:					
rpm	4500	4500	5000	5000	5000
degrees	26-31	27-31	26-30	26-30	26-30

F.H. Golf/Scirocco Automatic Gearbox

Begins:

rpm 1000-1200
rpm 2000
degrees ... ... 14° to 18°
rpm 4000
degrees ... ... 21° to 25°

End :

rpm 5000
degrees ... ... 26° to 30°

Vacuum advance (European models)

	F.A/F.J.	F.H/F.D.	F.H. automatic
Begins:			
m bar ...	107-153	280-333	267-333
mm Hg ...	80-115	210-250	200-250
Ends:			
m bar ...	247	433-440	440-453
mm Hg ...	185	325-335	330-340
degrees ...	10°-14°	11°-15°	11°-15°

Vacuum advance and retard (USA models, engines F.C./F.G.)

Vacuum advance

	up to June 75	after June 75
Starts:		
mm Hg ...	280-333	200-245
Ends:		
mm Hg ...	340	350
degrees ...	10-12	11-15

Vacuum retard

Starts:		
mm Hg ...	160-220	150-220
Ends:		
mm Hg ...	250-300	250-300
degrees ...	8-10	8-9

Coil

Type ...	Bosch 12v. Fitted with ballast resistor.

Spark plugs

	Bosch	Beru	Champion
1.1 litre engine ...	W175 T30	175/14/3	N.12.Y
1.5 litre - Golf and Scirocco (F.H.) ...	W175 T30	175/14/3	N.12.Y
1.5 litre - Scirocco F.D. (85 HP) ...	W225 T30	225/14/3	N.7.Y
1.5 litre - Golf/Scirocco - with auto transmission ...	W175 T30	175/14/3A	N.7.Y
1.5 litre - Rabbit/Scirocco ...	W175 T30	175/14/3A	N.7.Y

Spark plug electrode gaps ...   0.7 mm (0.028 inch)

Ignition timing marks

1.5 litre manual European	1.1 litre		1.5 litre auto. European

H.5565

1.5 LITRE MANUAL EUROPEAN

O = TIMING MARK

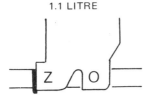

1.1 LITRE

Z = TIMING MARK 10° BTDC.

O = TDC

1.5 LITRE U.S.A.

O = TIMING MARK

1.5 LITRE AUTO EUROPEAN

O° = TDC

3° = 3° ATDC

1 General description

1 The ignition system is conventional. A 12 volt, negative earth supply goes from the battery to terminal '15' on the coil, via the ignition switch on the steering column and a ballast resistor. Removal and replacement of the ignition switch is dealt with in Chapter 11, Section 18. From terminal '1' of the coil the supply goes to the distributor points and, when they are closed, to earth. A small condenser is connected across the points to minimize sparking.

2 The resistor is so arranged that when starting the engine the value of the resistor is small and nearly all the full 12 volts is applied to the coil, As the current flows the resistor heats up and increases its resistance lowering the voltage applied to the coil. The coil is rated to work at 12v for comparatively short periods and if the resistor is short circuited the coil will overheat (photo).

3 The high tension winding is connected to the low tension winding inside the coil case and the other end is connected to the central terminal on the top of the coil casing. From here, via well insulated cable, the circuit goes to the centre of the distributor cap and from there via a small carbon bush inside the cap to the rotor arm.

This rotates causing a spark to jump across each rotor/segment gap in turn so that high voltage is led to the plugs where if all is correctly arranged a spark appears across the plug gap at the most propitious moment.

4 Because the engine requires only one spark per cylinder for every

1.2 The coil and ballast resistor

2.2 Undoing the screw securing the fixed point (1.5 litre)

2.5 Checking the points with a feeler gauge (1.5 litre)

two revolutions of the crankshaft the distributor rotates at half the speed of the crankshaft.

The distributors for the 1.1, 1.5 and 1.6 litre engines are all different. Those of the 1.5 litre and 1.6 litre are driven by a screw gear from the intermediate shaft. The 1.1 litre engine distributor is mounted on the end of the cylinder head and driven by the camshaft.

5   The central electrode of the spark plug is the one which gets hottest. Spark emission theory states that electron flow is from the hotter electrode to the cooler one. It is important therefore to keep the polarity correct. Connecting the LT winding of the coil incorrectly will cause all sorts of troubles and make starting difficult.

6   The heat path of the spark plugs has been carefully designed. Use only the recommended types or again performance will be badly affected.

7   With strict emission laws and the ever increasing cost of fuel it is most important that ignition timing should be exact and correct. It is now the accepted practice to set the distributor points gap by measuring the dwell angle. This requires a special meter and a tachometer. The gap can be set with feeler gauges in an emergency but this is not really accurate enough.

On the 1.5 litre and 1.6 litre engines the TDC sensor must be removed to see the flywheel on which is the timing mark to be set for optimum performance. On the 1.1 litre this job is done by a small bracket above the crankshaft pulley. This is good enough to get the engine running (Chapter 1, Sections 19 and 30) but the final adjustment needs a stroboscopic light and a tachometer. These jobs are described later in this Chapter.

8   On models after October 1975, the ballast resistor for the coil has been replaced by a resistance wire from the relay plate (see Section 10).

2   Contact breaker points (1.5 litre engine) - removal, replacement and adjustment

1   The contact breaker points require attention every 6000 miles. Depending upon how badly they are pitted or burned they may be cleaned and peaks removed with a fine oil stone. Do not try to remove craters. Points are cheap enough, it is difficult to set them accurately if they are worn.

2   To remove the points first take off the distributor cap and remove the rotor arm and seal. Two small leads are visible with spade terminals. Lift the spring away from them and pull the spring plus moving point up out of the distributor body. The fixed point is held to the mounting plate by a single screw. Undo this (photo) and the fixed point may be removed.

3   Examination of the points may be instructive. Normal wear gives pitting and small high points with light coloured surfaces. If the surface is grey then either the contact breaker spring is weak or the gap was too small. Yellow or black surfaces indicate over lubrication. A blue surface means that either the coil or condenser is defective.

4   This is a good moment to check side-play in the distributor shaft. If there is significant wear it will not be possible to set the points accurately, with feeler gauges, nor is it possible to obtain spares to remedy tolerence but that is only putting off the evil day; a replacement distributor is the answer. There is no reason to buy new points if you need a new distributor.

5   If the shaft and bearings are in good order replace the clean or new

points in the reverse order to dismantling. Make sure that the spade terminals are not short circuiting on the distributor body. Tighten the screw holding the fixed point so that it is just possible to move the point sideways. Turn the engine until the heel of the moving point rests on the highest point of the lobe of the cam on the shaft. The spring is now compressed to the maximum. Move the fixed point away from the moving point until a gap appears between them. Insert a 0.4 mm (0.016 in) feeler gauge between the points and close them with the screwdriver until the feeler gauge is just gripped (photo). Tighten the holding screw and recheck the gap again.

6   When using a dwell meter follow the instructions given with the meter concerning connection and timing. It is usual to connect one lead to No. 1 terminal on the coil and the other to earth.

7   Run the engine up to 1000 rpm. Read the value of the dwell angle. Now increase speed to 2000 rpm and read the dwell angle again. If the reading has altered by more than 1° the distributor shaft bearings are worn and a new distributor is required.

8   The readings should be compared with the specified figures, given at the start of the Chapter.

9   If they vary then the points gap is incorrect. To adjust slacken the fixed point holding screw and run the engine on the starter. It will not fire as the HT circuit is not connected. Move the fixed point until the correct angle is read on the meter. Tighten the screw, refit the rotor and cap and recheck the dwell angle as in paragraph 7.

3   Contact breaker points (1.1 litre engine) - removal, replacement and adjustment

1   It is much easier to take the distributor off the 1.1 litre engine for points adjustment than to try to peer in from the end of the engine.

2   Remove the battery earth strap and pull off the vacuum hose. Remove the distributor cap and undo the LT (green) lead to the coil at the coil end. Turn the engine so that the rotor arm points to the groove in the rim of the casing, a small saw cut, and remove the rotor arm. Using a scriber mark the distributor casing and the flange so that the casing can be replaced accurately on the flange, then remove the three bolts holding the distributor to the flange and take the distributor away. Note that the key on the end of the shaft is offset. Do not rotate the engine until the distributor is safely back in place.

3   Undo the two screws which clamp the outrigger bearing (see Fig. 4.2) to the housing (photo) and remove the bearing plate. The points are now accessible (photo). Pull the terminal connecting the points to the condenser off the tag, remove the screw holding the points to the plate and remove the points (photo).

4   Examination of the points is instructive. Normal wear gives pitting with small high points and a light coloured surface. If the surface is grey then either the contact breaker spring is weak or the gap was too small. Yellow or black surfaces indicate over lubrication. A blue surface indicates a defective coil or condenser. Clean the points with a rag moistened with petrol.

5   Depending upon the amount of wear the points may be cleaned up with a fine oil stone and the peaks removed. Do not try to remove craters, the surface of the contact point will be destroyed this way. If the points will not clean up easily fit a new set. It is not possible to set damaged points correctly.

6   Refit the points to the distributor, turn the shaft until the heel of

3.3a Remove the outrigger bearing (1.1 litre) ...

3.3b ... and the points are accessible (1.1 litre)

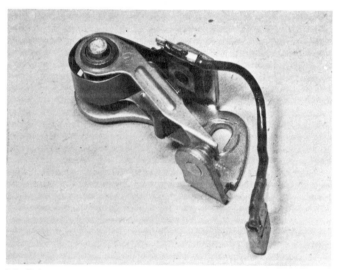

3.3c Points removed for examination (1.1 litre)

3.6 Check the points after the outrigger bearing is installed (1.1 litre)

the horn of the points is on the high portion of the cam on the shaft then move the static point of the pair away from the moving point and insert a 0.4 mm (0.016 in) feeler between them. Close the points until the feeler is just gripped by the points and tighten the screw. Check the gap again and adjust if necessary. Install the outrigger bearing and check again (photo). Adjust if necessary. Replace the shield and refit the distributor to the engine. Set the rotor to point to No. 1 cylinder mark and watch the offset of the key at the end of the shaft.

7   If you have a dwell meter read Section 2, paragraphs 6 to 9 inclusive and carry out the necessary check. Increasing the points gap reduces the dwell angle and vice-versa. If the gap is too small when the dwell angle is correct new points are required. The outrigger bearing **must** be in place when checking the dwell angle. A deviation of 20% may occur if the dwell angle is checked with the plate not installed.

4   Distributor - removal and replacement

1   The removal of the distributor from the 1.1 litre is dealt with in Section 3, paragraph 2. For the 1.5 litre it may be required to remove the distributor with the engine still in the car. Follow the procedure detailed below. Remove the TDC sensor.
2   Remove the valve cover and disconnect the battery earth strap.

3   Now bring No. 1 cylinder piston to the firing point. The TDC mark on the flywheel (not the timing mark) must line up with the pointer on the casing visible through the TDC sensor hole. Since the crankshaft revolves twice to the distributor's once you may be on the wrong revolution. Look at the cams on the camshaft for No. 1 cylinder. Both cams must be pointing upwards, valves closed. If they are not turn the engine one revolution. Remove the cap from the distributor.
4   Disconnect the LT lead from the distributor. Check that the rotor arm points to the mark for No. 1 cylinder on the rim of the distributor housing. This is a shallow groove. It can be seen in photo 2.2. just by the screwdriver.
5   Pull off the vacuum hoses. Now undo the clamp bolt and draw the distributor up and out. The shaft will turn a little as the gear is drawn away from the intermediate shaft. Note how much, If you are putting the same distributor back it is a good idea to centre-punch the casing and the block so that you get it back correctly.
6   Do not allow the crankshaft to rotate until you are ready to reinstall the distributor. Check the position of the oil pump drive before reassembly by looking down the bore for the distributor shaft. The slot in it should be parallel to the crankshaft.
7   Reassembly is the reverse of removal. Make sure the distributor is properly seated with the tongue on the end of the shaft firmly in the groove of the oil pump drive.

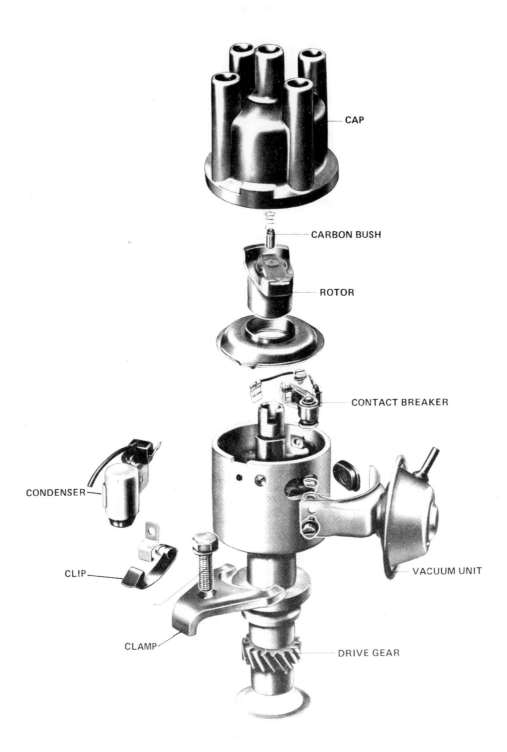

CAP

CARBON BUSH

ROTOR

CONTACT BREAKER

CONDENSER

VACUUM UNIT

CL!P

CLAMP

DRIVE GEAR

Fig. 4.1. Distributor fitted to 1.5 litre engine - exploded view

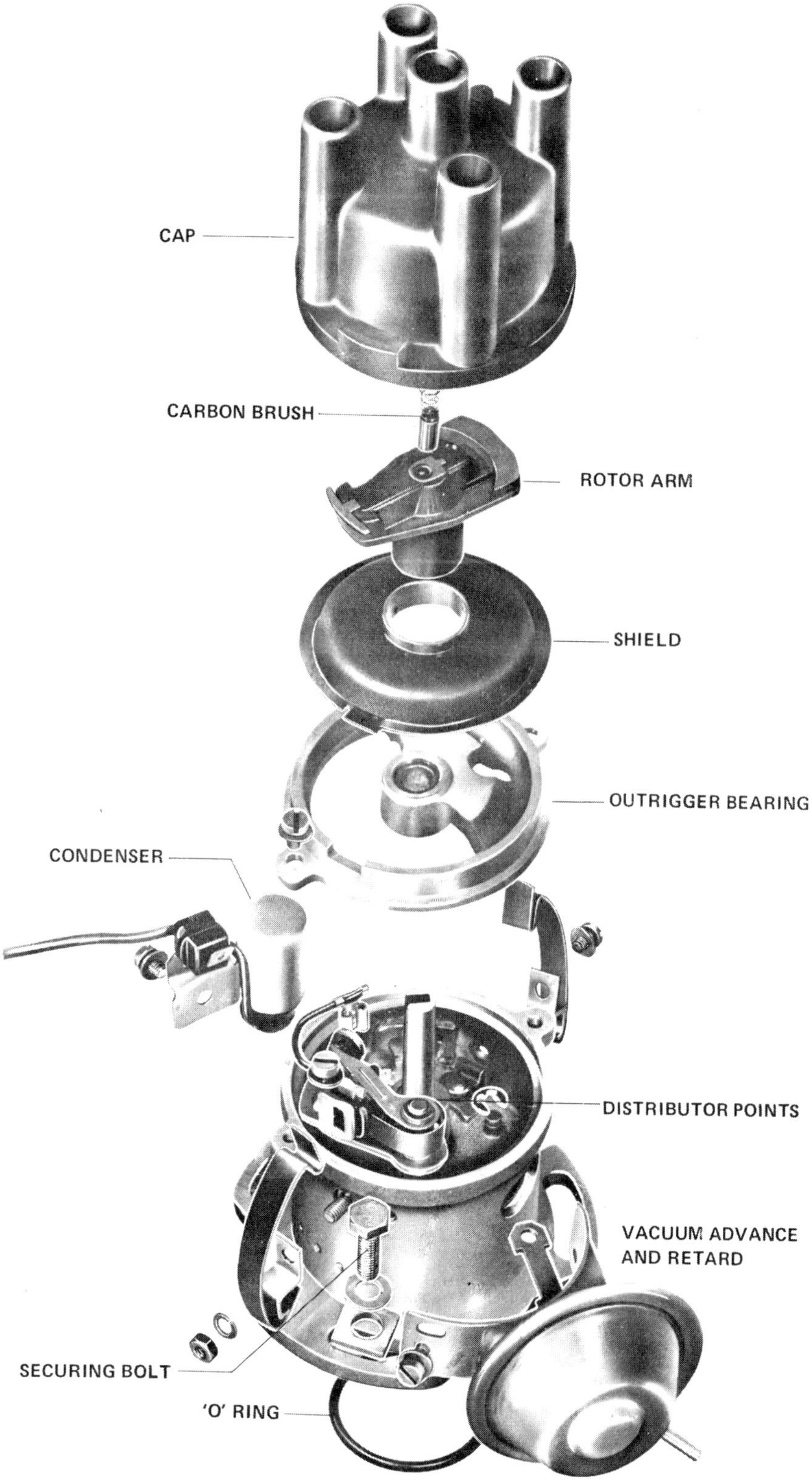

CAP

CARBON BRUSH

ROTOR ARM

SHIELD

OUTRIGGER BEARING

CONDENSER

DISTRIBUTOR POINTS

VACUUM ADVANCE
AND RETARD

SECURING BOLT

'O' RING

Fig. 4.2. Distributor fitted to 1.1 litre engine - exploded view

6.2 The opening in the distributor body giving access to inspect the centrifugal governer (1.1 litre)

6.3 Undo one screw and remove the condenser

6.4 Undo the circlip (A) and two screws and the vacuum unit may be removed from the housing

5 Distributor (1.5 litre) - overhaul

1　Refer to Fig. 4.1. Before starting to take the distributor apart check with the orficial agent what spares can be supplied.

2　The cap may have cracked, or chipped or the small carbon bush be faulty. Fine cracks will be visible and 'tracking' lines may also be found. When the cap is cleaned carefully, inside and out, what seem to be pencil lines are actually fine crackes harbouring carbon and are fine electricity conductors. All this means a new cap is necessary.

3　The rotor arm must not be cracked or chipped and the spring should be intact. The rotor arm segment has a resistance to suppress radio interference, this measured between the centre and the tip is up to 10000 ohms.

4　The vacuum unit is not removed and replaced easily, as this involves removing the mounting plate of the contact breaker and dismantling the centrifugal advance and retard mechanism. Unless the owner has had considerable instruction in these matters the job is best left to the expert.

5　The condenser can be removed easily and tested, or tested in position. A separate Section on this is included in this Chapter.

6　As stated before if there is wear in the bearings or shaft, replacement is not possible as spares are not available. If the teeth on the drive-gear are damaged this will also mean a replacement distributor.

7　To check the operation of the centrifugal advance and retard mechanism remove the distributor cap and rotor then grasp the shaft at the top and turn it a few degrees. It should turn easily and then stop. Do not force it, release it and it should return easily to the original position. If it does not then the springs are stretched or the mechanism is clogged. It would be as well to have it checked by the agent with his special tester. To clean the centrifugal governor it is necessary to remove the contact breaker and mounting plate. We do not recommend this as the governor should be set to exact readings if the emission control is to remain effective.

6 Distributor (1.1 litre engine) - overhaul

1　Refer to Fig. 4.2 which shows an exploded view of the distributor. This distributor differs in design from the conventional one fitted to the 1.5 litre. The shaft is in one piece and the rotor arm is not moved by the centrifugal governor. Instead the upper plate of the centrifugal governor moves the cam around the distributor shaft thus advancing the firing point as the engine speeds up. The movement is very slight and the operation of the governor can be checked by moving the cam relative to the shaft and checking its smooth return.

2　The contact breaker plate is crimped in to the body so that it is not possible to get at the centrifugal governor. It may be examined briefly through a small opening in the casing (photo) normally covered with a metal plate.

3　The condenser may be removed by undoing one screw (photo) having pulled off the points lead from the tag inside.

4　The vacuum advance and retard is easily removed. Pull off the hoses and remove the outrigger bearing. Remove the circlip (photo), undo the two screws which hold it to the body and withdraw the vacuum unit from the casing.

5　Apart from this no repair is possible. If it is not possible to obtain the correct dwell angle then the shaft or bearings are worn and it will be necessary to fit a new distributor.

7 Ignition timing (1.5 litre engine)

1　The timing marks are on the periphery of the flywheel. Remove the TDC sensor and a pointer on the casing will be visible. Turn the engine to find the timing marks on the flywheel.

2　A simple static method of setting the timing may be done using a test lamp. Set the engine so that the TDC mark shows in the sensor hole. Remove the distributor cap and check that the rotor arm points to the No. 1 cylinder mark.

3　Connect a 12 v test lamp across the No. 1 terminal of the coil and earth. Slacken the clamp nut on the distributor, switch on the ignition, and rotate the distributor body gently until the light goes off. At this position the points are closed and the lamp is shorted out. Reverse the direction of rotation of the body until the lamp *just* comes on. Tighten the clamp nut and reassemble the distributor. Have the timing checked dynamically as soon as possible.

4　The dynamic method may be done only if you have a tachometer and a strobe lamp. First find from the Specifications the engine speed, flywheel markings and connection of hoses for your engine.

5　The stroboscopic light should be connected in No. 1 spark plug lead. The instructions with the lamp explain how to do this. Usually a special connector is supplied to which the No. 1 plug lead from the distributor is connected. A lead from the connector goes to No. 1 plug and the lamp is also tapped into the connector. The other lead from the lamp goes to the battery positive (+) terminal.

6　The test must be carried out with the engine at normal operating temperature. Run the engine up to the specified rpm, as indicated on the tachometer, check the hose position on the vacuum unit and flash the lamp onto the hole for the TDC sensor. Read the timing mark illustrated and compare it with the Specifications. If adjustment is necessary slacken the clamp holding the distributor body and rotate the distributor body, clockwise to advance the timing, anticlockwise to retard it. It will be only a small amount. When the setting is correct tighten the clamp, reconnect the hoses, if necessary and replace the TDC sensor.

8 Ignition timing (1.1 litre engine)

1　The correct method of timing the ignition on this engine is to use a strobe lamp. It is also essential to use a tachometer to measure the engine speed. The contact breaker must be set correctly and, if possible, the dwell angle corrected. The carburettor setting should be correct and the idling speed adjusted. The operation should be done with the engine oil temperature between 30°C and 70°C (85 to 165°F).

2　Connect the strobe lamp as per manufacturer's instructions, and the tachometer. Remove the vacuum hose from the distributor. Run the engine at idle speed (900 rpm) and aim the flash of the strobe lamp at crankshaft pulley. Check that the notch in the pulley rim is in line with the left-hand edge of the timing marker (photo 9.4a, Chapter 1 and Fig. 4.2). The Vee cut is TDC, the left-hand edge is the timing mark 'Z'. Slacken the three bolts holding the distributor to the cylinder head and move the distributor until the timing marks coincide. Tighten the bolts and refit the hose.

3   There is another way if you do not have a strobe lamp. However it is as well to have the timing checked dynamically as soon as possible afterwards.

4   Take off the distributor cap and turn the engine until the rotor arm points to the small notch on the distributor housing rim. This is the TDC mark for No. 1 cylinder. The easiest way to turn the engine is by using a 19 mm socket spanner on the crankshaft pulley nut. Use a simple test-lamp or a voltmeter connected between the LT terminal (green wire) on the coil and earth. Turn the engine slowly until the timing mark on the crankshaft pulley is opposite the timing mark 'Z' on the bracket. Turn the engine in an anticlockwise direction through 90°. Now switch the ignition on and turn the engine clockwise until the timing marks coincide. The bulb should light, or the meter register. If the lamp comes on too soon, slacken the distributor holding bolts and turn the casing in an anticlockwise direction until you get the correct angle. If it comes on late, turn the distributor case in the other direction. Once the correct adjustment has been determined, tighten the clamping bolts and refit the cap.

9   Vacuum advance and retard mechanism - checking

1   A simple test to accertain whether the unit is working is given below. Remove the TDC sensor.

2   Connect a stroboscopic lamp to the ignition system and run the engine as though checking the ignition timing, shining the lamp on the flywheel through the TDC sensor hole (1.5) or the timing bracket (1.1). The hose position for the test should be as in the setting up procedure. When the timing mark is located correctly reverse the hose position (ie; if it was on, pull it off or vice-versa). The timing mark should seem to move. If it does not then the vacuum unit is not working, and must be exchanged.

3   This assures you only that it is working. It does not check that it is working correctly. To find this out requires gauges and switches and a control valve. It is best for this to be done by the agent.

10   Ignition coil - testing

1   It is well to remember that the test voltage output of the coil is in the region of 18000 volts. To test it accurately a special tester is needed. However, a coil is either all right or all wrong, there are no repairs possible, and there are three simple tests which will determine its condition.

2   Remove the wiring from the top of the coil and clean it carefully. Look for tracking marks and cracks. Check the servicability of the wires and connections and replace them if necessary. Refit the LT wires to the coil and the HT lead to the centre terminal of the coil but remove it from the middle of the distributor. Hold the distributor end of the lead about 3/8 in (10 mm) from the cylinder block and get a helper to switch on the ignition and operate the starter. A spark should jump from the lead to the block. You will jump too if you haven't taken the precaution of holding the lead with insulated pliers or wearing a rubber glove. If there is a big fat spark then the coil is working satisfactory. If no spark emerges then the LT circuit must be tested.

3   Connect a voltmeter between terminal '15' on the coil and earth. With the ignition switched on the reading should be minimum of 9 volts. Less than this, or zero, means that there is a faulty ballast resistor, ignition switch or faulty wiring. If this test registers a minimum of 9 volts then check the continuity of the remiander of the circuit. Connect the voltmeter between terminal '1' and earth. Remove the distributor cap and rotor. Turn the engine so that the points are closed, Switch on the ignition. There should be no voltage between terminal '1' and earth. Open the points with a piece of wood. There should be now a reading on the voltmeter. Finally check that the lead from the coil to the distributor is not shorting to earth when the points are open. If the lead is in order and there are no volts when the points are opened then the LT system of the coil is faulty and it should be removed for expert testing by the agent or a reputable Auto Electric specialist.

4   Even though the coil responds to all these tests it may still be the fault in the system. It can develop faults as it warms up. If you have persistent ignition trouble when the engine is warm after an excellent cold start suspect the coil and have it tested by the VW agent.

5   After October 1975 the ballast resistor is left off the coil, and its place taken by a resistance wire from terminal 'A.12' on the relay plate

to coil terminal '15'. The wire length, 1280 mm (50.4 inches) is critical, it is insulated by a transparent cover with violet stripes and its resistance in 0.9 ohms. The coil is designed to work at 9.0 volts, and on normal running the series resistance wire gives a drop of 3 volts. When starting the battery volts drop to approximately 9 volts and the coil is supplied with this voltage via starter terminal '16'. This supply ceases when the engine starts and the starter is disconnected. To check the resistance wire pull the multipin-plug off the relay plate and identify the series resistance wire. Disconnect the other end. Measure the resistance of the wire. It must be 0.9 ohms±0.5 ohm. If it differs fit a new wire in parallel with the old one, insulating both ends of the old one which must be left in place in the harness. The series resistance on the old coil may be tested the same way.

11   Condenser - testing

1   If the contact breaker points are badly burned or pitted the fault is probably with the condenser. This small unit will also cause problems with the HT circuit for it helps the rapid decay of the magnetic field in the coil and if it is defective the operating voltage of the HT circuit will be much reduced.

2   There are two faults that can affect it. A short circuit, either in its construction or lead will render it inoperative, as will an open circuit.

3   Disconnect cable '1' from the coil and connect a test lamp in series with cable '1' and cable '15' of the coil (in other words put the lamp in place of the coil). Switch on the ignition. If there is a short circuit then the lamp will not light, and the condenser must be replaced.

4   Open circuits are very rare. If the short circuit test shows that the condenser is in good condition and extensive pitting of the points has happened then remove the condenser and take it to someone who can measure its insulation resistance and capacitance. If this is not possible then replace it straight away.

12   Spark plugs and HT leads - general

1   Spark plugs should be removed, cleaned and the gaps reset every 12000 miles or more often if the engine shows signs of burning oil. The best policy is to have two sets of plugs and have a clean set ready to fit when necessary. The dirty ones may then be taken to a garage to be cleaned in the shot blast machine, reset and tested under pressure. In this way the carbon is removed from the plug. Trying to clean it with a wire brush only pushes the carbon inside the plug. Never try to clean plug with solvent.

2   The plug gap is set by bending the outer electrode. Do not attempt to move the centre electrode or you will break the insulator. If you are setting the gap with feeler gauges measuring inches aim at 0.028 in.

3   It is essential to use only the recommended grade of plug. Three choices are given in the Specifications but other makers produce equally good plugs. There is a comparison table concerning grades in most garages.

4   When refitting plugs make sure the washer is not flattened or the plug will be damaged by leaking gases. Be careful not to cross the threads or expensive repairs to the cylinder head may be necessary besides all the bother of taking off.

5   HT leads are special high resistance cable to deal with suppression of radio interference. If they are frayed or soaked in oil then replace them. Do not use insulating tape on HT systems and make sure the terminals are securely crimped on the cable. The resistance of a lead should be between 5000 and 10000 ohms.

6   The condition of the plugs gives an interesting comment on the state of the engine. A study of Fig. 4.3 will show why.

13   Ignition system - fault diagnosis method

1   Before assuming that there is an ignition fault check that there is fuel being supplied to the engine, the battery is in good condition and that there is compression in all four cylinders.

2   Ignition faults can be most exasperating. Read the whole Section and then work quietly through it, check everything and if you cannot find the answer go to the expert. He has instruments specially designed for finding faults. If you explain how you have checked methodically it may help him, if you have been pulling wires off in the hope of curing the fault quickly it may take him a long while to put things right and he

*White deposits and damage
porcelain insulation indicating
overheating*

*Broken porcelain insulation
due to bent central electrode*

*Electrodes burnt away due to
wrong heat value or chronic
pre-ignition (pinking)*

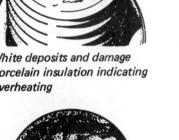

*Excessive black deposits
caused by over-rich mixture
or wrong heat value*

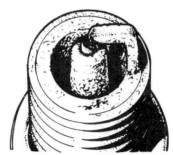

*Mild white deposits and electrode
burnt indicating too weak a
fuel mixture*

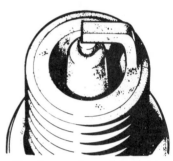

*Plug in sound condition with
light greyish brown deposits*

Fig. 4.3. Plug chart

may never find out which the original fault was that caused all the trouble.

Engine will not start

1   If the car will not start check first that the engine is not covered with moisture from mist, or rain or other sources. If it is, then dry inside the distributor cap, dry all leads and covers and generally clean up. A cold engine will not start if it is damp and you will only run the battery down.

2   If the engine is dry then remove one of the plug leads and turn back the insulation. Hold the lead near the block about 3/8 in (9.525 mm) away from it, and get someone to spin the engine with the starter. If there is a fat spark then the ignition is working alright but the timing may have slipped. This will be one of two things on this engine, the clamp holding the distributor has come loose or the timing belt is loose. The latter will make itself known by the noise it makes fouling the guard.

3   Check the ignition timing as in Sections 7 and 8.

4   If there is not a fat spark when testing as at the start of paragraph 2 then the fault is with the ignition circuit. However, check with another plug lead before doing anything else.

5   There is a tendency to test haphazardly but it is better to stick to a routine even if it takes a little longer. This way you will find the faults and cure them. There may be more than one. Begin by checking the LT circuit in the following order:

(i)   Are the points opening and closing correctly? Are they clean?

(ii)   Switch on the ignition and check the voltage at terminal '15' on the coil. It should be at least 9 volts. if it is less check the wiring switch and ballast resistor.

(iii) Check the voltage at terminal '1' on the coil. Points closed there should be no volts, points open there should be a reading. Check the LT lead from the distributor to the coil for short circuit to earth (points open). If the lead is correct and there are no volts with the points open then the coil is faulty.

(iv)   Ignition switched on check the voltage across the points. Points closed - no volts; points open the meter should read, if it does not the condenser is faulty.

6   Now proceed to test the HT circuit.

(i)   Pull the HT lead from the centre of the distributor, hold it close to the cylinder block, switch on the engine and spin it with the starter. No spark - faulty HT winding in the coil. Switch off the ignition and proceed to test the coil.

(ii)   Check the condition of the rotor and distributor cap.

(iii) Check the centrifugal automatic advance and retard.

(iv)   Remove the plugs and service them. Oily plugs mean worn cylinders; wet plugs, flooding in the carburettor.

7   A comprehensive chart is included (Section 14).

14 Fault diagnosis - Ignition system

See also Section 13

Symptom	Probable cause	Remedy
Engine sluggish, hard to start	CB points not set correctly	Check and set.
	Plug gaps incorrect	Check and set.
	Ignition timing incorrect	Check and adjust.
	Wrong fuel used	Check octane rating of fuel.
Engine misfires, cuts out at low revolutions	CB points gap too large	Reset.
	Distributor shaft and bearings worn	Fit new distributor.
Engine misfires at high revolutions	CB gap too small	Reset.
	Distributor shaft and bearings worn	Fit new distributor.
Engine starts and runs well for 15 mins then cuts out	Coil defection, fault only when warm	Test coil when warm, replace if necessary.
Engine runs irregularly with loss of power	Plug lead open circuit	Replace.
	Plug fouled	Clean and reset.
Engine overheats	Ignition retarded too much	Check timing.
Engine 'pinks' or pre-ignites	Ignition advanced too much	Check timing.
	Wrong fuel	Check RON rating of fuel and use correct one.
Engine sluggish, lacks power on hills, pinks, overheats.	Vacuum advance and retard not working	Check and repair as necessary.
	Centrifugal advance and retard not working	Check and repair as necessary.

Chapter 5 Clutch

Contents

Specifications

Type	... ...	Single plate, dry spring operated, activated by a clutch cable.

1.1 litre ... ...   Flywheel bolted to crankshaft, pressure plate bolted to flywheel.
1.5 litre ... ...   Pressure plate bolted to crankshaft, flywheel bolted to pressure plate.

Free-play at clutch pedal (1.1 litre and 1.5 litre) ... ...   15 mm (5/8 inch).

Driven plate (friction disc)

Max. out of true (at 179 mm dia) ... ...   0.4 mm (0.015 ins)
Min. depth of lining above rivets ... ...   0.6 mm (0.023 ins)

Drive plate

Max taper access drive face ... ...   0.3 mm (0.012 ins)
Diaphragm fingers (1.1 litre) max depth of scoring ... ...   0.3 mm (0.012 ins)

Clutch cables

Model	Engine Code	Cable length Production mm	in	Replacement mm	in	Part number replacement
Golf L.H.D.	F.A. F.J.	1055	41.5	1055	41.5	171 721 335C
Scirocco L.H.D.	F.A. F.J.	1055	41.5	1055	41.5	171 721 335C
Golf R.H.D	F.A. F.J.	1427	56.2	1427	56.2	172 721 335C
Scirocco R.H.D	F.A. F.J.	1457	57.4	1427	56.2	172 721 335C
Golf R.H.D.	F.H.	1216	47.8	1216	47.8	172 721 335B
Scirocco R.H.D	F.H. F.D.	1246	49.0	1216	47.8	172 721 335B
Scirocco L.H.D	F.H. F.D.	915	36.0	915	36.0	531 721 335A
Scirocco U.S.A	F.C.	915	36.0	915	36.0	531 721 335A
Golf L.H.D	F.H.	855	33.7	855	33.7	171 721 335B
Rabbit	F.C.	855	33.7	855	33.7	171 721 335B
Scirocco L.H.D*	F.H. F.D.	915	36.0	915	36.0	531 721 335

Note: L.H.D. left-hand drive. R.H.D. right-hand drive.
*This cable fitted to production models, no longer available. Use 531 721 335A.

Torque wrench settings

1.1 litre engine		mkg	lbs ft
Pressure plate to flywheel		2.5	18
Flywheel to crankshaft**		7.5	54

1.5 litre engine			
Pressure plate to crankshaft**		7.5	54
Flywheel to pressure plate		2	14

**Note: Use LOCTITE 270 or similar compound.

1 General description

1   The clutches of the 1.1 litre and the 1.5 litre are very different. The 1.1 litre is fitted with a conventional car type single plate, dry clutch with a diaphragm spring clamping the friction disc to the flywheel. Refer to Fig. 5.1. The flywheel is bolted to the crankshaft and the pressure plate to the flywheel. A normal clutch withdrawal mechanism consists of a release bearing operated by a forked shaft mounted in the gearbox bellhousing. The shaft is turned by a lever operated by a bowden cable from the clutch pedal.

2   The 1.5 litre clutch has the pressure plate bolted to the crankshaft flange. Refer to Fig. 5.2. The flywheel, which is dish shaped, is bolted to the pressure plate, holding the friction disc between them. This is in effect the reverse arrangement of the 1.1 litre clutch. The release mechanism consists of a metal disc called the release plate which is clamped in the centre of the pressure plate by a retaining ring. In the centre of the release plate is a boss into which the clutch pushrod is fitted. The pushrod passes through the centre of the main driveshaft of the gearbox, which is tubular, and is housed in a release bearing situated at the back of the gearbox. A single finger lever passes on this bearing when the shaft to which it is splined is turned by operation of the bowden cable from the clutch pedal. In effect the clutch lever pushes the clutch pushrod, which in turn pushes the centre of the release plate inwards towards the crankshaft. The outer edge of the release plate presses on the spring plate fingers forcing them back towards the engine and removing the pressure plate friction face from the friction disc, thus disconnecting the drive. When the clutch pedal is released the spring plate reasserts itself clamping the friction disc firmly against the flywheel and restoring the drive. A cross-section of this clutch is shown at Fig. 5.4.

3   It is not possible to dismantle the clutch pressure plate of either type.

4   It will be noted that seven different lengths of clutch cable have been fitted to the various models. This is to suit LHD and RHD and because the clutch lever of the 1.5 is in a different place relative to the frame than the 1.1 litre, due to the slope of the engine. Note also that replacements sometimes differ in length from the cable fitted at the factory. See the table in the Specifications

2 Clutch pedal - adjustment of free-travel

1   There should be 15 mm (5/8 inch) of free-travel downwards on the clutch pedal before the lever on the gearbox begins to turn the withdrawal mechanism shaft. At this point the additional load can be felt at the pedal. This ensures that the withdrawal mechanism is not in contact with the clutch and is not wearing out during normal operation. It also makes certain that the clutch is fully engaged. Of course this is provided you keep your foot off the clutch pedal. It is not a footrest!

2   The easiest way to measure the free-play is to use a short wooden strip. Hold it against the pedal with the end on the floor of the car. Mark the position of the top of the clutch pedal. Next make a mark 15 mm (5/8 inch) from the first mark, and replace the strip alongside the pedal as before. Press down the pedal until the end of the free-play is felt and make another mark. This mark should coincide with your second mark. If it does not then the cable must be adjusted until it does. An eighth of an inch (3 mm) either way does not matter. Keep the piece of wood in your tool box for subsequent checks.

3   The cable is adjusted at the gearbox end. At the bracket on the gearbox where the outer cable (cable sheath) ends on the 1.5 litre are two locknuts. Slacken these, and turn the adjuster. Undo it to shorten the free-play, screw it in to increase free-play. Two people make the job easier, one to check the measurement, one to do the adjustment. A photo of the adjustment point on the 1.1 litre and a diagram of the 1.5 litre is given (Fig. 5.3).

4   It will be seen from the photo that the adjustment on the 1.1 litre is by turning the nut behind the bracket which anchors the inner cable to adjust the position of the pedal. A spring holds the lever in the right place and thus the outer cable in the right place. Slacken off the nut to give more free-play and vice-versa.

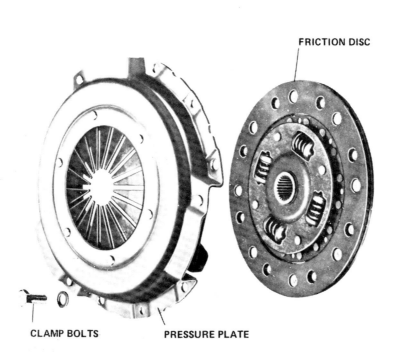

FRICTION DISC

CLAMP BOLTS   **PRESSURE PLATE**

Fig. 5.1. Exploded view of clutch - 1.1 litre

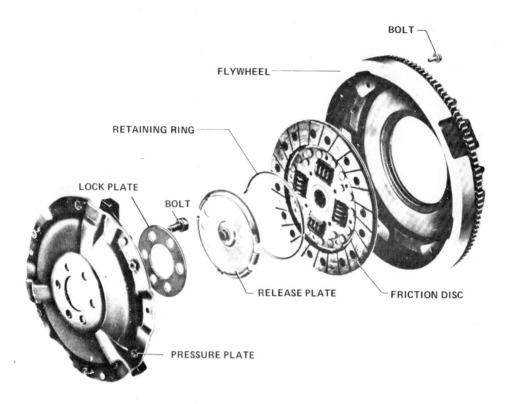

BOLT

FLYWHEEL

RETAINING RING

LOCK PLATE

BOLT

RELEASE PLATE

FRICTION DISC

PRESSURE PLATE

Fig. 5.2. Clutch - 1.5 litre - exploded view

2.4 The clutch withdrawal lever. 'A' is the adjuster nut on the 1.1 litre

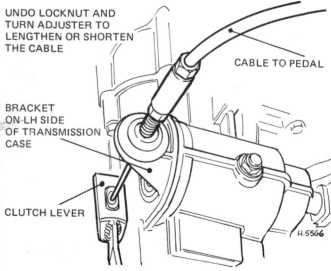

UNDO LOCKNUT AND TURN ADJUSTER TO LENGTHEN OR SHORTEN THE CABLE

CABLE TO PEDAL

BRACKET ON-LH SIDE OF TRANSMISSION CASE

CLUTCH LEVER

H-5566

Fig. 5.3. Clutch cable anchorage and free-travel adjustment - 1.5 litre (Sec. 2)

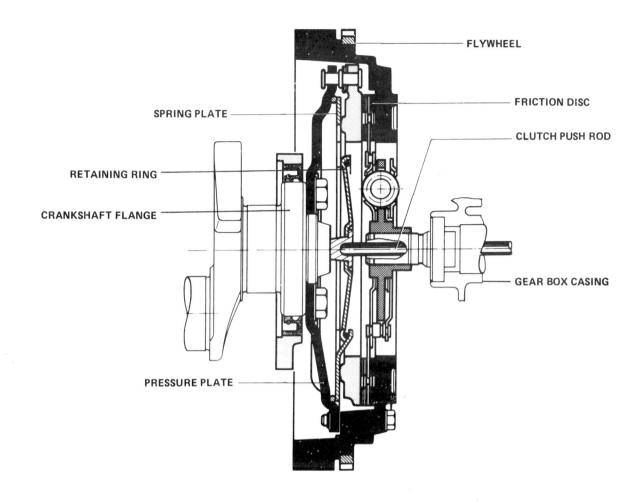

SPRING PLATE

RETAINING RING

CRANKSHAFT FLANGE

PRESSURE PLATE

FLYWHEEL

FRICTION DISC

CLUTCH PUSH ROD

GEAR BOX CASING

Fig. 5.4. Clutch 1.5 litre - cross-section

3 Clutch cable - removal and replacement

1   Slacken off the adjusters until it is possible to disconnect the cable from the operating lever and remove the inner and outer cable from the anchorages.

2   On some models it is necessary to remove the covering under the fascia to get at the clutch pedal. At the upper end of the clutch pedal the inner cable is attached to the pedal. On early 1.5 litre models the attachment is by loops and pins. On 1.1 litre and later 1.5 litre models it is held by a clip. Diagrams are given (Fig. 5.5). The outer cable fits in an anchorage on the column bracket. Unhook the inner cable and withdraw the cable through the grommet in the bulkhead. Fit the necessary parts of the bottom anchorage to the new cable on the pedal and then install it through the grommet. The end of the pedal will accommodate either old or new anchorages. Install the cable on the pedal and then fit it to the clutch lever. Fit the cable to the anchorage points and adjust the free-play.

3   When ordering a new cable consult the table in the Specifications; also, tell the storeman the chassis number of your vehicle — there may have been further changes since this book was written.

4 Clutch (1.1 litre) - removal and replacement

1   Make arrangements for the support of the engine and remove the transmission, this is described in Chapter 6.

2   The clutch may now be removed from the flywheel. This is described in Chapter 1, Section 9, paragraph 13. Installation is described in Chapter 1, Section 32, paragraph 12.

3   Be careful to centre the clutch disc carefully and to fit the pressure plate in the right position. To ensure that this is done scribe a line round the edge of the plate onto the flywheel and a line across the flange onto the flywheel before removing the pressure plate. There is no need to make a continuous line all round.

4   It will help if you make a short clip out of a piece of steel bar which will fit over a bolt through one of the transmission case bolt holes to hold the plate in position as you undo the pressure plate holding bolts. Watch which way the boss on the friction disc goes. Undo the holding bolts in a diagonal pattern, and replace them that way.

5   The friction disc must be centred properly or the gearbox main shaf· splines will not enter. This is particularly important when overhauling the clutch with the engine in the car. It will help if you make a mandrel a wooden one will do, to hold the friction disc while tightening the pressure plate bolts. The professionals use an old main shaft, but you are not likely to have one of those.

6   Once again it is emphasised that there must be no grease or oil on the friction surfaces, so wash your hands before starting assembly.

5 Clutch (1.5 litre) - removal and replacement

1   Support the engine and remove the transmission as described in Chapter 6. Clamp the flywheel to prevent it turning and remove the bolts holding the flywheel to the pressure plate in a diagonal fashion. Release each one two or three threads at a time until they are all slack and then take them out. The flywheel and the friction disc may now be removed. Note which way the disc is fitted.

2   Examine the pressure plate surface. If it is clean and free from scoring there is no reason to remove it unless the friction disc shows

EYE OF CABLE
HELD BY PIN

TOP OF CLUTCH PEDAL

CLIP
GOES
OVER
HOOK

A

B

H.5569

Fig. 5.5. Attachment of clutch cable to top of clutch pedal (Sec. 3)

A   *1.5 litre early models*   B   *1.1 litre and later 1.5 models*

6.1 The thickness of lining over the rivets must be measured

6.3a Measuring the taper of the pressure plate friction surface

6.3b Examine the tips of the diaphragm springs (1.1 litre). The pencil points to the danger spot

6.3c The surface of the pressure plate. The marks seen are probably casting faults but do not affect the operation of the clutch

signs of oil contamination.

3   If the plate surface does not pass test then it must be removed. Note exactly where the ends of the retaining ring are located (the ring must be reinstalled this way later), and prise the ring out with a screwdriver. The release plate may now be removed. The pressure plate is held to the crankshaft flange by six bolts installed with Loctite. These will be difficult to remove as they were tightened to 54 lbs ft (7.5 mkg) before the locking fluid sets so the plate must be held with a clamp.

4   Replacement is the reverse of dismantling. Watch that the retaining ring is correctly seated. Again be careful that no oil or grease is allowed to get onto the friction disc or friction surfaces.

5   When assembling the friction plate use a fixture similar to that described in Chapter 1, Section 31, paragraph 10, to centre the friction disc. Tighten the flywheel bolts in a diagonal fashion. If the pressure plate was removed from the crankshaft flange the bolts must be re-installed with locking fluid.

6   When installing the transmission put a smear of multipurpose grease on the end of the clutch pushrod at the release plate end.

6   Clutch components - inspection

1   The most probable part of the clutch to require attention is the friction disc. Normal wear will eventually reduce its thickness. The lining must stand proud of the rivets by a 0.6 mm (0.025 inch). At this measurement the lining is at the end of its life and a new friction plate is needed (photo).

2   The friction disc should be checked for run-out if possible. Mount the disc between the centres of a lathe and measure the run-out at 175 mm diameter. The quoted limit is 0.4 mm (0.016 ins). However, this requires a clock gauge and a mandrel. If the clutch has not shown signs of dragging then this test may be passed over, but if it has we suggest that expert help be sought to test the run-out.

3   Examine the pressure plate. There are three important things to check. Put a straight-edge across the friction surface and measure any bow or taper with feeler gauges (photo). This must not exceed 0.3 mm (0.012 ins). The fingers of the diaphragm will be rough (photo). Scoring of up to 0.3 mm (0.012 ins) is acceptable according to VW, but how you measure this is a good question. If the surface is rough enough to damage the release bearing remove the burrs with a stone. If in doubt consult the VW agent.

The rivets which hold the spring fingers in position must be tight. If any of them are loose the pressure plate must be scrapped. Finally, the condition of the friction surface. Ridges or scoring indicate undue wear and unless they can be removed by light application of emery paper it would be better to replace the plate. However, marks such as shown in photo 3c are probably casting faults and need cause no concern. They have been there a long while without causing problems.

4   The flywheel friction surface must be similarly checked.

5   So far the inspection has been for normal wear. Two other types of damage may be encountered. The first is overheating due to clutch slip. In extreme cases the pressure plate and flywheel may have radial cracks. Such faults mean that they require replacement. The second problem is contamination by oil or grease. This will cause clutch slip but probably without the cracks. There will be shiny black patches on the friction disc which will have a glazed surface. There is no cure for this, a new

friction disc is required. In addition it is **imperative** that the source of contamination be located and rectified. It will be either the engine rear oil seal, or the gearbox front oil seal, or both. Examine them and replace the faulty ones before fitting a new disc. Failure to do this will mean dismantling the transmission again very shortly. The fitting of new seals is discussed in **Chapters 1 and 6.**

6   The inspection so far concerns both 1.1 litre and 1.5 litre. However, on the 1.5 litre these are a few more things to look for. The seating for the pushrod on the release plate must not be worn or distorted. The retaining ring must sit securely in place, and the pressure plate must run truly with the crankshaft. Any sign of distortion is **suspect,** and expert advice should be sought before reassembly.

7   Clutch withdrawal mechanism (1.1 litre) - removal, overhaul and replacement

1   Before anything can be done with the withdrawal mechanism the transmission must be removed from the engine. (Chapter 6).

2   Undo the spring holding the release lever (photo) then undo the clamp bolt and take the lever off the clutch withdrawal shaft. Mark the angle at which the lever fits on the shaft relative to the clutch shaft fingers.

3   Inside the bellhousing is the release bearing held to the shaft fingers by clips. Note how these clips fit and then press the bottom leg down to clear the lever and pull the top leg out of the bearing shoulder (photo). Lift the release ring bearing off the shaft (photo).

4   From outside remove the bush round the release shaft (photo). The shaft may now be moved over and drawn out of the bearing inside the housing (photo).

5   The bearing guide may be removed if there is any sign of wear, or to examine the oil seal (photo).

6   The release bearing may be examined for wear or signs of roughness. Failure of the bearing will have transmitted vibration to the pedal when in operation, and a rumbling noise. Do not attempt to wash it with solvent, it is prepacked and cannot be recharged with lubricant. If in doubt do not reassemble it but seek advice from the agent. A bearing which is beginning to wear will wear rapidly thereafter.

7   Check the fit of the shaft in the bushes. The outer bush may be replaced, if necessary.

8   Assembly is the reverse of removal. Put a little molybdenum disulphide powder on the gearbox shaft before reassembly. Fit the springs carefully and be sure the actuating lever goes back on the shaft at the correct angle.

8   Clutch release mechanism (1.5 litre) - removal and replacement

1   Refer to Fig. 5.6 and Fig. 6.7. The release mechanism is approached through a plate on the end of the gearbox. Remove the five screws and then the plate, the shaft with its fingers is then visible (Fig. 5.7). The finger is held in place by circlips and a spring. The circlips may be lifted off and the spring disconnected so that the finger may be turned for the release bearing to be extracted. There is very little room to do this while the engine is in the car, but it is worth a try. The push-rod, of course, cannot be extracted. Be careful with the circlips, they

7.2 The clutch release lever and spring (1.1 litre)

7.3a The release bearing is held by clips (1.1 litre)

7.3b Remove the clips and lift the bearing off (1.1 litre)

7.4a Remove the bearing bush ...

7.4b ... and move the release shaft over to release the inner bearing

7.5 The guide sleeve may be removed to examine the oil seal

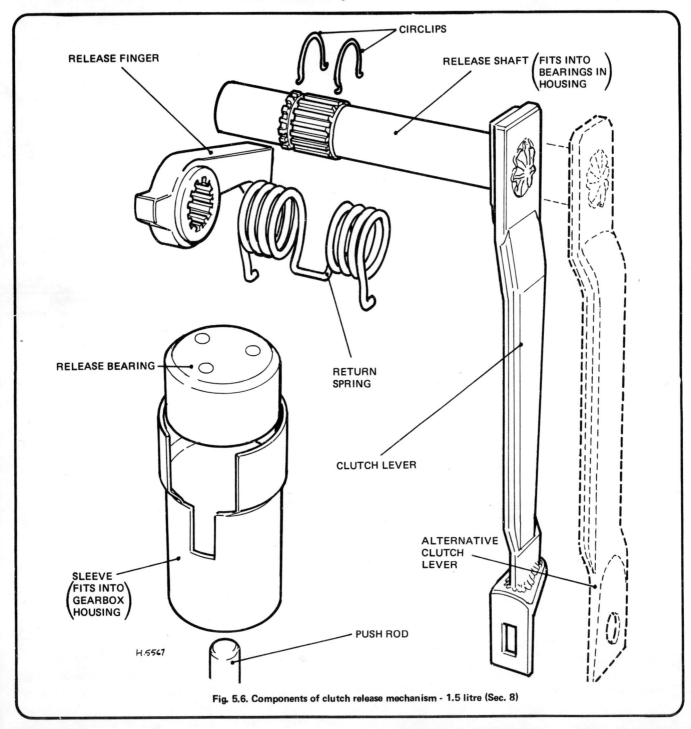

Fig. 5.6. Components of clutch release mechanism - 1.5 litre (Sec. 8)

Fig. 5.7. Clutch release mechanism - 1.5 litre; view of mechanism with cover removed. The arrows point to the circlips (Sec. 8)

spring out smartly and the spring can be awkward. The bent ends bear against the gearbox casing and the centre part hooks into the clutch finger.

2   Fit a new gasket when assembling the end cover.

9   Clutch faults - general

1   The various points at which the engine and transmission are bolted to the frame should be checked before beginning to dismantle the clutch. If any of them are loose, or the rubber perished, then the vehicle will shake when moving off and the fault will be diagnosed as clutch judder which is incorrect. When describing clutch faults the following terms are used.

2   'Judder' or 'grabbing' is a term used to describe the situation that occurs that when the clutch is engaged the vehicle vibrates excessively and moves off in jerks.

3   'Dragging' or 'clutch spin' means that the clutch will not disengage and the gears cannot be selected.

4   'Clutch slip' means that the engine is driving the flywheel faster than the flywheel is driving the plate. The physical symptom is that the engine accelerates but the vehicle does not, particularly on heavy load or when climbing steep hills. To confirm this diagnosis stand the vehicle on level ground, put the handbrake hard on, and start the engine. You will need a little help for the next bit. Disengage the clutch engage top gear, accelerate the engine slightly and with the footbrake hard on, engage the clutch. The engine should stall. If it does not the clutch is slipping. If the engine stalls at low engine revolutions, try again with a slightly higher engine speed. This test is best done after the vehicle has been running for an hour. Be gentle and if the clutch does slip, stop the test at once.

10 Fault diagnosis - clutch

See also Section 9

Symptom	Probable cause	Remedy
1 Clutch slipping	Oil on linings	Dismantle and replace linings. Repair oil seals.
	Free travel on clutch pedal incorrect	Adjust free-travel.
	Cable damaged in sheath and sticking	Replace cable.
2 Clutch judder	Engine or transmission mountings loose	Tighten nuts and bolts.
	Diaphragm plate distorted or fractured	Replace.
3 Clutch spin	Pedal free-travel too large	Adjust.
	Release bearing or shaft faulty	Dismantle and replace.
	Main driveshaft splines damaged or rusty	Dismantle, and clean splines. Lubricate with lithium grease.
	Friction plate distorted or broken	Replace friction plate.
	Pilot bearing in flywheel damaged	Dismantle and replace.
	Excessive clutch dust on driveplate	Dismantle and clean.
4 Clutch noisy	Pilot bearing worn	Replace.
	Diaphragm fingers loose or damaged	New clutch required.
	Release bearing defective	Replace.
	Splines worn, driven plate fouling the driveplate or pressure plate	Replace driveplate and/or driven plate.

Chapter 6 Manual gearbox and final drive

Contents

Specifications

Type	Four forward speeds, one reverse, mainshaft driven from clutch disc, driving pinion shaft. Final drive integral with main gearbox, helical gear containing differential. Transfer to front wheel by C.V. jointed driveshafts.

Gearbox application

	1.1 litre	1.5 litre
Gearbox code letter	G.F.	G.C.
Gearbox code number	084	020

Gear ratios

	1.1 litre	1.5 litre
1st gear	3.45 (11:38)	3.45 (11:38)
2nd gear	2.05 (20:41)	1.95 (19:37) 1.94 (18:35)*
3rd gear	1.35 (46:62)	1.37 (27:37)
4th gear	0.96 (55:53)	0.97 (32:31)
Reverse	3.38 (44:13)	3.17 (12:38)
Final drive	4.57 (14:64) 4.26 (15:64)	3.9 (19:74)

Oil capacity

	Litres	Pints (US)	Pints (Imperial)	Litres	Pints (US)	Pints (Imperial)
Up to December 1974:						
Initial filling	2.25	4.87	3.8	1.25	2.65	2.2
Oil change	2.0	4.25	3.5	1.25	2.65	2.2
After December 1974: **						
Initial filling	2.35	5	4.2	Remains the same		
Oil change	2.25	4.9	3.8	Remains the same		

*New ratio from mid-December 1974. **Due to modified breather (084 only)*

1 Gearbox (084 and 020) - general description

1   Although the casings are different in appearance the gearboxes for the 1.5 litre and 1.1 litre are basically similar. Gear ratios are different and because of the different types of clutch the 1.1 litre has a bell-housing containing the withdrawal mechanism whereas the withdrawal mechanism for the 1.5 litre is housed at the opposite end of the gear casing. The gearbox for the 1.5 litre has code letter 'GC' and code number '020'. The codes for the 1.1 litre are 'GF' and '084'. Hereafter, the boxes will be referred to by their code numbers.

2   The older gearbox, '020', has had nine modifications to date, one slightly modifying the second speed ratio. Gearbox code '084' has had five modifications, mainly to overcome teething troubles. These modifications are referred to in the text, where appropriate.

3   The method of dismantling is basically the same, but the '020' box has a requirement for the driveshaft gears to be removed in-situ, whereas the '084' box is so arranged that the mainshaft and driveshaft may be removed complete. To co-ordinate with VW nomencalatune the shafts are called 'driveshaft' and 'output shaft'. These replace the older names of 'mainshaft' and 'pinion shaft' and are used throughout the Chapter.

4   This Chapter describes in detail the removal and installation of the transmission, the dismantling and reassembly of the '084' box and then the '020' box. Shift mechanisms are dealt with at the end of the Chapter.

5   The dismantling of the final drive is described as far as removing the differential. It is not thought that the overhaul of the differential is within the capacity of the owner who does not have the necessary jigs and fixtures and therefore, this has not been included. However, the drive flanges may be removed without taking the gearbox out of the car and the oil seals renewed. For all other repairs to the transmission the gearbox must be removed.

2 Gearbox (084 and 020) - removal and replacement (general)

1   Although the removal of the transmission from the vehicle leaving the engine in place involves almost identical work, the order of doing it varies between the 1.5 litre and the 1.1 litre. It is not essential to stick to these suggested methods but they do give a logical sequence.

2   The gearbox is removed downwards so the vehicle must be raised from the ground sufficiently to withdraw the box from underneath. The ideal is to work over a pit but axle stands or similar support under the body can be arranged. However, note that you must be able to turn the wheels to disconnect the driveshafts. Do not raise it too much or you will be unable to get at the box through the opening in the engine compartment. About 24 inches (60 cm) clearance is required. The methods suggested here complete the work at the top of the car first,

and then go on to the underneath jobs so perhaps the lifting may be conveniently done when all the top jobs are finished.

3   Since the engine will be left unsupported at the rear it is necessary to make provision to take the weight of it almost from the outset. If you have a block and tackle or a garage crane this will be simple, but if not it is possible to make a simple support similar to that used in the VW agency. Fig. 6.1 shows a simple beam which is supported on either side of the vehicle in the channels which house the bonnet sides on the top of the wings. The item shown has a screw and chains with hooks to fit into the engine lifting eyes. This is luxury indeed. We used an old nylon tow rope as a sling and since the engine mounting at the front of the engine is not going to be disconnected the sling need only be used on the rearmost lifting hook. Whichever way it is done this is the first job to do. Using a beam such as this has an additional advantage. If you want to move the car during the operation the engine will move safely without having to move the support. As on all work of this sort remove the battery earth strap before commencing work. We also recommend the removal of the bonnet (hood). The professionals scorn to do this but either they have harder heads than most of us or permanently bent backs! When two people are struggling to get the box off the dowels a little elbow room is most acceptable!

3 Gearbox (084) - removal and replacement

1   Read through Section 2, support the engine and remove the battery earth strap.

2   Disconnect the clutch cable (Chapter 5) and pull the wire off the TDC sensor. It is right on top of the bellhousing (photo 7.3, Chapter 1)

3   The torque strut which goes from the gearbox to the body frame just below the radiator is next removed (Chapter 1, photo 4.14a).

4   Remove the speedometer cable (Chapter 1, photo 4.12b).

5   Now remove the upper starter bolts and bend the metal tab back. It is not necessary to disconnect the starter cables.

6   At the back of the gearbox is a support going to the frame. Remove this completely from the top of the box. You may have to remove it from the vehicle as it is an awkward business cleaning the bolts Chapter 1, photo 4.16b) now, still from the top remove top bolts holding the gearbox to the engine.

7   At this point start working underneath. Disconnect the gearshift linkage from the gearbox by undoing the square headed bolt and take the lever away. (Chapter 1, photo 4.13). Remove the socket-head bolts holding the right-hand driveshaft flange to the transmission, cover the CV joint with a polythene bag and tie it out of the way. This is difficult unless you can turn the roadwheel because if you cannot then some of the bolts are behind the CV joint and they are difficult enough to remove with an Allen key even when you can see them.

8   Remove the remaining starter bolt and hang the starter out of the

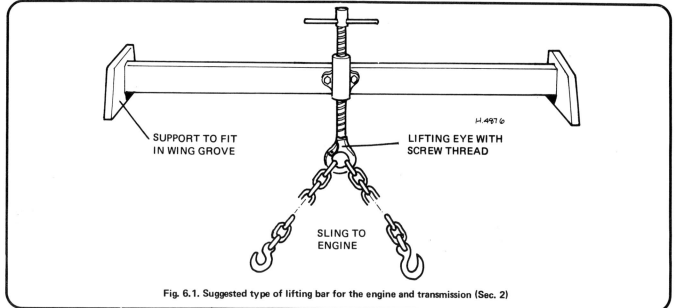

H.4876

SUPPORT TO FIT
IN WING GROVE

LIFTING EYE WITH
SCREW THREAD

SLING TO
ENGINE

Fig. 6.1. Suggested type of lifting bar for the engine and transmission (Sec. 2)

way. It must be removed because its rear bearing is in the gearbox housing.

9   The bottom of the flywheel is protected by a small casting bolted to the gearbox. Remove these bolts. The cover may stay with the engine.

10 There is one more mounting to remove, the one which goes from the gearbox to the body of the car (Chapter 1, photo 4.15). Remove the three nuts and take the bracket away, the mounting pad remains on the gearbox.

11 Take the lower rear engine gearbox bolt out, this will leave one bolt holding the box to the engine, the lower front engine gearbox bolt.

12 Remove the leads from the reversing light switch (photo) and take off the gearbox earth strap (the braided lead to the end cap bolt).

13 Using an Allen key remove the socket-bolts from the left-hand driveshaft and pull the CV joint from the flange. Wrap it in a polythene bag and hang the shaft out of the way.

14 Remove the last engine/gearbox bolt. The gearbox will not fall off, it is held on two dowels, but support it with a sling until you are ready to remove it.

15 Now is the time to stop and think. Check round that nothing else holds the box and assess just how it is to be lowered. Apart from the dowels the gearbox driveshaft splines are engaged in the friction disc of the clutch and the box must be pulled back to withdraw the shaft from the boss of the disc. This must be done carefully or there will be damage to the friction disc. In fact, if the box is not kept level the shaft will jam in the splines.

16 **Do not** try to separate the box from the engine by driving a wedge between the flanges, this will damage the castings. This box can be pulled backwards easily enough if it is kept level. The dowels are a tight fit and when they come out of the dowel holes the weight of the box will be felt suddenly. **Do not** let the box drop at all or you will damage the gear driveshaft splines but move it away from the engine until you can see the shaft clear and then lower the box to the ground and remove it from under the car.

17 Finally the question of weight. The box can be lifted and carried by one man but easing it off the dowels and lowering it is too much for even the strongest man. To start with, his arms are not long enough. Nor will a man underneath be able to hold it up. The job requires two men. It is as well to rehearse the way to do the job. It is probably best to do it in two stages, wriggle it clear of the engine and rest it on a support or sling, get a fresh purchase and then lower it. However remember that once it is clear of the dowels it will go down of its own accord and if allowed to fall will probably need a new gearbox case.

18 Lifting the box back into position after overhaul is much easier as you know the weight problem and can raise the box a bit at a time. Make sure the joint surfaces are clean put a little graphite or

molybdenum powder (not grease) on the splines and line the box up so that the gearbox driveshaft will enter the clutch friction disc. Slide the box gently forward over the dowels, install the bottom bolts and for good measure ease off the top ones and tighten them to 40 ft lbs (5.5 mkg).

19 Replace all the items taken off in the reverse order. The driveshaft flange bolts are tightened to 32 ft lbs (4.5 mkg). Check the operation of the gearshift mechanism (Section 25) and adjust the clutch free-play if necessary (Chapter 5).

---

4   Gearbox (020) - removal and replacement

1   Read through Section 2 and paragraphs 14, 15, 16, 17 and 18 of Section 3. Support the engine and remove the battery earth strap.

2   For purposes of this Section the front is the engine end of the gearbox, left and right are as if you are standing at the side of the car behind the gearbox looking towards the engine.

3   Remove the left gearbox mounting complete and take it away. Remove the TDC sender unit. This needs a specially short plug spanner. Turn the engine by pulling on the Vee-belt until the lug on the flywheel (33° BTDC) appears in the TDC hole (Fig. 6.2). This lines up the recess in the flywheel. Unless this is done the gearbox will not come away from the engine.

4   Remove the speedometer cable and plug the hole to stop the oil running out, when the box is removed (photo 4.3). Undo the upper engine/gearbox bolts and remove them. Pull the leads off the reversing light switch, which is just below the end of the clutch lever. Disconnect the clutch cable and tie it out of the way.

5   Refer to Fig. 6.3 and remove the earthstrap from the gearbox.

6   Working underneath the car remove the starter leads, tag them for easy replacement and remove the starter from the engine and take it away.

7   Remove the torque strut from the body and the engine.

8   Remove the mounting which goes from the gearbox to the mainbody of the car. It is on the right-hand side of the gearbox but for some reason is called the rear mounting by VW, presumably when referring to the engine and gearbox as an entity. It is best to take it right away from the rubber mounting on the gearbox (Fig. 6.4).

9   Undo the socket bolts holding the left driveshaft to the gearbox flange with an Allen key and remove the CV joint from the flange. Cover the CV joint with a plastic bag and tie the shaft out of the way. Turn the roadwheels to get at each bolt in sequence, do not try to work on bolts behind the CV joint.

10 Repeat for the right-hand driveshaft. Just below this driveshaft flange

3.12 The reverse light switch on the transmission casing

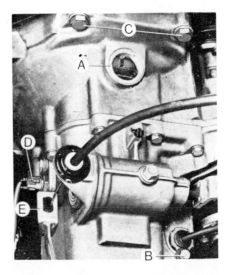

Fig. 6.2. View of the top of the transmission (Sec. 4)

A TDC hole with lug showing,   B Speedo drive,   C Engine/
gearbox top bolts,   D Reverse light switch,   E Clutch lever

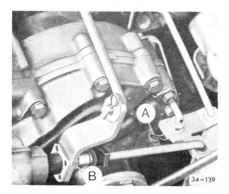

Fig. 6.3. Gearchange mechanism on top of the gearbox (Sec. 4)

A   *Shift linkage/relay lever*   B   *Shift linkage/rod lever*
    joint   *joint*

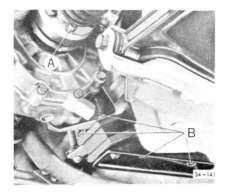

Fig. 6.4. Rear transmission support (A), and left-hand drive shaft (B)
(Sec. 4)

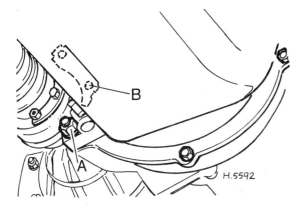

Fig. 6.5. Right-hand driveshaft and cover plates. Remove nut 'A' and
small plate 'B' as well as the driveshaft and flywheel cover (Sec. 4)

Fig. 6.6. The recess in the flywheel must be lines up with the
driveshaft flange (Sec. 4)

is a nut (Fig. 6.5) remove this and then take the bolts for the flywheel
cover plate and the smaller cover plate on the sump.
11 Pull the gearbox off the dowels and lower it to the ground. Keep
the box level with the engine until the clutch pushrod and the gearbox
driveshaft are clear of the boss on the friction disc.
12 Replacement is the reverse of removal. When positioning the gearbox check that the flywheel recess is in the correct position (paragraph
3) before trying to slide the gearbox into position (Fig. 6.6). Torque the
engine/gearbox bolts to 40 ft lbs (5.5 mkg), the driveshaft flange bolts
to 32 ft lbs (4.5 mkg) and the gearbox selector shaft/shift linkage to 11
lbs ft (1.5 mkg). The engine support bolts tighten to 40 lb ft (5.5 mkg)
and the nut under the CV joint to 40 lb ft (5.5 mkg).
13 Dust the splines of the gearbox driveshaft with a little graphite or
molybdenum powder (not grease) before assembly.
14 Check the gear selector operation (Section 25) and adjust the clutch
free-play if necessary (Chapter 5).

5 Gearbox (084) - layout

1   The box is bolted to the rear of the engine. The large bellhousing
carries the clutch withdrawal mechanism. It also carries the right-hand
drive flange and bearing for the differential. It is known as the bearing
housing and carries one bearing each for the drive and driven shafts.
2   The gearbox housing carries the driveshaft and the driven shaft and
also the left-hand drive flange. The differential is housed between the
two casings. Fig. 6.7 refers. Bolted to the end of the gearbox housing
is a small casting which covers the drive and driven shaft bearings in the
gearbox housing.
3   The speedo drive is housed in the bearing housing by the side of the
right-hand drive flange and is actuated by a special gear on the

differential casing. The bearing housing also holds the inner shift lever
for the gearchange mechanism. A small arm terminating in a ball projects
from the inner shift lever and fits into the cup of the actuating lever
of the inner selector shaft in the gearbox housing.
4   Movement from the inner selector shaft operates one of the three
selector rod. These are controlled by gear detents and interlocks fitted
into the gearbox housing. The 1-2 gear selector rod operates a fork which
engages with the synchromesh hub for 1-2 gear on the output or driven
shaft. A similar arrangement operates 3-4 gearchange moving gears on
the driveshaft. The third selector rod operates the reverse gearchange by
means of a relay lever. Reverse gear sits in the end of the gearbox
housing on a short shaft which is pressed into the housing. This shaft
does not rotate. Reverse gear has a plain metal bush and no roller or ball
bearings.
5   Power is transferred to the differential by a helical gear with 14 teeth
on the driven shaft which mates with a similar gear on the differential
housing, the latter having 64 teeth.
6   As in all front wheel drives of this type the axis of the differential
is parallel to that of the gearbox shaft and the crankshaft which
dispenses with the problem of mating a crownwheel and pinion.

6 Gearbox (084) - overhaul (general)

1   The box must be cleaned externally thoroughly and dried. Drain as
much of the oil through the filter plug as possible and replace the plug.
A selection of containers for small bits and a pencil and paper to note
what they are and which way round they go; a set of metric spanners
both ring and open end, Allen keys, a bit of welding wire about 12 inch
long and a set of feeler gauges, are needed. A wheel puller is essential
and a bearing puller, are required. We found a way to dispense with the

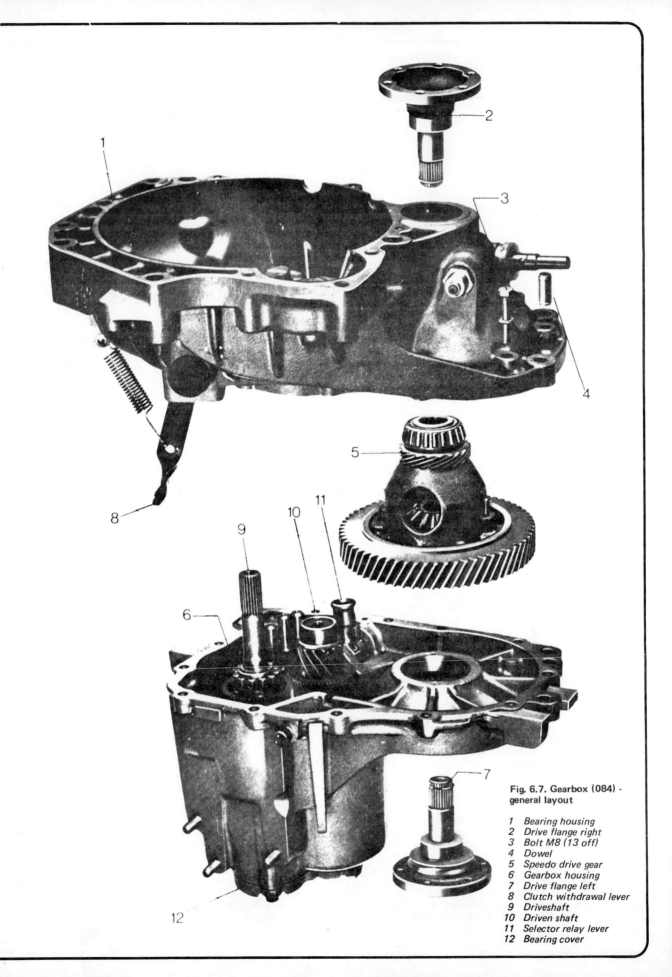

Fig. 6.7. Gearbox (084) -
general layout

1   Bearing housing
2   Drive flange right
3   Bolt M8 (13 off)
4   Dowel
5   Speedo drive gear
6   Gearbox housing
7   Drive flange left
8   Clutch withdrawal lever
9   Driveshaft
10 Driven shaft
11 Selector relay lever
12 Bearing cover

bearing puller, which is described later, but unless you have a lot of gearbox experience you could get into difficulties using this method (see Section 7, paragraph 24).

2 Before you start, read the whole of the Sections dealing with the 084 gearbox, and ponder about how much you can do. You may decide to opt for a replacement box.

3 There are a number of things you cannot do, in our humble opinion, as you have neither the jigs nor the tools to do them. A list is given below.

4 If the gearbox housing must be replaced then the shims on the driveshaft and drivenshaft bearings must be adjusted as well as the differential. We recommend a replacement gearbox.

5 If the bearing housing is damaged then the shims for the taper roller bearings holding the differential must be adjusted to fit the new housing. Similarly if the taper rollers are replaced they must be fitted in pairs and the tolerance adjusted. This is discussed in Section 12 but we think it is beyond the D-I-Y capacity.

6 If either of the shafts need replacement, or the bearings holding them, then once again a gauge is required and a box of shims. However, you can assemble the box and ask for it to be adjusted (ask before you do it) and so save a considerable sum. Read Section 13.

7 If it is necessary to fit a new thrust washer for first gear then again the (output) driven shaft shims must be adjusted.

8 Judging by this dismal list there is not a lot that can be done by the owner. Fortunately, the things in paragraphs 3 to 7 do not often go wrong, and more likely is trouble with oil seals, speedo drive, synchro-mesh hubs and wear on selector forks. These can be corrected, and chipped or spalled gears may be replaced.

9 On the driven shaft all of the gears may be replaced but 1, 3 and 4 must be pressed off. On the driveshaft 3 and 4 gears may be replaced, and of course the synchro hubs on both shafts. The shafts themselves are replaceable, but remember that the bearing shims must be adjusted if the shafts are renewed.

7 Gearbox (084) - dismantling and overhaul

1 Set the box firmly on the bench, undo the bolt holding the left-hand drive flange and lever the flange out of the oil seal (photo). Prior to October 1974 no bolt was fitted to the centre of the flange but since then a centre bolt has been fitted. It is torqued to 2.5 mkg (18 lb ft). A cross-section of the new layout is shown at Fig. 6.8. Examine the seal carefully, it has an interrupted annular grove round its face and an arrow points the direction of rotation of the shaft (photo).

2 Turn the box round and remove the right-hand flange in the same way (photo). Note that this oil seal has a continuous annular groove (photo).

3 The oil seals may be levered out and replaced if necessary. This job can be done with the box still attached to the engine if that is all that is necessary.

4 Note that the driveshafts have different contours. Fig. 6.9 shows the dimensions.

5 Undo the hexagon and remove the speedometer drive (photo).

6 Now remove the 13 bolts holding the two castings together. Note which bolts go where. The castings are still held by dowels. There are two, locate these and tap them through (photos) and then lift the bearing housing off the gearbox housing (Fig. 6.7).

7 This will leave the differential and the shafts exposed (photo). Lift the differential out (photo) and lay it on one side, cover it to keep it clean.

8 Turn the bearing housing on its back and inspect the inside. Check the movement of the inner shift lever and its fit in its bearings. The inner race of the driven (output) shaft is still on the shaft, leaving the rollers in the bearing housing but the inner race and rollers of the driveshaft have remained on the shaft, leaving only the outer race in the bearing housing (photo). As the shafts are dismantled these bearings must be assembled for checking.

9 Turn the case on end, and remove the cover plate (photos). Obtain two lengths of freezer tape each about 12 inches (300 mm) long. Remove the shim, circlip and inner shim from the driveshaft (photo) and stick them on one peice of tape. Label it. Repeat for the driven shaft. These shims and circlips must be replaced on the correct bearing.

10 Remove the gear detents. There is a set for each gear selector rod. At the bottom of the case (see Fig. 6.12) there are three plugs. Using a 6 mm Allen key remove the plugs and extract from each bore, a spring in its case and a plunger (photos).

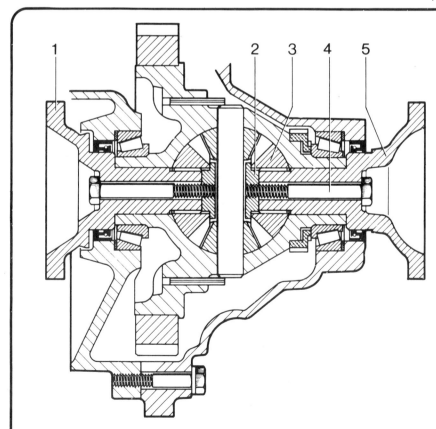

Fig. 6.8. Final drive - cross-section (Sec. 7)

1 Drive flange, left
2 Threaded plate
3 Differential gear
4 Threaded bolt installed in later models
5 Drive flange, right

7.1a Remove the centre bolt and lever out the left-hand driveshaft

7.1b The left-hand driveshaft oil seal has an interrupted annular groove

7.2a Remove the RH driveshaft

7.2b The right-hand driveshaft oil seal has a continuous annular groove

7.5 Remove the speedometer drive

7.6a The dowels must be pushed out ...

7.6b ... by tapping with a punch

7.7a The differential and shafts will be exposed

7.7b Lift the differential out and lay it on one side.

7.8 Examine the inside of the bearing housing

7.9a Remove the cover plate ...

7.9b ... and the bearings are accessible

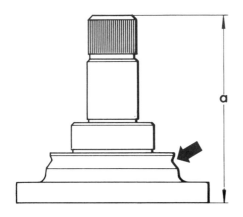

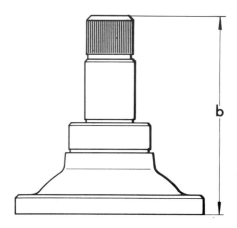

Fig. 6.9. Drive flange identification (Secs. 7 and 8)

Left: left-hand flange (gearbox housing - note groove)
a = 3.3 in (84.6 mm)

Right: right-hand flange (bearing housing)
b = 3.5 in (89.6 mm)

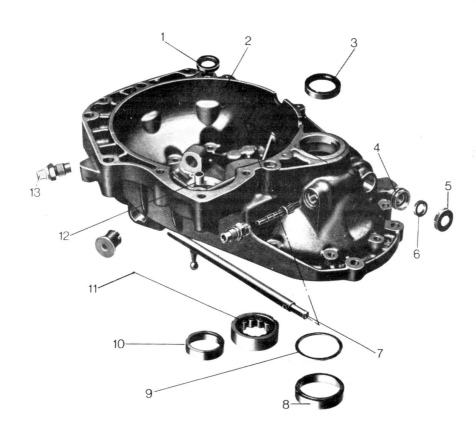

Fig. 6.10. Gearbox (084) - bearing housing exploded view
Note: Clutch withdrawal mechanism not shown

1 Driveshaft oil seal	5 Cap	8 Outer race - differential bearing	11 Outer race - driven shaft bearing
2 Bearing housing	6 Oil seal - inner shift lever	9 Shim S2	12 Starter rear bearing bush
3 Drive flange right - oil seal	7 Inner shift lever	10 Outer race - driveshaft bearing	13 TDC sender unit
4 Bush, inner shift lever			

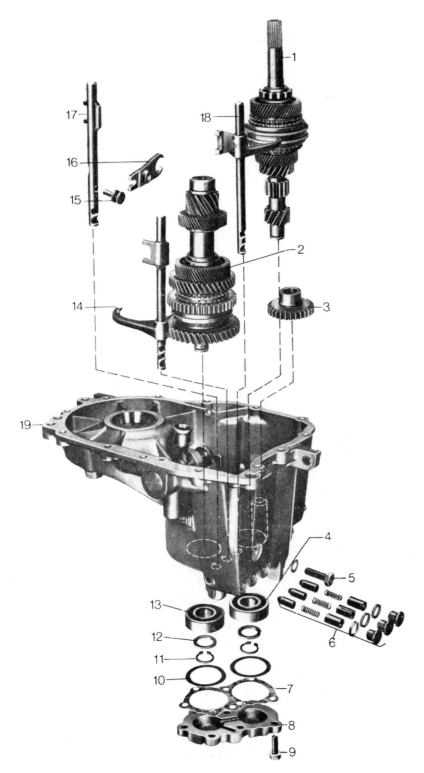

1 Driveshaft assembly
2 Driven shaft assembly
3 Reverse gear
4 Driveshaft bearing
5 Reverse gear relay lever screw
6 Detents
7 Gasket
8 Bearing cover
9 Bolt
10 Large shim
11 Circlip
12 Small shim
13 Driven shaft bearing
14 Selector rod and fork 1/2 gear
15 Pin
16 Relay lever - reverse gear
17 Selector shaft - reverse gear
18 Selector rod and fork 3/4 gear
19 Gear housing

Fig. 6.11. Gearbox (084) - gear housing   and shafts - exploded view

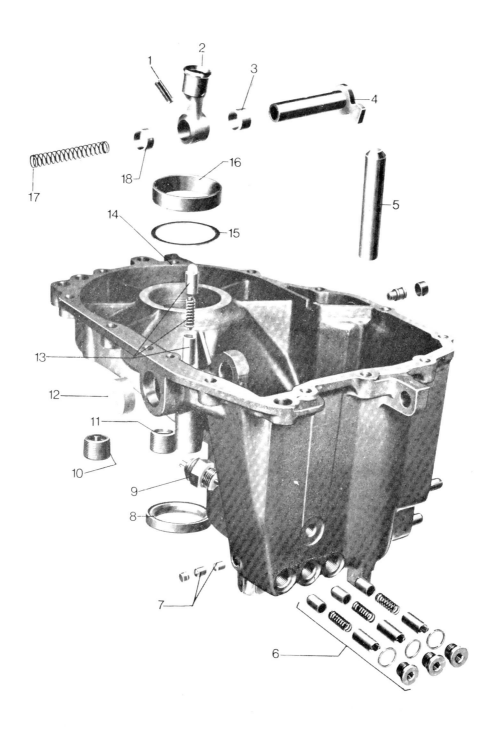

Fig. 6.12. Gearbox (084) - gearbox housing exploded view

1 Pin	6 Detents	11 Filler plug	15 Shim S.1
2 Cup lever	7 Interlock plungers	12 Plug	16 Bearing outer race
3 Bush 12 mm long	8 Oil seal - drive flange L	13 Reverse lock	17 Spring
4 Selector shaft	9 Reversing light switch	14 Gearbox housing	18 Bush 9.5 mm long
5 Shaft - reverse gear	10 Magnetic drain plug		

7.9c Remove the circlips

7.10a Removing the detents

7.10b The detent has a spring held in a split tube

7.11a Removing the reverse gear selector rod

7.11b The reverse gear selector rod and relay lever

7.11c Unscrewing the pivot pin of the reverse relay lever

11 Remove the relay lever and take out reverse gear selector shaft and the relay pin (photos). Before the shaft is withdrawn the pivot of the relay lever must be screwed out (photo and Fig. 6.13).

12 The actuating shaft for the selector mechanism is held in bearings on the casting. It is spring-loaded. Push the cap over to the side of the casting, against the spring, and jam the shaft with a chisel. Better still cut and bend a piece of steel to form a small clip and install this.

13 The next job is to remove the driveshaft. Using a bearing puller extract the bearing from the gearbox housing. The experts use VW 30-207 which is VW nomenclature for a bearing puller. We suggest that you contact the agent with a view either to hiring the tool or having a look at it so that you can buy a similar proprietary item.

14 Once the bearing is out the driveshaft together with the selector rod and fork for 3/4 gears may be lifted out. This is where you need the piece of welding wire. Form it into a small hook and lift the reverse gear a little, to ease the driveshaft out.

15 Set the driveshaft and selector rod on one side (photo).

16 The next job is to take out the driven (output) shaft. Extract the bearing from the gearcase housing (Tool 30-207, again) and lift the shaft out of the casing with the selector (photo). Remove the reverse gear. The case is now empty. Clean it carefully and inspect for damage.

17 The dismantling and reassembly of the shafts is discussed in the next two Sections.

18 The shaft bearings must be carefully checked before assembly is started. The two extracted from the gearbox housing should be washed in white spirit and then checked for tolerance. If all is well, lubricate them with a little engine oil and then install the driven (output) shaft bearing in the gearbox housing. It is best to press it in but it can be tapped in using a suitable drift. Press only on the outer race (photo). Do not assemble the driveshaft bearing until the shaft is back in place. The other two may be checked as the shafts are dismantled. They can be fitted together with the outer races still in the bearing housing.

19 The detents should be cleaned carefully and the bores into which they fit. There must be no grit or old grease left to cause them to stick or you will be in trouble with gear selection. Assemble them later as the shafts are replaced.

20 The selector shaft is carried in two bushes and these may be renewed

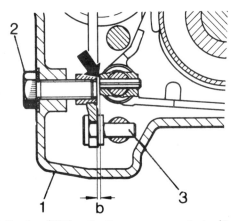

Fig. 6.13. Gearbox (084) - adjusting reverse gear selector (Secs. 7 and 8)

Screw in the bolt (2) until the play at the arrow is 1.3 to 2.8 mm. A hacksaw blade may be used as a gauge. '1' is the casing and '3' the reverse selector rod

if necessary. The outer one is 9.5 mm long, the inner one 12 mm long. The actuating cap is held to the shaft by a pin and a spring inside the shaft keeps the shaft at the right place.

21 The interlock plungers (2) which fit between the detents (see Fig. 6.14) are removed after pulling out a plug in the side of the casing (photos).

22 If for some reason the reverse gear shaft must be replaced it may be pressed out of the housing and a new one pressed in. The measurement from the top of the shaft to the housing should be 62 mm (2.44 ins). Put a little drop of thread locking fluid on the hole in the housing before pressing the shaft into place.

23 The reverse lock plunger should also be checked for ease of operation. See Fig. 6.12 for its location.

7.15 The driveshaft and selector rod. 3/4 gear

7.16 The driven (output) shaft and selector 1/2

7.18 Replace the driven shaft bearing in the housing. We used a 36 mm socket spanner as a drift. Push only on the outer race

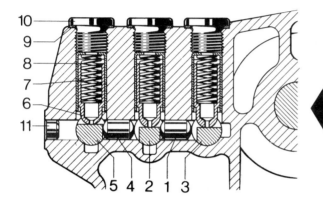

Fig. 6.14. Gearbox (084) - arrangement of interlocks and detents (Secs. 7 and 8)

Fit in the order as numbers. 6 to 11 repeat three times

1 Interlock plunger
2 Shift rod 1/2 gear
3 Shift rod 3/4 gear
4 Interlock plunger
5 Shift rod 4th gear
6 Bush

7 Spring
8 Sleeve
9 Seal
10 Threaded plug
11 Plug in interlock bore

7.21a Remove the plug or the side of the casing and ...

7.21b ... The interlock plungers may be removed

7.24a Removing the pin from 3/4 selector fork

24 We did say that it is possible to get the box to pieces without wheel pullers. Indeed we did manage it but it is tricky and could lead to damage being done if care is not taken. The problem is to get the driveshaft out and this cannot be done unless the bearing is removed. However, it is possible to remove the two shafts together. Remove the detents and put them in a container. Using a long punch tap out the pin from the 3-4 gear selector fork (photo). Once the pin is out the selector shaft may be withdrawn. Remove the screw holding the reverse gear relay lever and ease out the reverse gear selector shaft. Through the hole in the casing in which fits the screw for the reverse gear relay lever it is possible to get a centre punch on the pin holding the 1-2 selector fork to its selection shaft. With care this pin may be tapped out and the shaft removed (photo). Then using great care and a hammer and a soft brass drift, the two shafts may be driven out of the bearings together. It is necessary to watch that reverse gear does not jam. The selector shafts must be supported carefully while the pins are driven out. We strongly recommend the use of a bearing puller, and if you break something using the alternative method, well you have been warned.

7.24b The pin holding 1/2 selector fork can be approached through the hole for the reverse relay lever holding bolt

8 Gearbox (084) - reassembly

1 The overhaul of the shafts is described in Sections 9, and 10. The overhaul of the casing in Section 7. Now comes the big moment. Everything must be clean, including your hands, Take your time, it goes together quite easily but the sequence must be followed.

2 Install the driven (output) shaft bearing in the gearbox housing (if it is not already there). Do not fit the driveshaft bearing yet. Fit the clip to the inner selector rod to keep it out of the way (see photo 8.3). Push the interlock for 3 - 4 gear into position (see Fig. 6.14). Put a screwdriver in the 3-4 selector shaft bearing to stop the detent falling into the bore. Put reverse gear in place on its shaft.

3 Support the inner bearing race of the output (driven) shaft and holding the 1-2 selector rod and fork to the synchro-hub of the driven shaft (photo 7.16) place the driven shaft and its selector rod in their respective bearings. Tap the driven shaft into the bearing as far as it will go. The selector rod will follow down with the driven shaft (photo).

4 Fit the selector fork and shaft to the driveshaft (photo 7.15). Remove the screwdriver from the 3-4 selector shaft bore, check the interlock plunger is still there, and fit the driveshaft and its selector shaft into place. The driveshaft bearing is not fitted yet. It is quite a fiddle, lift the reverse gear with a wire hook and wriggle the shaft, at the same time guiding the selector shaft (photo).

5 Be careful not to disturb the synchro hubs. It is possible inadvertently to let the gear slide off the blockers. If this happens you must start all over again. We had to, so you will be in good company! (see Section 11).

6 Reverse the casing and support the casing and shafts in mesh. Refit the driveshaft ball bearing into the case over the shaft (photo). Both races must be pressed simultaneously. It may help if you warm the casing a little, but not too much say up to 100°C (212°F). The closed side of the cage faces the gearbox housing.

7 Next get the pieces of freezer tape with the shims and circlips and fit these to the correct shafts. Tap the shaft back into the case until the shim is just held. Fit the large shim a new gasket and replace the bearing cover (photos). Consult Section 13 for shim adjustment.

8 Now insert the second interlock plunger and replace the plug in the casing.

9 Refit reverse selector rod with the guide pin and relay lever. Engage the relay lever with reverse gear, turn the selector rod to the right, and fit the relay lever into position (see photo 7.11a and 7.11b). Refer to Fig. 6.13. Screw in the bolt for the relay lever and check the play between the lever and fork for 1-2 gear. It should be between 1.3 and 2.8 mm (0.052-0.110 in). We found that a hacksaw blade made a good feeler gauge for this job. Torque the bolt to 3.5 mkg (25 lbs ft).

10 Remove the clip from the inner selector shaft, fit a bar in the cap socket and check that the gears engage correctly. Only one shaft must move at a time, and it must not be possible to move the two shafts simultaneously.

11 Now assemble the detents. Make sure the springs fit snugly in their cases. Screw in the plugs with an Allen key. Refer to Fig. 6.14 if in doubt about the sequence. Check the gearshift again.

12 The next job is to fit the bearing housing. Reverse the case, clean the joint and smear a little gasket cement over the flange.

13 Replace the differential, the speedometer drive should be on top (see photo 7.7a). Refer to photo 7.8. The bearing housing should be fitted with a new oil seal for the driveshaft. To do this remove the clutch withdrawal mechanism(Chapter 5) and lever the seal out. Fill the space between the lips of the new seal with multipurpose grease and push it in squarely. It must go the same way round as the old seal.

14 Lower the bearing housing onto the gearbox housing. Guide the shafts into their bearings and make sure the ball on the arm of the inner selector shaft of the bearing housing fits into the cap of the inner selector shaft of the gearbox housing. When the flanges meet tap the dowels into position.

15 Fit all thirteen of the bolts (five inside, eight outside) and torque them to 2.5 mkg (18 lbs ft).

16 Refit the clutch withdrawal mechanism (Chapter 5).

17 Refit the drive flange. Make sure the correct ones go to the correct side (Fig. 6.9). If necessary, fit new seals before installing the flanges (paragraph 3). Install the flanges by driving them fully home with a rubber hammer. Tighten the centre bolts (if fitted) to 2.5 mkg (18 lb ft).

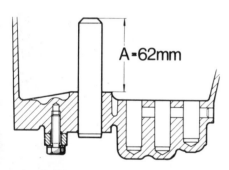

A = 62mm

Fig. 6.15. Gearbox (084) - fitting reverse gear shaft (Sec. 8)

A = 62 mm

8.3 Fit the clip (A) over the inner shift lever. Install reverse gear and then fit the driven shaft and its selector

8.4 Fit the driven shaft and its selector. Use a piece of wire to lift reverse gear, if necessary

8.6 Install the drive shaft bearing into the gearbox housing

8.7a Refit the small shims and the circlips to the shafts

8.7b Refit the large shim, a new gasket, and replace the cover

18 If the reverse light switch was removed then replace it.
19 Refit the speedometer drive (photo 7.5).
20 Fill the box with oil as per specification and it is ready to go back in the vehicle.

9 Driveshaft (084) - dismantling and reassembly

1 Refer to Fig. 6.16. The outer race of the top bearing has remained in the bearing housing. Remove the circlip retaining the inner race (photo) and hold 4th speed gear in a cloth. Tap the end of the shaft with a hide hammer and the inner race will come off (photo).
2 Slide off the thrust washer, note which way the chamfer goes and then pull off 4th gear (photo). Now remove the needle race (photo).
3 Remove the circlip (photo) and shim and press the synchro-hub off the shaft (photo). The rear synchro ring may remain. Remove this and third speed gear (photo). It may be necessary to warm third speed gear a

little. Next remove the needle roller bearing (photo). **This leaves the driveshaft stripped (photo).**
4 Assembly is the reverse of removal. Do not forget the shim and circlip. Note that the chamfer on the thrust washer should be toward 4th gear. In fact the one we took apart did not have a chamfer on the washer.
5 Drive the inner race onto the end of the shaft (photo) until you can insert the circlip (photo).

10 Driven (output) shaft (084) - dismantling and reassembly

1 Refer to 6.17. Fit a wheel puller under 1st speed gear and pull off the gear with the thrust washer (photo).
2 Remove the needle bearing noting which way round it goes.
3 Remove the shim and then the circlip holding the synchro-hub in place (photo).

9.1a Remove the circlip and ...

9.1b ... press off the inner race, and thrust washer

9.2a Remove 4th speed gear and ...

9.2b ... the needle race

9.3a Remove the shim and circlip and ...

9.3b ... the synchro hub

9.3c The rear synchro ring may remain. Press this off with 3rd speed gear

9.3d Remove the needle bearing

9.3e The driveshaft stripped

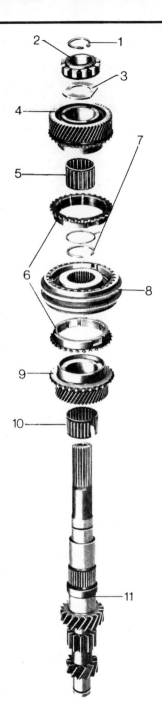

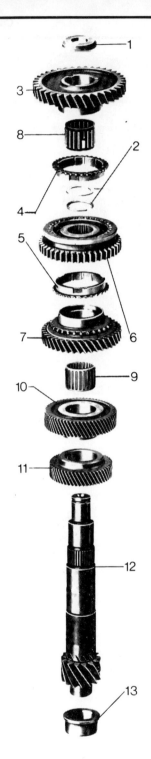

Fig. 6.16 Gearbox (084) - driveshaft exploded view (Sec. 9)

Fig. 6.17 Gearbox (084) - driven shaft exploded view (Sec. 10)

1	Circlip	7	Shim and circlip
2	Bearing - inner	8	Synchro hub 3/4 gear
3	Thrust washer		(for detail see Fig. 6.19)
4	4th speed gear	9	3rd gear
5	Needle race	10	Needle bearing
6	Synchro rings for	11	Driveshaft
	3 and 4 gear		

1	Thrust washer	7	2nd speed gear
2	Circlip and shim	8	Needle bearing
3	1st speed gear	9	Needle bearing
4	Synchro rings	10	3rd speed gear
5	1/2 gear	11	4th speed gear
6	Synchro hub 1/2 gear	12	Output shaft
	(for detail see Fig. 6.18)	13	Inner bearing race

9.5a The chamfer of the 4th speed thrust washer must be towards 4th speed gear. Press the outer race onto the shaft with a piece of tube

9.5b Press on the outer race until the circlip may be installed

10.1 Fit the wheel puller behind 1st gear and pull off the gear with the thrust washer

10.3 Remove the shim and then the circlip

10.4 Fit the wheel puller behind 2nd gear and pull off the gear with the synchro hub

10.5 Remove the needle race exposed when 2nd gear is removed

10.6 The shaft with 3rd and 4th gear still in place

10.7a Install the synchro hub and fit the circlip

10.7b Refit the shim. The pencil points to the shim

4   Using the wheel puller again behind 2nd gear (photo) remove second gear and the synchro-hub. This will expose the needle race. Remove this race (photo).

5   The shaft will now be left with 3rd gear and 4th gear in place (photo). It will be necessary to warm these gears to 130°C (266°F) if they are to be pressed off. The inner race of the bearing in the bearing housing is left on the end of the shaft. This may be pressed off if necessary.

6   Assembly is the reverse of dismantling. If 3rd or 4th gear have been disturbed, or a new output shaft fitted then the shim under the circlip on the bearing in the gearbox housing must be checked for clearance when the shaft has been reassembled (see Section 13). If a new shaft is fitted, count the teeth on the gear and get the right one. Some have 14 teeth, others 15 teeth.

7   Assemble the needle bearing and press on 2nd gear. Then install the synchro-hub and refit the circlip (photo). Install the shim (photo).

8   Refit the needle bearing (photo) and then press on 1st gear and finally the first gear thrust washer (photo).

11 Synchroniser hubs (084 and 020) - checking for wear

1   Unless the transmission is the victim of neglect or misuse, or has covered very high mileages, the synchro-hub assemblies do not normally need replacement. If they do they must be renewed as a complete assembly. It is not practical to fit an inner hub or outer sleeve alone - even if you could buy one.

2   When synchro baulk rings are being renewed it is advisable to fit new blocker bars (sliding keys) and retaining springs in the hubs as this will ensure that full advantage is taken of the new, unworn cut-outs in the rings.

3   Whether or not a synchro hub is dismantled intentionally or accidentally there is one basic essential to remember: the splines of the inner hub and outer sleeve are matched - either by selection on assembly or by wear patterns during use. Those matched on assembly have etched lines on the inner hub and outer sleeve so that they can be easily realigned. For those with no marks, a paint dab should be made to

10.8a Install the needle bearing and fit 1st speed gear

10.8b Fit the thrust washer and press it into position

11.4 Measuring the clearance between the selector forks and the synchro hub grooves

11.5 Measuring the gap between the synchro rings

ensure correct reassembly. If the hub falls apart unintentionally and there are no marks made then you will have to accept the fact that it may wear more quickly (relatively speaking) in the future. But do not have a heart attack if this happens - it will still work for a long time to come. Figs. 6.18 and 6.19 show the exploded views of the synchro-hubs.

4   When examining for wear there are two important features to look at:

a) *The fit of the splines. With the keys removed, the inner and outer sections of the hub should slide easily with minimum backlash or axial rock. The degree of permissible wear is difficult to describe in absolute terms. No movement at all is exceptional, yet excessive 'slop' would affect operation and cause jumping out of gear. Ask someone with experience for advice.*

b) *Selector fork grooves and selector forks should not exceed the maximum permissible clearance of 0.3 mm (0.012 inch). The wear can be on either the fork or groove so it is best to try a new fork in the existing hub first to see if the gap is reduced adequately. If not, then a new hub assembly is needed. Too much slack between fork and groove induces jumping out of gear. Where a hub also carries gear teeth on the outer sleeve these should, of course, be in good condition - that is unbroken and not pitted or scored.*

Measuring the clearance is shown in the photo.

5   The fit of the synchro-hub ring on the gear is important. Press the ring onto the gear and check the gap with feelers (photo). Consult Fig. 6.20 and check measurement (a) against the following table:

Gear	Code of box	new mm	ins	minimum mm	ins
		Measurement 'a'			
3-4	084	1.1-1.7	0.043-0.067	0.5	0.020
1-2	084	1.1-1.7	0.043-0.067	0.5	0.020
3	020	1.15-1.75	0.045-0.069	0.5	0.020
4	020	1.3-1.9	0.051-0.075	0.5	0.020
1-2	020	1.1-1.7	0.043-0.067	0.5	0.020

12 Final drive (084) - inspection

1   If the bearings on the gears are damaged, the unit should be taken to the agent. Since the crownwheel is not matched with the gear on the driven shaft a new differential may be installed without upsetting the drive and driven shaft.

2   The differential must be adjusted if the gearbox housing, the bearing housing or the differential bearings are replaced by new parts. This involves use of tools VW 402, 409, 415a, 433 and 459, and fitting the correct shims. There are 22 to choose from and when the shims are fitted the torque required to turn rhe differential must be measured with tool

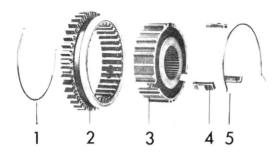

Fig. 6.18. Synchro hub 1/2 gear - exploded view (Sec. 11)

1 *Spring*
2 *1/2 operating sleeve - groove for shift fork faces 1st gear*
3 *1/2 synchroniser hub - groove on splines faces 1st gear*
4 *Synchroniser key*
5 *Spring. Fit 120° offset from '1', angled end fits in hollow key*

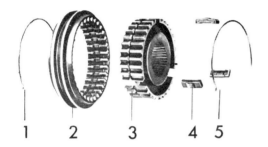

Fig. 6.19. Synchro hub 3/4 gear - exploded view (Sec. 11)

1 *Spring*
2 *3/4 gear operating sleeve*
3 *3/4 gear synchroniser hub - chamfer on internal splines faces 3rd gear*
4 *Key*
5 *Spring. Fit 120° offset from '1'. Angled end fits in hollow key*

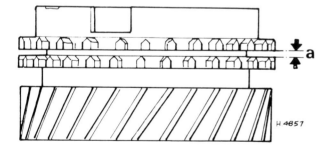

Fig. 6.20. Checking synchro rings (Sec. 11)

a Must not be less than 0.5 mm (0.020 in)

VW 249. This is a bit too much for the D.I.Y owner.
3 If only the crownwheel is damaged, a new one may be fitted, but this again needs special tools and must be left to the experts.
4 If the taper bearings are replaced, the whole adjustment process must be done. Altogether it is not possible to dismantle the differential at home and we recommend a replacement unit.

---

13 Driveshaft and driven shaft bearings (084) - adjustment

1 These shafts must be adjusted if a new gearbox housing is fitted. If the ball bearings, thrust washer from 1st gear or the shafts themselves

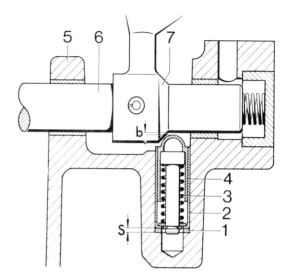

Fig. 6.21. Gearbox (084) - reverse safety catch, cross-section

1 *Adjusting washer*   6 *Selector shaft*
2 *Sleeve*   7 *Relay lever*
3 *Spring*   *Clearance 'b' = 0.4 to 0.8 mm*
4 *Plunger*   *(0.015 to 0.030 in)*
5 *Gearbox housing*   *Adjust washer 'S' to suit*

have been replaced by new ones then again the adjustment must be done.
2 The adjustment of the small shim under the circlip does not present too much difficulty. Measure the play between the circlip and the small shim with a feeler gauge. The shaft must be fully pressed in. The ideal measurement of play is zero, but 0.05mm (0.002 inch) is acceptable. Above this the shim must be replaced. The shims are graded in mm with 0.05 mm difference, the thinnest being. 1.75 mm and the thickest 2.025 mm.
3 The large shim is determined by the distance the outer race is below the machined part of the bearing housing. VW use a clock gauge with a special tool VW 382/7 which should be set to a 2 mm preload.
4 When this gap is measured, determine the gap thickness and fit a shim according to the table below:

Dial reading (mm)	Shim thickness (mm)
0.29 - 0.33	*0.60*
0.34 - 0.38	*0.65*
0.39 - 0.43	*0.70*
0.44 - 0.48	*0.75*
0.49 - 0.53	*0.80*
0.54 - 0.58	*0.85*
0.59 - 0.63	*0.90*
0.64 - 0.68	*0.95*
0.69 - 0.73	*1.00*

Example: Dial reading 0.50 - shim required 0.80.
5 If you do not have access to VW 382/7 we suggest you take the assembled box to the agent for him to measure and fit the shim.

---

14 Gearbox (084) - major modifications

1 Three important modifications have been introduced during the production of this gearbox.
2 Difficulty has been experienced in engaging reverse gear in gearboxes fitted prior to October 1974. A spring balance attached to the top of the gear lever and pulled in the direction used to engage reverse gear should move the lever with a force of less than 11 kiloponds (24 lbs or 108 N). If the force required is more than this action should be taken. The reverse safety catch which pushes the plunger up under the inner selector rod (Fig. 6.21) may need adjustment. The box must be

dismantled and the washer under the plunger corrected. When the
selector shaft is in the neutral position the clearance between the
plunger and the shaft should be 0.4 to 0.8 mm (0.015 to 0.03 in). If it
is not a new washer must be fitted of the correct size. The hole for the
catch must be drilled centrally and the plunger must move in and out
smoothly.

3 A modified version of the safety catch was introduced in October
1974. This version will not need modification and cannot be adjusted.

4 Oil leaks from the gearbox lid to the installation of a new type of
breather from December 1974. The older parts are not interchangeable.
If persistent leaks occur check with the agent and/or replace the gearbox.

5 There does not seem to be any other action so unless the leak is
excessive it may be as well to leave it alone rather than install a new
gearbox. Note that the new gearbox requires slightly more oil than the
older one (Specifications).

6 Heavy and difficult gear changes on the earlier models led to
modification from Chassis 1753 119 525 onwards. The front bearing
bush and plate have been modified slightly by increasing the diameter
of the bearing bush to 24 mm. However, stiff change mechanism may
usually be made easier by lubricating all linkage and bearing surfaces
with molybdenum disulphide powder.

15 Gearbox (020) - layout

1 The layout is very similar to the 084 gearbox but the clutch withdrawal mechanism and the selector arrangements are very different. The
larger casting, the gearbox housing is withdrawn from the bearing
housing leaving the gear trains and the differential in the bearing
housing.

2 The driven shaft may be removed complete quite easily, but the
driveshaft must be dismantled completely while held in the bearing
housing before it may be removed. Only then can the differential be
taken out. The speedometer drive is supplied by the helical teeth on the
driveshaft. A modified gear was introduced in July 1974 when the
black plastic drive gear was replaced by a new pattern. The new pattern
may replace the old one but the cable must be renewed.

3 Adjustments are critical and the overhaul requires a number of
special tools if the job is to be done successfully. For this reason we do
not recommend that the average do-it-yourself should attempt a
complete overhaul. However, it can be dismantled and the next Section
suggests a logical sequence. It is a more difficult task than the 084
gearbox and is somewhat heavier.

4 Section 4 of this Chapter deals with the removal and replacement of
the 020 gearbox. Having removed it clean it externally and dry it.
Remove the drain plugs and set the box firmly on the bench.

16 Gearbox (020) - separating the casings

1 Refer to Fig. 6.23. Set the box on the bench as shown in the
illustration. Undo the four screws from the cover plate and remove the
coverplate. This will give access to the clutch release bearing. There are
two circlips, one on each side of the clutch lever. Remove these and slide
the shaft out of the housing, collecting the spring and lever as the shaft
comes out. Note that the lever will fit on the shaft splines in one way
only.

2 Hook out the release bearing and its sleeve. There is a circlip visible
on the top of the driveshaft. Remove this and stick it on a piece of
freezer tape.

3 Prise out the plastic cap from the centre of the drive flange and
remove the circlip. The next job is to withdraw the flange from the
casing. This requires VW tool 391. Use two M8 x 30 bolts to fasten the
puller to the flange. Now screw the puller nut in a clockwise direction
and withdraw the flange.

4 The selector shaft must now be removed. On the side of the housing
below the clutch withdrawal shaft housing is the cover for the selector
shaft, (opposite side to the differential). Using a plug spanner remove
this cover (photo) and lift off the spring seat (Fig. 6.23). Inside are two
springs, remove these. On the face of the housing level with the selector
shaft is the selector shaft locking bolt. Undo this and pull out the
selector shaft.

5 On top of the gear carrier shaft housing, (where the clutch withdrawal shaft is located), are two plastic plugs. Prise these out and undo the
nuts underneath them. These hold the clamp bolts which locate the
bearing on the top of the driveshaft. There is a third nut inside the
space from which the withdrawal mechanism is taken. This must be
undone as well. If these nuts are not taken off, the bearing cannot be
pulled out of the casing and the casing will fracture if pressure is
applied to draw it off the bearing housing. A diagram is given in Fig.
6.22. Now go to the joint between the castings and remove all 14 bolts
holding them together. Twelve of these bolts are M8 x 50, two are M8 x
36: note where the shorter one go. The next problem is to separate the
housings.

6 Again tool VW 391 is needed. This time use two 7 mm bolts and fix
the plate in the holes for the coverplate. Remove the clutch pushrod.
Screw the centre screw down on the top of the driveshaft until it *just*
touches. Fasten a bar or piece of angle across the bell housing in such a
manner as to support the end of the driveshaft and then screw in tool
VW 391. This will pull away leaving the driveshaft bearing complete on
the driveshaft. On top of this is a very important shim, secure this and
label it. The needle race for the driven shaft will remain in the gearbox
housing. It may be removed by using an extractor 18.5 to 23.5 mm.
Kukko 21/3 is suggested. The two castings are separated and further
overhaul may be done.

16.4 Removing the cover of the selector shaft

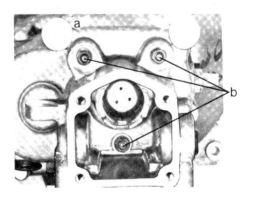

Fig. 6.22. Gearbox (020) - diagram showing nuts on clamp bolts of
the bearing on the driven shaft (Sec. 16)

A Plastic plugs   *B Clamp bolts (3)*

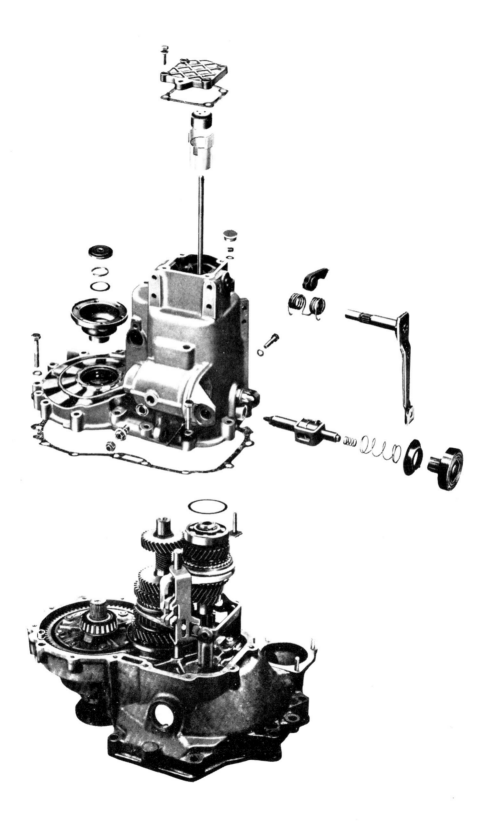

Fig. 6.23. Gearbox (020) - exploded view

Details of the various parts are named in subsequent diagrams

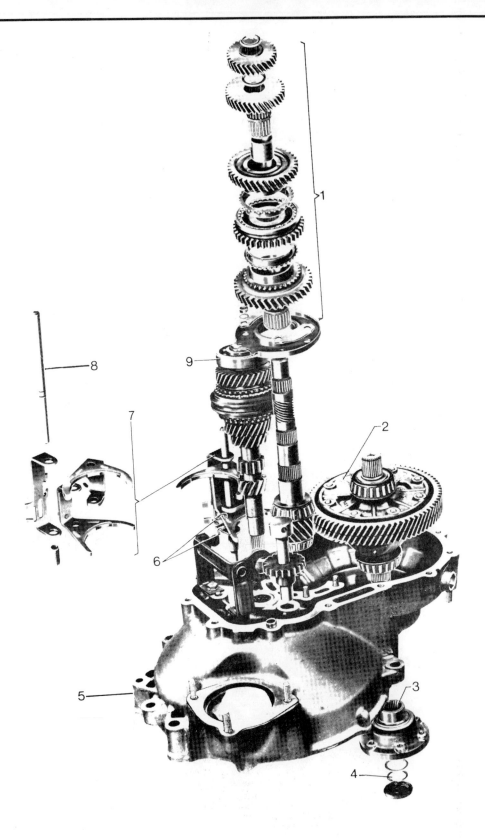

Fig. 6.24. Gearbox (020) - bearing housing, final drive and shafts - exploded view with gear housing removed (Sec. 17)

1 Driven shaft gear which must be removed before driven shaft may be removed
2 Final drive
3 Drive flange
4 Circlip

5 Bearing housing
6 Circlips on selector gear
7 Selector mechanism
8 Selector shaft
9 Driveshaft

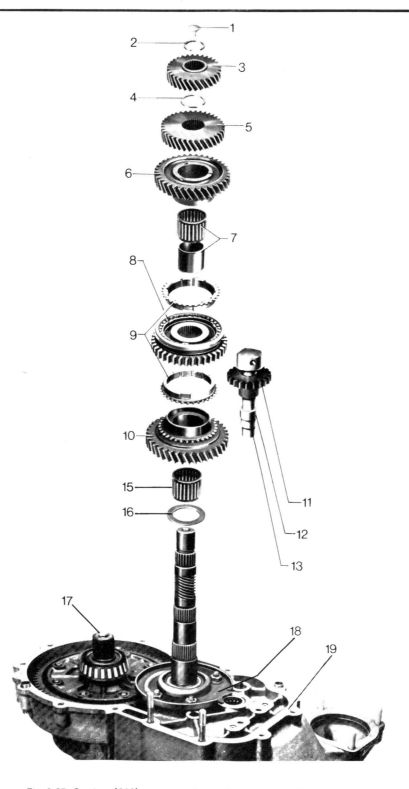

Fig. 6.25. Gearbox (020) - removal of gears from driven shaft prior to removing shaft and final drive (Sec. 17)

1	Peg	10	1st gear
2	Circlip	11	Reverse gear
3	4th gear	12	Bush
4	Circlip	13	Shaft
5	3rd gear	14	Needle bearing
6	2nd gear	15	Thrust washer
7	Needle bearing and inner race	16	Driven shaft
8	Synchro hub 1/2 gear	17	Final drive
	(for detail see Fig. 6.18)	18	Bearing cover
9	Synchro rings	19	Bearing housing

17 Driveshaft, driven shaft and differential (020) - removal

1   Refer to Fig. 6.24. The driveshaft may be removed quite easily, but the driven shaft must be dismantled partially before the differential and the shaft proper may be removed.

2   First get the driveshaft selector fork out of the way. Take off the shift fork circlip and pull the fork shaft out of the bearing housing. Now swing the shift fork to one side (Fig. 6.25).

3   On the driven shaft, yes, the other one, remove the circlip on the top of 4th speed gear. Pull the driveshaft out of its bearing at the same time removing 4th speed gear from the driven shaft. This may need a wheel puller on the driven shaft. The driveshaft needle bearing and oil seal will remain in the bearing housing. Set the driveshaft on one side for overhaul.

4   Return to the driven shaft. The fourth speed gear is already off, note that the shoulder of the gear faces upwards. On top of 3rd speed gear is a circlip. This circlip is used to adjust the axial play of 3rd speed gear. This particular circlip must go back in the same place so label it carefully.

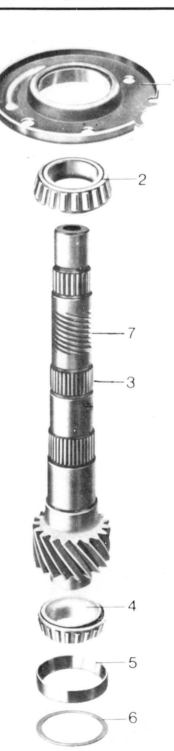

Fig. 6.26. Gearbox (020) - driven shaft. Arrangement of taper bearings (Secs. 17 and 20)

1   Bearing cover with outer race
2   Upper taper race
3   Driven shaft
4   Lower taper race
5   Outer race
6   Shim
7   Helical gear for
    speedo drive

Pull the gear off, It may need a wheel puller again.

5   Remove 2nd gear and then the needle race from over its inner sleeve.

6   To remove the rest of the gears a long hooked puller will be required. It is suggested that a 'Kukko 10-20' is used with 10 in (250 mm) hooks. However, before this can be done the reverse gear must be removed. Working from the other side of the bearing housing tap the reverse shaft out of its seating and lift the shaft and gear away. It is likely that the stop bush will come with the shaft. Now install the wheel puller under the 1st gear and pull the gear and synchro hub off the shaft. Tape the synchro unit together to prevent it coming apart.

7   The needle bearing can now be removed and the thrust washer. Note that the shoulder of the washer is towards the taper roller bearing. Label the washer.

8   Remove the four nuts from the bearing cover and lift the cover away. The bottom of the driven shaft sits in a taper roller. It is now possible to lift the driven shaft out of the bearing housing.

9   The differential may not be removed until the second drive flange is extracted. Using tool VW 391 repeat the same procedure for the other flange. The differential may now be lifted out of the bearing housing and the dismantling job is complete. The next jobs are to overhaul the shafts and the housings. We do not recommend trying to overhaul the differential, you will not get spares for it anyway, only an exchange differential, so if there is anything wrong with the differential, seek advice from the VW agent.

18 Bearing housing (020) - overhaul

1   Refer to Fig. 6.27. Carefully clean the housing, removing all oil and sludge. Replace both the oil seals with new ones. Fill the space between the lips of the seal with multi-purpose grease before installing. The drive flange oil seal must be driven in as far as it will go. A new type of oil seal was introduced for the driveshaft in October 1974. From that date a groove is cut in the bearing housing. When fitting a seal to the new housing the seal must be lubricated. If a new seal is fitted to the old pattern housing the seal must be coated on the surface contacting the housing with adhesive (VWD12 or D21.1).

2   As stated the driveshaft needle bearing may be extracted if necessary using an extractor 18.5 to 23.5 mm. A 'Kukko 21/3' is suitable.

3   The outer race of the driven shaft may be removed with an extractor

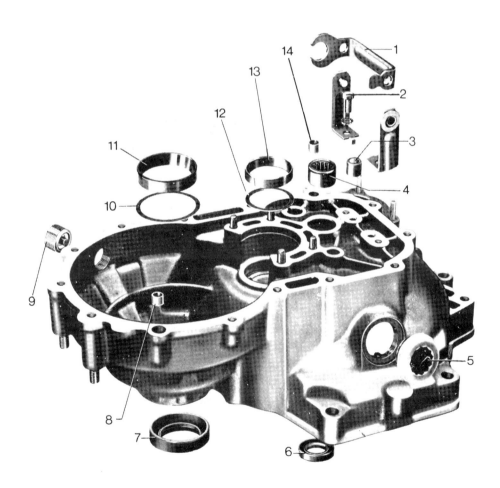

Fig. 6.27. Gearbox (020) - bearing housing exploded view (Sec. 18)

1 Reverse gear shift fork	5 TDC sensor	9 Magnetic drain plug	12 Shim S.3
2 Screw	6 Driveshaft oil seal	10 Shim S.2	13 Outer race, driven shaft bearing
3 Starter rear bearing bush	7 Drive flange oil seal	11 Outer race, differential bearing	14 Dowel sleeve
4 Needle bearing - driveshaft	8 Dowel sleeve		

of 37-46 mm (Kukko 21/6) using a spindle with an internal thread and support from 'Kukko 22/2'.

4   If the outer races of the differential bearings are damaged then it will be necessary for the casings and the differential to be taken to the VW agent for servicing.

5   The starter shaft may be tried in the starter bush. If undue wear is present remove the bush with a puller and fit a new one.

6   If the housing is damaged then we suggest you consult the agent and ask for the unit to be rebuilt, or accept a replacement unit.

19 Gearbox housing (020) - overhaul

1   Refer to Fig. 6.28. In North America this is referred to as the gear carrier housing. There are three oil seals to replace, the one for the clutch operating lever, the selector shaft oil seal, and the larger one for the drive flange. In each case lever out the old one noting which way round it goes, fill the new seal lips with multi-purpose grease and drive the seal in squarely using a suitable mandrel.

2   The needle bearing for the driven shaft is difficult to extract unless the correct extractor is available. Size 18.5 to 23.5 mm 'Kukko 21/3' or 'US 1088' are suitable. The shaft may be tried in the bearing without pulling the bearing out.

3   Again if the outer race of the final drive is renewed the whole unit

must be taken to the agent for setting up with the correct shims.

4   If the housing is damaged, then we recommend that the complete unit be taken to the agent for rebuilding or exchange.

20 Driven shaft taper bearings (020) - overhaul

1   Refer to Fig. 6.26. The movable gears have already been taken off but the problem of the taper races remains. These locate accurately the shaft gear with the crownwheel of the differential. If either bearing is faulty both must be removed. In the process the bearings are destroyed. New ones must be shrunk on (temperature $100^{\circ}C/212^{\circ}F$) and the shim under the lower outer race replaced with one of the correct size.

2   This operation is quite complicated and involves not only preloading the shaft and the use of a special clock gauge, but also measurement of the torque required to turn the new bearings once installed. The correct torque is between 5 and 12 cm kmg for new bearings. In addition the shim at the top of the driveshaft and the axial play at the circlip of the 3rd speed gear of the driven shaft will be affected. This means selection of a new shim and also a circlip. There are six different thicknesses of circlip. You will begin to see that one needs instruction in the adjustment of tolerances, for this gearbox, and this is given only to VW mechanics. So take the box back to the man who can deal with it correctly.

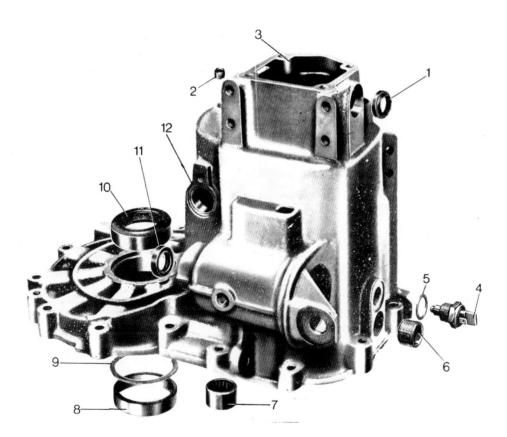

Fig. 6.28. Gearbox (020) - gearbox housing exploded view (Sec. 19)

1 Oil seal - clutch operating lever	5 Seal	9 Shim S.1
2 Oil control plug	6 Oil filler plug	10 Oil seal - drive flange
3 Clutch withdrawal race socket	7 Driveshaft needle bearing	11 Oil seal - selector shaft
4 Reverse light switch	8 Drive flange outer race	12 Speedo drive bore

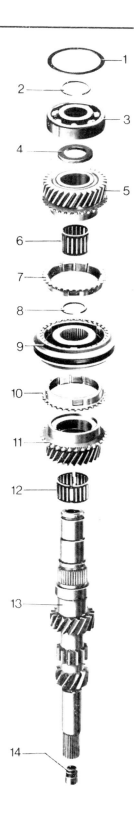

Fig. 6.29 Gearbox (020) - driveshaft exploded view (Sec. 21)

1	Shim	9	Synchro hub 3/4 gear
2	Circlip		(for detail see Fig. 6.19)
3	Bearing	10	Synchro ring
4	Thrust washer	11	3rd speed gear
5	4th gear	12	Needle race
6	Needle bearing	13	Driveshaft
7	Synchro ring	14	Bush
8	Circlip		

21 Driveshaft (020) - overhaul

1   The removal of the parts from the input shaft requires the use of a press and suitable supporting tools.

2   Refer to Fig. 6.29. Remove the circlip from the top of the bearing and then, supporting the bearing under the inner race press the shaft out of the inner race. On assembly this bearing is pressed into the gearbox housing and the shaft pressed into the race.

3   There is a very small space available between 4th gear and the synchro-hub so that supporting 4th gear for pressing it off is a problem. VW use a special appliance, 'Kukko 15-17' (size 1). If this is not available it may be possible to use a puller with thin jaws, after warming the gear a little. Pull the gear off together with the thrust washer. Remove the needle bearing and the circlip from the top of the synchro unit.

4   Now support 3rd gear and press the shaft out of it at the same time removing the synchro-hub complete. Tape the synchro unit to stop it falling apart.

5   Remove the needle bearing and the shaft is dismantled.

6   In the rare event of the clutch pushrod being loose in the shaft, the bush may be driven out of the end of the shaft and replaced with a new one. If the shaft is to be replaced then tolerances come into the business again, and back to the agent with his special tools and gauges. The problem is the play between 2nd speed gear on the driven shaft and 3rd speed gear on the driveshaft when both shafts are installed. This must be 1.0 mm (0.040 ins). Adjusting this also requires a new shim on the top of the ball bearing between the bearing and the gearbox housing.

7   If gears on either shaft are to be replaced then the mating gear on the other shaft must be replaced as well. This is logical for a damaged gear will have affected the mating gear, and a new gear must mate with an undamaged gear. They are sold in pairs anyway.

8   The inspection of the synchro-hub is dealt with in Section 11.

9   Assembly of the shaft is the reverse of dismantling. When pressing in the hub and sleeve turn the rings so that the keys and grooves line up, the chamfer on the inner splines of the hub must face 3rd gear. The closed side of the ball bearing cage must be toward 4th speed gear, so when the bearing is pressed into the housing the closed side will be the visible one.

22 Final drive (020) - inspection

1   A faulty differential will cause a lot of noise while the car is in motion. However, it may go a long way making a noise without getting any worse. If you decide it needs renewing then renew it as a unit.

2   There are several problems. If a new differential is fitted then a new crownwheel to an old shaft is inviting noise. It may be possible for the agent to build the old differential if only the taper bearings are at fault, and he may be able to fit a new crownwheel to your differential if only the crownwheel is damaged. It is worth asking, but most likely you will need a replacement differential.

23 Differential and shafts (020) - assembly to bearing housing

1   Install the differential. Using tool VW 391 install the drive flange to the bearing housing and fit the circlip.

2   Install the bearing for the driveshaft into the gear carrier and fit the clamp bolts. (Fig. 6.23). The plastic cage should be towards the casing.

3   Fit the driven shaft and its taper bearings into the gear carrier so that the shaft pinion gear meshes with the crownwheel. Fit the bearing cover and tighten the nuts to 2 mkg (15 lbs ft). Install the thrust washer to the driven shaft with its shoulder to the taper roller bearing, and fit the needle roller cage.

4   Now refit the reverse gear idler to its shaft (see Fig. 6.30). Heat the bush to install and press it over the shaft until the end of the bush is as shown in Fig. 6.30. Let the bush cool. Now drive the shaft into position in the housing, centre it as shown in Fig. 6.31.

5   Fit 1st gear over the needle bearing. Warm up the synchro-hub a little and press it into position. The hub will slide on if heated to 120°C 248°F) and it can be tapped into position. Make sure the grooves are in line with the shift keys. The shift fork slot in the operating sleeve should be toward 2nd gear and the groove on the hub towards 1st gear.

6   The inner race for 2nd speed must be next fitted and pressed down

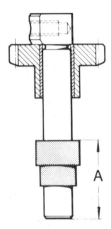

Fig. 6.30. Gearbox (020) - reverse gearshaft installing (Sec. 23)

A = 41 mm (1.61 ins)

as far as it will go. Fit the needle bearing and then 2nd gear with the shoulder downwards.

7   Warm up 3rd gear and press it down over the splines. The collar faces 2nd gear. Install the circlip and using a set of feeler gauges measure the play between the gear and the circlip. It must be less than 0.20 mm (0.008 in). If it is more, a thicker circlip must be installed. The following table gives the sizes:

Part no.	Thickness (mm)	Thickness (ins)	Colour
020 311 381	2.5	0.098	brown
020 311 381 A	2.6	0.102	black
020 311 381 B	2.7	0.106	bright
020 311 381 C	2.8	0.110	copper
020 311 381 D	2.9	0.114	yellow
020 311 381 E	3.0	0.118	blue

8   At this stage the driveshaft must be installed. Slide it into the needle bearing and install the shift forks in the operating sleeves. Insert the circlips (see Fig. 6.32).

9   Now refit 4th gear to the driven shaft and fit a new circlip. Finally put the stop button for the driven shaft needle bearing in the top of the driven shaft.

10 The casing and shafts are now complete ready for the gearbox housing to be fitted in place. At this point consider whether adjustments have to be made. If so then get them done, if not then proceed to fit the housing.

Fig. 6.31. Gearbox (020) - reverse gearshaft: Centre the shaft as shown by the arrows (Secs. 23 and 24)

24 Gearcase housing (020) - assembly

1   Check that the driveshaft ball bearing with the correct shim is in the casing correctly and the locating bolts and clips are fitted. They should be tightened to 1.5 mkg (11 lb/ft). The shim (S.1) must be between the housing and the bearing.

2   Check that the reverse gearshaft is in the correct position (Fig. 6.31) and set the gear train in neutral. Fit a new gasket to the bearing housing flange.

3   Lower the gearcase housing over the shafts onto the bearing housing check that the driven shaft is aligned with its needle bearing and drive the driveshaft into its bearing, using a mandrel on the inner race. A piece of tube is most suitable.

4   Replace the 14 bolts in the flange and torque them to 2 mkg (14 lb ft). Remember where the two M8 x 35 bolts were fitted (Section 16.5).

5   Refit the driveshaft flange using tool VW 391 and fit the circlip. Drive it in until the clip snaps into the groove.

6   Refit the clutch pushrod, and fit the circlip over the end of the driveshaft, working through the release bearing hole. Refit the sleeve and the clutch release bearing.

7   Fit the clutch release shaft and lever (Chapter 5). Watch that the spring is hooked over the lever in the centre and the angled ends rest against the casting. The shaft will enter the lever in one position only. Install the two circlips, one on each side of the lever. Fit a new gasket and replace the cover plate. Tighten the screws to 1.5 mkg (11 lb ft).

8   The gear train was set in neutral before the casing was installed. Lubricate the selector shaft and insert it into the casing. When it is in place refit both springs and screw in the shaft plug with a plug spanner. Tighten it to 4.5 mkg (32 lb ft).

9   Refit the selector shaft locking bolt. This has a plastic cap. Only if the housing, selector shaft or the screw are faulty and new ones are required should the screw setting need adjustment. This is shown at Fig. 6.33. The gearbox is now ready to go back into the car. Turn to Section 4.

25 Gearshift mechanism (084) - general

1   Refer to Fig. 6.34. The shift rod is joined to the gearlever by a bracket on the end of the shift rod which encloses a sphere on the gearlever. The rod passes through a bearing in the lever housing and another bolted to the steering gear. It is thus held firmly in the axial plane but may move axially and can rotate.

2   Movement of the gearlever knob causes the gearlever to pivot about its bottom end which is held firmly in a spherical bearing in the lever housing. This movement of the knob along the axis of the car moves

Fig. 6.32. Gearbox (020) - installation of circlips on selector gear (arrowed) (Sec. 23)

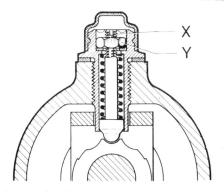

Fig. 6.33. Gearbox (020) - setting of selector shaft retaining screw (Sec. 24)

Screw in 'X' until it touches the selector shaft. When the stop is contacted nut 'Y' will move outwards. Turn 'X' back one-quarter turn. Fit the plastic cap.

the rod on this axis, but movement at right angles to this axis rotates the rod slightly. This motion is transmitted to the relay lever on the gearbox end of the rod. The shift finger, which is bolted to the gearbox relay lever by a square-headed bolt has a spherical joint in the relay lever, and as the rod moves or rotates that motion is passed onto the gearbox selector shaft.

3 The extent of movement of the gearlever is governed by a pair of guide plates which may be removed on their anchorages to adjust the correct engagement of the gears.

4 To remove the gearlever and shift rod first go to the gearbox end. Disconnect the shift finger from the gear selector shaft. (Chapter 1 photo 4.13). Now remove the two bolts holding the front bearing plate to the steering gear.

5 From underneath the car locate the lever housing by following the shift rod. Remove the rubber boot from the bearing plate, remove the nuts holding the bearing plate and pull the bearing plate away onto the rod. The front and rear bearing plates and the relay lever may now be removed from the rod.

6 Remove the two nuts holding the guide plates. These are under the rubber boot inside the car. Pull the boot upwards to get at them. The gearlever and shift rod may now be removed with the guide plate and the assembly taken apart. There are two small tabs on the lower guide plate which must be bent away to dismantle the gearlever.

7 Installation is the reverse of removal.

8 To adjust the mechanism slacken the two nuts holding the guide plate and move the guide plate so that when in neutral gear the lower part of the lever (where it joins the plastic ball) is vertical or inclined up to 5° to the rear. Tighten the nuts. This sets the longitudinal adjustment.

9 The lateral adjustment is done at the front bearing plate. Set the gearlever in reverse and slacken the nuts holding the bearing plate to the steering gear. Move the plate laterally until the gearlever inside the car is in a vertical plane along the axis of the car. Tighten the nuts. A diagram of the gearchange lever is also given at Fig. 6.35.

26 Gearshift mechanism (020) - general

1 The 1.5 litre gearshift is a complicated affair. The gearlever end of it is simple enough. (Fig. 6.36), but the linkage at the gearbox end is very complicated (Fig. 6.38 refers). Apparently the original bearing did not function too well as even more parts were added to the linkage in December 1974 (Fig. 6.40 refers).

2 There are two adjustments on the relay lever system. The bearing rod must be adjusted so that the distance from the gearbox casting face to the centre of the bearing rod housing in the relay lever is 30 to 32 mm (1.18 to 1.26 in). The detail is shown in Fig. 6.37. The length of the selector rod from the gearbox to the ball joint must be adjusted on early models to between 163 and 165 mm (6.42 to 6.50 in). Fig. 6.39 refers.

3 Adjustment of the gearlever is in two stages. To set it longitudually slacken the bolts holding the lever upper plate (Fig. 6.36) and move the plate until the lower part of the gearlever is vertical. This is done with the lever in neutral gear. The lateral (sideways) movement is done by moving the support plate of the front bearing of the shift rod. To do this undo the nuts holding it to the steering gear and with the gearlever in 1st gear move the plate until the gearlever is vertical.

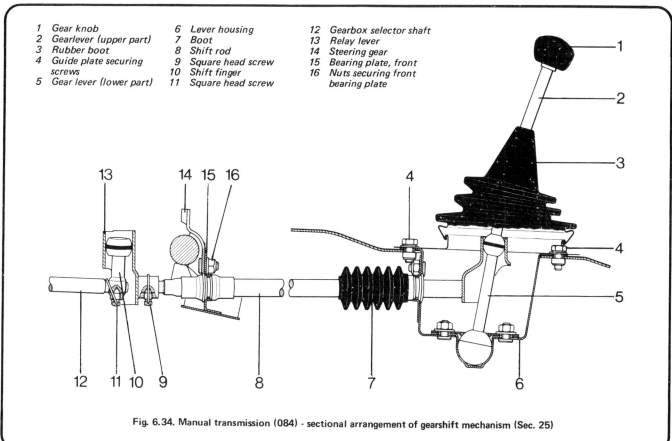

1 Gear knob	6 Lever housing	12 Gearbox selector shaft
2 Gearlever (upper part)	7 Boot	13 Relay lever
3 Rubber boot	8 Shift rod	14 Steering gear
4 Guide plate securing screws	9 Square head screw	15 Bearing plate, front
5 Gear lever (lower part)	10 Shift finger	16 Nuts securing front bearing plate
	11 Square head screw	

Fig. 6.34. Manual transmission (084) - sectional arrangement of gearshift mechanism (Sec. 25)

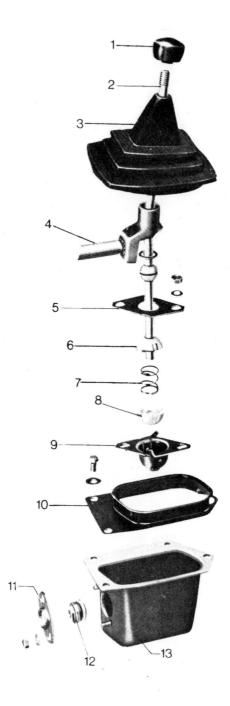

Fig. 6.35. Manual transmission (084) - gearlever, exploded view (Sec. 25)

1	Gear knob	4	Shift rod	7	Spring	10 Casing
2	Gear lever	5	Upper guide plate	8	Ball shell - lower	11 Bearing plate - rear
3	Boot	6	Ball shell - upper	9	Guide plate - lower	12 Bush
						13 Lever housing

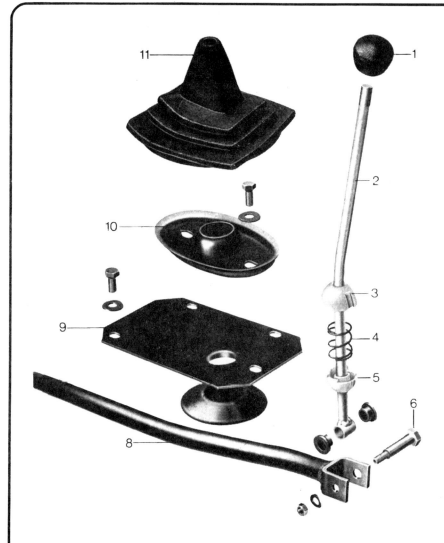

Fig. 6.36. Gearbox (020) - gearshift
lever - exploded view (Sec. 26)

1 Knob
2 Gear lever
3 Bearing upper shell
4 Spring
5 Bearing lower shell
6 Pivot pin
7 Fork
8 Selector shaft
9 Lever plate lower
10 Lever plate upper
11 Boot

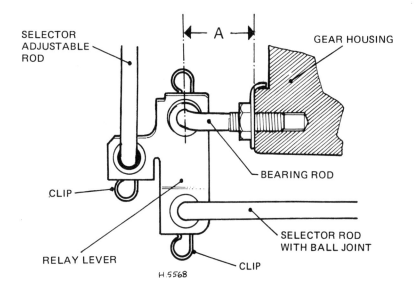

Fig. 6.37. Gearbox (020) - adjustment
of bearing rod (Sec. 26)

A = 30 to 32 mm (1.18 to 1.26 in)

Fig. 6.38. Gearbox (020) - layout of relay levers and shafts - early models (Sec. 26)

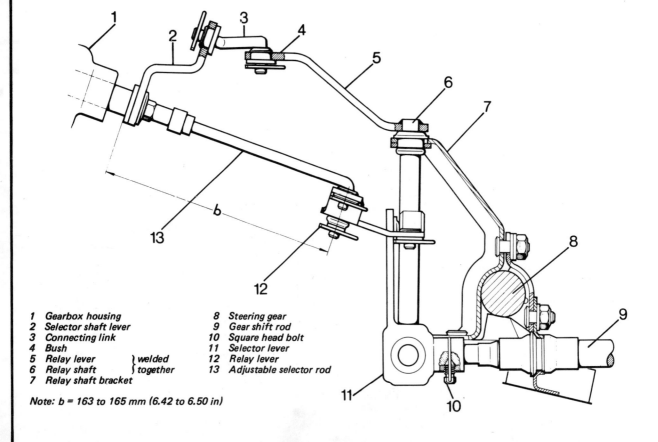

1 Gearbox housing	8 Steering gear
2 Selector shaft lever	9 Gear shift rod
3 Connecting link	10 Square head bolt
4 Bush	11 Selector lever
5 Relay lever } welded	12 Relay lever
6 Relay shaft } together	13 Adjustable selector rod
7 Relay shaft bracket	

Note: b = 163 to 165 mm (6.42 to 6.50 in)

Fig. 6.39. Gearbox (020) - adjustment of selector rod (early models only) (Sec. 26)

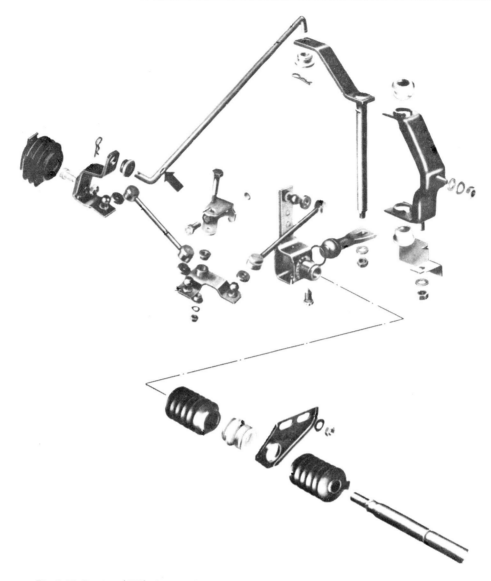

Fig. 6.40. Gearbox (020) - layout of relay levers and shafts after December 1974 (Sec. 26)

27 Fault diagnosis - manual gearbox (084 and 020)

It is sometimes difficult to decide whether all the effort and expense of dismantling the transmission is worthwhile to cure a minor irritant such as a whine or where the synchromesh can be beaten by a rapid gearchange. If the noise gets no worse consideration should be given to the time and money available, for the elimination of noise completely is almost impossible, unless a complete new set of gears and bearings is fitted. New gears and bearings will still make a noise if fitted in mesh with old ones.

Symptom	Reasons	Remedy
Synchromesh not giving smooth change	Worn baulk rings or synchro hubs	Fit new ones.
Jumps out of gear on drive or over-run	Weak detent springs	Fit new ones.
	Worn selector forks	Fit new ones.
	Worn synchro hubs	Fit new ones.
Noisy rough whining and vibration	Worn bearings, chipped or worn gears	Dismantle and fit new.
Gear difficult to engage	Clutch fault	Check free-play.
	Gearshift mechanism out of adjustment	Check and adjust.

Chapter 7 Automatic transmission and final drive

Contents

Specifications

Gearbox code ... ...   EQ

Gearbox code number   010

Gear ratios
1st gear 2.55
2nd gear 1.45
3rd gear ('D')   1
Reverse ('R') 2.42

Final drive
Ratio 3.76 (21;34:79)

Torque converter
Stall speed ... ...   1900 to 2100 rpm. This will fall about 125 rpm per 3000 ft of altitude

Oil capacity

Torque converter and gearbox (ATF):	litres	pints (US)	pints (Imp)
Initial filling	6	12.5	10
Refitting	3	6	5
Final drive (Hypoid SAE)	0.75	1.6	1.3

Oil type
ATF ... ...   Use only automatic transmission fluids labelled DEXRON R with a five figure number with prefex B; do not use additives

Hypoid SAE ... ...   SAE 90 MIL-L-2105 B

Shift points ... ...   These vary according to engine code. Consult the VW agent for particulars of your model

1 Automatic transmission - general description

1 Refer to Fig. 7.1. The unit consists of three parts and is contained in castings which are bolted together and then attached to the engine casing at the rear. They, together with the engine, form an integral power unit.
2 The torque converter casing is bolted to the engine flywheel. Inside the casing are two turbine discs, one (the middle one) is mounted on a one way clutch (freewheel) so that it may turn only in the same direction as the engine, and the other may rotate independently but is mounted on a shaft which is splined to the drive-gear in the automatic gearbox. On the inside face of the casing next to the flywheel are turbine vanes (the impeller). The middle one is called the stator and the third one the turbine.
3 The drive goes from the turbine to the planetary gear system contained in the transmission box. Here by means of a number of epicyclic gear trains with brakes and clutches operated by hydraulic pressure through a complicated valve chest the necessary reduction in rpm is determined for the load and speed of the vehicle. Three main control devices provide the correct combination, the manual valve operated by the gearshift cable and lever by the driver, the second primary valve operated by vacuum from the engine intake manifold which makes the gearbox sensitive to engine load and speed, and the third control is the governor which controls ATF (Automatic Transmission Fluid) pressure and is sensitive to the road speed.
   Thus it will be appreciated that the setting of the various springs and plungers in the valve chest is critical, as is the adjustment of clutches and brake bands, and for that reason we do not recommend that the unit be dismantled.
4 The drive is carried from the epicyclic system through the pinion shaft which is splined into the output gear of the train. The pinion

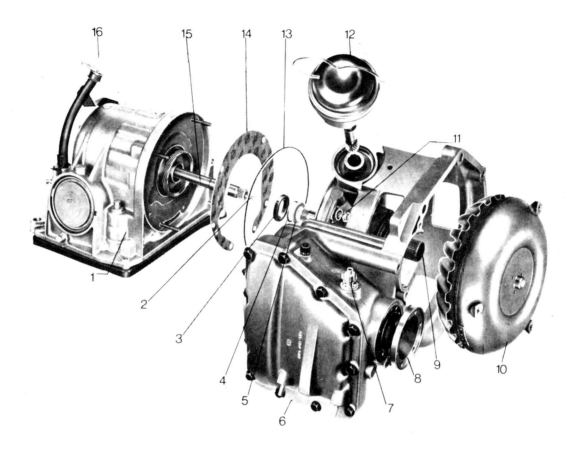

Fig. 7.1. Automatic transmission (010) - exploded view (Secs. 1 and 4)

1 Epicyclic gearbox	*6 Differential cover plate*	*10 Torque converter*	*13 'O' ring*
2 Pump driveshaft	*7 Speedometer drive*	*11 Nuts (4) securing final drive*	*14 Gasket*
3 Pinion oil seal	*8 Drive flange*	*to gearbox*	*15 Impeller shaft*
4 'O' ring	*9 Torque converter shaft (one*	*12 Governer*	*16 A.T.F. filler pipe*
5 Shim	*way clutch)*		

shaft is supported at the rear end by a taper roller bearing in the second casting which also houses the differential and carries the driveshaft flanges. The bellhousing at the end houses the torque converter round which it goes and is bolted to the engine casing.

The final drive is carried in bearings at the side of the gearbox. The drive flanges are splined into the differential. An intermediate gear is installed between the pinion and the crown wheel.

5 The pinion shaft is hollow and through it goes yet another hollow shaft which is driven by the torque converter primary rotor and takes power to the ATF pump which is situated at the extreme end of the epicyclic box.

6 The transmission case of the epicyclic box is filled with ATF, as is the torque converter and the ATF is pumped round both of them providing lubrication, cooling and a means of transmitting power in the torque converter. The final drive casing is isolated from the ATF circuit and contains Hypoid oil. Oddly enough, the governor is mounted on the final drive casting, driven by a helical gear from the pinion shaft, and is in the ATF circuit. It will be appreciated that the governor shaft seal is an important item.

7 When the engine is started the torque converter casing commences to rotate with the flywheel and the ATF pump is driven supplying ATF under pressure to the torque converter and the valve chest.

As speed builds up the ATF is driven by centrifugal force out of the ends of the impeller into the vanes of the turbine (the one connected to the epicyclic system). It causes the turbine to turn and throw the oil back towards the impeller. At this point it meets the centre disc (stator) which is turning with the primary rotor (impeller) because of its one way clutch. This impedes the flow of oil increasing the pressure of the flow through the secondary rotor (turbine) and speeds up the turbine by multiplying the torque. As the speed of the turbine approaches the speed of the impeller the oil flows easily through the stator and the multiplication factor decreases until the speed ratio between the two wheels is 0.84:1. At this point the engine torque and the turbine torque are the same and the torque converter ceases to act as a torque converter and acts as a fluid coupling only.

8 What happens to the torque depends upon the position of the manual selector valve. If the gearlever is in 'N' or 'P' then the epicyclic rotates freely and no power is transmitted to the wheels. When the lever is moved to 'D', '1', '2' or 'R' the various valves in the chest operate and move the controls of the clutches and brake bands so that the epicyclic train produces the correct ratio to the final drive. The second primary valve operates as the vehicle goes along according to engine load, causing the gear to change to suit the load, and the governor presides over the whole operation regulating the pressure of the ATF delivered by the pump according to the road speed of the vehicle.

9 It will be seen now why we suggest you leave well alone. It will also

be appreciated that If the engine is not running the pump will not circulate the ATF so the vehicle cannot be push started because the turbine will not work. Furthermore, if the ATF is not circulating the oil will get hot and since the lubrication is done by the ATF if the vehicle is towed for any length of time the oil will boil and the bearings suffer accordingly.

2 Automatic transmission - operation

1 These instructions are defined in the excellent vehicle handbook issued with the car, but to recap briefly.
2 *'P' or Parking lock,* only used when stopped. Locks the front wheels.
3 *'N' or Neutral,* as for manual transmission, engine running, oil pump working but no gears engaged.
4 *'R' or Reverse,* as for manual transmission. Vehicle must be stopped before this gear is engaged.
5 *'D' or Drive.* When this position is selected, the handbrake on, and the engine running at tick-over speed, the car will remain stationary. Release the handbrake and press the accelerator pedal and the car will move off, change into 2nd and 3rd gear according to load and speed.
6 *'2' or Second gear.* As for 'D' but the box will not select 3rd gear. Maximum speed in '2' is 70 mph/115 kph so do not select '2' at speeds above this, because the move from 'D' to '2' will take place and may cause skidding or mechanical damage. Useful for hilly country but expensive fuel-wise.
7 *'1' or First gear.* As for '2' but will not select 2nd or 3rd gear. Maximum speed for selection on full throttle 40 mph (65 kph). With engine idling the change will happen at 22 mph (35 kph).
8 For the full driving technique read the Instruction Book.
9 There are five more operational points to remember.
   a) *It is not possible to push or tow start the car as the transmission oil pump works only when the engine is running.*
   b) *If the car is towed the selector should be in 'N', and a limit of 30 miles of towing should not be exceeded as lubrication of the transmission is inadequate when the engine is not running and overheating and seizure may occur. Do not tow at more than 30 mph (40 kph).*
   c) *If there is a fault in the transmission the car must be towed with the driving wheels clear of the road; ie: a suspended tow.*
   d) *If '2' or '1' are selected for overrun braking when on a slippery surface the gear will change and there may be a skid you did not expect. Do not change down at high speeds in these conditions.*
   e) *The cooling fins and areas must be kept clean. The transmission fluid heats up and on long climbs can get very hot indeed.*

3 Kick-down position

1 When the accelerator pedal is pressed right down past the 'hard spot' to the kick-down position yet another control valve is brought into the system. Its effect is to move the gearshift points of first and second gears to correspond with maximum engine revolutions. The valve is operated by a solenoid controlled by a switch under the acceleration pedal.
2 So, if you are in a hurry and stamp on the pedal when you are in top gear, the gearbox will change into second, the engine will move up to maximum revolutions, the vehicle will accelerate very quickly and then change back into top with the engine at maximum power with the speedometer needle climbing rapidly. Be careful where this is done for it can cause wheel spin and possibly skidding.
3 When the pedal is lifted back through the 'hard spot' normal gearchange points are resumed.

4 Automatic transmission - maintenance and lubrication

1 According to VW there is no need to change the oil in the final drive during the normal life of the vehicle.
2 If the fluid drive is dismantled for repair then it should be refilled as per specification.
3 Check the level of ATF whenever the engine oil level is checked. Locate the dipstick in the engine compartment (see Fig. 7.1). Set the vehicle on a level surface and with the selector at 'N' run the engine at idling speed until the ATF is warm and check the level of the oil on

the dipstick while the engine is still running. The oil level should be between the two marks on the dipstick. Check twice to see that the dipstick was properly seated.
4 The difference between the two marks is about 0.4 litres (1 US pint, 0.7 Imperial pint). Top-up as necessary but do not overfill or the ATF will need to be drained down to the top mark. Use a funnel and a piece of plastic tube if ATF is to be poured in, it is an unpleasant fluid so do not spill it on the engine.
5 While checking the ATF level take a sample from the end of the dipstick and check its appearance for carbon and smell of burnt linings. If these are present the fluid should be changed and the reason for the burning located and corrected.
6 It is recommended that the ATF be changed every 30,000 miles (45,000 km) but this will be at shorter intervals if the car is used in hilly country or for towing. The interval should then be 20,000 miles.
7 The changing of ATF is a messy job and is best left to the service station. Do not attempt it unless you have a clean dust-free garage. If you must do it then take out the drain plug and let the fluid run out. Replace the plug and remove the automatic gearbox sump. Wash the sump clean and dry it thoroughly. Fit a new gasket and refit the sump to the box. Tighten the bolts to 7 lb ft (1 kg cm), leave for 15 minutes and tighten again to the same torque. Fill via the dipstick tube with 4 Imperial pints (5 US pints, 2.4 litres) of Dexron R ATF. Any Dexron R with a five figure number preceeded by the letter B may be used.
8 Start the engine and engage all the gears in turn. Do not drive more than a few yards. Check the level of the ATF and add ATF until the oil level just shows on the dipstick. Now go for a short drive and then check the level again. Fill with ATF until the level is between the marks. Check the sump bolts for tightness again.
9 **Do not tow the vehicle or start the engine while the gearbox is not full of ATF.**
10 If the ATF level is above the top mark ATF must be drained off until the level is correct or damage to the mechanism will result.
11 Apart from checking oil levels, keeping the box clean to assist cooling and checking connections, no further maintenance is necessary.

5 Tests and adjustments (general)

1 Before any accurate adjustments to the automatic transmission may be carried out the engine must be running correctly. Ignition and carburettor settings must be within the specified limits (eg: idling adjustments, valve tappets, ignition timing, etc). If these are all in order then inspect the transmission for leaks or external damage and correct these before proceeding.

6 Kick-down switch - testing

1 Check the kick-down switch operation. With the ignition switched on, press the accelerator pedal down as far as it will go. There should be a distinct click from the kick-down solenoid in the gearbox, as the valve is operated. If there is not then the system is not working. The switch is under the accelerator pedal (see Fig. 7.12). It is possible to move it slightly by loosening the screw. There are two wires to it, one from the supply and the other going to the automatic gearbox solenoid.
2 Check that when the ignition is on there is current in the supply cable. Now check that the accelerator pedal is not prevented, by maladjustment at the carburettor end of the operating cable, from going right down to its stop. The throttle operating lever should be resting on the spring. If the accelerator is not going right down, adjust the cable so that it will (see Section 16). At this point the switch should operate. It can be checked by putting a test lamp between the terminal of the kick-down switch which goes to the automatic box and earth. With the accelerator fully depressed the switch should be closed and the lamp alight. If the adjustment is correct at the point stated the switch should open and the lamp go out. The switch may be moved to adjust it or removed and replaced, if necessary.

7 Selector cable - checking operation

1 Correct adjustment for the 'P', 'R', 'N', 'D' and '1' ranges are necessary. The system will not work if they are out of adjustment in the selector mechanism. Adjustment is discussed in Section 15, paragraph 4. To test, switch the engine on and run up to 1100 rpm

with the lever at 'N' and the handbrake on.

   a) Move the lever to 'R'. The engine speed should drop noticeably.
   b) Move to 'P' and drop the safety stop. The speed should increase. Pull the lever against the stop - the speed must not alter.
   c) Engage 'R' again - speed should drop.
   d) Move to 'N' - no gears engaged so the speed should rise again.
   e) Move to 'D' and again the engine speed should drop noticeably.
   f) The lever should move from 'D' to '1' and back again, through '2', without any resistance.

8 Automatic transmission - stall speed test

1   The engine must be warm and the ATF lukewarm. **Do not carry out this test for more than 20 seconds** or the transmission will overheat.
2   The object is to check whether the torque converter is functioning correctly, and the running symptoms are poor acceleration and low maximum speed. A tachometer to measure engine speed is necessary.
3   Put all the brakes hard on and with the lever at 'D' run the engine for a brief period at full throttle. The engine speed should drop to between 2200 rpm and 1900 rpm immediately and remain constant.
4   If the stall speed is above 2200 rpm then either the forward clutch is slipping, or 1st gear one way clutch is slipping.
5   If the stall speed is about 1700 rpm then the engine needs overhaul but if it drops to 1500 rpm then the stator one way clutch in the torque converter is defective.

9 Automatic transmission - road test

1   As it is your vehicle, you will know whether there are any rough changes, slipping clutches or odd noises and at what point in the journey they occur. However, after a reasonably long run examine the transmission for oil leaks. These may come from several sources. The bellhousing may be dripping ATF. This means the torque converter seal is leaking. You can overhaul this yourself. Oil leaks from the final drive

may be rectified without removing the transmission, and there may be an ATF leak from the transmission box sump plate, which you can rectify. If the final drive contains ATF then the pinion seal has failed and you cannot do that one yourself.

There may be the obvious bearing noises from the final drive. This is discussed later.

10 Automatic transmission - action after testing

1   When you have decided what you think is wrong it would be a sensible idea to make a plan of action and then discuss this with the VW agent. If there are problems in the final drive, torque converter, or automatic gearbox that you cannot solve you can still save a lot of cash by taking the transmission out of the vehicle and sending the faulty unit to the agent for exchange or repair. It would be a good idea to get his agreement to that action first though. If you decide it is a job you can do yourself check that the spares are available. Finally, although we have found the agents are most helpful, they do not run Schools of Instruction and a busy man may give a short answer to an ill considered question.

11 Automatic transmission unit - removal and replacement

1   Disconnect the battery earth strap and the starter cable from the battery. Undo the bolt holding the speedometer drive to the bellhousing and remove the speedo cable (refer to Fig. 7.2).
2   Refer to Chapter 6, Section 2, paragraph 3 and using the method suggested there support the engine. Ultimately the gearbox is lowered to the ground. The ideal would be to work over a pit, if this is not possible refer to Chapter 6, Section 2, paragraphs 2 and 3.
3   Remove the upper engine/transmission bolts (2). Next remove the three nuts from the bracket holding the gearbox to the frame of the car. This bracket must be removed while working under the car, it is on the right-hand side of the box if you stand at the side of the car and look

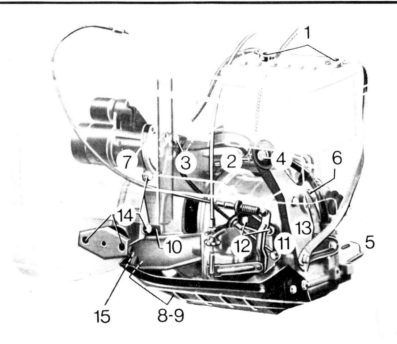

Fig. 7.2. Gearbox (010) - key to parts removed when taking out transmission (in order of removal) (Sec. 11)

1	*Battery connections*	*7*	*Starter*	*11*	*Selector lever cable*
2	*Speedometer cable*	*8*	*Cover plate*	*12*	*Cable bracket nuts*
3	*Upper engine/transmission bolts*	*9*	*Cover plate*	*13*	*Gearbox carrier - side*
4	*Gearbox carrier - side*	*10*	*Torque converter*	*14*	*Torque strut*
5	*Gearbox carrier - rear*			*15*	*Lower transmission/engine bolts*

over the box towards the engine. Sling the gearbox to the support bar to take the weight.

4 Remove the gearbox side carrier nut from the body. Undo the bolts and remove both driveshafts. (Chapter 12).

5 Remove the starter (see Chapter 12). Tag the cables for easy reconnection. The third bolt is between the engine and the starter.

6 Remove the screws holding the small cover plate and the large cover plate over the drive plate.

7 Working through the hole left by the starter locate and undo the three bolts holding the torque converter to the flywheel. These can be seen also in the gap left when the bottom cover plate is removed.

8 Set the selector lever to 'P' and disconnect the cable from the lever.

9 Remove the cable bracket and disconnect the accelerator cable and the pedal cable but do not alter the settings.

10 Now remove the side carrier from the gearbox.

11 Undo the nuts and remove the torque strut from the left-hand side of the engine.

12 Remove the lower bolts securing the gearbox to the engine.

13 The gearbox may now be removed. Lift it a little and push the LH drive shaft up and out of the way. Pull the gearbox off the dowels and lower it gently, at the same time supporting the torque converter,

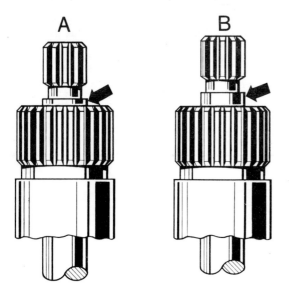

Fig. 7.3. Gearbox (010) - fitting of pump shaft splines (Sec. 11)

When the torque converter is fitted to the gearbox check BEFORE fitting that the pump shaft is fully engaged with the pump at the rear of the epicyclic gearbox. 'A' is correct. If the pump shaft protrudes from the one way clutch support splines as shown in 'B' the pump drive is not connected.

Fig. 7.4. Gearbox (010) - installation of side carrier (Sec. 11)

X must equal X

which will fall out if not held in place. There are two shafts and two sets of splines, be careful not to bend either of them or you will have a leaking torque converter.

14 The box is too heavy for one person to lift so a sling and tackle must be used. There is a convenient lifting eye on the converter housing.

15 Installation is the reverse of removal. The pump drive shaft is inside the impeller shaft. It must be fully engaged with the pump splines, before the converter is installed (see Fig. 6.3). The actual fitting of the converter is a tricky job. You may have removed the converter for repair, in which case it can be fitted to the final drive and installed with it. You may decide to remove the converter and fit it to the drive. Do not tilt the converter or you will spill ATF. There is a drawback about this method. It adds a lot of weight to an already heavy gearbox. The box can be fitted to the engine with the converter still in position. It is a question of preference. Lift the box into a position roughly level with the final position and about six inches from the final position horizontally. Remove the strap holding the torque converter in position. Do not tilt the converter or you will spill ATF. Ease the pump driveshaft into the converter and then pick up the splines in the converter hub with those of the impeller shaft. It is quite a performance as they are both fairly heavy, however if the box is slung firmly the converter can be moved about to suit. Once the two sets of splines are engaged slide the box towards the engine until the dowels engage. If the oil pump drive does not fully engage turn the driveplate of the converter a little when the impeller shaft has taken the weight of the converter, and pick up the oil pump drive splines in the casing cover. The converter must turn easily by hand.

16 When the box is located on the dowels and the converter in place then insert the bolts connecting the engine/gearbox housing and torque to 5.5 mkg (40 lbs ft).

17 Tighten the torque converter to driveplate bolts to 3 mkg (22 lb ft) and the driveshaft bolts to 4.5 mkg (32 lb ft).

18 It is essential to install the side carrier (Fig. 7.4) so that the dimensions marked 'A' are equal.

19 Insert the selector lever cable in the clamp on the operating lever. Fit the cable bracket to the box and connect the accelerator and pedal cables. Check the adjustment of the accelerator cable. Connect the selector cable to the selector lever, lever at 'P', and check the adjustment. (See Sections 15 and 16).

20 Refit the speedo cable and the earth strap. Check that all the carrier brackets are in place and the two cover plates are fitted. Refit the starter and its cables.

21 Install the driveshaft flanges and torque the bolts correctly.

22 Fill the box with ATF and the final drive with Hypoid oil.

23 Run the engine and check the ATF level, adjust as necessary.

12 Torque converter - repairs

1 The unit is welded together and if seriously damaged must be renewed. However, two repairs are possible, both to cure an oil leak from the converter/shaft bearing.

2 Before discussing repairs a word of warning. When refitting the converter to the one way clutch support do not rock or tilt the converter. Turn the converter slowly to-and-fro when installing it on the splines.

3 If the transmission has overheated so much that the ATF is polluted with carbon or other debris then the converter must be drained of the contaminated fluid. It is possible to siphon this out. From the homebrewers shop or somewhere similar get a rubber bung 1 3/8 in (34.8 mm) diameter. Bore two holes to fit the bung, one about 6 in. (150 mm) and the other 8 in (205 mm) long. Bend the tubes so that the top piece is a right-angle bend about 2 in. (50 mm) radius, and the outlet is horizontal. Fit the bung in the converter bushing (the converter should be flat with the starter ring upwards) and adjust the tubes so that the end of the short one is flush with the bottom of the bung and the end of the longer one just touches the bottom of the converter. Connect a piece of plastic tube to the long tube and arrange a siphon. Now blow down the shorter tube to start the siphon going and leave the converter to drain for at least eight hours. Blow, don't suck, the fluid not only does not taste nice, **it is poisonous.**

4 The seal is held in spigot of the one way clutch support (see Fig. 7.5). It may be levered out and the seat cleaned with a sharp tool. The new seal is a very soft silicone compound which must not be exposed to petrol or paraffin. Dip it in ATF and push it in gently as far as it will go.

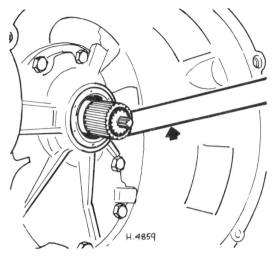

Fig. 7.5. Gearbox (010) - extracting the torque converter seal from the one way clutch support (Sec. 12)

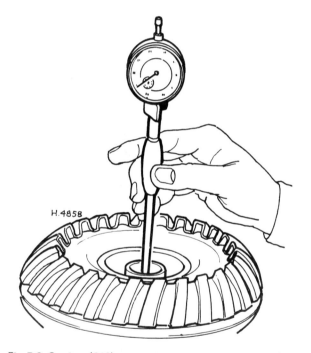

Fig. 7.6. Gearbox (010) - measuring the internal diameter of the torque converter bush (Sec. 12)

5   If the seal was damaged then there may be damage on the hub of the converter. Check the outside of the hub for scoring and uneven wear.

6   It is as well to check the bush inside the converter at this point. It must not be more than 1.436 in (34.25 mm) in diameter and not more than 0.001 in (0.03 mm) out of round. If it is then it must be replaced. (see Fig. 7.6). The new bush is finished to size and must not be reamed out. The limits are 1.347 to 1.375 in (34.025 to 34.095 mm). Unless you have an internal micrometer and a suitable press we suggest you leave this job to the agent, but it can be done with patience and the correct tools.

13 Final drive - overhaul

1   Refer to Figs. 7.9a and 7.9b. It will be seen that the differential is contained in a casting at the side of the final drive housing. The driveshaft from the automatic box mates with an idler gear which is held in taper bearings on the idler shaft.

Fig. 7.7. Final drive - The arrows show the circlips holding the drive flange shafts inside the differential. Remove these and draw out the flanges (Sec. 13)

Fig. 7.8. Final drive - Using Tool VW 182 to undo the differential adjusting ring (Sec. 13)

2   The idler gear mates with the crownwheel of the differential, thus the driveshaft and the final drive rotate in the same direction and the reduction is effected in easy stages, the gears having 21, 34 and 79 teeth respectively. In effect the idler gear replaces the driven shaft of the manual box in correcting the direction of rotation.

3   The drive flanges may be removed with the gearbox in the car and the oil seals may be levered out and replaced by new ones. Disconnect the driveshaft on the side of the faulty seal, remove the plastic plug, lever out the circlip and using tool VW 391 (see Chapter 6) pull out the flange. The seal may now be levered out and a new one fitted.

4   Any further work on the final drive means removing the gearbox, for the space available with the box in the car is too limited. Once the box is removed drain the oil and remove the cover plate. The drive flange shafts are held inside the differential by circlips. Press off these circlips and pull the flanges out complete with shafts (Fig. 7.7).

5   This type of box uses an adjusting ring similar to the VW 411/412 gearbox on one drive flange. The adjusting ring, which carries the oil seal and the outer race of the differential bearing, is screwed into the casting. It is held in place by a locking plate. Before disturbing anything make a mark across the adjusting ring and the housing so that you can screw the adjusting ring in to the same place on assembly. Now remove the clamp bolt and, using tool VW 182 or a similar device fitted in the slots on the face of the ring, remove the ring counting the complete turns to unscrew it from the thread. The first turn will be difficult as the bearing is preloaded, but after that the load eases considerably. (see Fig. 7.8). The differential bearing on the other side is held in a casting which is bolted to the main casting (see Fig. 7.9a). Undo the holding bolts and lever the casting out of the casing. The outer race of the differential will come out with the casting. Watch for the 'O' ring. Lift the differential clear and set it on one side.

6   If parts on the differential need renewing then we recommend the unit be taken to the VW agent for servicing or replacement. If the taper

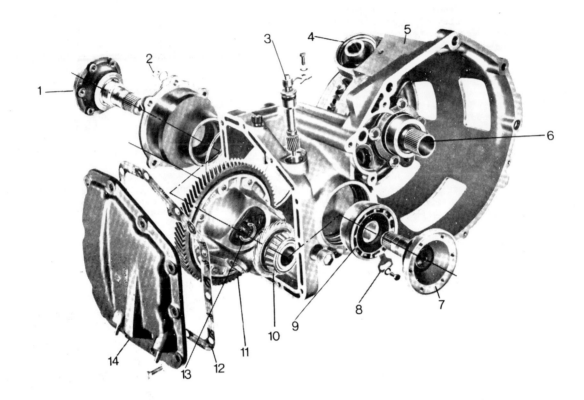

Fig. 7.9A. Final drive - exploded view, removal of differential (Sec. 13)

1 LH drive flange
2 Nut
3 Speedometer drive
4 Governer bearing
5 Drive housing
6 One way clutch support shaft
7 RH drive flange
8 Lock plate
9 Adjusting ring
10 Taper bearing
11 Crownwheel
12 Gasket
13 Circlip locking drive flange shaft
14 Cover plate

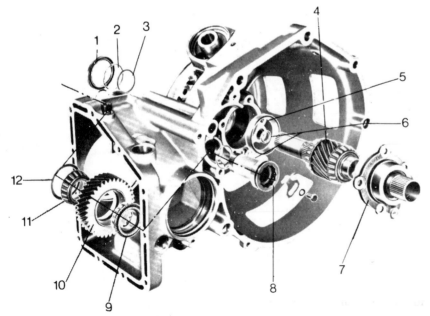

Fig. 7.9B. Final drive - exploded view, removal of idler gear and pinion shaft (Sec. 13)

1 Oil seal ⎫ Final
2 'O' ring ⎬ drive
3 Shim ⎭ housing
4 Pinion shaft
5 Bearing outer race
6 'O' ring/A T F drilling
7 One way clutch support shaft
8 Intermediate gear shaft
9 Taper bearing
10 Intermediate gear
11 Taper bearing
12 Shim

bearings are disturbed, as for example when fitting a new speedometer drive gear to the differential, then the bearings must be preloaded to the correct amount. You cannot do this: the bearings and final drive housing must be taken to the VW agent for correct assembly. Again we suggest you ask if he is prepared to do this work before dismantling the box, he may wish to do the whole job rather than a part of it, and an amicable agreement before the damage is done will pay in the long run.

7   The same technique is used to remove the idler gear shaft. Mark the shaft and housing and then remove the lockplate. A hexagonal tubular plug spanner will fit in the socket head of the shaft. Unscrew the shaft counting the turns and, holding the gear, withdraw the shaft and remove the gear. Watch out for the 'O' ring and the shim behind the inside race. The taper races will remain in the gearwheel. If either of them are to be replaced then once again the box must go to the VW agent for the bearings to be set correctly. This preloading in each case means also measuring the torque required to turn the final drive and calculating the thickness of shims needed. Without the special tools for the job you cannot do that, and the cost of the tools far exceeds the cost of a one off repair.

8   If the pinion shaft is to be removed then the epicyclic box must be removed from the final drive. Turn the casing so that the ATF cannot leak out and remove the four nuts from the studs inside the final drive casing and remove the final drive casing from the epicyclic box. Watch out for the large 'O' ring. The pinion shaft oil seal may now be levered out and replaced if necessary, but if the bearings are to be renewed then the final drive casing should be taken to the VW Agent. The refitting torque for the final drive/gearbox nuts is 3 mkg (22 lbs ft). You can't win, for this time as well as preloading there is the question of axial play as well as measuring the torque required for turning the shaft. **Do not** take it to bits and then take it to the agent. We agree with everything he will think, whether he says it or not!

9   We have described all this at length, apparently only to tell you what you cannot do. It is most unlikely that gears or bearings will require replacement, but you can replace oil seals, and you can do a lot of the dismantling and assembling yourself saving a lot of mechanics time. However, once again we urge you to talk to the VW agent *before* you take things to bits or your car may be off the road for quite a while.

10 Replacement of all the bits is the reverse of removal. Fit new gaskets and seals everywhere. When replacing the differential fit the large casting complete with a new 'O' ring. Torque the nuts to 3 mkg (21 lb ft). Install the differential and then refit the adjusting ring. Do not forget the shim. Screw the adjusting ring into the exact same place. The last two turns are hard work but it must be exactly the same place. When the differential is securely in place install the drive flanges and refit the circlips. Fit a new gasket and replace the differential cover. Torque the bolts to 3 mkg (21 lb ft).

---

14 Governor - dismantling and reassembly

---

1   The governor is driven by the helical gear on the pinion shaft.
2   If the transmission has failed due to burning of the brake bands or clutches then as well as draining the converter it will be necessary to clean the governor (refer to Fig. 7.10).
3   Remove it from the casing by undoing the clip and taking off the cover. The governor may now be extracted. Look at the thrust-plate and the shaft for wear. The shaft may be replaced by a new one if it is damaged but the new shaft must be fitted to the old governor. If a new governor is to be fitted the whole transmission must go to the agent for the governor to be reset on the test rig.
4   The seals should be replaced with new ones (lip toward the governor

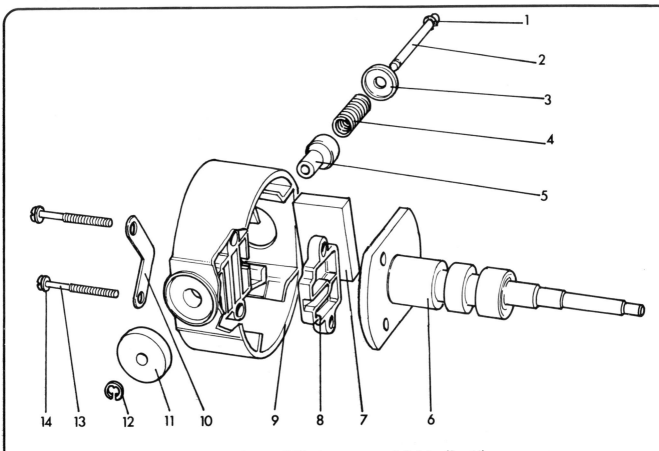

Fig. 7.10. Gearbox (010) - the governor, exploded view (Sec. 14)

1	Circlip	5	Valve	9	Housing	12	Circlip
2	Pin	6	Governor	10	Thrust plate	13	Bolt (M5)
3	Spring cup	7	Balance weight	11	Centrifugal weight	14	Washer
4	Spring					

body).

5   To clean the governor it is necessary to dismantle it. Remove the two screws from the thrust-plate and take off the thrust-plate and housing. The weight and the transfer plate will fall out. Remove the circlips from the pin and the remainder of the parts may be dismantled.

6   Wash it all carefully and dry it thoroughly. Reassembly is the reverse process. Dip the parts in ATF as you assemble them. The transfer plate drillings should have the narrow end of the taper next to the weight, and the thrust-plate apex must be at the centre of the housing.

7   Refit the shaft, install the governor and refit the cap and clip.

15 Gearshift mechanism - adjustment, removal and replacement

1   Refer to Fig. 7.11. The console is illuminated by a small bulb. The lever moves only in one plane pivotting about its bottom end. A small way below the pivot a cable is attached which transfers the motion to the valve chest of the automatic box.

2   To remove the selector lever first remove the gear knob. Remove the brushes and the console. Undo the screws which hold the bracket to the floor plate. Detach the cable from lever and take it away to the rear, undoing the sleeve nut in the casing. The gearshift should then come away. Installation is the reverse of removal.

3   To renew the cable remove the console and undo the cable from the lever at the bottom of the assembly. Now underneath the car, remove the circlip holding the cable end to the transmission selector lever. Draw the cable out of the gearshift mechanism.

4   To adjust the cable, set the lever in position 'P'. Take the cover plate off the lever assembly and loosen the clamp on the cable. Now under the car again push the levers on the gearbox right back against the stop. Push against the spring pressure with a pair of pliers. Hold the lever in this position and tighten the clamp on the cable in the gearshift.

5   Check the operation as in Section 7, of this Chapter. The Neutral/Park switch consisting of the contact bridge and the contact plate must be adjusted so that the starter motor operates only in the 'N' and 'P' positions.

16 Accelerator cable - removal, replacement and adjustment

1   Refer to Fig. 7.12. Pull the cable balljoint away from the lever at 'B' and screw the ball socket off the cable. Remove the boot and take

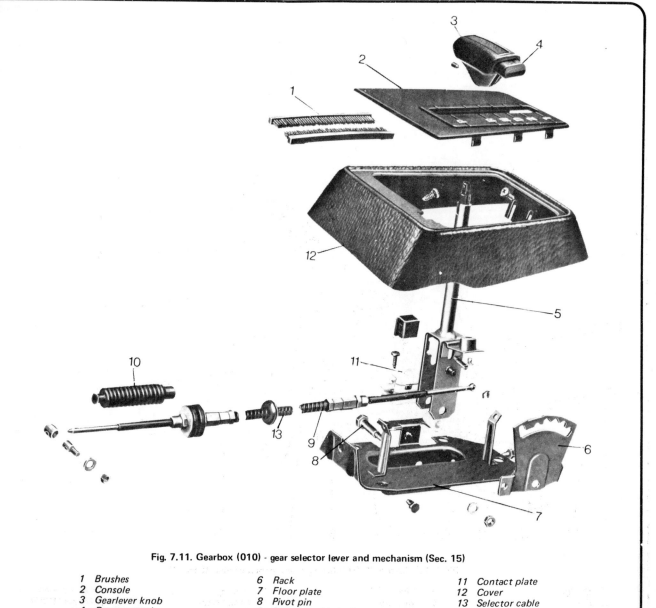

Fig. 7.11. Gearbox (010) - gear selector lever and mechanism (Sec. 15)

1 Brushes	6 Rack	11 Contact plate
2 Console	7 Floor plate	12 Cover
3 Gearlever knob	8 Pivot pin	13 Selector cable
4 Reverse catch	9 Selector cable locknut	
5 Selector lever	10 Boot	

the cable off the retaining bracket. Disconnect the cable from the throttle lever and remove the cable from the bracket on the carburettor.

2   Hold the cable outer at one end and lift it horizontally. If the cable droops down the steel strip the cover is in the wrong plane. Turn the outer cable until the cable droops in an 'S' position. This is the correct refitting position. Attach the cable to the bracket on the gearbox, push the outer cable in and fit the securing clip. Turn the ball socket to screw it onto the cable as far as it will go and then turn it back a little to fit it on the ball stud. Tighten the locknut and clamp the outer cable.

3   Push the cable into position through the hole in the carburettor

bracket and fasten it to the throttle lever. Squeeze the spring together with pliers and adjust the nuts on the bracket so that there is no strain on the cable.

4   To adjust the cable correctly first move the throttle lever on the carburettor to the end position so that the choke is open, the cam out of action, and the throttle closed. Now press the lever on the gearbox towards the accelerator cable as far as it will go and push the cable ball socket onto the ball stud. Turn the nut on the carburettor bracket until all play in the cable is eliminated. The lever on the gearbox must still be in the end position. Fasten the second (lock) nut again the

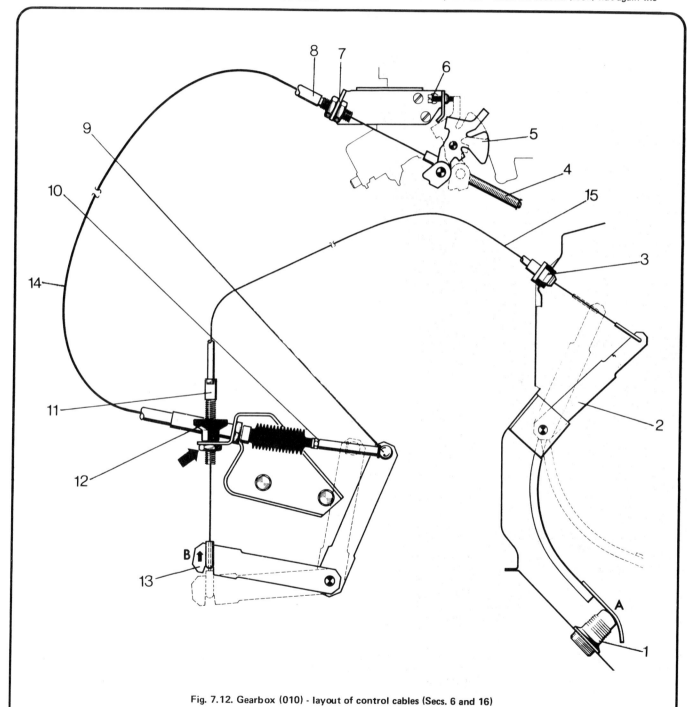

Fig. 7.12. Gearbox (010) - layout of control cables (Secs. 6 and 16)

1 Kick-down switch	5 Carburettor linkage	8 Outer cable	12 Adjusting nut and locknut
2 Accelerator pedal	6 Stop screw	9 Balljoint	13 Gearbox lever
3 Outer cable anchorage	7 Adjusting locknuts	10 Locknut	14 Cable
4 Spring		11 Cable anchorage	15 Cable

bracket.

5　Now check the gearbox control cable. Refer to Fig. 7.12 again. Move the pedal to kick-down position, slacken the locknut under the knurled knob where the cable from the pedal enters the bracket on the gearbox and turn the knurled knob until there is no play at 'B' in the direction of the arrow.

17 Automatic transmission - repairs

1　We do not recommend any d-i-y repairs to the automatic gearbox other than replacement of the ATF and the cleaning of the sump. Dismantling is simple, overhaul is limited to replacing worn parts, but the box has to be assembled again. There are 12 different springs, each operating a valve, of different wire diameters, free-lengths etc, in the valve chest alone, an oil pump and a complicated epicyclic gear train. If tests show that gears are slipping, or the ATF smells of carbon or burning leave the repair of the automatic gearbox to the official agent whose mechanics have done a course of instruction and have all the jigs, gauges and adjustment schedules. It will be much more economical in the long run.

18 Fault diagnosis - automatic transmission

This list is by no means complete but it contains all that the owner can rectify. The official agent is the best person to consult about a faulty automatic transmission

Symptom	Reason/s	Remedy
No drive in any gear	ATF fluid level low Transmission box defective	Fill. Official agent.
Drive in some gears but not all	Transmission box defective	Official agent.
Power output unsteady engine surges on	ATF fluid level incorrect Selector mechanism out of adjustment Oil strainer requires cleaning	Measure and correct. Adjust. Remove pan and clean.
Speed shifts at too low speed	Governor dirty Primary throttle valve needs setting Valve body assembly dirty	Remove and clean. Official agent. Official agent.
Speed shifts at too high speed	Vacuum hose leaking Kickdown lever distorted Kickdown solenoid defective ATF pressure too low	Replace. Repair. Repair. Official agent.
Kickdown will not operate	Lever distorted, solenoid defective, wiring open circuit, switch broken	Trace and correct. Replace switch/solenoid
Heavy leakage of ATF on floor and vehicle	Torque converter seal casing defective or cracked	Replace seal. Fit new converter
Heavy loss of ATF. None on floor or vehicle. Smoky exhaust	Leaking vacuum chamber of primary throttle	Official agent.
Parking lock will not hold vehicle	Selector lever out of adjustment Parking lock linkage defective	Adjust. Repair.
ATF dirty and smells of carbon and burning	Brake bands or clutches wearing in auto transmission box	Dismantle and take box to Official agent (check with him first). Replace oil in converter.
Oil leaks from final drive flanges	Seals in flanges worn out	Replace.
Differential noisy	Differential or pinion bearings worn	Remove final drive unit and take to Official agent.
Bumpy shift from 'N' to 'R'	Due to design feature	No action.
Harsh gear shift from '2' to '1'	Excessive wear in one way clutch of transmission	Fit redesigned cage with 10 lugs. Action by Official agent.
Selector cable stiff movement	Cable rubbing on front cover peg Outer cable not fitted correctly at front end	Bend peg sideways to give cable free movement. Fit new cable.

Chapter 8 Rear axle and rear suspension

Contents

Specifications

Type ... ...   Torsion axle beam with trailing arms. MacPherson type struts with coil spring and shock absorber co-axial. Wheels carried on stub axles bolted to the trailing arms.

Coil springs ... ...   Initial installation three grades with 1, 2 or 3 paint stripes. Replacement only from the middle grade.

Shock absorbers ... ...   Hydraulic, telescopic, double acting. Golf and Scirocco type differ.

Geometry
Adjustment	All angles fixed with no adjustment
Camber	$-1^{\circ} \pm 30'$ (max deviation 40')
Total toe	$0^{\circ} \pm 15'$ (max deviation 15')
Track	1358 mm (53.4 inches)

Hub bearings ... ...   Taper roller

Torque wrench settings

	Mkg	lbs ft
Axle beam to body bracket	6.0	43
Body bracket to floor	4.5	32
Shock absorber to axle	4.5	32
Shock absorber to body	3.5	25
Shock absorber slotted nut	2.0	15
Stub axle to axle beam	6.0	43

1 General description

1 A fabricated axle beam is located across the vehicle body held on either side in mounting brackets which are bolted to the underside of the body. The axle is held in the mounting by a hinge bolt which passes through a bonded rubber bush. The cross beam is a 'T' section. On the 1.1 litre Golf model prior to June 1975 it is 3.5 mm thick, all other models and the 1.1 litre after June 1975 have beams 6 mm thick. Service replacements are all 6 mm section.

2 Welded to the beam and supported by gusset plates are trailing arms of circular section. These terminate in fabricated brackets which serve as lower anchors for the shock absorbers and as mounting pads for the stub axles and rear brake backplates.

3 The stub axle carries the rear hub, brake drum and wheel on two taper roller bearings. The movement of the wheel is thus a radial one in the vertical plane. The weight of the body and its contents is supported by a suspension strut on each side which is secured to the body at its upper end and the axle at the lower end. The strut consists of a coil spring and shock absorber mounted co-axially. The shock absorbers are of hydraulic telescopic construction. Approximately half way up the outer casing of the shock absorber is welded a spring platform which houses the lower end of the spring (photo). The upper end is housed in spring cup which is kept in place by a slotted nut fitted to the piston rod of the shock absorber. A rubber buffer is fitted on the piston rod to stop the spring being compressed until its coils are solid.

1.3 The suspension strut removed from the vehicle

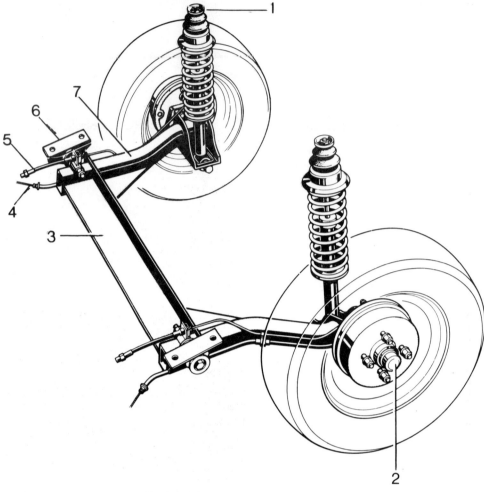

Fig. 8.1. Rear suspension - general layout

1	*Suspension strut*	3	*Axle beam*	5	*Hydraulic brake pipe*	7	*Trailing arm*
2	*Wheel bearing*	4	*Handbrake cable*	6	*Side mounting*		

4   The suspension strut is assembled complete away from the vehicle and then fitted, first to the body by a nut removable from inside the vehicle body and at the lower end by a hinge bolt to the bracket at the end of the trailing arm.

5   Two types of shock absorber are fitted, one for the Golf and a heavier type for the Scirrocco. The types of spring fitted also vary. This is discussed in Section 8.

6   The camber angle and toe-in are fixed. Details are given in the Specification for checking, should distortion be suspected.

7   The suspension struts may be removed without dismantling the axle, and once the brake hoses and the handbrake cable are disconnected the whole assembly may be removed from the car by removing six nuts.

8   If the axle beam, or the stub axles are distorted or otherwise damaged they must be replaced. Repair by straightening or welding is not permitted.

2   Rear wheel bearings - adjustment

1   The rear wheel bearings are normal taper bearings. To adjust them first raise the vehicle on a jack until the wheel may be rotated.

2   Remove the dust cap (photo) with a suitable lever, take out the split pin and remove the locking ring. Slacken off the nut and then tighten it to 1.5 mkg (about 12 lb/ft) rotating the wheel at the same time. Now slacken off the nut and then tighten it until the thurst washer may be turned with some difficulty. The bearing play will then be between 0.003 and 0.007 mm. In this way the bearings are firmly seated on the stub axle and then given the necessary running tolerance.

3   Refit the locking ring and a new split pin. If you must move the nut

2.1 Remove the dust cap, bend the split pin straight and extract it. Remove the locking ring

Fig. 8.2. Rear wheel bearing - exploded view (Sec. 3)

1 Dust cap	4 Nut	7 Brake drum
2 Split pin	5 Thrust washer	8 Inner bearing
3 Locking plate	6 Outer bearing	9 Oil seal

slacken it a little.

4   Fill the hub cap with multi-purpose grease and tap it into position.

3   Rear wheel bearings - removal and replacement

1   Slacken the wheel nuts, jack-up the rear wheel, support the vehicle on an axle stand and remove the wheel. Refer to Fig. 8.2.

2   Remove the hub grease cap, remove the split pin and locking ring. Undo the adjusting nut. Slacken the brake adjusters (Chapter 9), and remove the brake drum. The thrust washer and the outer bearing complete will come away with the drum, together with the oil seal and the outer race of the inner bearing. The inner race of the inner bearing will remain on the stub axle.

3   Remove the oil seal and tap the bearings out of the brake drum with a brass drift. Clean the drum and stub axle and oil them lightly. Wash the bearings in clean paraffin and then swill out all residue with more clean paraffin. Dry them carefully with a non-fluffy rag.

4   Examine the tracks of the races for scoring or signs of overheating. If these are present then the complete bearing should be replaced. Inspect the roller bearings carefully, there should be no flats or burrs. Lubricate the race with a light oil and spin the inner race in the outer race. Any roughness indicates undue wear and **the** bearing should be replaced. Once a bearing begins to wear the wear accelerates rapidly and may be the cause of damage to the stub axle or drum so if you are in doubt get an expert opinion.

5   Examine the oil seal. Ideally it should be replaced; if there is any damage or sign of hardening replace it anyway. Failure of an oil seal will mean contamination of the brake shoes and the minimum penalty will be new shoes on **both** rear wheels.

6   If all the items are correct and the stub axle bearing surfaces and brake drum bore are in good order then proceed to assemble the hub.

7   Pack the taper bearings with a lithium based grease, and smear the stub axle with a light film of grease. Fit the inner race, the inner bearing and the oil seal into the brake drum. Press the seal into place, tap it home with a rubber hammer taking care that it is squarely seated.

8   Fit the drum to the stub axle then the outer race and finally the thrust washer. Fit the nut and adjust the bearing as in Section 2. Fit the locking ring and a new split pin. Refit the dust cap, replace the wheel and test the bearing by spinning the wheel. Lower the vehicle to the ground.

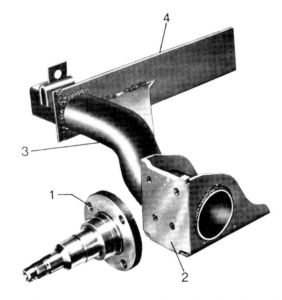

Fig. 8.3. Detail of axle beam and stub axle (Secs. 4 and 5)

1 Stub axle	3 Trailing arm
2 Axle beam trailing arm bracket	4 Transverse beam

4   Stub axles - removal, inspection and replacement

1   Apart from scoring on the bearing surfaces or ovality due to excessive bearing wear the only other defect to check on the stub axle is distortion due to bending. This could happen if the vehicle has been in an accident or has been driven heavily laden at excessive speed over rough ground.

2   The effect of a bent stub axle will be excessive tyre wear due to

4.4 The brake backplate and stub axle

6.1 The upper anchorage of the suspension strut is inside the vehicle

6.3 Lowering the suspension strut

the wrong camber angle and possibly incorrect toe-in. These angles are small with fine limits and, in our opinion, not measurable without the proper equipment. If irregular tyre wear occurs the owner is advised to have these angles checked right away. Before deciding the stub axle is bent read Section 5.

3   Alternatively the stub axle may be removed, bolted to a lathe face plate and checked for alignment with a dial gauge. The allowable run out is 0.25 mm (0.010 inches).

4   To remove the stub axle proceed as in Section 3 and remove the brake drum and bearings. The brake backplate and stub axle are held to the axle beam by four bolts. Unfortunately these are only accessible after the brake shoes have been removed (see Chapter 9). Remove the shoes and then the four bolts. The backplate and wheel cylinder may be moved out of the way to extract the stub axle (photo).

5   Replacement is the reverse of removal. Make sure the joint faces of the stub axle and axle beam are clean and free from burrs before assembly.

5   Axle beam - visual check for distortion

1   If irregular wear of the rear tyres is observed the reason will probably be incorrect camber angle. Before dismantling the stub axle check that the gusset plate of the axle beam is not distorted. If this fault is present the axle beam will be out of alignment. This will require a new axle beam. The removal and replacement of the complete rear axle is discussed in Section 10. Before deciding to replace the axle beam we suggest that the camber angle should be checked by the VW agent and your diagnosis confirmed.

6   Suspension strut - removal and replacement

1   Open the rear flap door and lift the parcel shelf. On either side of the body on top of the wheel arches are plastic caps. Remove these to find the upper anchorage nuts of the suspension struts (photo).

2   Lift the rear of the vehicle and support the body on axle stands. The best place for this is the recommended lifting place just forward of the wheel. If you look underneath you will see a narrow flat surface with a hole in it. Remove the roadwheel (refer to Fig. 8.4).

3   Remove the nut from the bolt holding the shock absorber to the trailing arm and tap out the bolt. It may be necessary to take the weight of the hub to extract this bolt. If the bolt fouls the brake drum then the brake backplate must be removed (Section 4).

4   Once the bottom anchorage is clear remove the nut holding the top of the shock absorber piston inside the body and lower away the suspension strut (photo). This needs two people; one to undo the nut and one to hold the strut.

4   Replacement is the reverse of removal.

7   Suspension strut - dismantling and reassembly

1   Refer to Fig. 8.4. The spring is held in compression by the slotted nut. There are two problems, the first to hold the spring in compression while removing the nut, and the second to stop the piston rod turning whilst undoing the nut. Fortunately the rod is fitted with flats which

may be held with a spanner, but the slotted nut requires a special tool, VW50-200, to turn it, and it must be retightened to the correct torque (2 mkg, 15 ft lbs).

2   The recommended method of holding the spring is to clamp it in a vice, but few people will have a vice that big, so a few turns of very strong lashing should be used to keep it compressed until the nut is removed, when the lashing may be slackened.

3   The coil spring may now be lifted off the shock absorber.

4   Assembly is the reverse of dismantling. The spring will need compressing enough to start the nut properly. After that progressive tightening to the correct torque will compress the spring.

8   Coil springs - inspection and modification

1   Although one would imagine that the coil spring was a mundane affair this is not so for the Golf/Rabbit/Scirroco and care must be taken if the spring is to be replaced.

2   Three faults may occur: either the spring is broken, which is very rare, or more often a rattling noise coming from the region of the back axle when the vehicle is driven over rough surfaces. The latter fault may be due to the end coil of the spring at the top coming into contact with the next coil. Finally the spring may just have got tired and distorted. In any case the suspension strut must be removed and dismantled as in Sections 6 and 7.

3   If the spring is broken then a careful examination of the fracture is indicated. Should the surface of the fracture show a crystaline form plus a smaller portion of clean metal then the spring was probably faulty when assembled. It would be worhwhile pointing this out to the agent. Anyway a straight replacement is indicated about which more in paragraph 7.

4   If the metal shows a clean break with no flaws, then a careful examination of the rest of the suspension is indicated for the force required for such a fracture will be of very large proportions indeed.

5   If the top coil has been banging on the next coil there will be evidence in the form of marking. In this case a piece of damping sleeve may be fitted (Part No. 321 511 125A) over the top two coils. This is plastic tube. There is enough for top and bottom so cut it in half. The spring must be cleaned carefully and coated with Tectyl. Avoid air bubbles or rust will form. Tectyl should be obtainable from the VW agent. Once the plastic tube is in position the spring may be put back on the strut. The coils will still bottom but the noise will stop, for a while at least.

6   If the spring has distorted, then it has just got tired and it must be replaced. The cause could be one of several: incorrect material, wrong heat treatment, or even the wrong spring. These occasions are mercifully rare and distortion is usually brought on by continuous over-loading.

7   When the springs are fitted they are selected for the purpose. Three grades are used, denoted by one, two or three paint stripes. When a replacement is required VW state that only the spring with two stripes is available. They further say that it is not necessary to renew both springs if only one is faulty. So fit a spring with two stripes and do not worry.

In June 1975 a modified spring was produced for the 1.1 litre Golf (not L models). This does not apply to the Rabbit or Scirrocco either. Before this date 'progressive' springs were installed. After this date

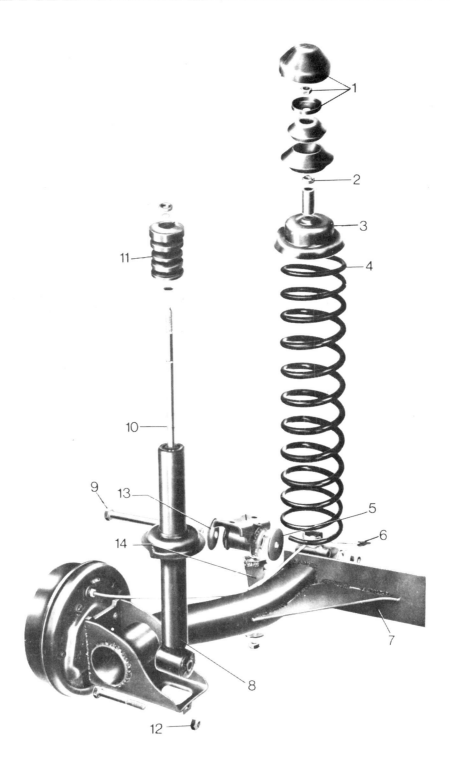

Fig. 8.4. Suspension strut - general layout, exploded view (Secs. 6 and 7)

1	Cap and details inside car	6	Washer (22 mm)	11	Buffer
2	Slotted nut	7	Axle beam gusset	12	Shock absorber anchor bolt and nut
3	Spring cap	8	Shock absorber	13	Concave washer
4	Coil spring	9	Axle mounting bracket hinge bolt	14	Parking brake cable holder
5	Disc (52 mm)	10	Mounting bracket		

'linear' springs are used. At the same time the thicker axle beam is
fitted. This, in effect, means that if you own a Golf (not Golf L) with
a 1.1 litre engine built before June 1975 and you need a new rear
spring you must get a progressive spring which has two white marks on
it. After that date you need a linear spring with two blue marks. The
following table will help:

Linear spring	Length	Dia top coil	Dia middle coil
pt no. 171 511 105H	352 mm	9.6 mm	9.6 mm
2 blue marks	(13.6 ins)	(0.38 ins)	(0.38 ins)
Progressive spring			
pt no. 171 511 105C	389 mm	7.6 mm	10.2 mm
2 white marks	(15.3 ins)	(0.3 ins)	(0.4 ins)

Both types are supplied as replacements, and when a spring is renewed
a spring of the same type should be installed.
8   The buffer fitted on the piston rod also varies with the type of
spring fitted. The buffer for the linear spring is Part No. 171 511 105H
marked with two blue marks. It is 89 mm long, 36 mm diameter at the
base and 60 mm dia on the larger diameter.
    The buffer for the progressive spring is Part No. 171 511 105C
identified by two white marks. This one is 71 mm long, 36 mm dia at
the base and 48 mm dia on the larger diameter.

9 Shock absorbers - testing

1   A defective shock absorber usually makes a rumbling noise as the
car goes over rough surfaces. A quick test to confirm this suspicion is to
press the rear of the car down on the suspected side and release it
sharply. The car should rise and settle at once, if it oscillates at all the
shock absorber is not working correctly.
    A small leakage of fluid round the piston seal is normal and need
cause no worry, but a large leakage indicates that the shock absorber
must be changed. There is no repair possible.
2   Remove the suspension strut as in Sections 6 and 7. Hold the
lower portion of the shock absorber in a vice with the piston rod in a
vertical position. Pull the rod right up and press it down again. The
force required in each direction should be even and equal. Repeat this
test several times. If the stroke is uneven or jerky then the unit must be
replaced with a new one.
3   Examine the lower anchorage. The bush must be a good fit on the
locating bolt, and the rubber mounting in good condition.
    If either of these are faulty enquire whether a new bush and
mounting are available from the VW stores. Should this be so get a new
locating bolt at the same time. Press the bush out of the eye with the
mounting and press both of them into the eye. Lubricate the eye with
a little rubber grease or soap before pressing the mounting home and be
careful to enter it squarely. This must be done on a flypress or in a large
vice, do not attempt to hammer it in. Alternative an arrangement of a
draw bolt with a nut and two large washers may be used.
4   The units used on the Scirocco differ from those of the Golf/Rabbit
so be careful to obtain the correct type. It is not necessary to renew both
units if only one is defective.

10 Rear axle assembly - removal and replacement

1   If the rear axle beam is distorted the entire rear suspension must be
removed. It is not possible to remove the pivot bolts from the

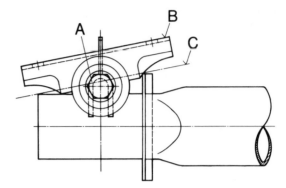

Fig. 8.5. Angle for setting axle beam mounting (Sec. 11)

*Align the mounting so that the top edge 'B' is parallel to line 'C',
then tighten nut 'A'*

mountings as the bolts foul the body (refer to Fig. 8.1).
2   Support the vehicle body on axle stands (Section 6) and remove the
wheels. Remove the brake drums and dismantle the brake shoes to free
the handbrake cables (Chapter 9). Unclip the handbrake outer cables
from the trailing arms.
3   Disconnect the hydraulic brake lines and plug the hoses to prevent
dirt or grit entering the system.
4   It may be necessary to remove parts of the exhaust system of the
Rabbit before proceeding further.
5   Each mounting is held by two studs and nuts. These must now be
slackened off. Be careful not to shear off the studs. If you do, refer to
Section 11.
6   From inside the body remove the caps from the suspension struts and
slacken off the nuts holding the shock absorber pistons to the body
(photo 6.1).
7   Support the axle and remove all the retaining nuts. It will be best
to have three people to do this job. The axle beam and suspension
struts may now be lowered to the ground and removed.
8   Seperate the mountings by removing the hinge bolts. Note how the
large washer is situated between the axle beam and the mounting. The
dished washer is fitted with the bolt.
9   If the axle beam is to be replaced note that the beams for the
1.1 litre models prior to June 1975 are of thinner material than the
other models.
10 When assembling lubricate the dished washer to prevent squeaks.
11 Assembly is the reverse of removal. Remember to adjust the
handbrake and bleed the hydraulic cylinders. When the car is back on
its wheels check the torque of the hinge bolt nuts.

11 Rear axle mountings - removal and replacement

1   If you have the misfortune to snear one of the studs then the stud
must be drilled out and the resultant hole tapped for a 10 mm thread.
Use an 8 mm drill and be careful to drill exactly in the centre of the
stud. We advise caution. Unless you have experience in this type of work
get a trained mechanic to do it for you. If you drill in the wrong place,
the result will be very expensive. After tapping the hole fit a 10 mm bolt
x 40, tensile class 10.9.
2   When refitting the mounting align it as shown in Fig. 8.5.

12 Fault diagnosis - rear axle

Symptom	Probable cause	Remedy
Excessive tyre wear or uneven tyre wear	1 Stub axle bent, check camber 2 Axle beam distorted 3 Wheel bearings defective 4 Shock absorber defective 5 Brake binding	1 Renew if necessary. 2 Check and renew if necessary. 3 Check and renew. 4 Check and renew 5 Check and adjust
Rumbling noise from rear axle	1 Shock absorber defective 2 Wheel bearing defective	1 Check and renew. 2 Check and renew.
Chattering or banging from rear axle	1 Top coil of spring banging on next layer 2 Lower mount of shock absorber worn	1 Fit plastic tube over spring coil (Section 8). 2 Renew.
Squeak from rear axle	1 Disc washer on hinge bolt rubbing on the bonded rubber bush 2 Guide sleeve of handbrake cable	1 Lubricate bush and washer. 2 Lubricate sleeve with 'Molykote' lubricant.

Chapter 9 Braking system

Contents

Specifications

Type	Hydraulic master cylinder, may be servo assisted. Front brakes disc or drum according to model. Rear brakes drum, may be self-adjusting according to model. Hydraulic system - dual circuit diagonally connected. Handbrake - cable operated, equalizer on brake lever.

Front brakes (drum)

	mm	in
Inside dia of drum	230	9.05
Wheel cylinder diameter	25.4	1.00
Lining thickness (new)	4	0.016
Lining width	40	1.57

Front brakes (disc - floating caliper)

	Standard		1.1 litre after Aug. 1975	
	mm	in	mm	in
Caliper piston diameter	44	1.73		
Disc diameter	239	9.4	mm	in
Disc thickness (new)	12	0.47	10	0.40
Disc thickness after machining (min)	10.5	0.41		
Pad thickness (new)	14	0.55	10	0.40

Rear brakes (drum)

	mm	in
Drum diameter	180	7.08
Drum diameter after machining (max)	181	7.13
Wheel cylinder diameter	14.29	0.56
Linings thickness:		
Rivetted	5	0.020
Bonded	4	0.016
Linings width	30	1.2

Rear brakes (drum with automatic adjuster)

	mm	in
Drum diameter	200	7.87
Drum diameter after machining (max)	201	7.92
Wheel cylinder diameter	14.29	0.56
Lining thickness:		
Rivetted	5	0.020
Bonded	4	0.016
Lining width	30	1.2

	mm	in
Master cylinder diameter	17.46	0.68
Master cylinder diameter (with servo)	20.64	0.81
Brake servo factor	2.12	
Master cylinder piston free-play	1	0.004

Wheels and tyres	Tyre size	Standard wheel	Offset (mm)	Tyre size	Optional wheel	Offset (mm)
Golf (with drum brakes)	5.95/145-13	4½J x 13	50	155 SR 13	4½J x 13	50
				175/70 SR 13	5J x 13	45
Golf (with disc brakes)	6.15/155-13	5J x 13	45	155SR 13	5J x 13	45
				175/70 S R13	5J x 13	45
Gold L, S, LS	155 SR 13	5J x 13	45	175/70 SR 13	5J x 13	45
Scirocco	155 SR 13	5J x 13	45	175/70 SR 13	5J x 13	45
Rabbit	155 SR 13	5J x 13	45			

Tyre pressures
Front and rear (all loads) ... ...   26 psi (1.8 bar)

Torque wrench settings

	mkg	lbs ft
Axle nut front brakes (drum and disc brakes)	24	174
Caliper to wheel bearing housing	6	43
Disc to hub	0.7	5
Splash plate to hub	0.8	6
Backplate to stub axle	3	22
Wheels to drums	9	65
Servo to adaptor	1	14
Master cylinder to servo	1.5	11
Brake hoses to caliper/wheel cylinder	1	7
Brake hoses to master cylinder	1	7

1 General description

1 The main braking system is operated hydraulically. The master cylinder is fitted with a servo-system on the 70 HP models. On automatic models a pressure limiter is fitted to the rear brakes. The system is fail/safe, with dual hydraulic systems connecting the brakes diagonally. If one system fails there still remain one front and one rear brake working on the other system. The out of balance on the steering caused by this is taken care of by the negative roll radius in the steering geometry.

2 Drum brakes are fitted to the rear axle, the more powerful models having self-adjusting shoes.

3 On some early models drum brakes were fitted to the front wheels, but the majority of the vehicles have disc brakes with floating Calipers. Two kinds of caliper may be found, those made by Girling, and those made by Teves.

4 The handbrake is cable operated, and applies the rear wheel brakes only. The balance bar is situated at the bottom of the handbrake lever.

5 The sequence of bleeding the brakes is:

1 Rear wheel right cylinder
2 Rear wheel left cylinder
3 Front right caliper or cylinder
4 Front left caliper or cylinder

When bleeding the brakes of a vehicle fitted with a pressure regulator the lever of the regulator should be pressed towards the rear axle.

2 Braking system - inspection

1 The braking system is such a tribute to design that most drivers are taken by surprise when it goes wrong. The way to avoid this unpleasant happening is by regular inspection and by understanding the symptoms of ailing brakes.

2 Many vehicles are fitted with self-adjusting rear brakes - which means that no active maintenance is required. For the few not so fitted a regular inspection of the shoes and adjustment as necessary is imperative. The handbrake will tell you when excessive wear is taking place. This is discussed in the Section on rear brakes. If the shoes of the front drum brakes are wearing unevenly the steering of the vehicle will be affected when braking. The drums must be removed to investiate the trouble.

3 The front discs are self-adjusting but again inspection does not entail much hard labour and may save not only a lot of money but also heartache. This operation is explained in the Section on front brakes.

4 The maintenance of pipes and hoses is also gone into at some length.

5 At the conclusion of this Chapter a fault diagnosis chart is included, but this only diagnoses trouble when it has happened, the smart operator gets busy before then.

6 The brakes should operate smoothly and consistently. Any variation in performance must be investigated and cured right away.

7 Pulling to one side or the other, however slight, means that all four brakes must be checked for adjustment forthwith. It only means jacking-up the vehicle and spinning each wheel in turn. Get someone to apply the footbrake gently and it is easy to find which wheel is at fault.

8 Loss of fluid from the header tank is serious. It is going somewhere it shouldn't and it is no use just topping-up and carrying on. Leaks at the front calipers or the various pipes can be spotted by just looking underneath the car. Leaks in the rear wheel cylinders may require removal of the drums before they can be located. This will apply to the front drum brakes too.

9 If the pedal goes much further down than usual when there are no leaks in the system and the brakes are properly adjusted then the trouble is at the master cylinder. **Do not** wait until it goes right down to the floor, there will not be any braking force at all then.

10 If the brakes drag, get hot, or even lock on then the trouble is probably either maladjustment of the connecting rod, or foreign matter clogging the compensating ports in the master cylinder. It may be as simple as something stopping the footbrake pedal from returning to its stop. It may be a problem in the servo which will not allow the master cylinder pushrod to return fully and so it is closing the compensating ports when they ought to be open.

If only one brake gets hot then that one should be dismantled checked and readjusted. If both rear brakes get hot then the handbrake may be malfunctioning (or you may have left it on of course, this happens to everyone at sometime or other).

Generally speaking slight overheating will not do too much damage, but it will eventually melt grease and cause oil seals to fail. It can crack discs or even drums if left too long.

11 Although the servo gives very little trouble, when it does it can be difficult to track down the problem. If the pedal does not go right down but very high pressure is needed to operate the brake then the servo vacuum has failed. This is discussed in Section 24 and should be tackled right away.

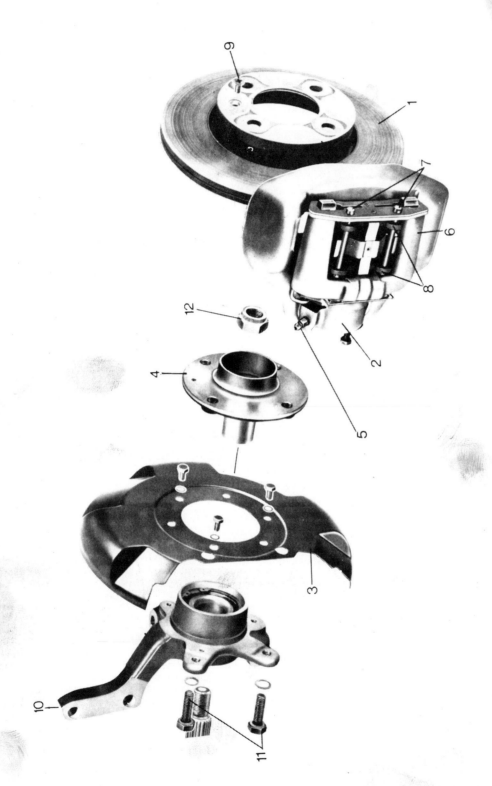

Fig. 9.1. Disc brake (Teves) - exploded view

1 Disc	4 Drive flange	7 Pins	9 Disc securing screw	11 Caliper fixing bolts
2 Floating caliper	5 Bleed screw	8 Brake pads under spreader	10 Wheel bearing housing	12 Axle nut
3 Splash plate	6 Fixed mounting			

12 Adjustment of rear brakes and the handbrake is discussed in Section 14. There is no adjustment for the front brakes.

13 Finally the question of 'sponginess' in the pedal. This is nearly always caused by air in the system. It can easily be cured by bleeding the brakes as discussed later on, but the worry is how did it get there. If having checked all the unions for leaks (and fluid at 800 lbs per square inch will come out of any small hole), and having bled the brake satisfactorily once, the sponginess returns then the next port of call is the official agent. It will be less expensive than the hospital!

3 Front disc brakes - general description

1 Two types of floating caliper are fitted. Those made by Teves, and after September 1974 those made by Girling may be installed. Refer to Fig. 9.2 to see the difference and 9.3 for detail of the Teves type.

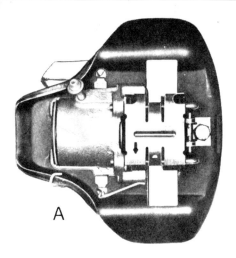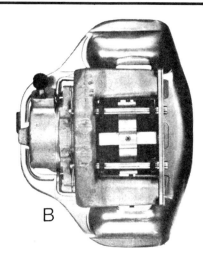

Fig. 9.2. Comparison of types of caliper fitted (Sec. 3)

A *Girling*   *Note the arrow on the spreader. This must point in the*
                  direction of rotation of the disc when the car moves forward.

B *Teves*

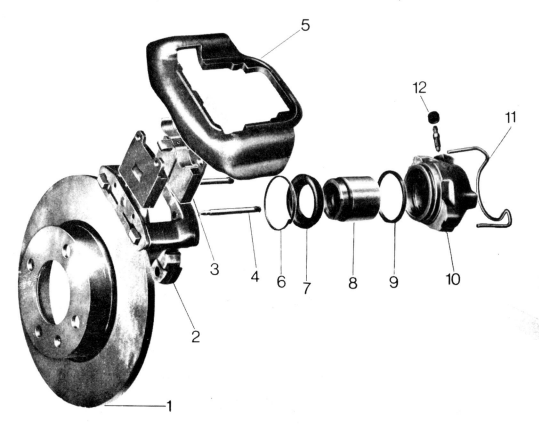

Fig. 9.3. Front disc brake (Teves) - exploded view (Secs. 3 and 6)

1 Disc	4 Pins	7 Dust cap	10 Cylinder
2 Mounting frame	5 Floating caliper	8 Piston	11 Guide spring
3 Brake pads	6 Retainer ring	9 Seal	12 Bleed nipple and cap

The Teves caliper has a fixed mounting frame bolted to the stub axle
and a floating frame held in position on the mounting frame and able to
slide on the mounting frame in a direction 90° to the face of the disc.
Fixed to the floating frame is a hydraulic cylinder with piston and seals.
The friction pads are held in the mounting frame by pins and a spreader
spring.

When the brake pedal is pressed the piston is forced against the
inner (direct) brake pad pushing it against the disc. The reaction causes
the floating frame to move away until the floating frame presses against
the outer (indirect) pad, pushing that one against the disc. Further
pressure holds the disc between the two pads.

2   The Girling, commonly known as the Girling A type single cylinder
caliper works on a different principle (refer to Fig. 9.4). The
cylinder is fixed to the stub axle and contains two pistons. The caliper
body which carries the pads is free to slide along grooves in the
cylinder body. One piston pushes the direct pad against the disc and
the other piston pushes the floating caliper so that the indirect pad is
forced against the disc.

3   Despite the obvious structural differences the two calipers are
interchangeable but must be changed as pairs (ie; two Teves or two
Girlings) but not one of each. In April 1975 a different type of hose
was fitted to the Girling caliper. The new hose is shorter and has a
left-hand thread. It has a groove machined all round the hexagon.
These hoses were installed on the Golf after Chassis 1753286959
and Scirocco 5352038023.

3   The same type of disc and pad was fitted to all models until
August 1975. Prior to this all models had discs 12 mm thick and pads
14 mm thick. After this date 1.1 litre models have discs 10 mm thick
and pads 10 mm thick.

4   Disc pads (Teves) - inspection and renewal

1   Brake pads wear much more quickly than drum brake linings. They
should be checked at least every 10,000 miles. The minimum lining
thickness is 1/8 in (3 mm). If the pads wear below this thickness then
damage to the disc may result. A badly worn pad is shown in the photo
and compared with a new one in the next photo. The dealer has a
gauge, tool VW/Audi 60-200, with which he can tell whether
replacement is required without taking the pads out. If this gauge is not
available then they must be removed for measurement.

2   The pads are different. The inner one is flat on both sides, the outer
one has a slot cut in its outer face (photo) which engages with a boss
on the caliper.

3   To remove the pads, jack-up the front of the car and remove the
wheels. Using a suitable drift tap out the pins (photo) securing the disc
pads. On some cars there may be a wire securing clip fitted round these
pins. This should be pulled off. If there is no clip the pins will have
sleeves.

4   Remove the spreader and pull out the inner, direct pad. If you are
going to put the pads back then they must be marked so that they go
back in the same place. Use a piece of wire with a hook on the end to
pull the pad out. Now lever the caliper over so that there is space
between the disc and the outer pad, ease the pad away from the caliper
onto the disc and lift it out.

5   Clean out the pad holder and check that the rubber dust cover is not
damaged. Insert the outer pad and fit it over the projection on the
caliper (photo). It will be necessary to push the piston in to insert the
inner pad. This will cause the header tank to overflow unless action is

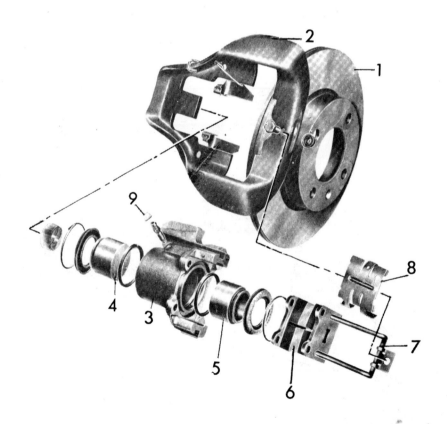

Fig. 9.4. Front disc brake (Girling) - exploded view (Secs. 3 and 7)

1 Disc	4 Piston pushing caliper	7 Pin
2 Floating caliper	5 Piston pushing brake pad	8 Spreader
3 Cylinder	6 Brake pads	9 Bleed screw and cap

4.1a This pad was worn well below the limit

4.1b Badly worn pad compared with new one

4.2 The back of the pad showing the slot

4.3 Tap out the pins and remove the spreader

4.5 Install the outer pad

4.6a View of empty caliper showing piston projection

4.6b Check the angle of the piston projections

4.7a Insert the inner pad. 'A' is the bleed nipple

4.7b Refit the spreader and pins. Install a new locking wire

taken to prevent it. Either draw some fluid out of the tank with a pipette or slacken the bleeder screw (see photo 4.7a). We prefer the first method but do not suck the fluid out with a syphon. It is poisonous. Use a pipette that has been used for brake fluid only, not the battery hydrometer.

6   Push the piston in and check that the angle of the edges of the raised face of the piston are at 20° to the face of the caliper (photo). Make a gauge out of cardboard as shown in the photo. If the angle is more or less turn the piston until the angle is correct.

7   Insert the inner pad (photo) fit the spreader and install the pins (photo). Fit a new locking wire if the type of pin requires it.

8   Do not forget to shut the bleed screw if it was opened as soon as the piston has been forced back. We do not like this method because there is a chance of air entering the cylinder and we do not like spare brake fluid about on the caliper while working on the friction pads.

10 Work the footbrake a few times to settle the pistons. Now repeat the job for the other wheel.

11 Replace the roadwheels, lower to the ground and take the car for a test run.

5 Disc pads (Girling) - inspection and renewal

1   In general, the method is the same as for the Teves caliper with the following differences.

2   Lever off the pad spreader spring with a screwdriver, and **pull** out the pins with pliers after removing the screw which locks them in position.

3   Remove and replace the pads as with the Teves caliper. Install the pins and the locking screw. A repair kit for brake pads will include new pins and retainer so use them.

4   The pad spreader spring is pressed on. The arrow must point in the direction of rotation of the disc when the car is travelling forward.

6 Calipers, pistons and seals (Teves) - removal, inspection and renewal

1   Support the front of the car on stands and remove the wheels.

2   If it is intended to dismantle the caliper then the brake hoses must

be removed, plugged and tied out of the way.

3   Mark the position of the brake pads and remove them (Section 4), if the caliper is to be dismantled.

4   Remove the two bolts holding the caliper to the stub axle (photo). This should not be done while the caliper is hot.

5   Withdraw the caliper from the car and take it to a bench.

6   Refer to Fig. 9.3. A repair kit should be purchased for the overhaul of the caliper.

7   Ease the floating frame away from the mounting frame. Now press the brake cylinder and guide spring off the floating frame. The cylinder may now be dismantled.

8   Remove the retaining ring and the rubber boot. The next problem is to remove the piston which is probably stuck in the piston seal. The obvious way is to blow it out using air pressure in the hole which normally accommodates the hydraulic pressure hose. However, be careful. The piston may be stuck in the seal but when it does come out it will come quickly. Fit the cylinder in a vice with a piece of wood arranged to act as a stop for the piston. If you do not, as most people do not, have a ready supply of compressed air use a foot pump. If it will not come out that way then a trip to the local garage is indicated.

9   When the piston is out of the cylinder clean carefully the bore of the cylinder and the piston with brake fluid or methylated spirits.

10 It is difficult to define wear on the piston. When it has been cleaned it should have a mirror finish. Scratches or dull sections indicate wear. The inside of the bore must be clean with no scratches or distortion. If there is any doubt replace the whole unit. In any case replace the seal and dust excluder. Dip the cylinder in clean brake fluid. Coat the piston and seal with brake cylinder paste (ATE) and press the piston and seal into the cylinder. Use a vice with soft jaws. Install new dust excluder and its retaining ring. Fit a new locating spring and knock the cylinder onto the floating frame with a brass drift.

11 Refit the floating frame to the mounting frame and set the piston recess at an inclination of 20° to the lower guide surface of the caliper (where the pad rests).

12 Bolt the mounting frame onto the stub axle and install the pads. Refit the wheel and lower to the ground.

7   Calipers, pistons and seals (Girling) - removal, inspection and renewal

1   Refer to Fig. 9.4. The general rules for overhaul are the same as for the Teves but the complication of the extra piston is more work.

2   Remove the cylinder and floating mounting from the stub axle and press them apart. Again use compressed air to dislodge the pistons and be careful that they do not come out suddenly. Clean the pistons and bore carefully. Use a Girling kit of seals and parts. Wash the cylinder and pistons with clean brake fluid and reassemble.

3   In this case the pistons and cylinder are bolted to the front

6.4 The bolts holding the calipers are marked with arrows A

suspension. The caliper sliding frame must move easily over the cylinder casting. Torque the holding bolts to 6 mkg (43 lb ft).

8   Disc pad wear indicators - general

1   From September 1974 a built in method of indicating to the driver that the brake pads require renewing is installed on vehicles going to USA and certain other countries. Refer to Fig. 9.5 and 9.6. The chamfer, arrow 'B', on both sides of the disc has a lug about 25 mm (1 in) long flush with the face of the disc. The pads have a thin extension piece on the bottom which is coated with wear resistant material. When the pads are worn to the limit the extension on the pad makes contact with the lug in the disc. This causes to vibrate and the piston to oscillate a small amount, producing a vibration or pulse effect at the foot pedal. Pad replacement is then a matter of urgency. Discs and brake pads of this type may be service installed to vehicles not so

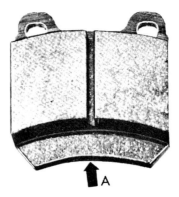

Fig. 9.5. Brake pad wear indicator - special brake pad (Sec. 8)

A points to the extension

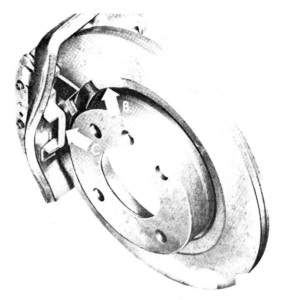

Fig. 9.6. Brake pad wear indicator - lug on disc (Sec. 8)

B points to the lug on the disc.
C is the reinforcement to be fitted to Teves calipers

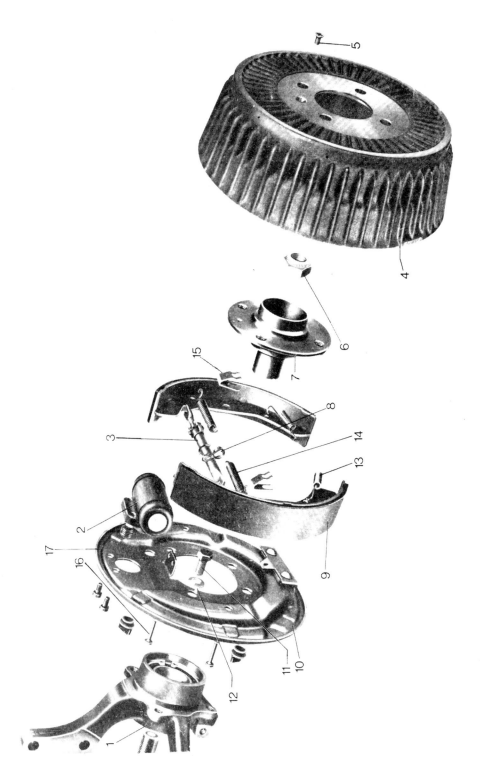

Fig. 9.7. Front drum brake - exploded view (Secs. 11 and 12)

1 Wheel housing
2 Hydraulic cylinder
3 Push rod

4 Brake drum
5 Securing screw
6 Axle nut

7 Hub
9 Brake shoes
10 Backplate

11 Securing screw
12 Double wave washer
13 Securing spring lower

14 Securing spring upper
15 Steady pin clip
16 Steady pin
17 Bleed nipple

fitted. However, although no further modification is required to Girling caliper an additional support (arrowed 'C') must be installed on Teves calipers.

9 Front disc brakes - squeaking pads

If the pads squeal or squeak excessively relief from this problem may be obtained by removing and cleaning the pads and holders and then applying a substance known as 'Plastilube'. This substance must not be applied to friction surfaces but to the ends, sides and back of the pad. It should also be applied to the pins and spreader and the sliding surfaces of the floating caliper.

10 Discs - removal, replacement and overhaul

1   Two thicknesses of discs are found, 12 mm and 10 mm. The discs are not interchangeable.
2   The discs may be removed and machined if scored until the thickness reaches a minimum of 8.5 mm (0.33 in) or 10.5 mm (0.41 in). The maximum run-out allowable is 1 mm (0.004 in). Variation of thickness is 0.02 mm (0.001 in) maximum.
3   Removal is quite simple. Remove the pads and calipers but do not disconnect the hydraulic hose. Hang the calipers out of the way.
4   The disc is held to the hub by one small screw. Remove this and the disc may be drawn off the hub for servicing.
5   If the vehicle has been left for a while and the discs have rusted seriously they can be salvaged by the agent without removing them from the vehicle. Special polishing blocks can be inserted in place of the pads and the wheels driven to polish the discs.
6   Machining the discs is a job which should be left to a specialist in a machine shop. It may be cheaper to buy a new disc. If a new disc is fitted then new pads should be installed, the old ones will have worn unevenly.
7   If one side is serviced then look at the situation on the other wheel. If the disc is in good condition fit a new set of pads or you will have problems later when the old pads wear.

11 Front drum brakes - general description

1   Refer to Fig. 9.7. The brake is considerably more powerful than the rear drum brake having a lining area of 358 sq cm as compared with the 223 sq cm of the larger rear brake and the 189 sq cm of the smaller one. It is 40 mm wide compared with the rear brake 30 mm, and 230 mm diameter compared with the 200 and 180 mm of the rear brakes. One of the more obvious problems is that of heat dissipation, for nearly all braking energy is converted to heat, and for this reason the substantial front drums are ribbed.
2   To cope with the extra force required the wheel cylinder is 25.4 mm diameter as compared with the 14.29 mm of the rear brake. Disregarding brake pressure limiters it may be assumed that the pressure in the front wheel cylinders is the same as that in the rear ones. The force thrusting the shoes against the drum is pressure times area of the cylinder pistons, since the brakes are of similar construction the force in the front brakes must be approximately three times that of the rear wheel cylinders.
3   All of the foregoing is of academic interest only, what is important is that the braking effort of the front drums is of paramount importance to your safety and that these brakes must be serviced carefully and regularly. They are not self-adjusting and they are fitted to a hub which already has the problems of steering and power transmission. If, when working on them, you have any doubts about the correctness of what you are doing seek expert advice, do not just carry on and hope for the best.
2   Many vehicles having front drum brakes employ two hydraulic cylinders producing a two leading shoe brake but this one is the simple leading - trailing shoe version. The shoes are pivotted at the bottom and held to the pivots by coil springs. Initial setting of the linings against the drum is governed by a pushrod which is adjustable for length. The adjustment is achieved by screwing one half of the rod into the other half. The shoes are held against the adjuster by coil springs attached to the shoe and backplate. The shoes are forced against the drum by the pistons of the wheel cylinder which is bolted to the back plate. A special spring holds the adjuster rod from turning unless deliberate action is taken to move the adjuster wheel. In the

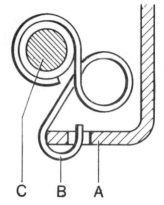

Fig. 9.8. Front drum brake: pushrod spring, installation position (Sec. 12)

A   Backplate   B   Spring   C   Pushrod

centre of each shoe is a steady pin secured by a clip. This prevents the shoe from moving across the face of the drum.
3   Operation is simple. When the brake pedal is depressed fluid pressure builds up in the hydraulic cylinder forcing the pistons out and pushing the shoes against the drum. When the pressure is released the return springs pull the shoes back against the adjuster rod.

12 Front drum brakes - removal, overhaul and reassembly

1   Jack-up the vehicle and set it on axle stands. Remove the front wheels. Undo the set scew holding the drum to the hub and remove the drum. Refer to Fig. 9.7. Unhook the lower return springs, remove the leaf springs from the steady pins, pull the shoes off the pivots and bring them forward so that they rest on the hub. Unhook the upper return springs and remove the shoes from the pushrod. Note how the pushrod spring is installed (Fig. 9.8). For overhaul of the shoes consult Section 17. For overhaul of the wheel cylinder consult Section 18.
2   The backplate may be removed only after removing the hub. (see Chapter 12). For adjusting the brakes see Section 14 and for bleeding the brakes, Section 27. Assembly is the reverse of removal.

13 Rear brakes - general description

1   Two types are found in the Golf/Scirocco/Rabbit range of cars. On the lower powered models and the Rabbit the 180 mm diameter drum, manually adjusted type, is fitted (refer to Fig. 9.9). A simple leading trailing shoe brake, wheel cylinder diameter 14.29 mm. The shoes are held against the connecting link by a 'U' spring. The shoes are adjusted manually through the hole in the backplate, as required. The more powerful models may be fitted with the 200 mm dia drum, self adjusting shoe, type of brake. Apart from the difference in size the construction of the brake is similar to the 180 mm type (refer to Fig. 9.10). The same diameter wheel cylinder is fitted but the 'U' spring is replaced by two coil springs and an adjusting lever is attached to the secondary or trailing shoe. When the brakes are operated and an appropriate amount of wear has taken place the adjusting lever moves the adjusting wheel on the connecting link due to the pull of the spring. The length of connecting link is thereby increased and the brake shoes automatically adjusted.

14 Drum brakes - adjustment (footbrake and handbrake)

1   The same method applies to front and rear drum brakes.
2   Locate the adjuster hole. It is just below the wheel cylinder and bleed screw. Remove the rubber plug from the hole.
3   Jack-up both wheels and set the vehicle on axle stands. Set the handbrake in the fully off position, if the rear drums are to be adjusted. If necessary, slacken the handbrake cable adjusting nuts.
4   Through the hole in the left-hand rear drum backplate a toothed

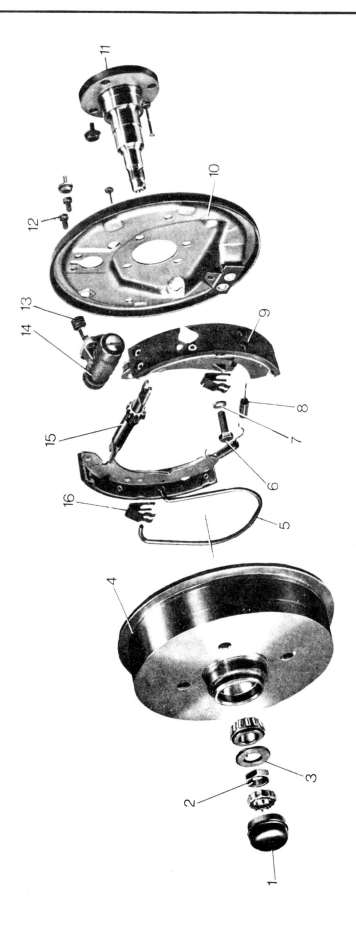

Fig. 9.9. Rear drum brake (180 mm diameter - manual adjuster) (Sec. 13)

1 Hub cap
2 Axle nut
3 Thrust washer
4 Brake drum

5 'U' spring
6 Bolt
7 Double wave washer
8 Retaining spring, lower

9 Brake shoe
10 Backplate
11 Stub axle
12 Wheel cylinder screw

13 Bleed nipple
14 Hydraulic cylinder
15 Pushrod
16 Steady pin leaf spring

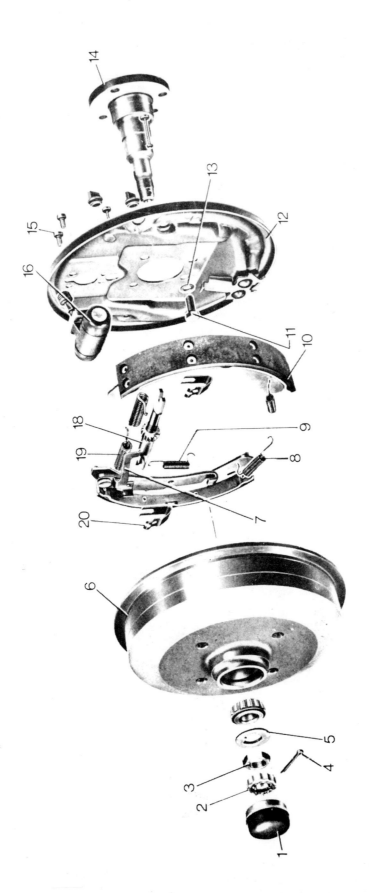

Fig. 9.10. Rear drum brake (200 mm diameter - self-adjusting) (Secs. 13 and 16)

1	Hub cap	5	Thrust washer	9	Adjuster arm spring	13	Double wave washer	17	Bleed nipple
2	Lock ring	6	Brake drum	10	Brake shoe	14	Stub axle	18	Pushrod
3	Axle nut	7	Adjusting arm	11	Bolt	15	Hydraulic cylinder screws	19	Retaining spring, upper
4	Split pin	8	Retaining spring lever	12	Backplate	16	Hydraulic cylinder	20	Leaf spring for steady pin

wheel is visible. Using a screwdriver (photo) lever the adjuster wheel teeth upwards (handle of the screwdriver down) until the lining binds on the drum. Now back off, (work the other way) until the wheel will rotate without the drum touching the shoes. Replace the plug.

5   Repeat on the other rear wheel but this time the adjuster works the other way, press the teeth downwards to contact the drum.

6   Adjustment on the front axle is in the same way. However, when backing the lining off from the drum turn the adjuster until the wheel may be turned by hand. A slight rubbing noise is permissible. Now turn the adjuster back two more teeth. This will make sure the front wheels turn freely even when the brakes are very hot.

7   Once the footbrakes are correctly adjusted the handbrake may be adjusted. Jack-up the rear wheels and set the vehicle on axle stands. Remove the handbrake lever boot. Refer to Fig. 9.16. The boot will require quite a bit of tugging to remove it. Pull the handbrake lever up two notches from fully off, or four notches if the vehicle is fitted with automatic brake adjusters. Tighten each of the adjuster nuts a little at a time keeping the equalizer bar level until neither of the rear wheels can be turned by hand. Release the handbrake lever and check that the rear wheels rotate freely. Tighten the locknuts. If the equalizer bar finishes up at an acute angle then one of the cables has stretched and must be replaced (see Section 31.)

15 Rear brakes (180 mm, manual adjustment) - removal and replacement

1   Slacken the wheel studs, jack-up the wheel and remove it. Support the vehicle on axle stands.

2   Take off the hub cap, remove the split pin and the locking cap. Undo the nut and pull the drum off the stub axle, the thrust washer and wheel bearing will come with it. Set the drum on one side for inspection (Section 17). The brake assembly is now exposed (photo). Remove the large 'U' spring (photo) and unhook the two springs at the bottom of the brake shoes. Take off the leaf springs from the steady pins (photo), and remove the shoes from the backplate. It will be necessary to unhook the handbrake cable to remove the shoes (photo).

This will leave the backplate clear (photo). The adjuster rod will come away with the shoes. The backplate may be removed if necessary with the stub axle by undoing the four bolts now accessible.

3   Overhaul of the shoes is dealt with in Section 16 and the wheel cylinder in Section 18.

4   Assembly is the reverse of removal. Fit the handbrake cable to the trailing shoe lever. This is a bit of a fiddle. The spring must be pulled back and held while the plunger is fitted. Actually we used a pair of blunt wire cutters to hold the spring once it was compressed, but be careful not to cut the cable. Once this is done put the shoes in place and fit the steady pins. Now install the bottom springs. Lever the shoes apart and install the adjuster rod. Finally fit the 'U' spring. Refit the drum and bearing, tighten the bearing correctly (Chapter 8) and then install the wheel. Adjust the brake shoes (Section 14).

16 Rear brakes (200 mm, automatic adjusters) - removal and replacement

1   Refer to Fig. 9.10. Proceed as in Section 15 up to the point where the drum is to be taken off. The automatic adjuster will have kept the lining right up to the drum and the adjuster must be turned through the hole in the backplate to slacken the linings back. Before this can be done the automatic adjuster lever must be pulled away from the gear. This is done by inserting a piece of wire with a hook on the end through a wheel bolt hole and pulling the lever back. You can see the approximate position from Fig. 9.10. Once the hook is in contact with the lever, the screwdriver through the hole in the backplate will tell you when the lever is clear of the gearwheel. Back the lining down enough to enable the drum to be withdrawn.

2   The method of dismantling is the same as detailed in Section 14 except that there is a pair of coil springs in place of the 'U' spring. A further coil spring holds the automatic adjuster rod in place.

3   Assembly is the reverse of removal. Hold the automatic adjuster lever away from the pushrod while doing the initial brake adjustment.

4   Tighten the axle nut to the correct setting (Chapter 8).

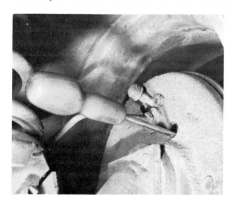

14.4 Using a screwdriver to adjust the rear brake

15.2a Once the drum is removed the brake looks like this

15.2b The brake shoe pivot at the bottom holds the lower shoe retaining springs and a clip for the handbrake cable

15.2c The leaf spring on the steady pin

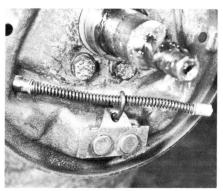

15.2d The handbrake cable inside the brake drum

15.2e The backplate

17 Brake shoes and drums - inspection and overhaul

1   Two types of shoe are fitted. The bonded lining does not have rivets. The new lining of the bonded type is 6.5 mm thick, 2.5 mm of shoe and 4 mm of lining. When the total thickness, lining plus shoe is reduced to 3.5 mm (0.134 in) the shoe must be replaced.

2   The rivetted type of lining is 7.5 mm thick (5 mm lining 2.5 mm shoe). The total thickness must be not be less than 5 mm (0.2 in) when measured with the shoe. The linings must be free from oil contamination have level, smooth surfaces and be free from scoring. If the existing shoes do not fulfil these conditions then new linings are required.

3   The four linings on the rear axle must be renewed simultaneously. It is not recommended that D-I-Y owners attempt to fit linings to the old shoes. It is much better to obtain replacement shoes which have been rivetted on in a jig and planished to a concentric radius.

4   Drums must be smooth and unscored. Any grooving or scoring must be machined away. There are two sizes of drum, the nominal 180 mm (7.08 in) drum must not be machined out to a diameter greater than 181 mm (7.13 in). The 200 mm (7.87 in) drum limit is 201 mm (7.92 in).

5   Inspect the drum for cracks, and ovality. Machining is a job for the specialist.

18 Wheel cylinders - dismantling, overhaul and reassembly

1   The wheel cylinder is fastened to the backplate by two screws. (photo) It may be removed only after the brake shoes are lifted away from it. It is not necessary to dismantle the shoes from the backplate.

2   Disconnect the hydraulic hose from the cylinder and plug the hose. The screws holding the cylinder to the plate may be difficult to extract. Brake fluid is a good penetrating oil so moisten the threads with a little fluid.

3   The front wheel cylinder is 25.4 mm diameter inside the bore. That of the rear cylinder is 14.29 mm. An exploded view of the rear wheel cylinder is shown at Fig. 9.11

4   To dismantle remove the dust caps and blow the pistons out with compressed air. Be careful when doing this that the pistons do not come out too quickly. Muffle the cylinder with a large piece of rag.

5   Wash the bores and pistons with clean brake fluid and examine for mirror finish and scratches. If there is any blemish discard the complete unit and fit a new one. Always fit new seals and dust caps. Coat them with a little brake paste before installing and make sure the seals are the right way round.

19 Master cylinder and servo - general description

1   The master cylinder and header tank together with the servo mechanism if fitted, stoplight and fail safe light switches are mounted in the engine compartment just in front of the brake pedal (photo).

2   This is a welcome change from other VW arrangements as the mud and water do not reach this all important item. Furthermore the pushrod operating the master cylinder is short and accessible (photo).

3   The master cylinder for vehicles without servo mechanism is 17.46 mm (0.687 in) diameter. It is illustrated in Fig. 9.13.

4   The master cylinder for vehicles with servo mechanism is 20.64 mm (0.813 in) diameter. It is illustrated in Fig. 9.14.

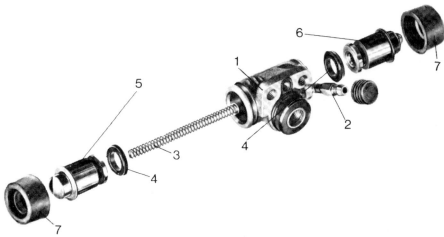

**Fig. 9.11. Drum brake rear hydraulic wheel cylinder - exploded view
(Sec. 18)**

1   Cylinder
2   Bleed screw
3   Spring
4   Seal
5   Piston
6   Piston
7   Dust cap

18.1 The wheel cylinder is bolted to the backplate

19.1 The master cylinder and header tank

19.2 The brake pedal and pushrod

155

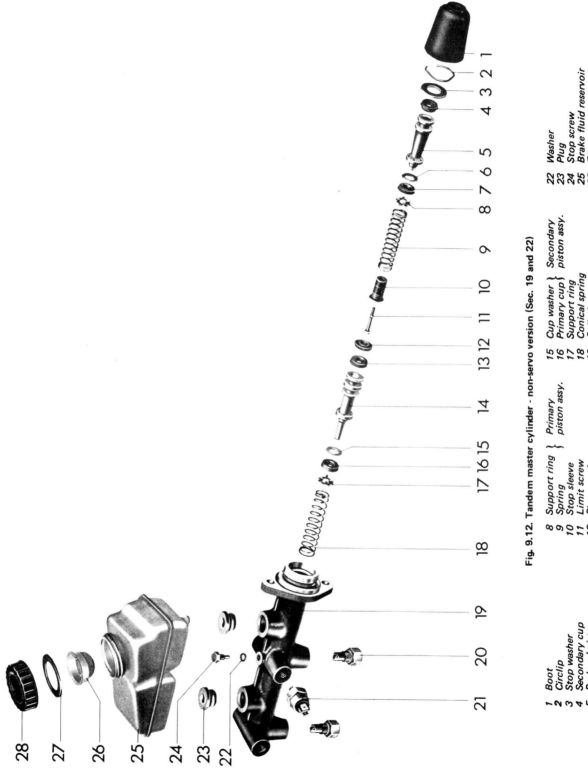

Fig. 9.12. Tandem master cylinder - non-servo version (Sec. 19 and 22)

1   Boot
2   Circlip
3   Stop washer
4   Secondary cup
5   Pushrod piston } Primary
6   Cup washer   } piston assy.
7   Primary cup

8   Support ring } Primary
9   Spring   } piston assy.
10   Stop sleeve
11   Limit screw
12   Piston seal
13   Piston seal
14   Secondary piston   S.p.a.

15   Cup washer } Secondary
16   Primary cup } piston assy.
17   Support ring
18   Conical spring
19   Cylinder
20   Residual pressure valve
21   Stop light switch

22   Washer
23   Plug
24   Stop screw
25   Brake fluid reservoir
26   Filter
27   Washer
28   Cap

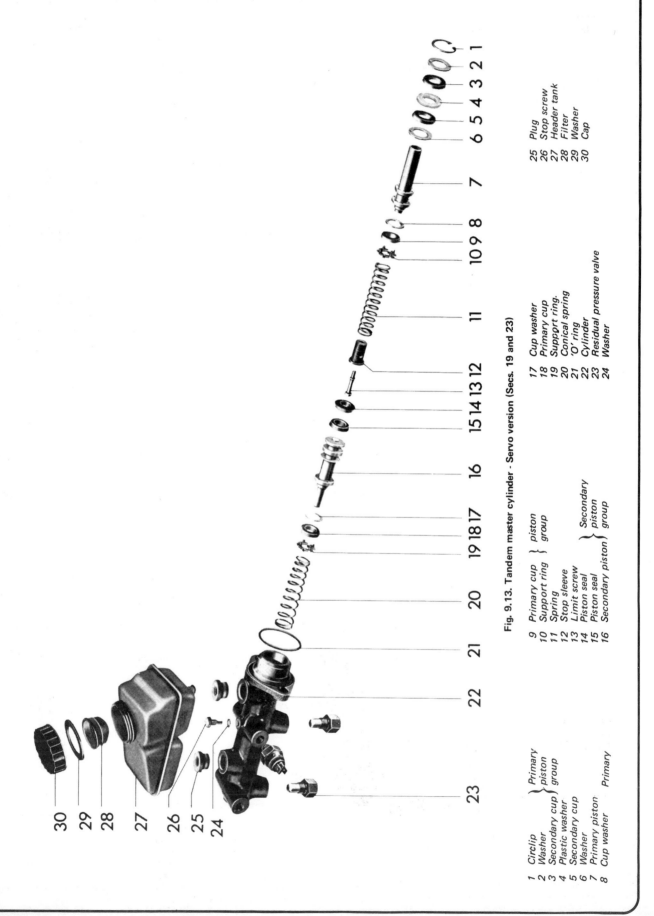

Fig. 9.13. Tandem master cylinder - Servo version (Secs. 19 and 23)

1   Circlip   ⎫ Primary
2   Washer   ⎬ piston
3   Secondary cup   ⎭ group
4   Plastic washer
5   Secondary cup
6   Washer
7   Primary piston   ⎫ Primary
8   Cup washer

9   Primary cup   ⎫ piston
10   Support ring   ⎬ group
11   Spring
12   Stop sleeve
13   Limit screw
14   Piston seal   ⎫ Secondary
15   Piston seal   ⎬ piston
16   Secondary piston   ⎭ group

17   Cup washer
18   Primary cup
19   Support ring.
20   Conical spring
21   'O' ring
22   Cylinder
23   Residual pressure valve
24   Washer

25   Plug
26   Stop screw
27   Header tank
28   Filter
29   Washer
30   Cap

20 Brake hydraulic system - description of operation

1   The master cylinder has two pistons, the front or secondary supplying pressure to the left-hand front wheel and the right-hand rear wheel. The rear, or primary, piston supplies pressure to the right-hand front wheel and the left-hand rear wheel. Inspection of the unit will show four pipes leading from the main casting to the hydraulic wheel cylinders.

2   Brake fluid is supplied from the header tank, the white plastic container which feeds both circuits through the master cylinder.

3   When the brake pedal is pressed the pushrod moves the primary piston forward so that it covers the port to the header tank. Further movement causes pressure to build up between the two pistons exerting pressure on the secondary piston which also moves forward covering the port to the header tank. The pressure now builds up in the pipes. The pipes are joined to the cylinder via unions containing residual pressure valves.

4   If the pipes of the secondary piston circuit fracture or the system fails in some way the secondary piston will move forward to the end of the piston compressing the conical spring and sealing the outlet port to the left front and right rear brakes. The primary piston circuit will continue to operate.

5   Failure of the primary piston circuit causes the piston to move forward until the stop sleeve contacts the secondary piston and the primary piston simultaneously when pressure will again be applied to the secondary piston circuit.

6   The various springs and seals are designed to keep the pistons in the right place when the system is not under pressure.

7   Pressure switches, are screwed into the cylinder body which operate the brake stoplights and warning lamps.

21 Master cylinder - removal, replacement and pushrod adjustment

1   Depending upon whether a servo unit is fitted or not the cylinder may be removed, after disconnecting the pipes and switches - marking them for easy replacement, either by undoing the nuts from the bolts connecting it to the servo unit, or by unbolting the cylinder from the bulkhead bracket. It will be necessary to hold the bolts from inside the car.

2   When replacing the cylinder to the servo unit, fit a new 'O' ring and bolt the cylinder to the servo unit. Connect up pipes and wires and bleed the system.

3   If no servo is fitted, then it may be necessary to adjust the free travel of the pushrod after bolting the unit in place and connecting up. The brake pedal is attached to the pushrod by a yoke which has a locking nut. Slacken off the locking nut and rotate the pushrod until a clearance (free travel) of approximately 2 to 4 mm (1/8 in) can be measured at the foot pedal pad.

4   If, for some reason, both servo and master cylinder have been removed the adjustment of the pushrod is a little different. Install the servo unit and the master cylinder. Remove the pin that secures the yoke to the brake pedal, slacken the locknut and with the pedal in the normal off position turn the pushrod until the yoke pin can be fitted between the yoke and pedal without moving the pedal. Replace the pin and tighten the locknut. The allowance is automatic in the servo unit.

22 Master cylinder (non-servo type) - dismantling, inspection and reassembly

1   Clean the outside of the cylinder carefully and set it on a clean bench. Work only with clean hands. Obtain an overhaul kit and a quantity of brake fluid in a clear jar. Refer to Fig. 9.13 for the cylinder without a servo mechanism.

2   Remove the header tank. Undo and remove the residual pressure valves and the brake light switch.

3   Remove the stop screw. Now remove the boot and the circlip may be levered out. With a little luck the contents of the cylinder will come sliding out of the bore if the cylinder is tilted. If they do not, apply gentle air pressure and blow them out. Take them out one at a time and lay them down in the order they should go back.

4   The front spring is slightly conical. The pistons may need new seals. These are not easy to fit. The VW mechanics use a special taper mandrel which just fits on the ends of the piston and ease the seal on over the taper. Assemble the two pistons with their groups of parts.

5   Examine the bore of the cylinder. If it is scored or rusty the cylinder must be renewed. It is possible to hone out slight marks if you can find someone with the right tools, but our advice is to fit a new one.

6   Wash out all passageways and holes with clean brake fluid, hold the cylinder vertical and install the complete secondary piston from underneath. If you do it any other way the bits will fall off.

7   Now install the primary piston, stop washer and circlip. Fit the stop screw. It may be necessary to move the secondary piston to fit the stop screw fully.

8   Fit the residual pressure valves, boot and install the brake fluid reservoirs. Refit to the car.

23 Master cylinder (servo type) - dismantling, inspection and reassembly

1   Refer to Fig. 9.14 and read Section 22. It will be seen that apart from the bore diameter there is little difference between the cylinders. The end of the cylinder is shaped differently to fit on the servo and there is an extra 'O' ring. The primary piston differs slightly and there is no rubber boot.

2   Dismantling, inspection and reassembly are as in Section 22. When the unit is complete it is installed onto the servo unit.

24 Servo unit - testing, repair, removal and replacement

1   If the brakes seem to need more or less pressure than normal a check of the servo is indicated.

2   First of all trace the hoses and check their condition. There must be no leaks or obstructions.

3   Check the vacuum check valve. This is to be found in the vacuum line between the induction manifold and the servo. Remove it from the hose line and clean it carefully. There is an arrow on the valve. Blow into the valve in the direction of the arrow, the valve should open. Blow in the opposite direction and the valve must seat. The valve is there to stop pressure from the manifold eg; a backfire, arriving in the vacuum side of the servo, ie; it is a non-return valve, so that the induction suction can only suck, and not blow.

4   If all of the above are correct and the servo is still not assisting the brakes the trouble is either a leaky servo diaphragm or something wrong with the master cylinder. Check that the sealing ring between the master cylinder and the servo is not leaking.

5   If the pedal pressure increases only at a certain position each time then there may be wear in the master cylinder pushrod allowing air to get into the vacuum side of the servo. This will only be on elderly brake cylinders, and it is time the master cylinder was overhauled.

6   The repairs possible to the servo are very limited. Refer to Fig. 9.14. The 'O' ring between the servo and the master cylinder should always be replaced with a new one when the units are separated. At the rear end of the servo the seals for the brackets should be renewed when the units are dismantled.

The cap damping washer may be removed from the sleeve and renewed, note that the slots in the damping washer and filter should be offset 180° on reassembly.

Apart from this the unit cannot be serviced further as it is sealed. Be careful when assembling the servo to the bracket not to tighten the nuts to torque greater than 9 lb ft (1.3 mkg) or damage to the case may occur and the servo must be scrapped.

7   To remove the servo, first remove the master cylinder from the servo. Plug the hydraulic lines, if disconnected. Remove the hoses from the servo. Undo the clevis pin at the brake pedal (photo 19.2), and disconnect the stirrup. Now remove the three nuts securing the servo to the bracket and take the servo away (see Fig. 9.14).

9   Assembly is the reverse of removal. When assembled bleed the brake system and adjust the brake pushrod.

25 Brake pressure regulator - description

1   This device is fitted to limit the hydraulic pressure in the rear wheel hydraulic cylinders and so limit the braking force. In effect it should stop the rear wheels being locked solid by the brakes and so avoid skidding.

2   It is fitted just in front of the rear axle, to which it is attached by

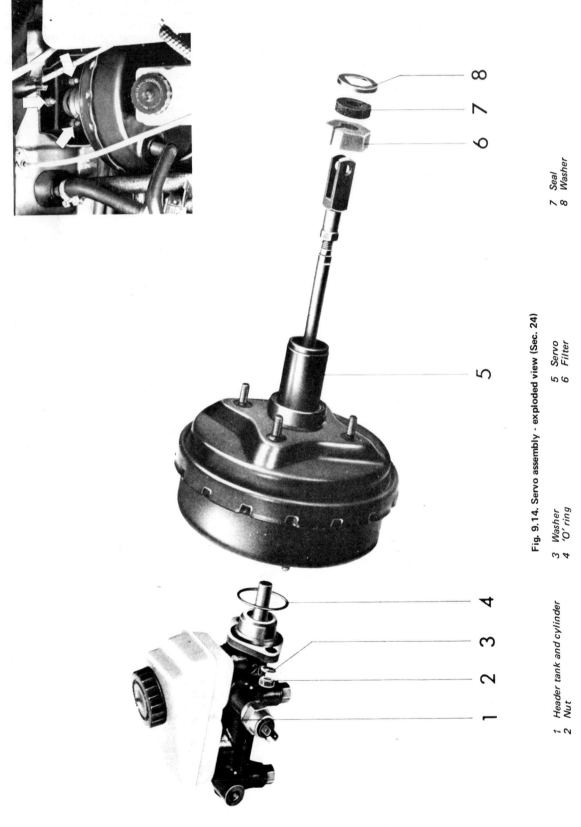

Fig. 9.14. Servo assembly - exploded view (Sec. 24)

1 Header tank and cylinder
2 Nut

3 Washer
4 'O' ring

5 Servo
6 Filter

7 Seal
8 Washer

Inset: Bracket - fixing nuts are arrowed.

a spring. When the brakes are applied sharply the front of the vehicle sinks and the rear rises a little. This causes the rear axle beam to pivot slightly in its mountings and the pressure on the spring is reduced a little. This enables a spring inside the valve to restrict the pressure available to the rear brakes.

3 It is necessary to position the vehicle body accurately and then to measure the pressures at the front and rear brake bleed nipples when the brakes are applied sharply, and then to adjust the tension in the spring between the regulator and the rear axle beam so that the correct pressures are obtained.

4 This requires special equipment to set the position of the rear suspension springs, and meters to measure up to 1420 psi.

5 The job must be left to the agent to do. Inaccurate setting will result in rear wheel skids of uncomfortable proportions.

26 Hydraulic pipes and hoses - inspection and renewal

1 The magnitude of the pressure in the hydraulic lines is not generally realized. The test pressures are 1420 lbs per square inch (100 kg sq cm) for the front brakes.

These pressures are with the braking system cold. The temperature rise in the drums and discs for an emergency stop from 60 mph is as much as 80°C (176°F), and during a long descent may reach 400°C (752°F). The pressure must be even further raised as the temperature of the brake fluid in the cylinder rises.

The normal pressure in the hydraulic system when the brakes are not in use is negligible. The pressure builds up quickly when the brakes are applied and remains until the pedal is released. Each driver will know how quickly the build up is when equating it to the speed of his own reaction in an emergency brake application.

2 Recent research in the USA has shown that brake line corrosion may be expected to lead to failure after only 90 days exposure to salt spray such as is thrown up when salt is used to melt ice or snow. This in effect makes a four year old vehicle automatically suspect. It is possible to use pipe made of a copper alloy used in marine work called 'Kunifer 10' as a replacement. This is much more resistant to salt corrosion, but as yet it is not a standard fitting.

3 All this should by now have indicated that pipes need regular inspection. The obvious times are in the autumn before the winter conditions set in, and in the spring to see what damage has been done.

4 Trace the routes of all the rigid pipes and wash or brush away accumulated dirt. If the pipes are obviously covered with some sort of underseal compound do not disturb the underseal. Examine for signs of kinks or dents which could have been caused by flying stones. Any instances of this means that the pipe section should be renewed, but before actually taking it out read the rest of this Section. Any unprotected sections of pipe which show signs of corrosion or pitting on the outer surface must also be considered for renewal.

5 Flexible hoses, running to each of the front wheels and from the underbody to each rear wheel should shoe no external signs of chafing or cracking. Move them about to see whether surface cracks appear. If they feel stiff and inflexible or are twisted they are nearing the end of their useful life. If in any doubt renew the hoses. Make sure also that they are not rubbing against the bodywork.

6 Before attempting to remove a pipe for renewal it is important to be sure that you have a replacement source of supply within reach if you do not wish to be kept off the road for too long. Pipes are often damaged on removal. If an official agency is near you may be reasonably sure that the correct pipes and unions are available. If not, check first that your local garage has the necessary equipment for making up the pipes and has the correct metric thread pipe unions available. The same goes for flexible hoses.

7 Where the couplings from rigid to flexible pipes are made there are support brackets and the flexible pipe is held in place by a 'U' clip which engages in a groove in the union. The male union screws into it. Before getting the spanners on, soak the unions in penetrating fluid as there is always some rust or corrosion binding the threads. Whilst this is soaking in, place a piece of plastic film under the fluid reservoir cap to minimise loss of fluid from the disconnected pipes. Hold the hexagon on the flexible pipe coupling whilst the union on the rigid pipe is undone. Then pull out the clip to release both pipes from the bracket. For flexible hose removal this procedure will be needed at both ends. For a rigid pipe the other end will only involve unscrewing the union from a cylinder or connector. When you are renewing a flexible hose, take care not to damage the unions of the pipes that connect into it. If

a union is particularly stubborn be prepared to renew the rigid pipe as well. This is quite often the case if you are forced to use open ended spanners. It may be worth spending a little money on a special pipe union spanner which is like a ring spanner with a piece cut out to enable it to go round the tube.

8 If you are having the new pipe made up, take the old one along to check that the unions and pipe flaring at the ends are identical.

9 Replacement of the hoses or pipes is a reversal of the removal procedure. Precautions and care are needed to make sure that the unions are correctly lined up to prevent cross threading. This may mean bending the pipe a little where a rigid pipe goes into a fixture. Such bending must not, under any circumstances, be too acute or the pipe will kink and weaken.

10 When fitting flexible hoses take care not to twist them. This can happen when the unions are finally tightened unless a spanner is used to hold the end of the flexible hose and prevent twisting.

11 If a pipe is removed or a union slackened so that air can get into the system then the system must be bled. This is discussed in Section 27 of this Chapter.

27 Brake hydraulic system - bleeding

1 First locate the bleed nipples on all four brakes. The rear wheel bleed nipples are at the back of the drum at the centre of the hydraulic cylinder (photo). A small dust cap covers the nipple. This will probably be covered with mud. Clean the mud from the back of the drum, wipe the dust cap and the area around it with a clean rag and the operation may start.

The front disc brake bleed nipples are on the inside surface of the caliper (photo).

When all four wheels have been cleaned sufficiently sweep up the mud and then wash your hands, this is a job where cleanliness pays.

2 As fluid is to be pumped out of the system make sure you have plenty of new clean fluid. It must conform to SAE recommendation J1703, J1703R but better still, get the official VW fluid. If the wrong fluid is used the whole system may become useless through failure of piston seals. Top-up the header tank generously, and keep topping it up at intervals throughout the whole job.

3 Start with the rear right-hand wheel. A piece of rubber or plastic hose 5/32 in. (4 mm) inside diameter and about two feet (600 mm) long is required. Fit this over the bleed nipple and immerse the other end in a jar or bottle with about 4 inches of clean brake fluid in it. Fix the hose so that the end of it cannot come out of the brake fluid, and stand the bottle on the ground in a secure place.

4 You will need a helper whose job is to depress the brake pedal when requested. It is as well to rehearse the operation before opening the bleed nipple valve. Open the valve about one turn and depress the pedal slowly to the floor of the vehicle. As soon as it is on the floor close the bleed valve **before** the pedal is released. Now release the pedal slowly. Brake fluid and air bubbles should have passed down the tube into the bottle. Repeat the operation until no further air bubbles are observed. Make the final tightening at the end of the last down-stroke. Check the header tank level after every two strokes and top-up if necessary.

5 When you are satisfied that the rear right-hand brake line is clear of air bubbles then wipe down the brake and proceed to the next task; in order left rear, right front caliper, left front caliper.

6 After each session clean down the brakes with care and wash your hands. Brake fluid is poisonous and it is a splendid paint remover. Use a soapy solution and wash any paintwork that has been splashed.

7 Finally, the brake fluid in the jar or bottle should be discarded. This is not too easy. I bury mine three spits deep - bubbles and all.

28 Brake hydraulic system - changing fluid

1 The brake fluid is hygroscopic, which means that allowed to come into contact with the open air will absorb moisture. If it does then when the brakes get hot the water will boil and the brakes will not work properly - at the moment they are needed most.

2 VW recommend that the fluid should be changed every two years - they give a variety of reasons - but the fact that they do recommend it should be reason enough.

3 The change over is simple to do. First of all clean the rear drums, particularly by the bleed nipples, and give the front calipers the same treatment.

27.1a The bleed nipple (A) on the rear drum

27.1b The bleed nipple, cap removed, on the caliper

4   Connect all four bleed nipples to plastic pipe and suitable containers, then open all four bleed nipples and get a helper to pump the brake pedal until no further fluid comes out.
5   Close the nipples, fill the system with clean brake fluid and then bleed the system as in Section 27.

29 Tyres - selection, inspection and maintenance

1   These can be an expensive problem if neglected. The most important matter is to keep them inflated at the correct pressure. A table of pressures is given at the start of the Chapter.
    If the vehicle is driven over rough ground, or over glass in the road the tread should be inspected to see whether stones or glass fragments are lodged in the tread. These should be removed forthwith.
2   A careful study of the tread once a week will pay dividends. Tyres should wear evenly right across the tread but they rarely do, they are usually replaced because of misuse. A table is given showing some of the main troubles. Study it and watch your tyre treads.

Wear description	Probable cause
Rapid wear of the centre of the tread all round the circumference	*Tyre overinflated.*
Rapid wear at both edges of the tread, wear even all round the circumference	*Tyre underinflated.*
Wear on one edge of the tyre *(a) Front wheels only* *(b) Rear wheels only*	*Steering geometry needs checking.* *Check rear suspension for damage.*
Scalloped edges, wear at the edge at regular spacing around the tyre	*Maybe wheel out of balance, or more likely wear on the wheel bearing housing or steering balljoint*
Flat or rough patches on the tread	*Caused by harsh braking.* *Check the brake adjustment.*
Cuts and abrasions on the wall of the tyre	*Usually done by running into the kerb.*

3   If the tyre wall is damaged the tyre should be removed from the wheel to see whether the inside of the cover is also damaged. If not the dealer may be able to repair the damage.
4   Tyres are best renewed in pairs, putting the new ones on the front and the older ones on the rear. Do not carry a badly worn spare type, and remember to keep the spare properly inflated.
5   The Specification to this Chapter gives the recommended grade of

tyre to fit the wheels for each model. We suggest you keep to this recommendation. However, if you wish to alter the arrangement there are two golden rules to remember:
    a) Do not fit a radial and a crossply on the same axle. In many countries this is illegal, and it ought to be in the others. The braking characteristics are different and you will be inviting an accident which the insurance company will rightly refuse to pay for.
    b) If you have two radials and two crossplys, the radials MUST be on the rear wheels. This again is bound up with braking characteristics and if you have them the other way the insurance company will be equally obdurate.
6   It is really best to stick to the original choice, but if you must change then change all five together (yes, even the spare).

30 Wheels - inspection and balancing

1   Tyres and wheels should be balanced dynamically when new tyres are fitted. Mark the position of the balance weights and note the size of them. They have been known to fly off. This will affect the steering in the case of the front wheel.
2   If you suspect a wheel is out of balance, jack-up that wheel and spin it gently. Mark the bottom position when it comes to rest. Spin it several times more and note the bottom position each time. If the wheel comes to rest in the same position each time then the wheel and tyre are definitely out of balance and should be taken for balancing. It is best to do this test with the wheel on the rear axle where it may spin more freely.
3   Even though the wheel may be balanced statically (as in paragraph 2) it may still be out of balance dynamically. The only way to check for certain is to have it tested by a specialist.
4   A table of wheels fitted to various models is given in the Specification. If a new wheel is to be purchased it must match the other four. The two types are shown in Fig. 9.15.
5   There are two simple checks to do on the wheel:
    a) Jack the wheel off the ground and spin the wheel. Place a heavy weight so that it almost touches the rim and watch the clearance between the weight and rim as the wheel spins to see that the rim is not distorted.
    b) Examine the holes through which the fixing bolts are fitted. If the bolts are allowed to get loose while the car is in service these holes may be elongated. Check the rim for cracks between bolt holes.

31 Handbrake - removal and replacement

1   Adjustment of the handbrake is discussed in Section 14. If the footbrake is working properly then adjust the handbrake only.
2   To remove the lever the plastic boot must be removed from the brake lever (photo). Refer to Fig.9.16. Slacken off the locking nut and

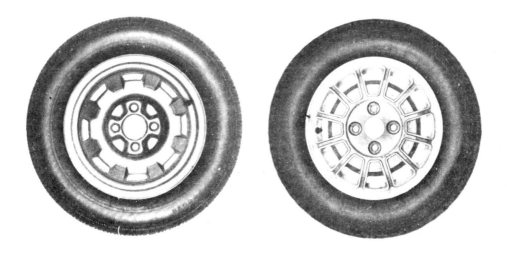

Fig. 9.15. Road wheels (Sec. 30)

(left): standard steel wheel, (right): optional alloy wheel

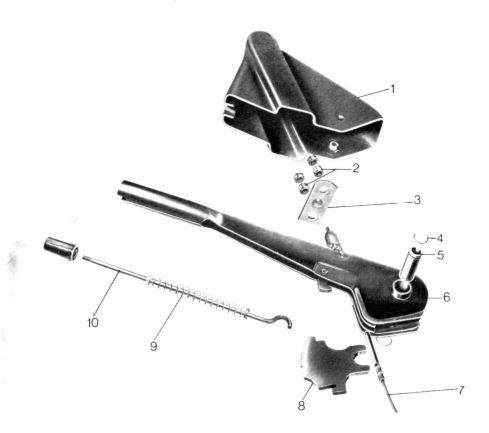

Fig. 9.16. Handbrake lever - exploded view (Secs. 14 and 31)

1	Boot	4	Circlip	7	Cable	10	Ratchet rod
2	Adjusting nuts	5	Pivot pin	8	Quadrant
3	Equalizer bar	6	Brake lever	9	Ratchet spring

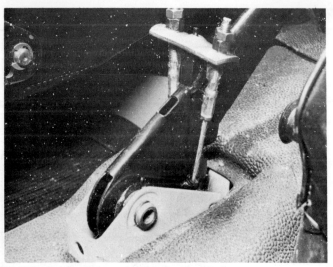

31.2 The handbrake lever showing the equalizer bar

31.3 The old pattern of handbrake cable. This has been replaced by a simple wire clip on later models

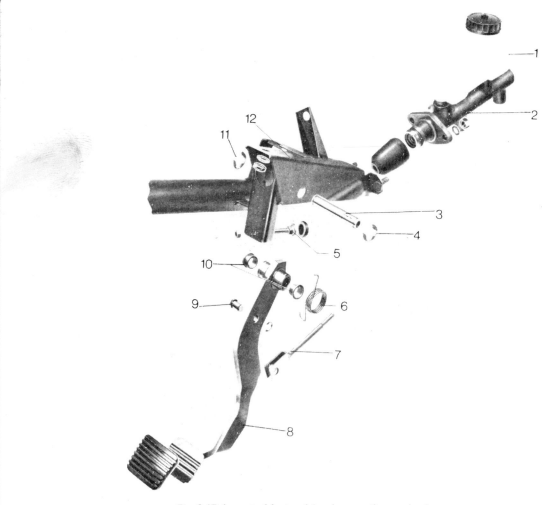

Fig. 9.17. Layout of foot pedal and connecting mechanism - non-servo type (Sec. 32)

1	Brake fluid reservoir	7	Pushrod
2	Master cylinder	8	Pedal
3	Pedal pivot pin	9	Pushrod pivot pin
4	Circlip	10	Pedal bushes
5	Pedal stop	11	Circlip
6	Return spring	12	Bracket

remove it and the adjusting nut from each cable. Lift off the equalizer bar. Remove the circlip from the pivot pin and push the pin out of the housing. The lever with the quadrant will now come out leaving the cables in place.

3   The cable runs through the sheath under the car, through the clip (photo) to the rear brake. It is necessary to remove the brake drum and shoe to unhook it from the lever on the shoe. It must then be extracted from the sheath and a new one inserted.

32 Brake pedals - description and modifications

1   The original pedal arrangements are shown in Fig. 9.17 and 9.18. Adjustment for the non-servo type system is given in Section 21. It will be seen on the servo type pedal an adjustable stop is fitted. Having adjusted the pedal as in Section 21 the stop is then screwed out until it just touches the lever, and locked in this position.

Fig. 9.18. Layout of foot pedal and connecting mechanism - servo-assisted type (Sec. 32)

1	Brake fluid reservoir and master cylinder	6	Bushes
2	Servo	7	Circlip
3	Bracket	8	Return spring
4	Pushrod stirrup	9	Pedal
5	Pivot pin	10	Bracket
		11	Pivot pin

2   In July 1975 a modified pedal was fitted. The distance from the centre of the pivot pin to the pushrod pin centre was decreased from 47 mm to 42.5 mm to give greater leverage. At the same time a wedge shaped plate is fitted on the master cylinder anchorage to align the pushrod with the piston. The new pedal may now be installed in older vehicles. The new pedal is not fitted to vehicles with servo mechanisms.

3   In August 1975 yet another modified pedal and pushrod were fitted. The **42.5 mm dimension** was decreased further to 41 mm and the bracket for the pedal moved forward to give more leg room. The distance from the pivot to the mounting face of the bracket was decreased from 120 mm to 100 mm. A new, shorter, pushrod is used, and a different method of securing the pivot pin.

4   Operation and adjustment are not affected but care must be taken when ordering spares as the parts are not interchangeable.

33 Fault diagnosis - braking system

Before diagnosing faults in the brake system check that irregularities are not caused by any of the following faults:

    1   Incorrect mix of radial and crossply tyres
    2   Incorrect tyre pressures
    3   Wear in the steering mechanism, suspension or shock absorbers
    4   Misalignment of the bodyframe

Symptom	Reason/s	Remedy
Pedal travels a long way before the brakes operate	Seized adjuster on rear shoes or shoes require adjustment	Check, repair and adjust.
	Disc pads worn past limit	Inspect and renew as necessary.
Stopping ability poor, pedal pressure firm	Linings, pads, discs or drums worn, contaminated, or wrong type	Renew pads, linings, discs and drums as necessary.
	One or more caliper piston or rear wheel hydraulic cylinder seized	Inspect and repair as necessary.
	Loss of vacuum in servo	Test servo.
Car veers to one side when brakes are applied	Brake pads on one side contaminated with oil	Remove and renew. Repair source of oil leakage.
	Hydraulic pistons in calipers seized or sticking	Overhaul caliper.
	Wrong pads fitted	Install correct pads.
Pedal feels spongy when brakes are applied	Air in the hydraulic system	Bleed brakes and check for signs of leakage. Top-up header tank.
	Spring weak in master cylinder	Repair master cylinder.
Pedal travels right down with no resistance	Fluid reservoir empty	Check refill and bleed all brakes.
	Hydraulic lines fractured	Trace through and replace as necessary.
	Seals in master cylinder head failed	Dismantle cylinder and rebuild with new seals.
Brakes overheat or bind when car is in motion	Compensating port in master cylinder blocked	Rebuild cylinder.
	Reservoir air vent blocked	Clean vent.
	Pushrod requires adjustment	Adjust.
	Brake shoes return springs broken or strained	Replace.
	Caliper piston seals swollen	Replace.
	Unsuitable brake fluid	Drain and rebuild system.
Brakes judder or chatter and tend to grab	Linings worn	Replace.
	Drums out of round	Replace.
	Dirt in drums or calipers	Clean.
	Discs run-out of true excessive	Replace.
Brake shoes squeak (rear brakes)	Dirt in linings	Clean.
	Backplates distorted	Fit new backplates.
	Brake shoe return springs broken or distorted	Fit new springs.
	Brake linings badly worn	Fit new linings.
Disc pads squeak (front brakes)	Wrong type of pad fitted	Fit new pads.
	Pad guide surfaces dirty	Clean.
	Spreader spring deficient or broken	Fit new spring.
	Pads glazed	Fit new pads.
	Lining on pad not secure	Fit new pads.
Foot pedal must be pressed harder in one position only	Groove in master cylinder pushrod due to wear at sealing cups. Air entering vacuum side of servo	Rebuild master cylinder, new pushrod required.
Very high pedal pressure required to operate brakes, linings found to be in good condition and correctly adjusted	Servo has failed	Check hoses are tight and vacuum check valve is working. If so, then remove and service servo. If necessary fit a new one.
Calipers rattle on poor road surface	Fit stronger locating spring	Spring part No. 171 615 169/70. This is fitted to Golf after chassis 1753029049 and Scirocco 5342012440.

Chapter 10 Electrical system Part I:
Starting and generating systems

Contents

Specifications

Generating system	AC generator with built-in rectification and voltage controller. Belt driven from the crankshaft pulley. Two makes used, Bosch and Motorola
Voltage	12V

Generator

Type	Rotating field with stator windings for output current. Rectification by diodes in the endplate

Maximum output:

Golf	35 amp
Rabbit and Scirrocco	55 amp

Stator winding resistance:

	35 amp	**55 amp**
Bosch	0.25 ohms + 0.025	0.14 ohms + 0.014
Motorola	0.23 to 0.25 ohms	0.15 to 0.17 ohms

Rotor winding resistance:

Bosch	3.4 to 3.7 ohms
Motorola	3.9 to 4.3 ohms
Slip rings, max. ovality	0.03 mm (0.001 inches)
Bearings	Prepacked ball races

Brushes:

Protrusion new	10 mm (0.4 inches)
Protrusion minimum	5 mm (0.2 inches)

Regulator	Transistorised. Bosch EE 14VS Part No. 0 192 052 004

Starter motor

Type	12V DC. Solenoid operated pinion drive with over-run clutch
Load current (max.)	Approx. 200 amps

Output (HP):

Manual transmission	0.7
Automatic transmission	0.8
Brush length (minimum)	13 mm (0.5 inches)
Commutator (min. diameter)	38.5 mm (1.52 inches)
Armature axial-play	0.1 to 0.15 mm (0.004 to 0.006 in)

Battery

Type	Lead acid 12V with centre tapping for computor analysis. Negative earth

Capacity (amp. hr.): *

Golf and Golf L	27
Golf S and Golf L.S.	36
Scirrocco	54
Rabbit	45
Rabbit with air conditioner	54

* Note: The larger capacity battery may be fitted as an optional extra.

1 General description

1   Two makes of generator may be found, the more usual one a Bosch, and on later models a Motorola. Both are similar in construction and have the same output with the same drive arrangements. Both types are shown in exploded diagrams (Figs. 10.5 and 10.11).
2   The 1.1 litre engine is fitted with a 35 amp generator, the 1.5 litre with a 55 amp generator. The main difference between them is in the stator windings which cause the larger output generator to have a slightly longer stator body.
3   Both generators are driven by Vee-belts from the crankshaft, but whereas on the 1.5 litre model the belt also drives the water pump, on the 1.1 litre type the water pump is driven by the timing belt and the Vee-belt drives only the generator.
4   The generator is mounted on the left front side of the engine. The method of mounting is different for each type but the principle is the same. Belt tension is adjusted by moving the alternator about a hinge bolt and fastening it in position with a clamp.
5   Rectification is done by a group of diodes mounted in a heat sink in the end plate of the generator.
6   A transistorized voltage regulator is an integral part of the alternator and carries the brush gear. The brushes may be replaced when worn below the minimum limit. The regulator with brushes may be easily removed without removing the generator from the engine. Connection to the wiring harness is by a multipin plug. An earth strap is fitted to the generator, the method being different in the case of the Motorola and Bosch. A condenser for radio interference suppression is fitted to the back face of the generator.
7   The battery is mounted on the left of the engine compartment and has a negative earth strap.
8   Two types of starter motor are fitted. For all models with manual transmission a Bosch E.F.12 is mounted on the right-hand rear of the engine. The rear bearing of the motor armature is carried in the clutch bellhousing. The motor fitted to the automatic transmission vehicles is slightly more powerful and has a larger armature. This is to cope with the higher starting torque required by the torque converter, especially in cold weather. It has a different pinion so be careful when ordering spares.

2 Battery - removal and replacement

1   The battery is mounted on the left-hand side at the front of the engine compartment (photo). Remove the earth strap (negative) and the positive cable terminal. The battery is held in position by a clamp which fits over a rim at the base. A 13 mm socket spanner, preferably with an extension is necessary to undo the clamp nut.
2   Lift the battery out and clean the battery platform. Any sign of corrosion should be neutralized with an alkali solution. Ammonia or ordinary baking powder will do the job. If the corrosion has reached the metal, scrape the paint away to give a bright surface and repaint right away.
3   Installation is the reverse. Smear the terminals with a little petroleum jelly (vaseline). **Do not** use grease.

3 Battery - maintenance and inspection

1   Normal weekly battery maintenance consists of checking the electrolyte level of each cell to ensure that the separators are covered by ¼ inch of electrolyte. If the level has fallen, top up the battery using distilled water only. Do not overfill. If a battery is overfilled or any electrolyte spilled, immediately wipe away the excess as electrolyte attacks and corrodes any metal it comes into contact with very rapidly.
2   As well as keeping the terminals clean and covered with petroleum jelly, the top of the battery, and especially the top of the cells, should be kept clean and dry. This helps prevent corrosion and ensures that the battery does not become partially discharged by leakage through dampness and dirt. If topping up the battery becomes excessive but the case has been inspected for cracks that could cause leakage, but none are found, the battery is being over-charged and the regulator should be checked.
3   When removing the battery be careful not to strain the terminal posts. If these are twisted too much they may cause the plates inside to move with consequent battery failure.

2.1 The battery is on the left-hand side of the engine compartment

4   With the battery on the bench at the three monthly interval check, measure its specific gravity with a hydrometer to determine the state of charge and condition of electrolyte. There should be very little variation between the different cells and if a variation in excess of 0.025 is present it will be due to either:

   a) *Loss of electrolyte from the battery at some time caused by spillage or a leak, resulting in a drop in the specific gravity of electrolyte when the deficiency was replaced with distilled water instead of fresh electrolyte.*
   b) *An internal short circuit caused by buckling of the plates or a similar malady pointing to the likelihood of total battery failure in the near future.*

5   The correct readings for the electrolyte specific gravity at various states of charge and conditions are:

	Temperate	Tropical
Fully charged	*1.285*	*1.23*
Half charged	*1.20*	*1.14*
Discharged	*1.12*	*1.08*

6   The hydrometer is a glass tube tapered at one end and fitted with a rubber bulb at the other end. Inside it there is a float.
   The tapered end of the tube is inserted into the filler hole of the cell to be tested and the bulb squeezed. When it is released acid is drawn into the tube. Enough must be drawn to allow the float to float freely.
   The float has a scale on it and where the surface of the acid meets the float is the point to be read on the scale.
7   It is rare indeed for a battery to freeze but it can happen. If the battery is discharged and the specific gravity is low it may happen more easily. It will not happen while the engine is running so the first intimation will be a refusal to start, for a frozen battery will not supply current. Remembering that there is a solid lump of acid take care how it is handled. It must be thawed slowly. If it can be removed from the car so much the better but if it is frozen in any attempt to remove it by force will break the case. Indeed, the case may have split due to the expansion of the electrolyte so watch carefully as it does thaw or there may be an acid leak of considerable proportions which will do a lot of damage. If this happens take the battery out of the car as quickly as possible, but wear rubber gloves, to avoid being burned.
   If the battery thaws out and no leaks appear then it will be of use again. However, check the specific gravity and charge if necessary.
   For interest value, acid at specific gravity 1.120 (ie; the battery is flat) will freeze at 12°F (−11°C), at 1.200 S.G. at −17°F (−27°C) and a fully charged battery at 1.285 is safe until −68°F (−90°C), so keep the battery well charged in cold weather, and if you do have to leave the car in a snowdrift get the battery out before it freezes.
8   If the battery loses its charge repeatedly then it is probably sulphated or damaged internally. First check the specific gravity of each cell. If some are high (1.285) and the odd one is lower then that is where the trouble lies. The S.G. throughout the six cells should not vary by more than 0.025.

The remaining test is a brutal one, which will probably kill an ageing battery anyway. It consists of short circuiting the battery through a "pair of tongs" equipped with a shunt and a voltmeter in such a way that a current of about 110 amps is passed for 5 to 10 seconds. The voltage between the terminals should not drop below 9.6 volts.

4 Battery - charging

1 In winter time when heavy demand is placed upon the battery such as when starting from cold and much electrical equipment is continually in use, it is a good idea occasionally to have the battery fully charged from an external source at the rate of 3.5 to 4 amps. Always disconnect it from the car electrical circuit when charging.

2 Continue to charge the battery at this rate until no further rise in specific gravity is noted over a four hour period.

3 Alternatively, a trickle charger, charging at the rate of 1.5 amps, can be safely used overnight. Disconnect the battery from the car electrical circuit before charging or you will damage the alternator.

4 Specially rapid 'boost' charges which are claimed to restore the power of the battery in 1 to 2 hours can cause damage to the battery plates through over-heating.

5 While charging the battery note that the temperature of the electrolyte should never exceed 100°F (37.8°C).

6 Make sure that your charging set and battery are set to the same voltage.

5 Battery - electrolyte replenishment

1 If the battery has been fully charged but one cell has a specific gravity of 0.025, or more, less than the others it is most likely that electrolyte has been lost from the cell at some time and the acid over diluted with distilled water when topping-up.

2 In this case remove some of the electrolyte with a pipette and top up with fresh electrolyte. It is best to get this done at the Service Station, for making your own electrolyte is messy, dangerous, and expensive for the small amount you need. If you must do it yourself add 1 part of sulphuric acid (concentrated) to 2.5 parts of water. **Add the acid to the water**, not the other way round or the mixture will spit back as water is added to acid and you will be badly burnt. Add the acid a drop at a time to the water.

Having added fresh electrolyte recharge and recheck the readings. In all probability this will cure the problem. If it does not then there is a short circuit somewhere.

3 Electrolyte must always be stored away from other fluids and should be locked up, not left about. If you have children this is even more important.

6 Alternator - safety precautions

1 The alternator has a negative earth circuit. Be careful not to connect the battery the wrong way or the alternator will be damaged.

2 **Do not** run the alternator with the output wire disconnected.

3 When welding is being done on the car the battery and the alternator output cable should be disconnected.

4 If the battery is to be charged in-situ both the leads of the battery should be disconnected, before the charging leads are connected to the battery.

5 Do not use temporary test connections which may short circuit accidentally. The fuses will not blow, the diodes will burn out.

6 When replacing a burnt out alternator clear the fault which caused the burn out first or a new alternator will be needed a second time.

7 Alternator (1.5 litre) - drivebelt adjustment

1 The alternator is driven by a belt from the crankshaft pulley. The belt also drives the water pump.

2 The alternator has two lugs on its casing. A bolt threaded through these is mounted in a bracket bolted to the cylinder block. This bolt forms the hinge on which the alternator is mounted. The head of the bolt is a hollow (socket) hexagon which is accessible through a hole in the timing belt cover. This bolt must be slackened before the alternator belt tension may be adjusted.

3 On the top of the alternator is yet another lug (photo), through which a bolt is fitted to a slotted strap. The strap is hinged on the cylinder block.

4 Thus the alternator may be rotated about the hinge bolt to tighten the drivebelt. The tension in the drivebelt is correct when the belt may be depressed with a thumb a distance of 3/8 in. (9.5 mm) halfway between the crankshaft and alternator pulleys. The bolts should be tightened to hold the alternator in this position.

5 It may be difficult to slacken the socket head bolt. In this case do not go on until the bolt hexagon is destroyed, do as we did, remove the strap, and then remove the bracket with alternator complete. Undo the wiring plug, remove the belt and then take the alternator away. The socket head bolt may then be held in a vice and undone that way.

8 Alternator (1.1 litre) - drivebelt adjustment

1 On the 1.1 litre engine the Vee-belt drives only the alternator. It is situated at the front left-hand side of the engine (photo).

2 To adjust the belt, slacken the hinge bolt a little. In this case it is the top bolt and will need a spanner on each end. Now slacken the bolt on the adjusting strap (photo). The head of the bolt is square and is held between lugs on the strap.

3 Lever the body of the alternator away from the cylinder block until the belt may be depressed with the thumb about 3/8 in. (9.5 mm) halfway between pulleys. Hold the alternator in this position and tighten the square-headed bolt, then tighten the hinge bolt.

4 On the later 1.1 litre engines a different method of holding the alternator has been installed. A rigid one-piece bracket holds the top hinge bolt and is fastened to the cylinder block with one bolt. This has not been completely satisfactory as if the tolerances between the alternator endplates are such that the alternator is not gripped firmly when the hinge bolt is tightened correctly, then the alternator can move on the bolt and a rattling noise will be produced when the engine is

7.3 The alternator mounted on the side of the engine (1.5 litre). Note the adjusting strap on the top of the alternator

8.1 The alternator on the 1.1 litre engine. The adjusting strap is below the alternator in this engine

8.2 The head of the bolt on the adjusting strap is square and held between lugs

running.

5 The cure for this is rather drastic. Refer to Fig. 10.1 which is a sketch of the bracket. Remove the bracket from the alternator and saw through the weld at the end of the bracket. Do not cut the plate. Refit the bracket using a stronger bolt in the hinge 8 mm x 80 which has VW part number N 10.378.2 and nut N 11.008.8. Tighten the hinge bolt to 3 mkg (22 lb ft).

9 Alternator - testing

1 There is a way of testing the alternator in the car, but it requires a lot of expensive equipment and does not provide much conclusive evidence. Refer to Fig. 10.2. The following are required. A battery cut-out switch, a variable resistance capable of consuming up to 500 watts, an ammeter reading 0-30 amps, a voltmeter reading 0-20v, and a tachometer.

2 The battery cut-out switch is illustrated in Fig. 10.3.

3 Connect up as shown in the diagram in the following manner. Disconnect the battery earth strap and the positive cable. Connect the cut-out switch to the battery positive terminal and then connect the car positive lead to the cut-out switch.

4 So far no interference with the normal circuit. Now arrange an alternative one to take the place of the battery. From the battery cut-out switch connect the variable resistance and ammeter in series to the chassis (earth) of the car. Arrange a voltmeter so that the volts drop between the battery cut-out switch and earth. Reconnect the battery earth strap. The following test figures are for both 35 amp and 55 amp alternators.

5 Start the engine and run it up to 2800 rpm. Set the variable resistance so that the ammeter reading is between 20 and 30 amps. Now open the battery cut-out switch, that is, cut the battery out of the circuit so that the current flows only through the resistance. Alter the resistance to bring the current back to 25 amps. Now read the voltmeter. It should read between 12.5 and 14.5 volts.

6 If the voltmeter reading is outside these limits close the cut-off

switch, stop the engine and replace the alternator regulator with a new one (or a borrowed one). Repeat the test. If the desired 12.5 to 14.5 volts is obtained then the old regulator was faulty. If not then the alternator is faulty and must be changed. It seems a lot to do for little reward but the only other way is to take the alternator to an official agent for testing.

10 Alternator (Bosch K.1 14v) - overhaul

1 The regulator is fitted into the alternator housing. Remove a small screw and it may be removed. Refer to Fig. 10.5.

2 Inside it will be seen the two slip ring brushes. These must be free in the guides and at least 5 mm (0.2 in) long. The new length is 10 mm (0.4 in). The brushes may be renewed by unsoldering the leads from the regulator, fitting new brushes and resoldering the leads (Fig. 10.4).

3 Undo the pulley nut and remove the pulley, the spacer ring, the large washer and the fan. Note which way the fan fits to make assembly easier. There is an arrow showing the direction of rotation.

4 Remove the bracket from the housing which held the wiring plug and if not already removed, take away the regulator (photo).

5 Undo the housing bolts and separate the components. The armature will stay in the endplate and the housing bearing will stay on the shaft (photo). Have a good look at the various components. Clean off all the dust using a soft brush and then wipe clean with trichlorethylene. Any smell of burnt carbon or signs of over-heating must be investigated. Check the slip-rings for burning scoring and ovality. You will have had reason to check the bearings before dismantling, but have a further look now. At this point you must make up your mind whether to do the repair yourself, or whether to take the alternator to a specialist. If you have the tools and the skill, it is possible to replace the bearings, replace the diode carrier complete, clean up the slip-rings and to fit a new rotor or stator. It is not possible to repair the winding, replace individual diodes, replace the slip-rings or repair the fan.

6 Dealing with the rotor first. The rotor may be removed from the endplate by using a mandrel press. Then take the screws out of the

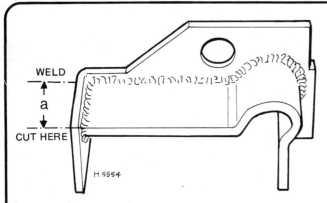

Fig. 10.1. Alternator mounting bracket (1.1 litre engine - later models) - modification to prevent rattle (Sec. 8)

Saw along the line of the weld marked 'a'.
Do not cut the back of the bracket

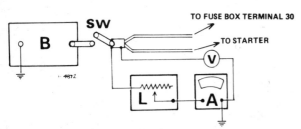

Fig. 10.2. Circuit diagram for testing alternator (Sec. 9)

B	Battery	A	Ammeter (0—30 amps)
SW	Battery cut-out switch	V	Voltmeter (0—20 volts)
L	Variable resistance (bad)		

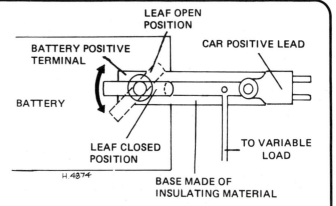

Fig. 10.3. Diagrammatic arrangement of the battery cut-out switch. VW recommend Sun electric No. 7052—003 (Sec. 9)

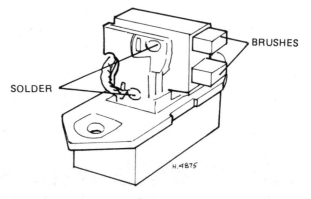

Fig. 10.4. Regulator with carbon brushes (Sec. 10)

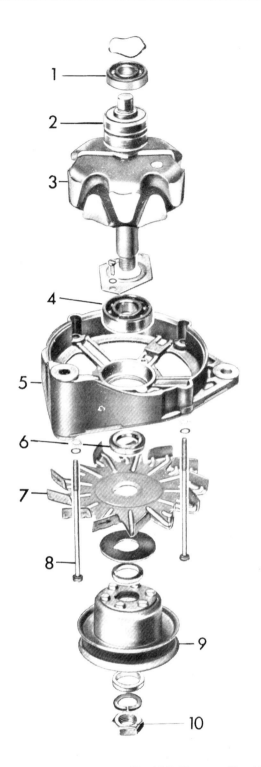
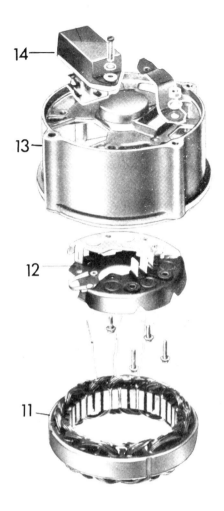

Fig. 10.5. Alternator (Bosch) - exploded view (Sec. 10)

1	Bearing	8	Through bolt
2	Slip rings	9	Pulley
3	Claw pole rotor with field windings	10	Nut
4	Bearing	11	Stator with windings
5	Endplate	13	Alternator housing
6	Spacer ring	14	Regulator with carbon brushes
7	Fan		

10.4 The regulator removed from the alternator

10.5 The alternator rotor in the housing removed from the stator

10.9 The diode plate showing the stator connections. The pencil points to one connection

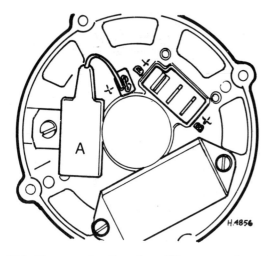

Fig. 10.6. Alternator - install condenser 'A' to prevent damage from surging (Sec. 10)

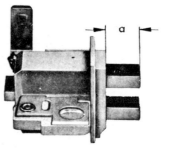

Fig. 10.7. Generator (Motorola) - brush gear (Sec. 11)

a) Brush length, new 9 mm, wear limit 5 mm

cover over the endplate bearing and press the bearing out of the frame. The slip-ring end bearing may be pulled off using an extractor on the inner race. If you pull on the outer race the bearing will be scrapped. Replace the bearings with new if necessary.

7   The slip-rings may be cleaned up by setting the rotor in a lathe and either cleaning them with emery or by taking a very fine skim.

8   Test the rotor electrically. Check the insulation resistance between the slip-rings and the shaft. This must be infinity. If it is not there is a short circuit and the armature must be replaced. Get an auto-electrical specialist to confirm your findings first. Check the resistance of the winding. Measure this between slip-rings. It should be about 4 ohms. If there is an open circuit or high resistance, then again the rotor must be renewed.

9   The stator and the diode carrier are connected by wires. Make a simple circuit diagram so that you know which wire goes to which diode and then unsolder the connections. This is a delicate business as excess heat will destroy the diode and possibly the winding. Grip the wire as close as possible to the soldered joint with a pair of long nosed pliers and use as small a soldering iron as possible (photo).

10 The stator winding may now be checked. First check that the insulation is sound. The resistance between the leads and the frame must be infinity. Next measure the resistance of the winding. It should be of the order of 1.3 ohms between leads. A zero reading means a short circuit, and of course a high or infinity reading, an open circuit.

11 The diode carrier may now be checked. Each diode should be checked in turn. Use a test lamp or an ohmmeter. Current must flow only one way; ie, the resistance measured one way must be high and the other way (reverse the leads), low. Keep the current down to 0.8 milliamps and do not allow the diode to heat up. If the resistance both ways is a high one, then the diode is open circuited, a low one, short circuited. Of only one diode is defective the whole assembly (diode plate) must be replaced.

12 Reconnect the stator winding to the diode circuit, again be careful

not to overheat the diode, and reassemble the stator and diode carrier to the housing.

13 A new diode carrier, or a new stator may be fitted, but be careful to get the correct parts.

14 Assembly is the reverse of dismantling. Be careful to assemble the various washers correctly.

15 It has been found that voltage surge in the electrical system damages the alternator diodes. If this happens when requesting repair of the diode plate ask for and install a condenser (part no. 059 035 271) to prevent this occurring again (Fig. 10.6).

11 Alternator (Motorola type) - overhaul

1   Refer to Figs. 10.8 and 10.11. It will be seen that although the construction is basically the same as the Bosch generator the Motorola differs considerably in detail.

2   The stator and rotor have the same form as those of the Bosch but the cover, housing and diode plate are of different construction. The earth strap is bolted to the cover, not the hinge as in the case of the Bosch.

3   The same principles apply for overhaul. The rotor should be checked for earth short circuit and continuity. The resistance between slip rings must agree with the Specification, ovality of slip rings must be within limits. Bearings may be drawn off with a puller and replaced if necessary.

4   The stator may be disconnected from the diode plate and the winding tested for open and short circuit. The resistance should agree with specification.

5   Once isolated the diode plate may be tested, as in Section 10, and a new one fitted if required. It is not recommended that any attempt be made to replace diodes.

6   The routing of the 'D+' wire inside the cover is important. It must be fitted in the two sets of clips provided or it will become involved with the armature.

7   The voltage regulator connections must be checked. The green wire goes to 'DF' and the red wire to 'D+' (see Fig. 10.10).

8   The connections on the cover must be checked carefully. A diagram is given for information.

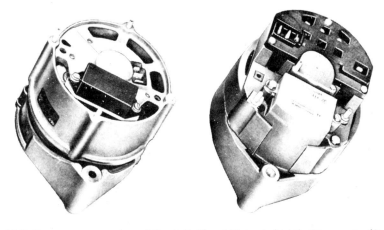

Fig. 10.8. Generator - comparison of Bosch (left) and Motorola (right), AC generator (Sec. 11)

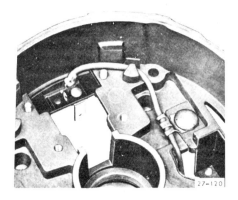

Fig. 10.9. Generator (Motorola) - routing of 'D+' (red wire) lead in the cover plate (Sec. 11)

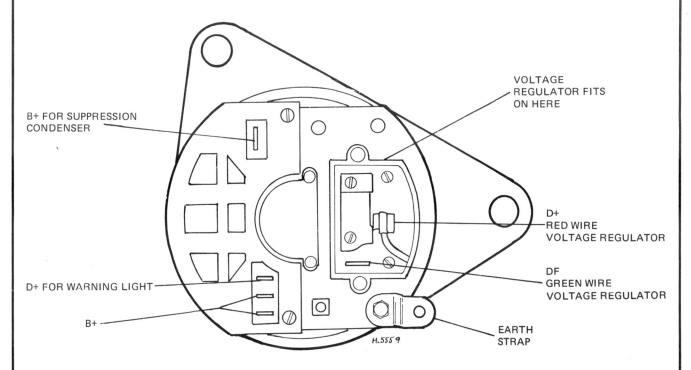

Fig. 10.10. Generator (Motorola) - diagrammatic view of endplate showing connections (Sec. 11)
Note voltage regulator has been removed to show 'DF' and 'D+'
(red wire)

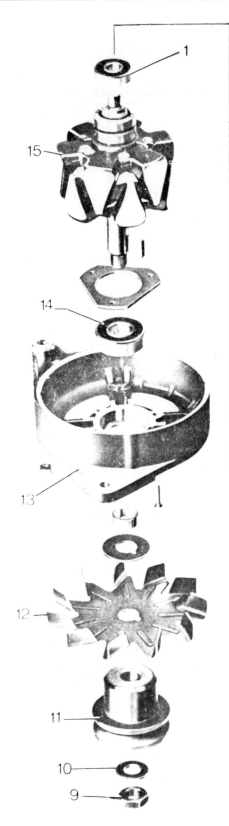
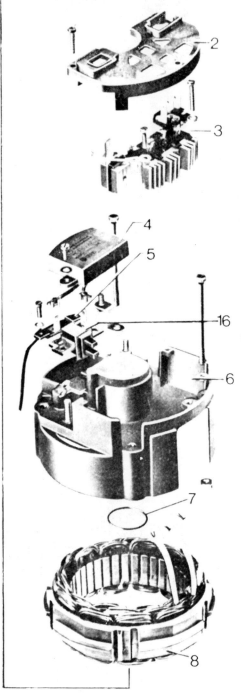

Fig. 10.11. Generator (Motorola) - exploded view (Sec. 11)

1	Armature ball bearing	5	Connector plate 'D+'	9	Nut	13	Endplate
2	Cover plate	6	Housing	10	Thrust washer	14	Bearing
3	Diode plate	7	'O' ring	11	Pulley	15	Rotor
4	Voltage regulator	8	Stator	12	Fan	16	Brush gear

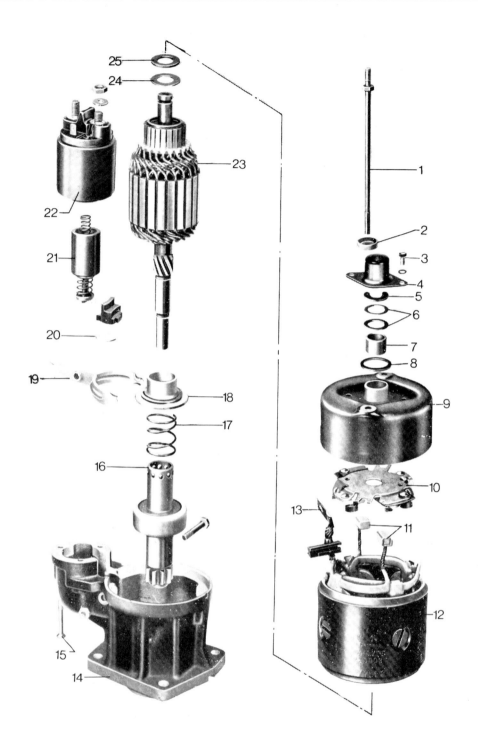

Fig. 10.12. Starter motor - exploded view (Sec. 14)

1	Housing screw (through bolt)	7	Bush	13	Terminal tag for solenoid (field winding)	19	Stirrup
2	Cupped washer	8	Washer			20	Disc (lug toward armature)
3	End cap screw	9	Housing	14	Mounting bracket	21	Solenoid plunger
4	End cap	10	Brush plate	15	Solenoid switch screw	22	Solenoid
5	Circlip	11	Brushes	16	Drive pinion	23	Armature
6	Shims	12	Stator	17	Spring	24	Shim
				18	Bush		

12 Starter motor - testing in car

1 The starter motor is bolted to the bellhousing. There are four connections to the solenoid (see photo). Terminal 'A' (terminal 50) goes to the ignition starter switch, 'B', (terminal 15a) goes to terminal 15 on the battery positive terminal direct.

2 If when the ignition is switched on the starter will not turn the engine over it does not necessarily mean the starter is at fault. So before taking the starter out a routine check should be done.

3 Check the state of charge of battery. Remove the leads from the battery terminals, clean the leads and terminals and reassemble correctly. The quickest way to check the battery is to switch on the headlights. If the lights come on brightly and stay bright then the battery is in good order. If the lights are dim, or come on bright and dim quickly then the battery is discharged. Remedy this state of affairs before dismantling the starter.

4 If the battery is in good order and the ground strap (earth lead) is firmly fixed to the chassis then turn to the starter connections. Are they tight, free from corrosion and water. On automatic transmission vehicles check that the starter cut-out switch is in good order (Chapter 7).

5 Get down by the starter and have someone operate the ignition switch. Does the solenoid work (make a clunking noise), if so disconnect the cable from terminal 30 and fit it to the connector strip terminal (D). If the starter now revolves when the ignition is switched on then the solenoid contacts are worn or faulty and the starter must be removed for overhaul.

6 If the starter still does not work, bridge terminals '30' and '50'. If the starter works then the fault is in the ignition switch wiring, not the starter.

7 If all the above tests have been done and there is still no life then the starter must be removed for test and overhaul.

8 If the starter turns the engine slowly, and the battery and connections are in good order then the starter should be removed for

testing and overhaul. It is probably brush or commutator trouble, or it may be problems with the field windings.

9 If the starter works erratically or will not disengage then the fault is a mechanical one, and the starter must be removed for overhaul.

10 Only after checking all these points should the starter be dismantled.

13 Starter motor - removal and replacement

1 Remove the battery earth strap. Disconnect the large lead from the starter and pull the leads off the two solenoid terminals '15a' and '50' noting which one goes where.

2 Remove the bolt holding the aluminium end-bracket to the cylinder block. Remove the bolts holding the starter mounting flange to the gearbox. Undo the nuts holding the end-bracket to the starter and remove the bracket. Replace these nuts hand-tight. Withdraw the starter from the engine (photo).

3 When replacing the starter care must be taken not to fit the end bracket in such a way as to strain the starter casting.

4 Insert the starter into the gearbox housing and fit the armature shaft into the rear bearing. Replace the flange nuts and bolts and tighten them to 1.6 mkg (11 lb ft). Fit the bracket on the end of the starter loosely with plain and spring washers and tighten the 5 mm nuts hand-tight. Now fit the 8 mm bolt to the bracket and tighten it to 1.6 mkg (11 lb ft). Check that the holes in the bracket which house the starter bolts have clearance all round. If they do not and the bracket is bearing on the starter through bolts, the bracket must be removed and the holes filed out until there is clearance. Tighten the 5 mm nuts to 4 lb ft (0.5 mkg). Reconnect the starter leads and replace the battery earth strap.

14 Starter motor - overhaul

1 Clean the exterior carefully and clean and oil the pinion and shaft (refer to Fig. 10.12).

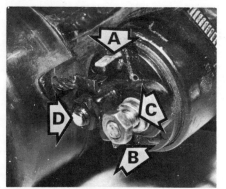

12.1 The starter and solenoid on the engine. Terminals 'A' to starter switch, 'B' to terminal '15', 'C' to battery, 'D' solenoid to starter field winding

13.1 Removing the starter

14.3a Remove the end cap ...

14.3b ... then the circlip and shims

14.4 Remove the through bolts. These must be sealed on assembly.

14.5 Lift off the brush plate. This commutator needs attention

14.19a Using two clips to hold the brush spring on assembly

14.19b The wire clip (A) fits under the brush spring so that the brush may be lifted easily to enter the plate over the commutator

2   Remove the connector strip terminal nut (D) and from the other end remove the two bolts holding the solenoid to the mounting bracket. Now lift the solenoid pull rod so that it is clear of the operating lever and remove the solenoid.

3   At the front end of the starter is a cap held by two screws. Remove this (photo) and under it there is a shaft with a circlip and bush. Remove the circlip (photo).

4   Now remove the through bolts (photo) and remove the cover.

5   The brush gear is now visible (photo). Lift the brushes out of the holder and remove the brush holder. The starter body holding the field coils may now be separated from the endplate. This will leave the armature still in the mounting bracket.

6   To remove the mounting bracket from the drive end of the shaft, first push back the stop ring with a suitable tube so that the circlip underneath may be released from its groove. It is now possible to remove the mounting bracket and pinion from the shaft.

7   Finally remove the operation lever pin from the mounting bracket and remove the pinion assembly.

8   Clean and examine the pinion, shaft and lever and inspect for wear. If possible run the armature between centres in a lathe and check that the shaft is not bent. Check the fit of the drive pinion on the shaft. Check that the pinion will revolve in one direction only (one way clutch) and that the teeth are not chipped.

9   Examine the commutator. Clean off the carbon with a rag soaked in petrol or trichlorethylene. Minor scoring may be removed with fine emery paper. Deep scoring must be removed by machining in a lathe. Commutator copper is harder than the commercial grade, and requires the lathe tool to be ground differently. Unless you have had instruction on machining commutators we suggest that the skimming and under-cutting be left to the expert. The minimum diameter for the commutator is 1.358 in (34.5 mm).

10 Test the armature electrically. Check the insulation between the armature winding and the shaft. To do this connect the negative terminal of the ohmmeter to the shaft and place the positive probe on each commutator segment in turn.

11 Burning on the commutator is usually a sign of an open circuited winding. If you have access to a 'growler' have the armature checked for short circuits.

12 Inspect the field windings fir signs of abrasion or stiff and damaged insulation, particularly where the leads leave the coil. Check the field coil for short circuit to the pole piece and for open circuits. Replace if necessary.

13 The brushes must be atleast ½ in. (13 mm) long and must slide easily in the holder. There are two schools of thought about brush replacement. One says that the entire field coil must be replaced or the brush plate with the armature current brushes. The VW/Audi method is somewhat different.

14 Isolate the brushes, pull them out of the holders and hold them away from the winding and crush the old brush with a powerful pair of pliers until the lead is free from the brush. Clean the end of the lead

and prepare it for soldering. The new brush, obtainable from official agents, is drilled and has a tinned insert. Push the end of the lead into the drilling and splay it out, then using silver solder, solder the brush to the lead.

15 If it is your first attempt at soldering it could be better to get expert help. Use a large soldering iron (250 watts plus) do not let any of the solder creep along the wire and file off any surplus. Do not let the lead get too hot, or damage will occur to the field coils. Use a flat pair of pliers to hold the lead as close to the brush as possible while soldering. These will act as a heat sink and will also stop the solder getting in the core of the lead.

16 One final word about brushes. Check that you can get new ones before crushing the old ones.

17 Assembly is the reverse of dismantling. Fit the drive pinion and operating lever to the mounting bracket. Fit the drive pinion to the armature shaft. Refit a new lock ring (circlip) and install the stop ring (groove towards the outside) over the lock ring. Check that the stop ring will revolve freely on the shaft. The stop ring is not shown in the illustration. It fits on the armature shaft outside the pinion.

18 Fit the starter body over the armature to the mounting bracket. See that the tongue on the body fits in the cut-out of the mounting bracket and that the body seats properly on the rubber seating. Smear a little joint compound round the joint before assembly.

19 Fit the two washers onto the armature shaft and install the brush holder over the commutator. This we found easier to write about than to do. In order to get the holder, in place with the brushes correctly assembled we found that we didn't have enough fingers so we cut two lengths of wire and bent them as shown (photos) to hold up the brush springs while the brushes were fitted over the commutator. Once the four brushes are in place the wires may be withdrawn.

20 Wipe the end of the shaft and oil it, then fit the endcover onto the housing and install the through-bolts. Again seal the joint, and seal the ends of the through-bolts. Now refit the shims and the circlips. If a new armature has been fitted the endplay must be checked. It should not exceed a maximum of 0.072 in., minimum of 0.004 in. (0.1 to 0.3 mm) and is adjusted by fitting appropriate shims.

21 Check that the solenoid lead grommet is in place and refit the solenoid. Use a seal compound on the joint faces, move the pinion to bring the operation lever to the opening and reconnect pullrod. Seat the solenoid firmly on the mounting bracket in the sealing compound and install the bolts. Reconnect the wire to the starter body (D).

22 The starter may now be refitted to the car.

23 The pinion end of the shaft fits into a bearing in the clutch housing and this can be checked only when the transmission is dismantled. The commutator end of the shaft fits into a bearing bush in the endplate. The old bush may be pressed out if necessary and a new one pressed in. The endplate should be dipped into hot oil for five minutes before the bush is pressed in to give a shrink fit. Grease the bush with multi-purpose grease before installing the shaft.

15 Starter motor -bench test

1   Because the pinion end bearing is in the clutch housing,it is not possible to rotate the starter under load or at speed when not fitted to the engine. The customary bench tests are therefore not applicable to this starter.

16 Fault diagnosis - charging circuit

Symptom	Reason/s	Remedy
Alternator warning light does not come on when the ignition switch is closed	1 Bulb burned out	Replace.
	2 Battery flat	Charge.
	3 Connector between alternator and relay not correctly fitted	Refit.
	4 Carbon brushes not seating on slip ring	Check for length and free movement. Replace if necessary.
	5 Open circuit between battery, ignition switch and warning light	Check continuity.
	6 Rotor windings damaged	Check and fit new rotor if necessary.
Alternator warning light does not go out as engine speed increases	1 Regulator damaged	Check and replace if necessary.
	2 Field winding diodes open circuit	Dismantle alternator, check diodes. Replace diode carrier if required.
Alternator warning light remains on when the ignition is switched off	1 Positive diode (main load diode) short circuited	Dismantle alternator, check diodes, replace diode plate if necessary.

17 Fault diagnosis - starting circuit

Symptom	Test and possible reason	Remedy
Starter does not operate when key is turned to 'start' position. Turn on the lights for this test	1 Lights go out - loose connections, corroded terminals, flat battery	Check circuit and replace battery.
	2 Lights go dim - battery run down	Recharge or replace battery.
	3 Connect a cable between terminals '30' and '50'. If starter now turns either cables or ignition switch is faulty	Replace cables, starter to ignition switch and/ or ignition switch.
	4 Lights stay bright. Connect cable from terminal '30' to connector strip terminal - starter now turns	Solenoid needs service or replacement.
Drive pinion sticks in mesh with starter ring	1 Coarse thread damaged	Overhaul starter.
	2 Solenoid not working	Replace solenoid.
Starter turns slowly and will not start engine	1 Battery run down	Charge or replace.
	2 Loose connections	Check circuit.
	3 Brushes not making proper contact	Overhaul or replace starter.
	4 Commutator dirty, burnt or damaged	Overhaul or replace starter.
	5 Windings damaged	Overhaul or replace starter.
Erratic starting ie; sometimes it will and sometimes it will not, particularly from cold	1 Battery has internal fault Load test battery with tongs	Replace battery if necessary.

Chapter 11 Electrical system Part II:
Lights, instrument panel and electrical accessories

Contents

Specifications

Bulb chart

	DIN Designation	Part no.	Type
Headlamp:			
Round (filament)	A12V 45/40W	N17 705 3	Twin filament
Round (halogen)	YD 12V 60/55W	N17 763 2	Halogen H.4
Double headlamp (halogen)	YA 12V 55W	N17 761 2	Halogen H.1
Parking light	HL 12V 4W	N17 717 2	Tubular
Front turn signal	RL 12V 21W	N17 732 2	Ball
Rear turn signal	RL 12V 21W	N17 732 2	Ball
Brake	SL 12V 21W	N17 738 2	Ball
Reversing light	RL 12V 21W	N17 732 2	Ball
License plate light	HL 12V 4W	N17 717 2	Tubular
Interior light	K12V 10W	N17 723 2	Festoon
Glovebox	J12V 2W	N17 722 2	Tubular
Warning lamps for switches and heater levers	W 12V 1.2W or JG 12V 1.2 W	N17 751 2	Glass base
Instrument lights	W 12V 1.2W	N17 751 2	Glass base
Fog lights (halogen)	YC 12V 55W	N17 762 2	Halogen H.3
Rear fog light	RL 12V 21W	N17 732 2	Ball

Sealed beam lamp (USA) ... ...   G.E.C. sealed beam SBM 1AE 122.7 in. diameter, 45 watt

Wiper motor ... ...   12V, 2 speed, worm-drive permanent magnet field

Rear window demister ... ...   110 - 120 watt

Fan blower ... ...   65 watt, 2 speed

Air-conditioner blower ... ...   180 watt, 3 speed

Fuses *

1   Left headlamp - low beam
2   Right headlamp - low beam
3   Left headlamp - high beam
4   Right headlamp - high beam
5   Rear window heater
6   Interior light - door switches
7   Brake light, glovebox light, cigar lighter
8   Turn signal and emergency flasher
9   Back-up light, horn
10 Rear window heater - warning light, headlamp washer circuit
11 Fresh air fan
12 License plate lamps
13 Tail light right, parking light right, side marker front
14 Tail light left, parking light left, side marker front
15 Foglamps

* This table is typical. Consult the handbook supplied with your car and, if necessary, the VW agent.

Relays

The number of relays fitted depends on the equipment connected. The following list is not comprehensive, consult the VW agent for details for your model.

J1	Headlight combi relay
J2	Indicators and emergency flasher
J5	Fog light
J9	Heated rear window
J20	Towing attachment relay
J26	Radiator fan relay
J31	Wash/wipe intermittant relay
J34	Seat belt warning relay (Rabbit and Scirocco USA)
J39	Headlight washer relay
J42	Catalytic converter relay (behind dashboard) (USA)

1 General description

1   The various models have a common system of electric wiring and accessories although the number and exact type of accessories depends on the option package and year of the vehicle. In most cases wiring and fixing provision is already built in to models not fitted with extras such as fog lamps, and fitting of these extras is a simple task. All such extras must be earthed to the chassis with a separate connector.

2   A very marked step in technique is evident. The fuse and relay console under the dashboard contains 15 fuses and a number of relays. The purpose of these relays is two-fold. Firstly, the heavy current required for headlamps, fog lamps, air-conditioner, horn, rear window heater and flashers, may be routed only from the generating circuit, via the relay, to the accessory. The operation of the relay switching on the current is by a much smaller current from the switch on the dashboard (fascia) which enables the second step. By using relays the current to and from instruments may be carried by a printed circuit and the size of switches and wiring behind the fascia board reduced to a minimum. Indeed it would not be very difficult to install all the accessories if the main current had to be lead to switches on the fascia.

3   Measuring instruments on the fascia have a controlling voltage stabilizer built into the instrument.

4   The car is wired to a computor plug so that the official agents computor may check the car against standard values in a very short time. In our opinion this service is invaluable and should be used as intended. It does,, however, preclude the addition of extra electrical accessories, unless these are VW standard ones, or can be easily disconnected before the check is done. The operator must be informed of any such additions before he starts his inspection.

5   The more expensive types of vehicle have built in tachometer (rev counter), oil pressure gauge and voltmeter fitted as standard. These may be added to the standard vehicle and will assist considerably in maintenance.

6   The Golf and Rabbit have single round headlamps on each side. The Golf may be fitted with ball type or halogen bulbs. The Rabbit has **sealed beam units.** The Scirocco has twin headlamps, round or rectangular in shape. European versions have ball or halogen type bulbs, USA versions may have the sealed beam type.

7   The speedometer is included in this Chapter because it is part of the fascia. The drive arrangements of the Golf/Rabbit and the Scirocco are slightly different.

8   Instruments are governed by a voltage stabilizer fitted in the printed circuit behind the dashboard.

9   Guide lines are given concerning the fitting of fog lamps, radios and provisions for lighting to trailers. If items other than VW accessories are fitted the owner may be confronted with problems we cannot foresee so comment is confined mainly to what not to do in such cases.

10 Current flow type wiring diagrams with a short explanation of how to use them, are included.

2 Headlamps - general

1   The fixing and beam adjustment for the Golf/Rabbit is generally the same. The main differences are in the type of bulb and method of renewal. The same dictum applies to the double lamp Scirocco.

3 Single headlamp (round reflector) - removal, replacement and bulb renewal (Golf)

1   To remove the bulb first extract the rubber grommet at the back of the headlamp cover (photo). Then pull off the cover.

2   Under this will be found another cover and a plug (photo). Remove the plug and pressing in the cover remove it from the retaining ring (photo).

3   This now exposes the lamp holder (photo) which may be turned in its bayonet fitting and pulled out carrying the bulb. Using a duster remove the bulb and replace it with a serviceable one. **Do not** touch the bulb with bare fingers, it won't hurt you but the moisture from your skin will etch lines on the bulb when it lights up.

4   Assembly is the reverse of removal. Make sure the covers seat properly or the lamp will leak water and will require a new reflector. A typical layout is shown at Fig. 11.1.

5   To remove the reflector it is necessary first to remove the grille. This is held by five screws. The screws holding the headlamp (not the focus screws) may then be undone and the lamp drawn out from the front. The frame and reflector are held together by clamps (photos) which must be turned to separate the parts. It would be better to replace them

as an assembly.

6 Focusing is done by moving two screws one for vertical and the other for horizontal adjustment (photo). Although for clarity's sake the photo shows the lamp out of the car, the adjustment may be done without disturbing the headlight as the screws are accessible from inside the engine compartment without undoing any part of the lamp.

4 Single headlamp (round reflector) - removal, replacement and sealed beam unit renewal (Rabbit)

1 Remove the front grille, there are two screws in each side and four along the top edge (see Chapter 13). Refer to Fig. 11.2.

3.1 Remove the plug from the back of the cover. 'A' is one of the focussing screws

3.2a The plug and inner cover may be removed to show ...

3.2b ... the lamp socket. Turn this and ...

3.3 ... pull it out with the bulb

3.5a With the grille removed the lamp may be detached

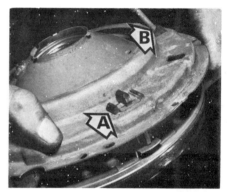
3.5b The fastener clips are at 'A' and the focussing screw 'B'

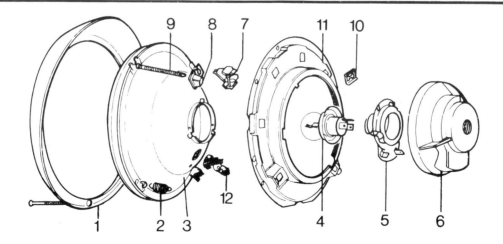

Fig. 11.1. Single headlamp, round pattern, ball or halogen bulb - typical layout (Sec. 3)

1 Rim	4 Bulb - headlight	7 Retaining clip	10 Clip
2 Spring	5 Bulb holder	8 Adjuster screw nut	11 Retaining ring
3 Headlight unit	6 Cover	9 Adjuster screw	12 Parking light

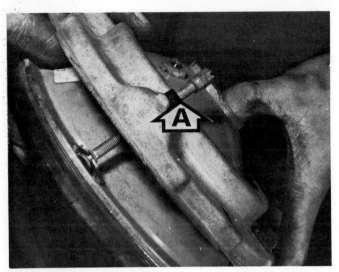

3.6 The focussing screw. Do not turn this unless you wish to refocus the lamps

2   Remove the three screws holding the headlamp securing ring (do not touch the focusing screws). Pull out the sealed beam unit and disconnect the plug from the back (Fig. 11.3).
3   Fit the plug to a new unit and reinstall the lamp and grille. Be careful that the lettering on the headlamp housing and the chrome ring are at the top and that the lettering on the glass of the sealed beam unit is at the bottom.

5   Twin headlamps - removal, replacement and bulb renewal (Scirocco)

1   The twin lamps are mounted into a frame onto which they are held by chrome rings and mounting screws. Disconnect the grille and loosen the mounting screws drawing the headlamp forward. It will then be possible to disconnect the wires at the back of the reflector and remove

the cap at the back of the light. The bayonet socket may then be removed.
2   If it is only bulb renewal that is required, there is no need to dismantle the lamp assembly. From inside the bonnet locate the twin lamps. The outer one is dipped beam and the inner main or high beam. Pull the connector off the bulb, unhook the spring clip and swing it away. Remove the bulb and replace with a new one. After changing bulbs the headlamp alignment should be checked.

6   Square headlamp - removal, replacement and bulb renewal (Scirocco)

1   The lamp is basically the same as the round one, see Figs. 11.6 and 11.7. When renewing a bulb make sure that the gasket is seated correctly. The four retaining tabs (Fig. 11.8) must be pressed behind the bulb holder (Fig. 11.9).

7   Foglamps - fitting guidelines

1   These are fitted to some cars when new. The remainder are wired for the lamps and provision is made for the switch. A relay is also required. They do not appear to be fitted at all in the USA.
2   Reference to the wiring diagram of the Golf pt II will show the foglamps 'L22' and 'L23' in current tracks '51' and '53'. Further investigation shows that 'L22' is picked up from connector 'T1b', a single connector in the engine compartment. Similarly 'L23' from connector. 'T1f'. The connector is actually part of the harness so it is there, whether there is a lamp or not.
3   Refer to Fig. 11.12 and it will be seen that a blank space for the switch exists on the top left-hand of the dashboard. On R.H. drive vehicles it is on the top right of the dashboard. Push out this blanking piece and a switch may be fitted. It will be necessary to remove the fascia to fit the switch (Section 18).
4   Reference to the wiring diagram again shows one side of the switch connected direct to 'G4' on the fuse/relay plate and the other to 'T1e' a spare single connector behind the dash. The wires are white and grey.
5   The relay must be connected in the same way.
6   In the same way 'L20', the rear foglamp, can be plugged in to 'T1d' which is in the rear boot on a black and purple cable.
7   Note that the lamps all have separate earth wires.

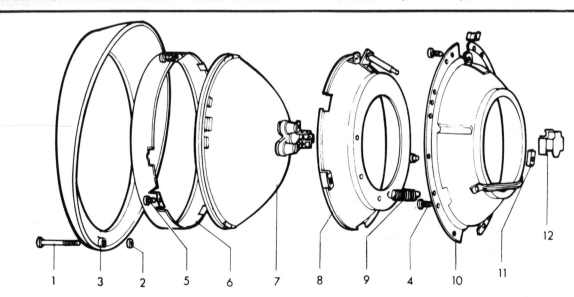

Fig. 11.2. Single headlamp, sealed beam - typical layout

1	Rim securing screw	5	Retaining ring screw	9	Retaining ring spring
2	Rubber washer	6	Retaining ring	10	Securing ring
3	Rim	7	Sealed beam unit	11	Tapped plates
4	Securing ring screw	8	Aiming ring with 2 aiming screws	12	Terminal

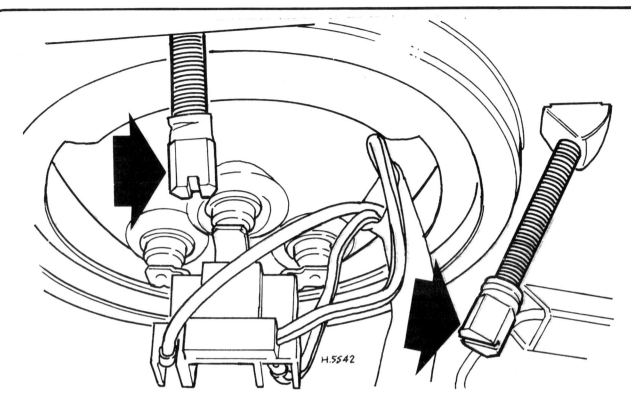

Fig. 11.3. The back of the sealed beam lamp on the Rabbit. The focusing screws are arrowed (Sec. 4)

Fig. 11.4. Scirocco (USA) twin headlamps - remove the cap (arrow) (Sec. 5)

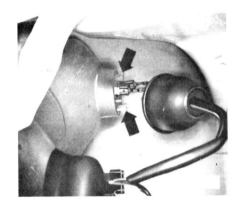

Fig. 11.5. Scirocco (European) - connections, twin headlamps (Sec. 5)

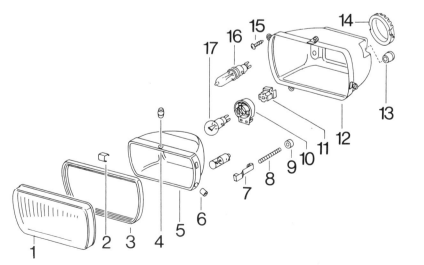

Fig. 11.6. Single headlamp, rectangular pattern, ball or halogen bulbs - typical layout (Sec. 6)

1 Lens
2 Clip
3 Frame
4 Plug
5 Reflector
6 Bush
7 Clip
8 Spring
9 Bush
10 Bulb holder
11 Plug
12 Lamp housing
13 Focus screw nut
14 Cover
15 Screw
16 Halogen bulb
17 Ball type bulb

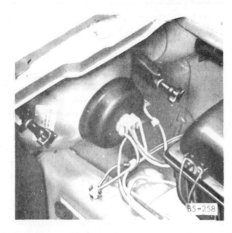

Fig. 11.7. Scirocco (European) - rectangular headlamp (Sec. 6)

Fig. 11.8. Scirocco (European) - rectangular pattern (Sec. 6)
There are four tabs inside the lamp cap (arrows) which ...

Fig. 11.9. ... be pressed behind the bulb holder (arrows) (Sec. 6)

8.1 The parking light bulb fits into the headlight reflector

9.1 Remove the lens from the bumper bar and the turn signal bulb may be removed

10.1 The bulb plate for the rear light cluster removed from its case

11.1 The interior light removed from the lining

12.1 The license plate lens always seems to be dirty

8   These are only guidelines. There are so many modifications continually appearing that we stress that you should buy these lamps from the VW agent and ask for fitting instructions.

9   If you have fitted the lamps successfully the lamps will work only when the ignition is switched on and the side lamps on low beam , headlights are on. The switch has two positions, the first one for front foglamps and the second one for front and rear foglamps. The warning light should work in both positions.

8   Parking light - bulb renewal

1   Refer to photo 8.1. The parking light is inside the headlight and attached to the headlight wiring.

9   Turn signal lamps (front) - bulb renewal

1   Refer to photo 9.1. Remove the two screws holding the lens to the bumper bar, the bulb may then be pressed into the holder, turned to the left and extracted. A new bulb may then be fitted. When replacing the lens see that the gasket is in good condition. Do not tighten the screws too much or you will crack the lens.

10   Light cluster (rear) - bulb renewal

1   Inside the boot, opposite the reflector glasses on the outside is a plastic cover with a knurled knob in the centre of it. Undo this and

remove the cover. The lamp plate may then be pulled clear (photo) and new bulbs inserted as necessary. The vehicle (Golf economy size) we dismantled did not have back up lights, although the switch was installed on the transmission, so that bulb is missing from the photo.

2   Do not remove the plastic lens from the outside unless it is broken. When fitting a new one tighten the screws very carefully and make sure the joint between the lens and the vehicle body is water tight.

11 Interior light - bulb renewal

These are held into the linings by a lug at one end and a spring clip at the other. The fitting may be levered out of the lining using a small screwdriver. Be careful not to damage the lining. The festoon bulb may then be extracted and replaced (photo). Install the housing at the switch end first and engage the lug. Now press the other end until the spring clip engages.

12 License plate light - bulb renewal

Undo the two screws holding the lens in place and remove the lens. The bulb may then be replaced. For some reason this light seems to collect more mud than the others (photo) and should be wiped clean frequently.

13 Side markers (USA) - bulb renewal

On the Rabbit and Scirocco USA version, there are four red lights, two on each side. Each one is fastened to the body by two screws. Remove these and gently pull the lens away from the body. The bulb may then be removed and a new one fitted. Be careful when refitting the lens that the joint is made water tight, these lamps get more than their share of spray in wet weather from passing traffic.

14 Headlamp - beam adjustment

1   Refer to photo 4.2b. The screws arrowed are the adjusting screws which tilt the reflector horizontally and vertically.

2   Because of the many different local regulations and the increasing argument about what is, and what is not, a correctly aimed headlamp beam we are not offering any advice as to where the beam should point, only how to make it point in that direction. The actual focus point should be obtained from your local dealer or police authority.

3   Having ascertained how the beam is to be aimed on dip, whether it must swing to the right or left when dipped, and the measurements of the displacement, set the car on level ground about 20 feet (6 metres) from a vertical wall or door. The vehicle tyre pressures should be correct and there should be the equivalent of the driver's weight in the driving seat.

4   Mark with relation to the centre-line of the car and the height of the lamps from the ground, the equivalent positions of the lamps on the wall. Using this as a datum, mark the area to which the lights should be

directed on dipped beam. Cover one light and switch on. Using the adjusting screws direct the beam to the area required. Cover that light and repeat with the other one.

When the beams are correctly focussed on dip the main beams will automatically be correct.

15 Direction indicators and emergency flashers - general

1   The direction indicators are controlled by the left-hand column switch.

2   A switch on the fascia board operates all four flashers simultaneously and although the direction indicators will not work when the ignition is switched off the emergency switch over-rides this and the flasher signals continue to operate.

3   All the circuits are routed through the relay on the console and its fuse.

4   If the indicators do not function correctly, a series of tests may be done to find which part of the circuit is at fault.

5   The most common fault is in the flasher lamps, defective bulbs, and dirty or corroded contacts. Check these first, then test the emergency switch. Remove it from the circuit and check its operation. If the switch is in good order replace it and again turn on the emergency lights. If nothing happens then the relay is not functioning properly and it should be renewed. If the lights function on emergency but not on operation of the column switch then the wiring and column switch are suspect (see Section 16).

16 Steering column switches - removal and replacement

1   There are four switches on the steering column:

   a) *The horn switch on pad in the centre of the steering wheel.*
   b) *The turn signal/headlight dip and flasher lever on the left of the column.*
   c) *The windscreen wiper/washer control lever on the right of the column.*
   d) *The steering lock/starter switch on the lower right of the column (see Section 17).*

2   Before commencing dismantling remove the earth strap from the battery.

3   To remove the horn pad simply pull it upwards. It takes a very strong pull, but it does come off that way. Remove the wire connection (photo). Undo the nut and remove the steering wheel.

4   Two crosshead screws hold the two halves of the cover for the column switches together. Remove these and take the lower half of the cover away. The various components of the switches are now visible (photo).

5   From below the switch pull out the three multipin plugs. There is one for each lever switch and one for the starter switch. They will go back only one way (photo) so there is no need to mark them. Refer to photo 16.4. Undo the four screws which hold the wiper/turn signal switch assemblies in place and lift the complete switch away (photo).

16.3 The connecting wire under the horn pad

16.4 The four screws must be taken out ...

16.5a ... the multipin plugs pulled off and ...

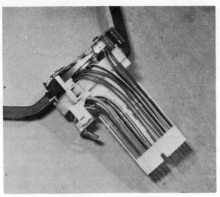
16.5b ... the switch assembly lifted out

16.5c The column, switch removed

16.7 The underside of the steering wheel. The cancelling lug (A) must be correctly aligned or the direction switch will be damaged

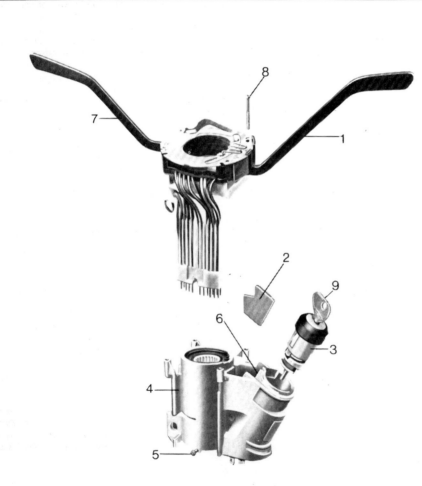

Fig. 11.10. Column switches - exploded view (Sec. 17)

1 Windscreen wiper/wash lever
2 Locking plate
3 Lock barrel
4 Housing
5 Set screw
6 Opening for withdrawing lock
7 Turn signal lever
8 Screw
9 Key

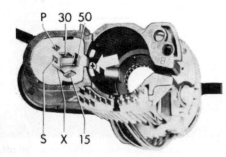

Fig. 11.11. Ignition switch/steering lock - view from below (Sec. 17)

Remove the set screw (arrow) to extract the terminal block

The top of the steering column is then cleared for dismantling (photo).
6   The action of the lever switches may now be tested. If the switch does not move decisively and there is slackness in the linkage, then the switch must be replaced.
7   Assembly is the reverse of removal. When refitting the steering wheel be careful to align the cancelling lug in the right place on the switch levers will be damaged (photo). The roadwheels should be in the 'straight-ahead' position, the turn signal switch in the neutral position and the lug to the right.

17 Ignition and steering lock switch - removal and replacement

1   Disconnect the battery earth strap.
2   Remove the steering wheel and column switches as in Section 16.
3   Refer to Fig. 11.10. Pull out the locking plate using a pair of pliers. Keep the key in the lock and turn the key clockwise approximately one thickness of the key and then pull the lock and key out of the switch housing. If you have had the misfortune to break the key in the lock, try turning the key with a small screwdriver. The key must be aligned before the barrel may be extracted. There isn't much to be done about the lock. If it is faulty take it back to the VW agent. They have a lot of spares and expertise, if you take all the bits they will be able to solve your problem.

4   The switch is removed after undoing a small screw (see Fig. 11.11). It may be necessary to remove the set screw and slide the whole assembly off the column to get at this.
5   Assembly is the reverse of removal. Put the lock barrel in without the key this time. When installing the locking plate tap it with a hammer to peen it into position.

18 Instrument panel - removal and replacement

1   Remove the horn pad and the steering wheel. You can do the job without this but it is much more difficult (photo).
2   Remove the heater control knobs, pull them off, and pull out the trim plate. This is a fiddle but it is held by clips and will come away with patience.
3   The radio is held in position with clips. First remove the control knobs, prise out the centres and pull the knob away. You can get at the clips from underneath. If you study photo 18.3 you will see that the clip on the side of the radio has to be pressed against the side of the radio and the radio pushed in a bit to clear the side of the hole in the fascia. Ease the radio out and disconnect the earth wire. Pull off the supply plug, speaker plug and aerial plug. Note which goes where, and pull the radio out. Note how the rear support fits.
4   Disconnect the speedo cable from the rear of the speedo. You can

18.1 Single instrument dashboard (steering wheel removed)

18.3 Radio removed. Note the spring clip

18.4 The strut behind the instrument panel. 'A' is where the locating screw sits

18.5 The instrument panel withdrawn

reach up from underneath to do this. Now comes the tricky bit. Behind the instrument panel is a plastic vertical support strut. It has a recess in it into which a screw fixed to the instrument panel fits. Remove this screw. Our photo shows the strut after the panel has been removed. Once this screw is out on the Golf the whole panel may be pulled forward for examination. On the Scirocco remove the two crosshead screws, an extra one on the right-hand side.

5   Ease the panel forward and turn it at the same time. You will see now why it is better to have the wheel out of the way (photo). Be very careful, there is a fragile printed circuit with no protection at all.

6   Comparison of Fig. 11.12 and photo 18.1 will show that there are two versions of dashboard, the one with only a speedometer and fuel gauge plus warning lights and switches, the other with two instrument inserts for speedometer plus clock or revolution counter. The figuration is shown in Fig. 11.13.

7   This does not affect the method of removal and replacement, but it obviously does affect inspection and testing.

8   If you want to take the board right out then there are a lot of wires to deal with. The switches may be removed from the board by opening the dovetails and pulling them out. Do not disconnect the wires to the

switches. The multipin plug may be removed. However, this will leave a number of wires still connected. These must be pulled off one at a time and labelled for correct replacement.

9   Instruments, light clusters or the printed circuit may then be removed and replaced but you may think it better to go to the expert. You will have to go to the VW stores to get the new bits, why not ask for them to be fitted and tested?

10 Replacement of the board is the reverse of removal. Fitting the securing screw into the strut is quite a task. We worked our panel into place and lined up the hole with a small screwdriver. On the Scirocco the panel foil must go under the sealing lip. Don't forget to reconnect the speedo drive. Do not switch on the radio if the speakers are disconnected.

19 Instrument panel - inspection and testing

1   Besides having two types of panel, the one with two major instruments has yet more variation. On the panel with a clock, the fuel gauge is at the bottom of the clock face and the temperature gauge at

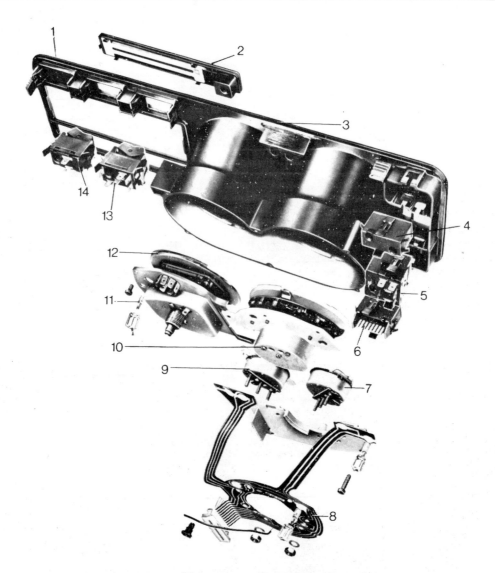

Fig. 11.12. Instrument panel - exploded view (Sec. 18)

1 Space for fog lamp switch	6 Warning light cluster, dual brake system	10 Tachometer or clock
2 Heater control cover	and rear seatbelt system	11 Speedometer light bulb
3 Instrument cluster	7 Temperature gauge	12 Speedometer
4 Warning lights cluster, oil and generator	8 Painted circuit	13 Emergency light switch
5 Light switch	9 Fuel gauge	14 Heated rear window switch

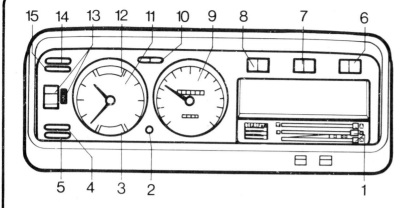

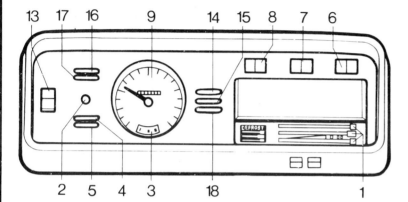

Fig. 11.13. Two types of instrument panel (Sec. 18)

1 Heater controls
2 Trailer warning lamp
3 Fuel gauge
4 Spare
5 Brake warning lamp
6 Fog light switch
7 Heated rear window switch
8 Emergency light switch
9 Speedometer
10 High beam/turn warning lamp (twin dial board)
11 Clock or revolution counter (twin dial board)
12 Temperature gauge (twin dial board)
13 Lighting switch
14 Generator warning lamp
15 Oil pressure warning lamp
16 Turn signal lamp (single dial)
17 High beam warning lamp (single dial)
18 Temperature warning light (single dial)

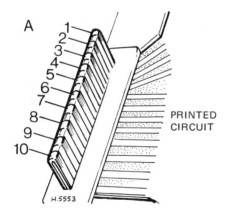

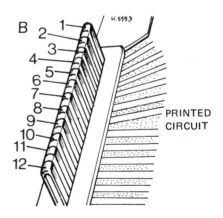

Fig. 11.14. Connections to printed circuit multipin plug (Sec. 19)

	A Golf European	Terminal		B Rabbit USA	Terminal
1	Turn signal warning lamp	49a	1	Turn signal warning lamp	49a
2	High beam warning lamp	56a	2	Alternator warning lamp	61
3	Rev counter or clock + ve	1 or 30	3	High beam warning lamp	56a
4	Earth	31	4	Tachometer or clock + ve	1 or 30
5	Instrument lights	58	5	Earth	31
6	Positive wire	15	6	Instrument lights	58b
7	Fuel gauge sender	—	7	Positive wire	15
8	Temperature gauge sender	—	8	Fuel gauge sender	—
9	Generator warning lamp	61	9	Temperature gauge sender	—
10	From oil pressure switch to warning lamp	—	10	Catalytic converter control	—
			11	From oil pressure switch to warning lamp	—
			12	E.G.R. (Cal. only)	

the top. Where a revolution counter is fitted the fuel gauge is at the right bottom and the temperature gauge at the left bottom.

2   On vehicles with only the speedometer the fuel gauge is at the top of the speedo face and there is a warning light for temperature problems.

3   This makes no difference to test procedures but obviously the wiring circuit varies so if a new printed circuit is required care must be taken to get the right one. There are also two types of speedometer.

4   The testing and checking of the various instruments is discussed separately. The checking of the panel involves testing the printed circuit. As can be seen from photo 19.4a one end of each of the circuits goes to an instrument or warning light, the other end goes to a multipin plug as shown in photo 19.4b. A diagram, Fig. 11.14 gives the key to this plug for a ten pin plug. The Rabbit and Scirocco USA have a twelve pin plug, also on Fig. 11.14.

5   Using the tables at Fig. 11.14 it is possible to trace circuits using a meter should there be a need to do this.

6   Examine the printed circuit carefully, use a magnifying glass if you have one. Any defects will show as breaks or unwanted short circuits.

20   Switches (lighting) - testing, removal and replacement

1   You cannot repair the switches; either they work or they don't. If you suspect the switch then the only way to test it is to take out the instrument panel. Disconnect the battery earth strap before you start. Move up the dovetail clips of the switch and extract it from the panel (photo), make a diagram of the wiring to the switch and pull off the connectors. Use a meter to test the operation of the switch. If it does not work satisfactorily, fit a new one.

21   Temperature gauge - testing

1   The first thing that seems odd is that there is no voltage stabilizer in the circuit. On models up to August 1975 the stabilizer is built into the instrument. After that date a single stabilizer is fitted for the fuel and temperature gauges. The printed circuit has been altered. The stabilizer must be in contact with the metal surface of the speedometer to assist cooling.

2   If the gauge refuses to indicate that the engine is getting warm, then either the gauge or the sender are not working, or perhaps, the wiring circuit is at fault.

3   A quick test is to pull the wire off the sender and using a 12v 6 watt bulb as a series resistance and with the ignition switched on touch the bulb centre pin to earth momentarily. Have someone watch the gauge. It should move right across the scale. It is essential to have the bulb in series with the wire or you may damage the gauge. If there is no reading then press a bit harder with your contact. Still no reading, then either the wiring or the gauge are at fault. Check the fuse, if there is one in the circuit for your vehicle. If there is still no reading then the gauge must be extracted for testing separately.

4   If there is a reading then the gauge is not at fault but the sender is suspect. To test the gauge for accuracy disconnect the sender and fit resistances in its place. Ordinary radio resistances will do. A 47 ohm resistance should indicate that the engine is hot. Replace this with a

150 ohm resistance and the needle should move to the middle zone. Finally use a 270 ohm resistor and the needle should register 'cold'. If the gauge does not pass this test then it is not accurate and should be replaced. If the gauge passes the test, but still refuses to indicate that the engine is getting warm then the sender unit should be renewed.

22   Fuel gauge and sender unit - testing

1   Read the notes in Section 21, paragraph 1 before reading this Section.

2   The handbook states that when the needle of the fuel gauge reaches the reserve mark there is about one gallon of fuel in the tank. It is important therefore that the gauge is accurate.

3   There is a very good way of checking the reserve mark. Buy one gallon of petrol, empty the petrol tank, put in the one gallon and check the reading against the reserve mark. If it is possible to arrange to fill the tank from empty to full, one gallon at a time, a piece of thin cardboard fitted to the face of the gauge glass may be marked at each gallon and you will know exactly how much fuel is in the tank at all times.

4   If the gauge is not reading then a simple test is required. A 47 ohm resistor and a 0-12v meter are needed. Underneath the car at the rear on the right-hand side of the petrol tank is the combined fuel hose and fuel gauge wires entry. Switch on the ignition and measure the voltage across the terminals. If there is no voltage pull off the terminal of the wire to the gauge (Fig. 11.15) and check the voltage between that terminal and earth. If there is now a reading the sender unit is at fault. Check that the other wire is in fact connected securely to earth. If there is still no reading then either the wiring or the gauge is faulty. Check that all the fuses are in order. To decide whether the gauge or the wiring is at fault the instrument panel must be removed. The end of the wiring is on the multipin plug for the printed circuit - see Fig. 11.14 and Section 19.

5   If the sender unit is faulty then the tank must be drained. Remove the hose clip and pull off the hose. Disconnect the battery earth strap and disconnect the wires from the sender unit. Turn the locking plate until the unit can be withdrawn from the tank, and then remove the fuel pipe and sender unit. There is little that can be done to the sender unit, it is best to take it to an expert, who may be able to repair it or supply a new one.

6   To test the accuracy of the gauge, if it is working, disconnect the gauge wires at the sender unit and insert a 47 ohm resistance between them. Switch on the ignition and the gauge should register full. Replace this with a 100 ohm and then a 220 ohm resistor in turn and the needle should be on the second mark and then the reserve mark respectively.

23   Fuse and relay panel - removal and replacement

1   Disconnect the battery earth strap. If you forget to do this something is bound to burn out this time.

2   Undo the screws holding the panel in place (photo) and lower it away from the bulkhead (for LHD see paragraph 6).

3   The underside of the board is shown in Fig. 11.17. Unplug the main multipin plugs 'A' to 'F'. Tag them as you pull them off. Fig. 11.16

19.4a The instrument end of the printed circuit

19.4b The multi-pin plug end of the printed circuit

20.1 The switches. Move the dovetail bits out and the switch can be pulled out

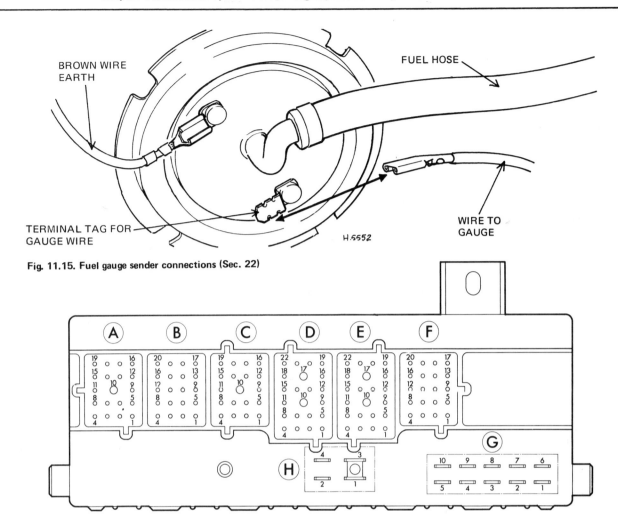

BROWN WIRE
EARTH

FUEL HOSE

TERMINAL TAG FOR
GAUGE WIRE

WIRE TO
GAUGE

H.5552

Fig. 11.15. Fuel gauge sender connections (Sec. 22)

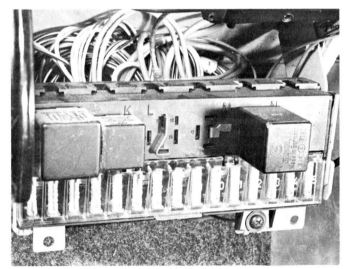

Fig. 11.16. Diagrammatic layout of fuse/relay plate - Rabbit (Sec. 23)

A   Wiring harness front left
B   Wiring harness diagnosis network
C   Wiring harness front right
D   Wiring harness instrument panel
E   Wiring harness instrument panel
   1   Z to G6 by fuse 15
   2   53c to wash pump contact in wiper switch
   3   15 to starter switch 15
   4   K to fuse S12
G   5   61 to alternator D+
   6   Z to G.1 by fuse 15
   7   X to starter switch X
   8   56b to 56a on headlight dimmer relay
   9   To oil pressure switch
   10   To 56 on light switch
H   1 and 5 (on later models) to terminal 30 (main supply)

23.2 The fuse and relay board. Remove the screws and lower away from the bracket. Note the bridge between terminals '13' and '14'. This is where the radiator fan relay used to fit

refers.

4   Take the 6 connectors from 'H' and whatever is connected to 'G' (Fig. 11.16 refers). Tag these wires. The board may now be removed complete with relays and fuses. A new board may be installed in its place and the connectors replaced.

5   The usual faults are loose connections in the multipin plug connector to the socket in the plate. Bent pins may be straightened but if the pins have spread then the plate may need replacement.

6   On left-hand drive cars it may be necessary to remove the steering column trim and the cubby hole before the relay plate may be removed.

7   On vehicles without the intermittent wash wipe relay contacts '19' and '21' are connected with a bridge.

8   From chassis 175 3 024 377 of the Golf and 535 200 1292 Scirocco the radiator fan relay is dispensed with. Sockets '13' and '14' in the 'L' relay are bridged. This is shown in our photo 23.2.

9   On later boards the number of flat connections in 'H' has been increased from 6 to 7. This presumably for more wires in search of terminal '30'.

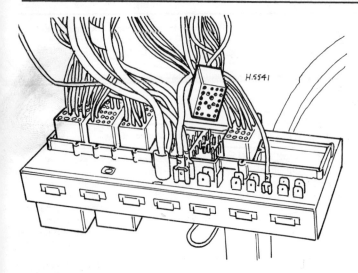

Fig. 11.17. The reverse side of the fuse and relay board (Sec. 23)

24.1 The horn on the Golf/Rabbit is located on the frame at the front of the vehicle. It is near the radiator.

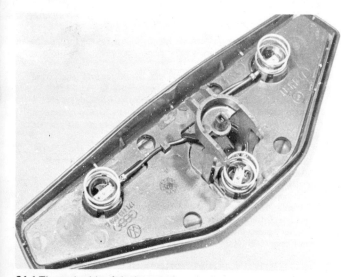

24.4 The underside of the horn pad

24 Horn - fault diagnosis

1 The Scirocco has twin horns, the Golf and Rabbit a single one (photo). To remove the horns disconnect the battery ground strap, pull off the connections, and remove the horns from the brackets. When refitting them make sure the horn case does not touch the body when the nuts are tightened or there will be vibration noises when the horn is blown.

2 If the horn blows continuously, or intermittently when the steering wheel is turned, disconnect the battery earth strap and then remove the fuse. You may then proceed on your way but do not replace the fuse until the fault has been located.

3 If the horn will not sound when the horn pad is pressed, check the fuse. If this is blown do not replace it until you are ready to locate the fault.

4 Pry off the pad from the steering wheel and disconnect the horn wire from the pad. Three screws hold the switch to the pad (photo). Remove these and the switch may be examined for faults or damage. Check the circuit of the switch with a meter. If this is in order replace the pad.

5 The fault finding process should be done at home, not at the roadside. Check first that the gap between the steering wheel and the column switch is between 2 and 4 mm (0.08 to 0.16 in). Now replace the fuse and switch on the ignition during each test. If the fuse is correct the back-up light will work, if it is not, then the light will not work.

6 Disconnect the earth wire to the horn and using a stout piece of wire (say 1.5 mm^2) connect the negative terminal of the horn to the battery 16.5a). The right-hand plug is the one you want (not the one to the that there is voltage at the other horn terminal. If there is voltage and the horn does not work then the horn is defective and must be replaced.

7 If the horn works when connected to the battery as in paragraph 5, then it is probable that the steering wheel horn switch is defective. Remove the plug (pull it off) it is under the column switch (see photo 16.5a). The right-hand plug is the one you need (not the one to the ignition /starter). Look for the brown/blue wire, (current diagram Golf part II track '81'), and with the circuit live, earth the wire. If the horn works now, then the fault is between the plug and the horn pad on the steering wheel. Check the wire from the slip ring to the horn pad. If the horn does not work then the fault is in the wiring from the plug to the relay plate or the relay plate to the horn. Contact 'E 11', for the Golf (check the diagram for the others) is the point on the relay plate. If the test wire from the plug to 'E 11' makes the horn blow, then the fault is between the relay plate and the horn. Connect a test wire to the horn from 'A7' in the relay plate. If the horn works then renew the wire, if it does not then the fault is in the relay plate, which may mean a new plate.

8 Going back to paragraph 5. If there is no voltage at the horn positive terminal then check the black/yellow wire from the horn to the relay plate 'A 11'. To do this put the horn earth wire back again, take off the battery earth strap, connect a wire from the horn '+ ve' to 'A 11', refit the battery earth strap and try again. If the horn works this time, then fit a new wire. If it does not then the fault is probably in the relay plate.

9 Before deciding to renew the plate it would be as well to have your diagnosis confirmed by the VW electrician.

10 There is little to be done for a defective horn. Connect two stout wire to the terminals and to the battery and turn the adjusting screw a little. Do not keep the connections to the battery on more than a few seconds. Turning the screw is a forlorn hope, you can vary the tone and pitch of a serviceable horn this way but a silent one usually remains silent. The screw is under the seal on the back of the case.

25 Speedometer and speedometer drive - removal, replacement and renewal

1 In July 1974 the speedo cable for the 1.5 litre 020 gearbox model was replaced by an improved type of drive gear. If the speedo drive gear of the old type breaks up then the pieces may have fallen into the gearbox. If this is so, then the transmission must be removed and dismantled. How much depends upon whether the gears will engage easily or not. If they will then it is sufficient to remove the gearbox housing and clean out the pieces. If the gears will not engage easily then both the shafts must be dismantled.

2 The cable routing for the Golf/Rabbit and the Scirocco is different. In both cases the cable screws directly onto the rear of the speedometer

but with the Scirocco it will be found that the cable is secured to a bracket with a plastic band at the back of the instrument panel to stop it touching the clutch cable.

3   The cable can be extracted into the engine compartment once the bulkhead grommet is eased out of its hole. When fitting a new cable do not grease the cable, this will cause trouble in the speedometer head. Be careful not to kink the cable when fitting it.

4   Access to the back of the speedometer is gained by removing the radio (Section 18). It may be possible on some models to reach the speedo-nut from under the dashboard. It was on the Golf we dismantled but on the L and LS, there will be covers to remove before this can be done.

5   Removal of the speedometer instrument is described in Section 18. If you fit a new one there is the question of adjusting the mileage recorder. Consult the local regulations about this or you may be breaking the law.

26 Radio - fitting guidelines

1   The fitting of a radio to the Golf or the Scirocco presents no problems. It may be fitted to the dashboard, or, in the case of the Golf, a centre console with provision for storing small articles may be purchased and the radio installed in that.

2   VW provide a choice of three radios to suit the taste and pocket. Pushbutton or manual control are available, and a third option with a built in cassette tape player, speakers, a lockable arial and suppression kits are supplied, with full fitting instructions.

3   There does not seem to be any point in going elsewhere as fitting a set which is not tailored to suit will mean cutting the dashboard about and building separate supports which will get in the way of things in an already crowded space.

4   The console fitting is particularly attractive as the storage space is somewhat limited, and putting the radio in the dashboard involves pressing out the small glovebox and discarding it.

5   It is important to get advice from the local experts as to the best set for your requirements. V.H.F. gives patchy reception in built-up or hilly areas, if you do a lot of long distance work a set which functions well at home may be unsuitable in other areas.

6   If 'electrical noise' appears then it is probably due to some unit of the electrical system which is badly worn. Sparking at the alternator slip rings, a defective voltage regulator, a faulty ignition lead, fan motor or blower motor. The only way to find out is to isolate each item until the noise disappears and then overhaul that item.

7   It is recommended that a small fuse be inserted in the supply cable. A two amp one is sufficient.

27 Heated rear window - general

1   This item seems to be a standard fitting throughout the range after 1974.

2   A switch on the dashboard activates a relay 'J9' on the fuse/relay plate. There is a heavy fuse in the heater power circuit and a smaller one in the switch/warning light circuit. The circuit is easily followed in the circuit diagram. In the Golf part II current tracks '62' '63' '60' and '61' refer.

3   It will be seen that the window element is connected to a plug 'T1d' in the rear compartment.

4   Testing is mainly following the circuit through. However, before starting to work on the system disconnect the battery and only reconnect it to do specified tests.

5   The current consumption is large (about 8 amps) so turn the heater off as soon as the window is clear.

6   If the heater is not fitted the necessary parts, switch relay, warning light and heater panel may be purchased and installed on the existing wiring. The necessary points are clear on the wiring diagram.

28 Towing attachment - guidelines

1   A custom built towing attachment is available from VW dealers . This is supplied with fitting instructions and we recommend its use. It is designed to take the stress correctly. There are other reputable makes which also fit but there is always the question of overstraining the frame, a matter which the warranty does not cover.

2   There is also a standard electrical layout showing how to connect the trailer plug to the various sockets and switches in the vehicle harness. This is contained in VW workshop Bulletin 30 for the Golf/Scirocco dated November 1974.

3   **Do not** improvise. You will upset all sorts of current balances and possibly damage the vehicle circuit. If the information is not available then ask the dealer to install the wiring for you.

29 Windscreen wiper and washer - general description

1   The early basic vehicle was fitted with a two speed wiper and a mechanical foot pump for the washer system.

2   Subsequent models have an electric washer pump and an intermittent wiper control as well as two speed continuous wiping.

3   The early models may be converted by the installation of a different switch in the column switch set up and the washer pump. It is also necessary to fit a relay. The wiring circuit is shown in the various current flow diagrams. Details of the modification should be obtained from the dealer.

4   Some of the models are fitted with headlamp washers. A general description of this circuit is given in Section 35 and a current flow diagram in Fig. 11.18 for those who already have the system fitted.

5   A rear window wiper and washer is also available as an optional extra. The circuit diagram is shown in the current flow diagram (see Section 34).

6   The wiper/washer is controlled from the right-hand steering column switch. The speed control is fixed by the horizontal movement of the lever and the washer works when the lever is lifted towards the steering wheel.

7   The rear screen wash/wipe switch is fitted to the dashboard below the heating lever.

30 Windscreen wiper mechanism - removal, inspection and replacement

1   The nut holding the wiper arm is covered by a plastic cap. Prise this out and remove the nut. The arm may now be removed (photo). Under the wiper boss is a splined shaft and a rubber boot.

2   Remove the boot and the gland nut is accessible (photo). If you intend to dismantle any more remove the battery earth strap. Undo the nut and repeat the operation for the other spindle.

3   Unplug the connector from the motor terminals (photo).

4   The wiper motor and frame all held in position by a nut on a bracket (photo). Remove this nut and lift the motor and frame away from the car. (photo). The mechanism may now be examined at leisure.

5   The motor may be removed from the frame by undoing two nuts. Alternatively, the motor may be removed from the frame while the frame is still in position but we do not see the point in this as having got so far one might as well have a look at the frame joints as well.

6   Check that all the levers and pins are secure, not worn and are well lubricated.

7   Do not remove the crank from the motor unless the motor is to be replaced with a new one. If this is to be done, connect the multipin plug to the motor before installing the motor, switch on and let the motor run for four minutes. Switch off and the motor will stop in the parking position. Install the crank in the way shown in Fig. 11.19.

8   Repair is by replacement. Whatever is wrong with the electrical components may only be cured by fitting new ones. The replacement of the column switch is discussed in Section 18. The brush gear is not a service part so the motor must be replaced if faulty.

9   Inspect the linkage for wear or corrosion. The parts of the linkage are replaceable, if required. However, the links are different on left-hand and right-hand drive vehicles.

10 If electrical 'noise' has caused problems with the radio the motor may be replaced by a fully suppressed one.

11 Replacement is the reverse of removal. When assembling the arms they should be fitted to the splines in such a way that they come to rest in the park position as shown in Figure 11.20. Tighten the wiper arms to 0.7 mkg (5 lbs ft).

31 Windscreen wiper (two stage without intermittent wiping) - fault diagnosis

1   Check that the bridge between contacts '53s' and '53m' is installed

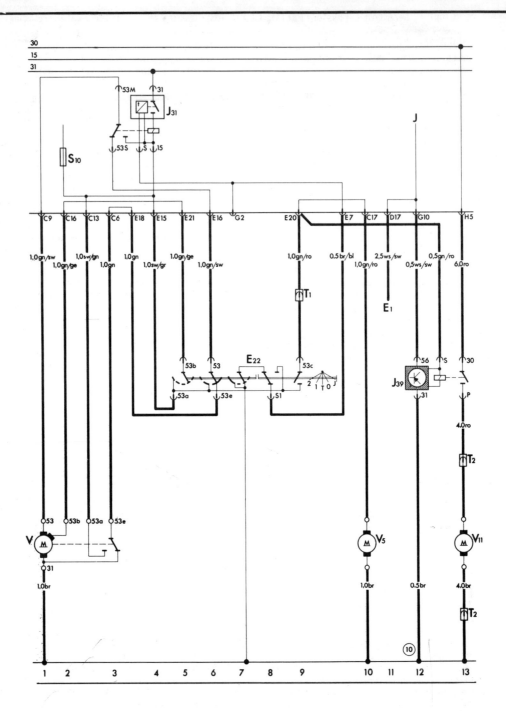

Fig. 11.18. Current flow diagram for the headlight washer system (Sec. 29)

Designation			In current track
E1	–	To lighting switch, terminal 56	11
E22	–	Wiper switch for intermittent operation	5,6,7,8,9
J	–	To dipper and headlight flasher relay, terminal 56 (see diagrams: Scirocco, part 2, current track 77)	12
		(see diagrams: Golf, part 2, current track 74)	
J31	–	Relay for wash-wipe intermittent system	3,4
J39	–	Relay for headlight washer	12, 13
S10	–	Fuse in fuse box (see diagrams: Scirocco, part 2, current track 61)	2
		(see diagrams: Golf, part 2, current track 62)	
T1	–	Connector, single, near fuse box	
T2	–	Connector, 2 pin, near headlight washer pump	
V	–	Wiper motor	1,2,3
V5	–	Windscreen washer pump	10
V11	–	Headlight washer pump	13
10	–	Earthing point, dashboard	

30.1 Remove the plastic cap, undo the nut and lever the arm away

30.2 Remove the rubber cap and undo the gland nut

30.3 Pull off the supply plug

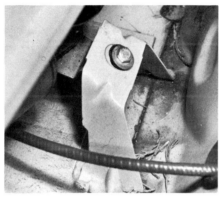
30.4a Undo the bolt securing the motor to the bracket (motor removed)

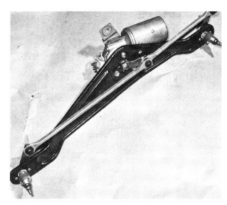
30.4b Pull out the motor and frame

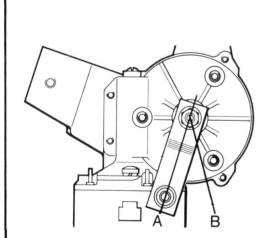

Fig. 11.19. Wiper motor crank - setting angle (Sec. 30)

Left-hand drive - The angle of the crank to the vertical in this position is 20° (A)
Right-hand drive - The crank should be 20° to the other side of the vertical line (B)

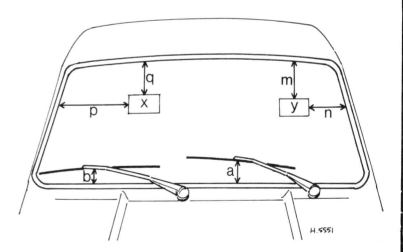

Fig. 11.20. Windscreen wiper arm park positions and washer jet aiming areas (Secs. 30 and 33)

Note: This is for a LHD, RHD will be a mirror image
Golf   — a, 35 mm (1.4 in)   b, 65 mm (2.6 in)
Scirocco — a, 25 mm (1 in)   b, 30 mm (1.2 in)
           p, 450 mm (17.7 in)   q, 260 mm (10.2 in)
           m, 350 mm (13.8 in)   n, 200 mm (7.9 in)

on the relay plate. The fresh air blower motor should be working to show that the fuse system is in order and the ignition should be switched on for each test.

2   *The motor is not working at all.* Check the voltage at terminal '53' on the wiper motor. Pull the multipin plug off the motor, set the switch lever to stage 1 and check the voltage at connection '53' (green/black). If there is voltage then the motor is defective. Connect a wire from terminal '53' (photo) of the motor to the battery '+ ve' and from the terminal '31' to earth. If the motor does not work now a new motor is needed. If it does work then the earth wire requires renewal.

3   If there was no voltage at terminal '53' when the connector was checked then the fault is probably in the wiper switch. Pull the multi-pin plug off the wiper column switch. Two wires, black/grey and black/green are connected to terminals '53' and '53a' of the plug. Slot these two out by connecting them with a piece of wire. If the motor now works a new column switch is needed. If it still does not work then there is a fault in wire '53' or wire '53a' which go to the relay plate. Disconnect the battery earth strap, pull connector 'E' off the relay plate and bridge contacts 'E 15' and 'E 16'. It will be necessary to remove the relay plate to do this (Section 23). Reconnect the battery and try again. If the motor works this time then wires '53' or '53a' are defective. Replace them. If the motor still does not work then there is fault in the relay plate. It must be removed and checked. Circuits 'E 16' to 'C 9' and 'E 15' to 'C 13' are the ones to test. If there is an open-circuit on these lines then a new relay plate is needed. If the circuits are in order then the wiring from the relay plate to the motor is at fault.

4   *The motor works on stage 1, but not stage II.* Set the lever to stage II. Connect terminal '31' on the motor (photo 31.2) to earth and terminal '53b' to the battery positive (+). If the motor works now then the fault is in the wiper switch. If the motor does not work then a new motor is needed. To test the switch: Fit the connector plug back on the motor and pull off the plug from the wiper switch. Bridge terminals '53a' and '53b' (wires black/grey and green/yellow). If the motor now works a new wiper switch is needed. If it does not then the problem is in the relay plate, between 'C16' and 'E21' (wire '53b'). The only way to find this out is to take the relay plate out, disconnect multiplugs 'C' and 'E' and check contacts 'C16' and 'E21' for continiuty. If there is a break in the circuit a new relay plate is needed. If the relay plate circuit is in order then check wire '53b' from the plate to the switch. If the break is in the wire then fit a new wire. If the wire is in order then the wiring from the relay to the motor must be renewed.

5   *The motor works on stage 1 and II, but not on intermittent wipe.* If both stages 1 and II are in order then the relay is suspect. Fit a new one. If the motor works now then the relay was faulty. If it does not put the old relay back and pull the connector off the wiper switch. Check switch contact 'S1'. It should be connected to earth with the lever at intermittent wipe. If it is connected to earth (zero resistance) then a new wiper switch is needed. If the 'S1' connection is not earthed properly then the 'S1' sire to the relay plate is shorted to earth. This time detach connector 'E' from the relay plate and check wire 'S1' for a short to earth. If it is defective replace the wire. If there is an open circuit, then the relay plate requires renewal.

6   There are other causes than wiring faults. A list is appended below.

31.2 The motor terminals: 'A' = terminal '53'; 'B' = terminal '31'; 'C' = terminal '53b'

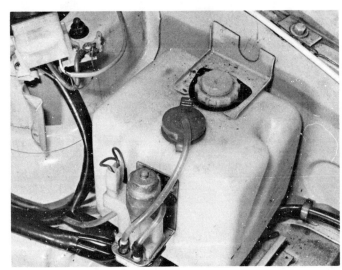

32.2 The washer motor and pump fixed to the tank in the engine compartment

Symptom	Probable reason	Remedy
Motor does not work, runs slowly or runs and then stops	1 Loose connections 2 Brushes worn 3 Linkage stiff or seized 4 Armature burnt out 5 Column switch defective	1 Check wiring. 2 New motor. 3 Dismantle, clean and lubricate. 4 Replace motor. 5 Replace switch.
Wiper arms do not park correctly	1 Cable to terminal '53' of the motor loose or broken 2 Drive crank not in correct position 3 Open circuit between terminals '53' and '31b'	1 Check and repair. 2 See Fig. 11.19. 3 Replace switch.
Motor continues to run when switched off	1 Switch burnt or defective	1 Replace switch.
Motor runs slowly with high pitched noise from the motor and gearbox	1 The gear housing is not seated properly, is not lubricated, or is worn badly	1 Examine gears and adjust if possible, otherwise replace motor

32 Windscreen washers - general

1   The early models of the Golf have a mechanical pump, foot operated, situated on the left near the pedals. This rarely gives trouble. Check the serviceability of the hoses and that the jets are clear. If the pump will not work then it must be disconnected, unscrewed from the frame and replaced with a new one. It is possible to install an electric pump with intermittent wash/wipe but this involves the use of a special tool to drive out the round connector sleeves of the multi-point socket connection. A wash/wipe switch, relay, and washer pump are required. The pump is connected to contact 'C17' of the relay plate.

2   The standard models now have the electric pump fitted and a two-speed wiper. The pump is situated on a bracket in front of the container. Keep the hoses and joints in good condition. If the motor does not work pull off the connector plug and check whether there is voltage at the + ve terminal when the lever switch is set to 'wash' and the ignition is switched on. Check also that the earth side is in order.

3   If there is voltage then the motor is defective and the complete pump motor unit must be replaced. To be quite certain rig a 12v supply and an earth wire to the motor terminals as a separate test. If there is no voltage the circuit must be traced back to the switch. There is no relay, the relay space on the board is bridged. The washer motor has not yet arrived in the Golf circuit diagram, but it is in current track '92' of the Rabbit, and in the Scirocco diagrams. The probable circuit trouble is that the bridge on the relay/fuse panel has become dislodged. Check for voltage here, and finally at the wiper switch plug. Use the same technique employed in Section 31, If the fuse was blown and you cannot find the fault check the fuse frequently. If it blows again then consult the VW agent.

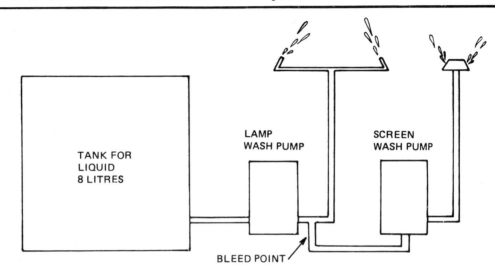

Fig. 11.21. Diagrammatic layout of hose connections for the screen and headlamp washer circuits (Sec. 32)

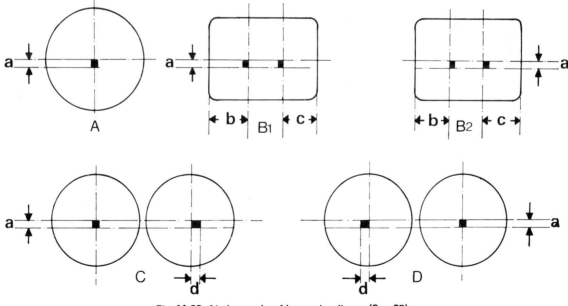

Fig. 11.22. Aiming marks of jets on headlamps (Sec. 35)

A   Single round lamp (both sides)
B1 LH rectangular (facing the lamps)
B2 RH rectangular (facing the lamps)
C   Twin headlamps L (facing the lamps)
D   Twin headlamps R (facing the lamps)

a = 10 mm
b = 70 mm
c = 60 mm
d = 15 mm

Width of area, except double headlamps = 1 mm

4 If the vehicle has an intermittent wash/wipe then the bridge is replaced by relay 'J31' and the turn signal switch has had a lug removed at a pre-determined breaking point to expose the location for intermittent wash/wipe to the wiper switch. There is also a variation in the wiring. Fault finding works the same way with the additional complication of the relay.

33 Wiper arm and washer jet - adjustment

To give the best results the wiper arms must be installed so that when parked they come to rest in the position shown in Fig. 11.20. This varies for different models. In the same way the jets should be directed to the area indicated in Fig. 11.20. The measurements seem to be to a fine limit. Mark the spot with a bit of sticky tape and direct the jet generally to this area. Do not fuss too much, the jet of liquid will be blown about by the wind anyway.

34 Rear screen wipe/wash - fitting guidelines

1 A very desirable addition is a rear screen wipe/wash. This may be supplied by VW as an optional extra, or a kit may be pruchased from Hella. The kit comprises switch motor, wiper arm, pump and washer unit with wire and hose. Full fitting instructions are supplied. It is not cheap, and requires holes to be drilled in the bodywork. It is not a job for the beginner, but it can be done with care and patience by the average mechanic. Do not fit a wiper without a washer, you will scratch the rear window this way.
2 For those who do have a service installed rear wiper a word of warning. If for some reason the motor must be disconnected, the reconnection is very important or the diode will be destroyed and a new motor required. If the wires to terminal '53' and '53a' are interchanged then this disaster will happen when the motor is switched off.

35 Headlamp washer system - general

1 This system is fitted to the higher range of vehicles only.
2 The system washes only, and does not wipe. An extra pump is installed which is operated by a relay allowing a jet for 0.3 seconds. The emission is further controlled by a pressure valve set at 35 psi (2.6 bar).
3 When the system is filled the lines must be bled (as with brakes). This is done by pulling off the hose at the junction leading to the headlamp jets until liquid emerges. Then reconnect the hose, switch on the ignition and the headlights and operate the column switch until water emerges from the jets. Be careful that all connections are correctly installed and use only the VW/Audi special water hose.
4 Training the jet is a difficult job unless the correct tool (VW 819) is available. This is a cylindrical mandrel which fits in the jet hole and reaches up to the lens. The top of the tool is moved about until it contacts the lens with certain limits.

36 Headlamp washer - fault diagnosis

37.2a The diagnostic computor terminal box is located in the engine compartment

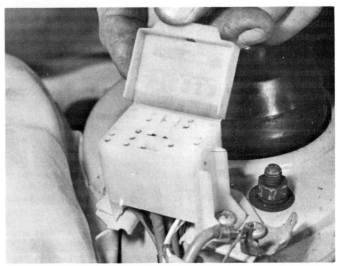

37.2b The cable fits in here. Keep this lid firmly shut and do not allow dirt or moisture to get in

Symptom	Possible cause	Remedy
One jet only squirts	Pressure valve stuck	Close off jet which does work and switch on to clear the blockage.
No jets, but pump can be heard to work	No fluid in tank Pressure valve defective	Fill. Replace.
No jets, pump not working	Column switch faulty	Check continuity - replace switch if necessary.
	Relay defective Pump defective	Check continuity - replace relay if necessary. Connect pump direct to 12V supply. If it does not work, remove and fit a new pump.
Jets squirt for longer than 1 second Jets squirt when lights are not switched on	Relay defective Relay defective	Replace relay. Replace relay.

37 Computer diagnosis - general

1   In 1970 VW introduced the computor diagnosis system. It is a truly immense step forward in preventative maintenance. The system is devised to assess the state of maintenance of all the major and many minor components of the vehicle. Over 80 points are checked, many of them automatically.

2   A multi-pin plug is installed in the engine compartment (photos). The operator at official agency will check the correct pressures of your tyres and then plug in a large cable to the diagnosis plug. He selects the correct master card for your vehicle, installs it, and from there on a computer takes over. The operator has a hand set connected to the computer which has a small window showing the number of the test to be carried out. As each check is done the print out is marked '+' if the measurement agrees with the vehicle specification or '−' where it is beyond tolerance.

3   The items which are not measured automatically are checked by the operator, where all is well he presses a button marked '+' on the hand set, where all is not well the '−ve' button is pressed.

4   The items which are measured by the equipment automatically are the steering geometry, ignition and charging systems and cylinder compression. Lights and battery condition are checked automatically.

The steering geometry is checked by photo electric beams and mirrors as the steering wheel is turned through 180°, 90° each side of the straight-ahead position. This is done within a 20 second period and measures toe and camber and prints out the answer in degrees and minutes. The ignition and charging systems are measured by the resistance of the various circuits. It is important that all connections are clean and that cable sizes are standard.

The cylinder compression is measured by calculating the load on the starter motor when the engine is turned over. The state of the battery and the temperature of the engine oil is measured and taken into account for this check.

There is no doubt that the system is quick, accurate and calculated to tell the unhappy customer all the awful things wrong with his vehicle in the shortest possible time.

5   If the vehicle is used a lot then this system is without doubt the finest way to take care of its working parts. The system does not repair, it diagnoses only, but a record such as the computer gives is worth many hours of hard work inspecting all these things manually, and of course it measures accurately items which the owner of the car cannot measure without expertise and a lot of expensive equipment.

6   Finally, it does away with opinion. It measures and compares with the vehicle specification. After that it is up to the owner what repairs he does, and which he leaves to the official agent to do. .

38 Wiring diagrams - explanation of the circuit structure

1   The vehicles of ten years ago were mostly supplied with current by D.C. generators. This effectively kept the charging rate down and in particular gave small charge at low engine rpm. The maximum speed of the generator was governed by commutator integrity problems. With the advent of the A.C. generator much better charging characteristics became possible, and greater loading of the electrical circuits without incurring cold starting problems due to uncharged batteries. At the same time minaturization of relays made it possible to use smaller and multi-contact switches. The possible number of appliances which could be used became much greater, and the number of circuits involved multiplied accordingly. Thus a vehicle of the Golf type which formerly would have rubbed along with four fuses now appears with fifteen fuses and a number of relays as well.

2   To date we have produced old fashioned circuit diagrams for all the VW family but they are rapidly becoming so involved that there is more black ink than white paper!

3   A circuit diagram bears little or no resemblance to the actual wiring of the car, for on the car all the wires are bunched in harness and the diagram may only be used to trace the terminal ends of the wiring, that is if your eyesight is good and you have a liking for finding your way in a maze. Some time ago VW took a firm line on this and produced a new idea called the Current Flow Diagram, which we reproduce in this book.

4   To understand the Current Flow Diagram it is necessary first to appreciate the change in wiring layout that has taken place. The Golf has four separate wiring harnesses. They are:

> a) *The wiring harness rear*
> b) *The wiring harness behind the dashboard panel.*
> c) *The wiring harness right front.*
> d) *The wiring harness left front.*

5   The ends of the wires terminate in plugs of various types ranging from multipin connectors to simple single pin or in the case of earth connections, eyelets. If you know how, the installation of a new harness is simply a matter of dismantling these plugs and refitting a new harness, but it is not a job for the amateur.

6   There are a number of single wire connections, mostly heavy duty cable, some of which are earth (ground) connections. These are very important as it is vital that there be minimal volts drop on the ground connections carrying large current loads.

7   A typical wiring harness is shown in Fig. 11.23. This one is an instrument board harness for the Rabbit.

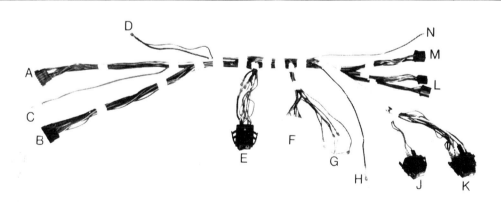

Fig. 11.23. Typical wiring harness - Golf/Rabbit (Sec. 30)

This is the wiring harness behind the instrument panel for the Rabbit

A   *Multipin connector D to relay plate*
B   *Multipin connector E to relay plate*
C   *Single wire H2 to terminal 30*

D   *Instrument panel earth*
E   *To headlamp switch*
F   *To panel cluster*
G   *Earth wires, instrument panel*
H   *Single wire to radiator fan motor*

J   *Rear window heater switch*
K   *Emergency light/switch*
L   *Steering column switch plug*
M   *Steering lock/starter switch*
N   *Earth wire*

8   Under the dashboard on the left-hand side of the vehicle is the fuse and relay plate, see (photo 23.2) and Fig. 11.16. This has six terminal plates 'A' to 'F' into which the wiring harnesses plug in, a section 'H1' to 'H4' all of which are connected to terminal '30', the main supply point in the starter circuit, and 'G1' to 'G10' which is provided for single wire contacts such as the oil pressure switch, ignition/starter switch terminal '15', all of which for some reason are better served with single wires. The board is so organized as to include the fuses in the correct circuits.

9   Relays, as required are plugged in to the face of the plate, the multipin connectors of the relays making the correct contacts automatically.

10 A table showing the connections for the Golf/Rabbit is given below:

Plate reference	Circuit connections
A	*Wiring harness left front.*
B	*Wiring harness diagnosis network.*
C	*Wiring harness right front.*
D	*Wiring harness behind the instrument panel.*
E	*Wiring harness behind the instrument panel.*
F	*Wiring harness rear.*
G 1 to 10	*Single wire connectors.*
H 1 to 4	*Connections to terminal '30'*

39 Wiring diagrams - explanation of usage

1   Before looking at the diagram study Fig. 11.24. This gives the explanation of the symbols used in the diagram. The majority of them are straightforward. The wire junction, fixed, means what it says - wires soldered or otherwise permanently fixed together. The wire jinction separable is a pull off tag or an eyelet held under a screw and washer. The wire connector is a plug and socket have one, two, or a multipin, connector which may be pulled apart easily, and assembled easily. These are referred to in the wiring key under letter 'T' and the type and location given.

2   Now refer to the diagram. For the examples given use

Diagram 1 - current flow diagram Golf: Part 1

3   A key of the explanation of the symbols is given. For instance 'E9' is the fan motor switch. Opposite this on the key is a number in this case '1' and '2'. This is the track number in which 'E9' may be found.

4   Now look at the diagram. At the front of it is a shaded portion with numbers running from '1' to '45'. This has two functions. First, it represents ground, earth, or things connected in one way or another to the battery negative terminal. The number represents the current flow track. Some of the tracks are connected to earth with heavy lines, sometimes with a number. These are actually earth wires. For example in track '2' the fan motor switch 'E9' is connected to earth via '10' which is the earth point of the instrument panel. In other cases, such as '19' the earth is by a thin line, which means no wire, the spark plug is screwed into the engine providing its own earth connection.

5   Returning to track '2' and 'E9'. The symbol for the switch shows a two stage switch and a resistor. This is connected to 'V2' the fan (blower) motor and then to 'T10'. The latter is the symbol for a 'wire connector-separable' and 'T10' in the key denotes a multipin connector on the instrument panel insert. This uses only one pin of 'T10', it crops up again in current tracks '12' to '17' and '43'. Each time a suffix denotes the pin number.

6   The other side of the multipin connector goes to the top shaded portion of the diagram. This represents the relay and fuse plate. Where the wire enters the relay plate is a small figure 'D5'. Reference to Fig. 11.25, the relay plate shows that one of the numbered terminals is 'D5'

so now we know where the blower motor terminal on the relay plate is located. A closer look at the diagram shows that 'D5' is connected inside the relay board to 'S11' which is a fuse. The wire from the fuse (internal connection) goes to track '46' which is at the right-hand end of the relay board. On part 2 of the diagram track '46' goes to terminal '31' which is the main supply point. On the way the line is joined in the relay board, a permanent connection, to 'E10' which leads externally to 'T', the cable adaptor behind the instrument board and thence to one contact of 'D' the starter/ignition switch.

7   In this way the blower motor circuit is traceable. The various connection points are identifiable and the circuit fuse is located. One further point. The wires are labelled with the colour code, and the breaks in the wire where small figures are inserted are the cross section area of the wire. Thus our blower motor switch line is brown and 1.0 mm area. The wire from the motor to the connector pink and 1.0 mm area. The wire from the connector to the relay board is black and pink and 1.0 mm area.

8   On part 1 of the flow diagram is a large block 'T20'. This is the diagnostic terminal connector. Scattered about the diagram are wires terminating in circles with numbers in them. For example track '8' terminates in a circle with '31' inside it. This means that the '31' terminal of the diagnostic box goes to earth (ground). Similarly in track '15' the TDC sensor, 'G7' is connected to terminals '21' and '22' of the diagnostic box.

9   It will be seen that the starter 'B' has only thin connecting lines, whereas we know large currents flow. The connections are internal to the starter and solenoid, the diagram deals only with external wiring.

40 Wiring diagrams - general advice

1   One of the truest things ever said is that a little knowledge is a dangerous thing. If you have read and understood the previous two Sections then you have a rough idea of how the connections are arranged. If you are an electrical engineer or an automotive electrician then we have supplied all you need. If you do not have this expertise you can still check connections and find out whether voltage is getting to the right point, but there you will stop if you are wise. Refer to the various Sections of this book to see what can and cannot be done to components but **do not take the wiring out of the car.** You can convert a simple fault which the VW electrician will quickly locate and correct, into a nightmare for which there is no logical reason, in a matter of seconds. We do not wish to be blamed for this. You will rightly feel foolish if the radiator fan does not work because the connector has pulled apart and only needs pushing together, but if you go to the expert and say that you have checked the circuit as far as possible, that 'T2b' is connected properly but that 'J26' does not seem to work or 'F18' (the thermo-switch) is doubtful then he will regard you with much more respect. But if you replace 'J26' without finding out what is really wrong (eg; a short circuit in the motor), and reintroduce current to where it should not go, then the VW electrician may not say anything, but he will think it, and we wouldn't like that.

2   The following wiring diagrams are included:

Fig. 11.25	Golf: part 1
Fig. 11.26	Golf: part 2
Fig. 11.27	Additional wiring Golf & Scirocco (Europe)
Fig. 11.28	Scirocco: part 1 (Europe)
Fig. 11.29	Scirocco: part 2 (Europe)
Fig. 11.30	Scirocco: part 1 (USA)
Fig. 11.31	Scirocco: part 2 (USA)
Fig. 11.32	Rabbit: part 1
Fig. 11.33	Rabbit: part 2

Although they are up-to-date at the time of publication it would be wise to consult the VW agent about possible modifications.

Fig. 11.24. Symbols used in current flow diagrams giving examples of useage

SYMBOL	EXPLANATION	Sample use
	ALTERNATOR WITH DIODE RECTIFIERS	Golf alternator
	MOTOR	Fan motor, radiator fan
	EXTERNAL WIRING WIRE 10 mm^2 sectional area	Wiring diagram
	WIRE JUNCTION FIXED (SOLDERED)	Relay plate, dash board printed circuit
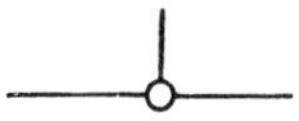	WIRE JUNCTION SEPARABLE	Screw on terminals and eyelets
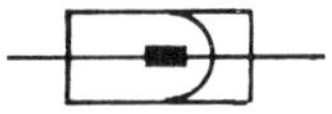	PLUG, SINGLE OR MULTIPIN	T10 written by the side means explanation in the key
	WIRE CROSSING, NOT JOINED	Wiring diagram
	GROUND, OR EARTH	Wiring diagram
	SWITCH CLOSED	Wiring diagram
	SWITCH OPEN	Wiring diagram
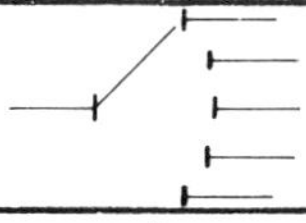	MULTI CONTACT SWITCH	Wiring diagram
	SWITCH, MANUALLY OPERATED	Wiring diagram
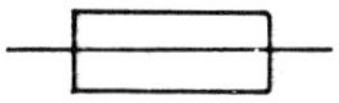	FUSE	
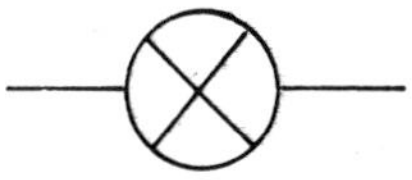	BULB	
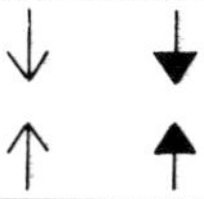	SPARK GAP	Spark plugs Distributor points
	CONDENSER	Distributor

H.5550

SYMBOL	EXPLANATION	Sample use
	TRANSFORMER, IRON CORE	Ignition coil
	DIODE	Alternator
	TRANSISTOR	Voltage regulator
	MECHANICAL CONNECTION MECHANICAL CONNECTION SPRING LOADED	Double switch Oil pressure switch
	RELAY, COIL	
	RELAY, ELECTRO MAGNETIC	(a) Headlamp (b) Cut off valve (carburettor)
	HORN	
	RESISTOR	
	POTENTIOMETER	
	THERMAL RESISTOR AUTOMATIC REGULATING	Temperature sender
	HEATING ELEMENT	Rear window heater
	BATTERY 12 volt	
	MEASURING GAUGE	Fuel gauge Temperature gauge
	SUPPRESSION WIRE	
	CLOCK	
	MECHANICAL PRESSURE SWITCH	Door switch for interior light

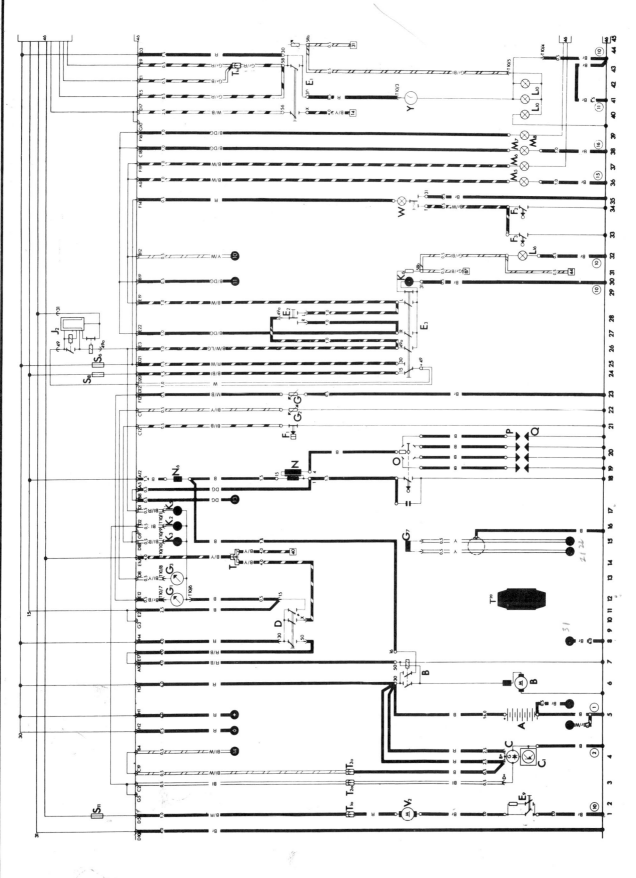

Fig. 11.25. Current Flow Diagram - Golf: Part 1 (see page 202 for 'Key')

Key to Current Flow Diagram - Golf: Part 1

Designation		in current track
A	Battery	5
B	Starter	6, 7
C	Generator	4
C1	Voltage regulator	4
D	Ignition/starter switch	8, 10, 11
E1	Lighting switch	40, 43, 44
E2	Turn signal switch	28
E3	Emergency light switch	24, 25, 26, 27, 29, 30, 31
E9	Fan motor switch	1, 2
F1	Oil pressure switch	21
F2	Door contact switch, front left	34
F3	Door contact switch, front right	33
G	Fuel gauge sender	23
G1	Fuel gauge	12
G2	Temperature gauge sender	22
G3	Temperature gauge	13
G7	TDC sensor	15
J5	Emergency/turn signal relay	26, 27, 28
K2	Generator warning lamp	17
K3	Oil pressure warning lamp	15
K5	Turn signal warning lamp	17
K6	Emergency light warning lamp	30
L10	Instrument panel light	40, 41, 42
L16	Heater lever light	32
M5	Turn signal, front left	36
M6	Turn signal, rear left	37
M7	Turn signal, front right	38
M8	Turn signal, rear right	39
N	Ignition coil	18
N6	Series resistance	18
O	Distributor	18, 20
P	Plug connector	19, 20
Q	Spark plugs	19, 20
S6, S8, S11	Fuses in fuse box	1, 24, 25
T	Cable adaptor, behind instrument panel	
T1a	Cable connector, single, behind instrument panel insert	
T1b	Cable connector, single in engine compartment, front, left	
T1c	Cable connector, single, in luggage compartment, left	
T1d	Flat connector, single, in luggage compartment, left	
T1e	Connector, single, behind instrument panel	
T1f	Connector, single, in engine compartment, front, right	
T2a	Flat connector, 2 pin, in engine compartment, right	
T2b	Flat connector, 2 pin, in engine compartment, front left	
T10	Multi-pin connector, instrument panel insert	
T20	Test socket	12
V2	Blower motor	1
W	Interior light	35
Y	Clock	41
1	Earth strap, battery to body	
2	Earth strap, generator to engine	
10	Earth point, instrument panel insert	
11	Earth point, body	
15	Earth point engine compartment, front left	
16	Earth point engine compartment, front right	

Key to Current Flow Diagram - Golf: Part 1

See Page 246 for Wiring Colour Code

Key to Current Flow Diagram - Golf: Part 2

Designation		in current track
E4	Headlight dimmer and flasher switch	72
E15	Heated rear window switch	62
E22	Intermittent wiper operation switch	67, 68, 69, 70, 71
E23	Fog and rear fog light switch	48, 49
F	Brake light switch	84
F4	Reversing light switch	79
F18	Radiator fan thermoswitch	89
H	Horn button	81
H1	Horn	82
J	Dimmer and flasher relay	72, 73, 74, 76
J5	Fog light relay	49, 50
J9	Heated rear window relay	60, 61
J26	Radiator fan relay	88, 89
J31	Wash-wipe, intermittent relay	65, 66, 67
K1	Headlight warning lamp	77
K10	Rear window warning lamp	63
K17	Fog and rear fog light relay	47
L1	Twin-filament headlight bulb, left	73, 74
L2	Twin-filament headlight bulb, right	75, 76
L15	Ashtray light	87
L20	Rear fog light	48
L22	Fog light, left	51
L23	Fog light, right	53
L28	Cigarette lighter lamp bulb	86
M1	Side light bulb, left	56
M2	Tail light bulb, right	59
M3	Side light bulb, right	58
M4	Tail light bulb, left	57
M9	Brake light bulb, left	83
M10	Brake light bulb, right	82
M16	Reversing light bulb, left	78
M17	Reversing light bulb, right	79
N1	Automatic choke	64
N3	Cut-off valve solenoid	63
S1, S2, S3, S4, S5, S7, S9	Fuses in fuse box	52, 54, 57, 58, 60, 62,
S10, S12, S13, S14, S15		73, 74, 75, 76, 80, 84
T	Cable adaptor, behind instrument panel	
T1a	Cable connector, single, behind instrument panel	
T1b	Cable connector, single, in engine compartment, front left	
T1c	Flat connector, single, in luggage compartment left	
T1d	Cable connector, single, in luggage compartment left	
T1e	Connector, single, behind instrument panel	
T1f	Connector, single, in engine compartment, front right	
T2a	Cable connector, 2 pin, in engine compartment right	
T2b	Flat connector, 2 pin, in engine compartment, front left	
T10	Multi-pin connector, instrument panel insert	
U1	Cigarette lighter	85
V	Wiper motor	65, 66
V7	Radiator fan motor	88
W6	Glove box light	84
X	License plate light	54, 55
Z1	Heated rear window	60
10	Earth point, instrument panel insert	
11	Earth point, body	
15	Earth point engine compartment, front left	
16	Earth point engine compartment, front right	

Key to Current Flow Diagram - Golf: Part 2

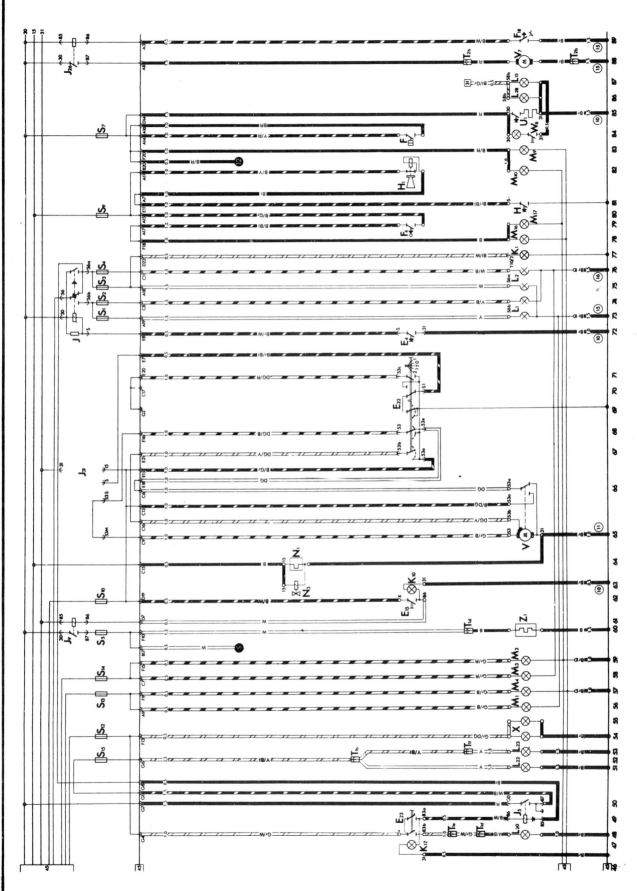

Fig. 11.26. Current Flow Diagram - Golf: Part 2

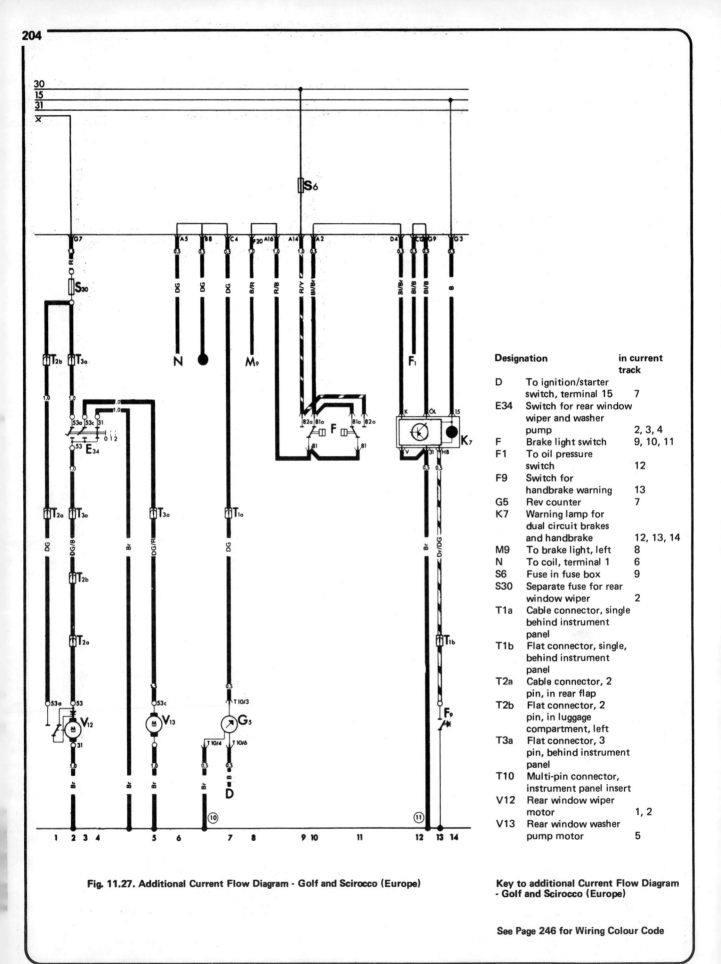

Fig. 11.27. Additional Current Flow Diagram - Golf and Scirocco (Europe)

Key to additional Current Flow Diagram
- Golf and Scirocco (Europe)

Designation		in current track
D	To ignition/starter switch, terminal 15	7
E34	Switch for rear window wiper and washer pump	2, 3, 4
F	Brake light switch	9, 10, 11
F1	To oil pressure switch	12
F9	Switch for handbrake warning	13
G5	Rev counter	7
K7	Warning lamp for dual circuit brakes and handbrake	12, 13, 14
M9	To brake light, left	8
N	To coil, terminal 1	6
S6	Fuse in fuse box	9
S30	Separate fuse for rear window wiper	2
T1a	Cable connector, single behind instrument panel	
T1b	Flat connector, single, behind instrument panel	
T2a	Cable connector, 2 pin, in rear flap	
T2b	Flat connector, 2 pin, in luggage compartment, left	
T3a	Flat connector, 3 pin, behind instrument panel	
T10	Multi-pin connector, instrument panel insert	
V12	Rear window wiper motor	1, 2
V13	Rear window washer pump motor	5

See Page 246 for Wiring Colour Code

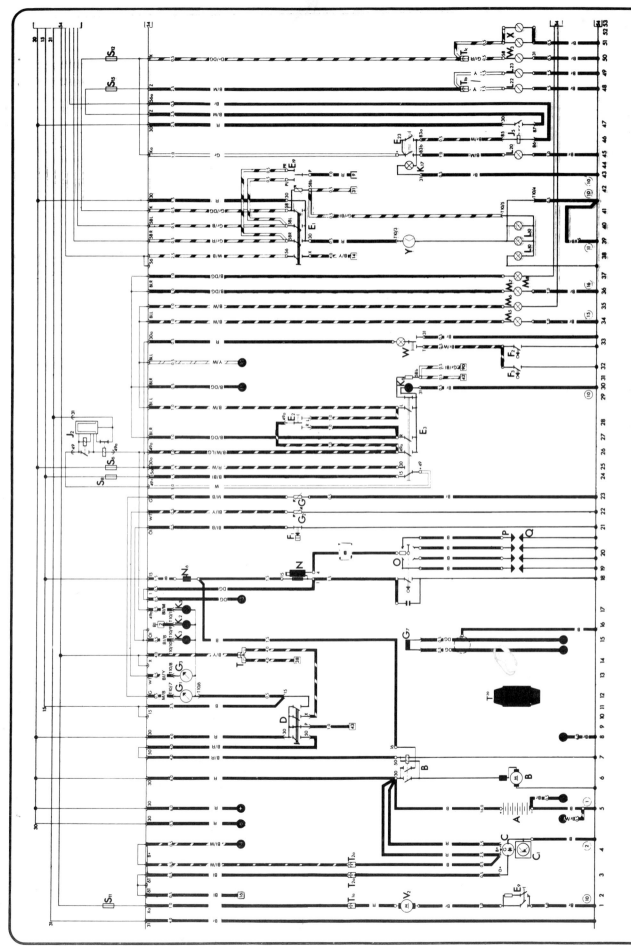

Fig. 11.28. Current Flow Diagram - Scirocco (Europe): Part 1 (see page 206 for 'Key')

Key to Current Flow Diagram - Scirocco (Europe): Part 1

Designation		in current track
A	Battery	5
B	Starter	6, 7
C	Generator	3, 4
C1	Voltage regulator	4
D	Ignition/starter switch	8, 9, 10, 11, 12
E1	Lighting switch	38, 39, 40, 41, 42
E2	Turn signal switch	28
E3	Emergency light switch	24, 25, 26, 27, 29, 31
E9	Fan motor switch	1, 2
E19	Side light switch	43
E23	Fog and rear fog light switch	45, 46
F1	Oil pressure switch	21
F2	Door contact switch, front left	33
F3	Door contact switch, front right	32
G	Fuel gauge sender	23
G1	Fuel gauge	12
G2	Temperature gauge sender	22
G3	Temperature gauge	13
G7	TDC sensor	15
J2	Emergency/turn signal relay	26, 27, 28
J5	Fog light relay	46, 47
K2	Generator warning lamp	16
K3	Oil pressure warning lamp	15
K5	Turn signal warning lamp	17
K6	Emergency light warning lamp	30
K17	Fog and rear fog light warning lamp	44
L10	Instrument panel light	38, 39, 40
L20	Rear fog light	45
L22	Fog light, left	48
L23	Fog light, right	49
M5	Turn signal, front left	34
M6	Turn signal, rear left	35
M7	Turn signal, front right	36
M8	Turn signal, rear right	37
N	Ignition coil	18
N6	Series resistance	18
O	Distributor	19, 20
P	Plug connector	19, 20
Q	Spark plugs	19, 20
S6, S8, S11, S12, S15 - Fuses in fuse box		1, 24, 25, 48, 50
T	Cable adaptor, behind instrument panel	
T1a	Cable connector, single, behind instrument panel insert	
T1b	Cable connector, single, in engine compartment, front, left	
T1c	Cable connector, single, in luggage compartment, left	
T1d	Flat connector, single, in luggage compartment, left	
T2a	Flat connector, 2 pin, in engine compartment, right	
T2b	Flat connector, 2 pin, in engine compartment, front left	
T10	Multi-pin connector, instrument panel insert	12
T20	Test socket	1
V2	Blower motor	33
W	Interior light	50
W3	Luggage compartment light	51, 52
X	License plate light	39
Y	Clock	

1	Earth strap, battery to body	
2	Earth strap, generator to engine	
10	Earth point, instrument panel insert	
11	Earth point, body	
15	Earth point, engine compartment, front left	
16	Earth point, engine compartment, front right	

Key to Current Flow Diagram - Scirocco (Europe): Part 2

Designation		in current track
E4	Headlight dimmer and flasher switch	75
E15	Heated rear window switch	61
E22	Intermittent wiper operation switch	69, 70, 71, 72, 73
F	Brake light switch	87
F4	Reversing light switch	82
F18	Radiator fan thermoswitch	92
H	Horn button	84
H1	Horn	85
J	Dimmer and flasher relay	75, 77, 79
J9	Heated rear window relay	59, 60
J26	Radiator fan relay	91, 92
J31	Wash-wipe, intermittent relay	66, 67, 68
K1	Headlight warning lamp	80
K10	Rear window warning lamp	62
L1	Twin-filament headlight bulb, left	76, 77
L2	Twin-filament headlight bulb, right	78, 79
L15	Cigarette lighter lamp bulb	89
L16	Heating lever lamp bulb	90
M1	Side light bulb, left	55
M2	Tail light bulb, left	58
M3	Side light bulb, right	57
M4	Tail light bulb, left	56
M9	Brake light bulb, left	86
M10	Brake light bulb, right	85
M16	Reversing light bulb, left	81
M17	Reversing light bulb, right	82
N1	Automatic choke	64
N3	Cut-off valve solenoid	63
S1, S2, S3, S4, S5, S7, S9	Fuses in fuse box	56, 57, 59, 61, 76, 77
S10, S13, S14		78, 79, 83, 87
T	Cable adaptor, behind instrument panel	
T1a	Cable connector, single, behind instrument panel	
T1b	Cable connector, single, in engine compartment, front left	
T1c	Flat connector, single, in luggage compartment left	
T1d	Cable connector, single, in luggage compartment left	
T2a	Flat connector, 2 pin, in engine compartment left	
T2b	Flat connector, 2 pin, in engine compartment, front left	
T10	Multi-pin connector, instrument panel insert	
U1	Cigarette lighter	88
V	Wiper motor	65, 66
V5	Washer pump motor	74
V7	Radiator fan motor	91
W6	Glove box light	87

1	Earth strap, battery to body	
2	Earth strap, generator to body	
10	Earth point, instrument panel insert	
11	Earth point, body	
15	Earth point engine compartment, front left	
16	Earth point engine compartment, front right	

See Page 246 for Wiring Colour Code

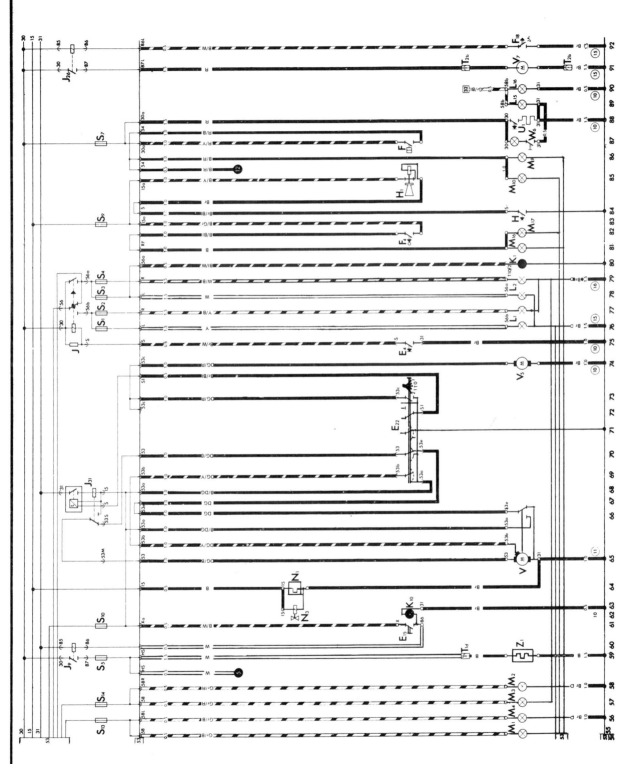

Fig. 11.29. Current Flow Diagram - Scirocco (Europe): Part 2

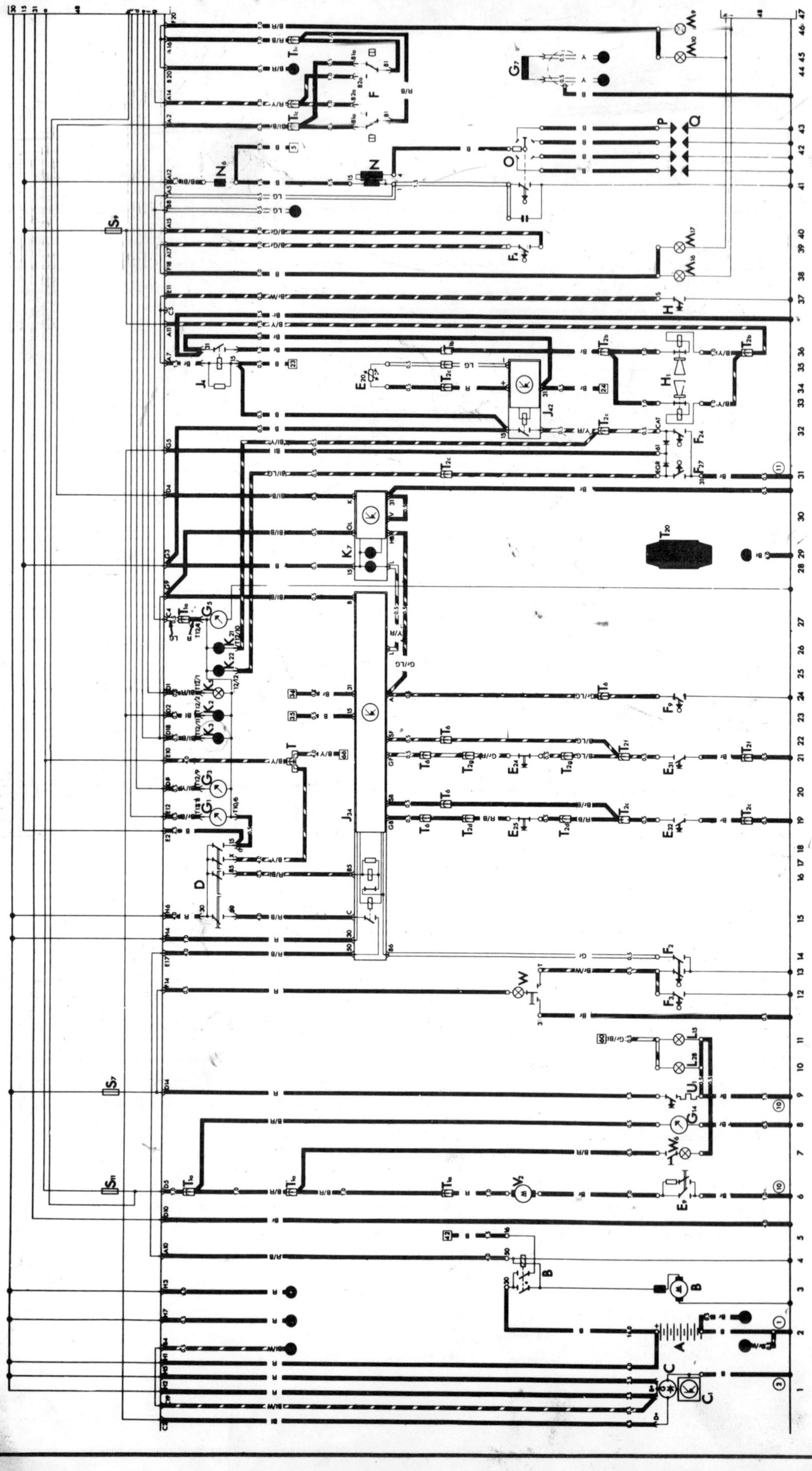

Fig. 11.30. Current Flow Diagram - Scirocco (USA): Part 1

Key to Current Flow Diagram - Scirocco (USA): Part 1

Designation		in current track
A	Battery	2
B	Starter	3, 4, 5
C	Alternator	1
C1	Regulator	1
D	Ignition/starter switch	15, 16, 17, 18
E9	Fresh air fan switch	6
E24	Safety belt lock with contact, left	21
E25	Safety belt lock with contact, right	19
E31	Contact strip in driver's seat	21
E32	Contact strip in passenger seat	19
F	Brake light switch	43, 44
F2	Door contact and buzzer alarm switch, left	13, 14
F3	Door contact switch, right	12
F4	Back-up light switch	39
F9	Parking brake control switch	24
F24	Switch in catalytic converter operating time recorder (on speedometer)	32
F27	Switch in EGR operating time recorder	31
G1	Fuel gauge	19
G3	Coolant temperature gauge	20
G5	Tachometer	27
G7	TDC marker unit	44
G14	Voltmeter	8
G20	Temperature sensor for catalytic converter	34, 35
H	Horn button	37
H1	Dual horn	33, 36
J4	Dual horn relay	34, 35, 36
J34	Safety belt warning system relay	14, 15, 16, 17, 19, 21, 22
J42	Relay for catalytic converter (behind dashboard)	32, 33, 34, 35
K2	Alternator charging warning light	23
K3	Oil pressure warning light	22
K5	Turn signal warning light	24
K7	Dual circuit brake warning, parking brake warning and safety belt warning light	28, 29, 30
K21	Catalytic converter warning light	26
K22	EGR warning light	25
L15	Ashtray illumination	11
L28	Cigarette lighter illumination	10
M9	Brake light, left	46
M10	Brake light, right	45
M16	Back-up light, left	38
M17	Back-up light, right	39
N	Ignition coil	41
N6	Series resistance	41
O	Ignition distributor	41, 42
P	Spark plug connectors	42, 43
Q	Spark plugs	42, 43
S9	Fuses in fuse box	6, 9, 40
T	Wire connector behind dashboard	
T1a	Wire connector, single, behind dashboard	
T1b	Wire connector, single, behind dashboard	
T1c	Wire connector, single, in engine compartment	
T1d	Wire connector, single, in engine compartment, front left	
T1e	Wire connector, single, in engine compartment, front right	
T1f	Wire connector, single, in engine compartment	
T1g	Wire connector, single, in luggage compartment, rear left	
T1h	Wire connector, single, in luggage compartment, rear right	
T1i	Wire connector, single, in luggage compartment	
T2a	Wire connector, double, in engine compartment	
T2b	Wire connector, double, in engine compartment	
T2c	Wire connector, double, behind dashboard	
T2d	Wire connector, double, on frame, right	
T2e	Wire connector, double, under passenger seat	
T2f	Wire connector, double, under driver's seat	
T2g	Wire connector, double, on frame, left	
T6	Wire connector, 6 point, behind dashboard	29
U1	Test network, test socket	9
U2	Cigarette lighter	6
W	Fresh air fan	12
W6	Glove compartment light	7
1	Ground strap, battery/body	
2	Ground strap, alternator/engine	
10	Ground connector, dashboard cluster	
11	Ground connector, body	
15	Ground connector, engine compartment, front left	
16	Ground connector, engine compartment, front right	

Key to Current Flow Diagram - Scirocco (USA): Part 2

Designation		in current track
E	Light switch	66, 67, 68, 69
E2	Turn signal switch	56
E3	Emergency flasher switch	52, 53, 54, 55, 56, 57, 58, 60
E4	Headlight dimmer switch	98
E15	Rear window defogger switch	85
E20	Instrument panel lighting control switch	70
E22	Windshield wiper intermittent switch	92, 93, 94, 95, 96
F1	Oil pressure switch	49
F18	Radiator fan thermo switch	106
G	Fuel gauge sender unit	51
G2	Coolant temperature gauge sending unit	50
J'	Headlight dimmer relay	98, 99, 100
J2	Emergency flasher relay	54, 55, 56
J9	Rear window defogger relay	84
J31	Windshield wash/wiper intermittent relay	89, 90, 91
K1	Headlight high beam warning light	105
K6	Emergency flasher warning light	59
K10	Rear window defogger warning light	85
L1	Sealed beam unit, left headlight, high and low beam	99, 101
L2	Sealed beam unit, right headlight, high and low beam	100, 102
L8	Clock illumination	69
L10	Instrument panel illumination	70, 71, 72
L16	Heater operation lever illumination	61
L17	Sealed beam unit, left headlight, high beam	104
L18	Sealed beam unit, right headlight, high beam	103
L25	Volt meter illumination	67
M1	Parking light, front left	77
M2	Tail light, right	82
M3	Parking light, front left	80
M4	Tail light, left	79
M5	Turn signal, left front	62
M6	Turn signal, left rear	63
M7	Turn signal, right front	64
M8	Turn signal, right rear	65
M11	Sidemarker, front	76, 81
M12	Sidemarker, rear	78, 83
N1	Automatic choke	87
N3	Electric magnetic cut-off valve	86
S1, S2, S3, S4, S5, S6 S8, S10, S12, S13, S14	Fuses in fuse box	80, 84, 85, 99, 100, 101, 102
T	Wire connector behind dashboard	
T1a	Wire connector, single, behind dashboard	
T1b	Wire connector, single, behind dashboard	
T1c	Wire connector, single, in engine compartment	
T1d	Wire connector, single, in engine compartment, front left	
T1e	Wire connector, single, in engine compartment, front right	
T1f	Wire connector, single, in luggage compartment	
T1g	Wire connector, single, in luggage compartment	
T1h	Wire connector, single, in luggage compartment, rear left	
T1i	Wire connector, single, in luggage compartment, rear right	
T2a	Wire connector, double, in engine compartment	
T2b	Wire connector, double, in engine compartment	
T2c	Wire connector, double, behind dashboard	
T2d	Wire connector, double, on body bottom, right	
T2e	Wire connector, double, on body bottom, right	
T2f	Wire connector, double, under passenger seat	
T2g	Wire connector, double, under driver's seat	
T6	Wire connector, 6 point, behind dashboard	
V	Windshield wiper motor	88, 89, 90
V5	Windshield washer pump	97
V7	Radiator fan	106
W3	Luggage compartment illumination	73
X	License plate light	74, 75
Y	Clock	67
Z1	Rear window defogger heating element	84
10	Ground connector, dashboard cluster	
11	Ground connector, body	
15	Ground connector, engine compartment, front left	
16	Ground connector, engine compartment, front right	

See Page 246 for Wiring Colour Code

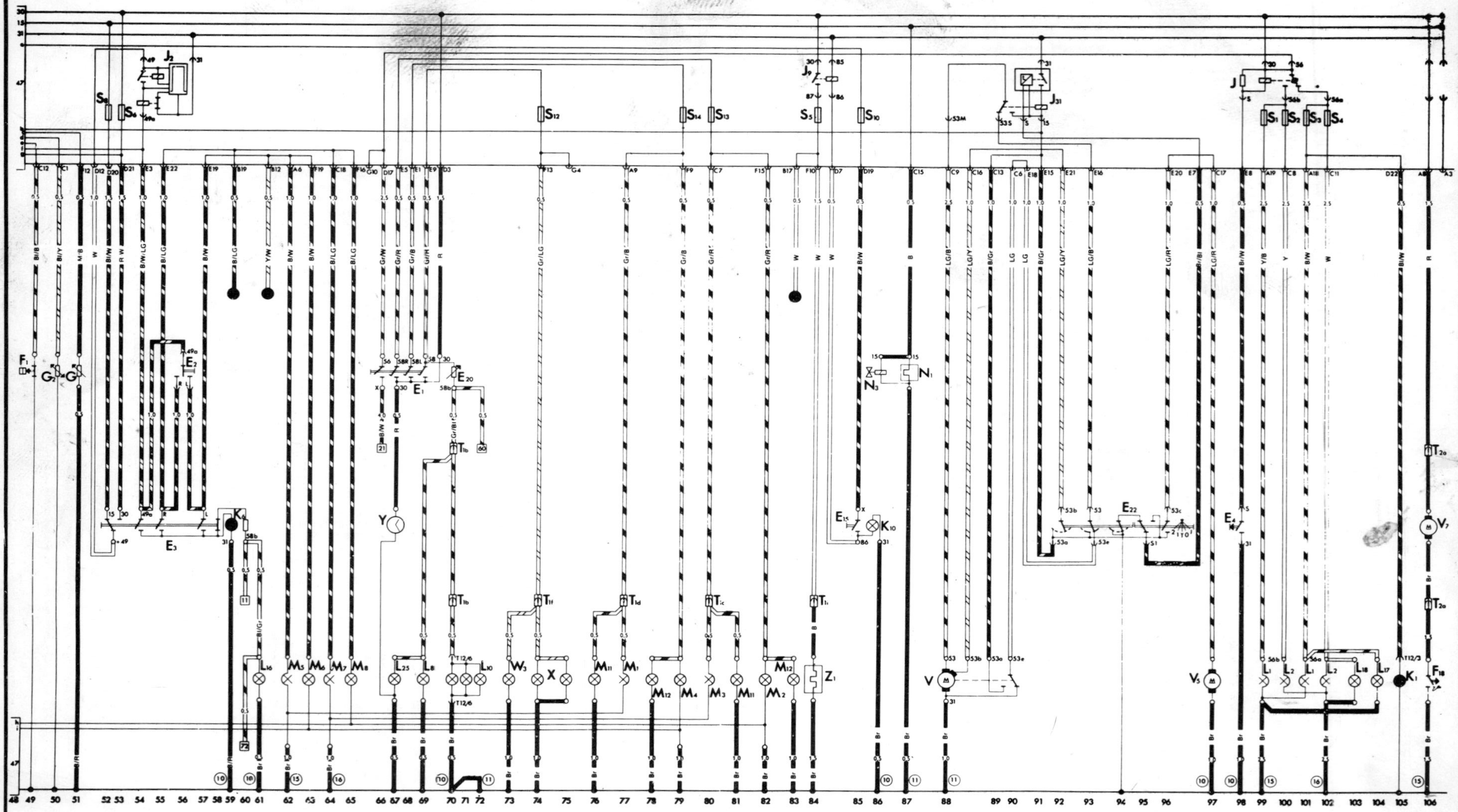

Fig. 11.31. Current Flow Diagram - Scirocco (USA): Part 2 (see page 209 for 'Key')

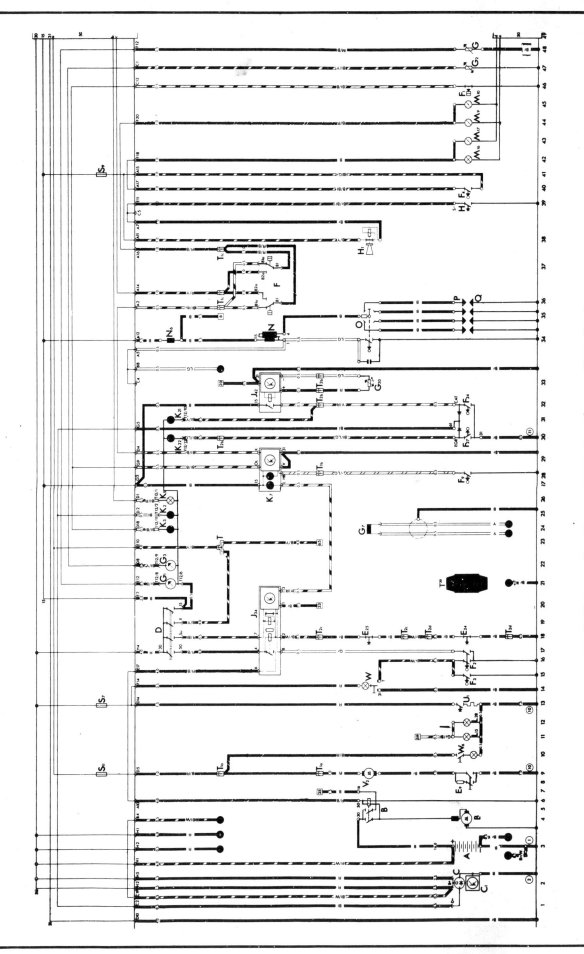

Fig. 11.32. Current Flow Diagram - Rabbit: Part 1 (see page 212 for 'Key')

Key to Current Flow Diagram - Rabbit: Part 1

Designation		in current track
A	Battery	3
B	Starter	4, 5, 6
C	Alternator	1, 2
C1	Regulator	2
D	Ignition/starter switch	17, 18, 19, 20
E9	Fresh air fan	8, 9
E24	Safety belt lock with contact, left	18
E25	Safety belt lock with contact, right	18
F	Brake light switch	46
F1	Oil pressure switch	36, 37
F2	Door contact and buzzer alarm switch, left	16, 17
F3	Door contact switch, right	15
F4	Back-up light switch	40
F9	Parking brake control switch	28
F24	Switch in catalytic operating time recorder converter (on speedometer)	32
F27	Switch in EGR operating time recorder (on speedometer)	29
G	Fuel gauge sending unit	48
G1	Fuel gauge	21
G2	Coolant temperature sending unit	47
G3	Coolant temperature gauge	22
G7	TDC marker unit	24
G20	Temperature sensor for catalytic converter	33
H	Horn button	39
H1	Horn	38
J34	Safety belt warning system relay	16, 17, 18, 19, 20, 21
J42	Relay for catalytic converter (behind dashboard)	32, 33
K2	Alternator charging warning light	25
K3	Oil pressure warning light	24
K5	Turn signal warning light	26
K7	Dual circuit brake, warning, parking brake warning and safety belt warning light	27, 28, 29
K21	Catalytic converter warning light	31
K22	EGR warning light	30
L15	Ashtray illumination	11
L28	Cigarette lighter illumination	12
M9	Brake light, left	44
M10	Brake light, right	45
M16	Back-up light, left	42
M17	Back-up light, right	43
N	Ignition coil	34
N6	Series resistance	34, 35
O	Ignition distributor	35, 36
P	Spark plug connectors	42, 43
Q	Spark plugs	
S7, S9, S11	Fuses in fuse box	
T	Test network, test socket	9, 13, 41
T1a	Wire connector, single, behind dashboard	
T1b	Wire connector, single, behind dashboard	
T1c	Wire connector, single, in engine compartment, front left	
T1d	Wire connector, single, in engine compartment, front right	
T1e	Wire connector, single, in engine compartment, front left	
T1f	Wire connector, single, in engine compartment, front right	
T1g	Wire connector, single, in luggage compartment, right rear	
T1h	Wire connector, single, in luggage compartment, left rear	
T2a	Wire connector, double, in engine compartment	
T2b	Wire connector, double, behind dashboard	
T2c	Wire connector, double, behind dashboard	
T2d	Wire connector, double, behind dashboard	
T3a	Wire connector, 3 point, in engine compartment, left front	
T3b	Wire connector, 3 point, in engine compartment, right front	
T12	Wire connector, 12 point, on dashboard cluster	21
T20	Test network, test socket	13
U1	Cigarette lighter	9
V2	Fresh air fan	14
W	Interior light	10
W6	Glove compartment illumination	
1	Ground strap, battery/body	
2	Ground strap, alternator/engine	
10	Ground connector, dashboard cluster	
11	Ground connector, body	
15	Ground connector, engine compartment, front left	
16	Ground connector, engine compartment, front right	

Key to Current Flow Diagram - Rabbit: Part 2

Designation		in current track
E1	Light switch	65, 66, 67
E2	Turn signal switch	55
E3	Emergency flasher switch	51, 52, 53, 54, 56, 57, 59
E4	Headlight dimmer switch	93
E15	Rear window defogger switch	83
E20	Instrument panel lighting control switch	68
E22	Windshield wiper intermittent switch	88, 89, 90, 91
F18	Radiator fan thermo switch	99
J	Headlight dimmer relay	93, 94, 95
J2	Emergency flasher relay	53, 54, 55
J9	Rear window defogger relay	81, 82
K1	Rear window defogger warning light	98
K6	Emergency flasher warning light	58
K10	Rear window defogger warning light	84
L1	Sealed beam unit, left headlight	94, 96
L2	Sealed beam unit, right headlight	95, 97
L10	Heater operation lever illumination	60
L16	Instrument panel illumination	68, 69, 70
M1	Parking light, left front	74
M2	Tail light, right	79
M3	Parking light, right front	77
M4	Tail light, left	76
M5	Turn signal, left front	61
M6	Turn signal, left rear	62
M7	Turn signal, right front	63
M8	Turn signal, right rear	64
M11	Sidemarker, front	73, 78
M12	Sidemarker, rear	75, 80
N1	Automatic choke	85
N3	Electromagnetic cut off valve	84
S1, S2, S3, S4, S5, S6, S8, S10, S12, S13, S14	Fuses in fuse box	51, 52, 71, 76, 77, 81, 83, 94
T	Wire connector, behind dashboard	86, 87
T1a	Wire connector, single, behind dashboard	
T1b	Wire connector, single, behind dashboard	
T1c	Wire connector, single, in engine compartment, front left	
T1d	Wire connector, single, in engine compartment, front right	
T1e	Wire connector, single, in engine compartment, front left	
T1f	Wire connector, single, in engine compartment, front right	
T1g	Wire connector, single, in luggage compartment, right rear	
T1h	Wire connector, single, in luggage compartment, left rear	
T2a	Wire connector, double, in engine compartment	
T2b	Wire connector, double, behind dashboard	
T2c	Wire connector, double, behind dashboard	
T2d	Wire connector, double, behind dashboard	
T3a	Wire connector, 3 point, in engine compartment, left front	
T3b	Wire connector, 3 point, in engine compartment, right front	
T12	Wire connector, 12 point, on dashboard cluster	81
V	Windshield wiper motor	86, 87
V5	Windshield washer pump	92
V7	Radiator fan	99
X	License plate light	71, 72
Y	Clock	66
Z1	Rear window defogger heating element	81
10	Ground connector, dashboard cluster	
11	Ground connector, body	
15	Ground connector, engine compartment, front left	
16	Ground connector, engine compartment, front right	

See Page 246 for Wiring Colour Code

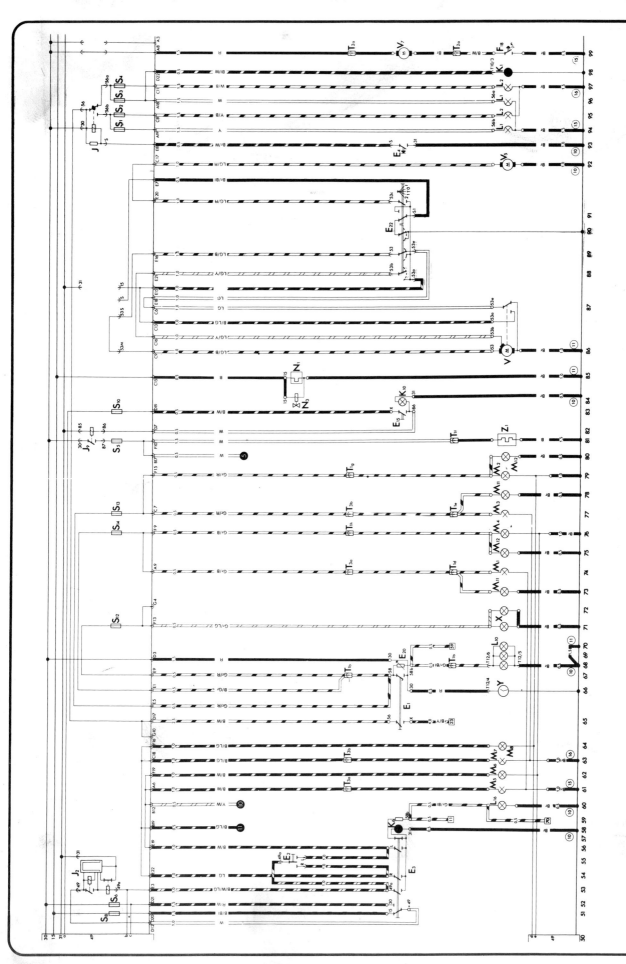

Fig. 11.33. Current Flow Diagram - Rabbit: Part 2

Chapter 12
Front suspension, steering and driveshafts

Contents

Specifications

Front suspension

Type	Independent MacPherson strut, co-axial coil spring and shock absorber with wishbones. Stabilizer bar is not fitted
Coil springs	There are six grades which must be matched. See Section 6
Shock absorbers	Hydraulic, telescopic, double acting
Steering knuckle, ball joints, maximum allowable play	2.5 mm (0.01 inches)

Steering gear

Type	Rack and pinion, progressive ratio, with safety column
Steering overall ratio	17.37
Steering wheel turns, lock-to-lock	3 1/3
Turning circle *:	
Between kerbs	10 metres (33 ft) } Safe limits for all
Between walls	10.6 metres (34½ ft) } models
Front wheel track	1390 mm (57.4 inches)

Note: This dimension was reduced in April 1975 (see Section 13)

Steering geometry

Camber, straight-ahead position	+ 30' ± 30' } Maximum tolerance between
Castor	+ 2º ± 30' } L and R is 1º
Toe-in (not pressed)	− 10' ± 15'
Toe-in (pressed)	+ 10' ± 15' at pressure 10 kg ± 2 kg (22 lb ± 4 lb)

Steering roll radius (negative):

		Standard equipment		Optional equipment	
		Tyre	Radius	Tyre	Radius
Golf (drum brakes) †	... ...	5.95 14.5 13	13.8 mm	155 SR 13*	12.9 mm
				175/70 SR13	13.2 mm
Golf (disc brakes)	... ...	6.15 155	15 mm	155 SR 13	12.9 mm
				175/70SR13	13.2 mm
Golf (L, LS and S)	... ...	155 SR 13	12.9 mm	175/70SR13	12.9 mm
Rabbit †	... ...	145-13 *	13.8 mm		
Scirocco ††	... ...	155 SR 13	12.9 mm	175/70/SR13	13.2 mm

*† Note: Tyres fitted to wheels 5J x 13 except those marked * fitted to wheels 4½J x 13.*
†† Note: Scirocco USA are fitted with 175/70/SR13 wheel size 5J x 13.

Driveshafts (Golf, Rabbit and Scirocco): **

		Right	Left
Gearbox 020 (manual) ...	... ...	17.5 in (445 mm)	25.9 in (658 mm)
Gearbox 084 (manual) ...	... ...	18.4 in (467 mm)	25.9 in (658 mm)
Gearbox 010 (automatic) ...	... ...	17.5 in (445 mm)	25.9 in (658 mm)

*** Note: The right-hand (short) shaft is solid, the left-hand shaft is tubular.*

Torque wrench settings

Suspension

	Mkg	lbs ft
Self-locking nut on top of the shock absorber inside the engine compartment (m8)	8	58
Nut on shock absorber for compressing the spring	2	14
Wheel bearing housing to suspension strut clamp nut to wheel bearing housing	8	58
Steering ball joint to clamp nut (m8)	3	21
Wishbone front hinge bolt (m10)	7	50
Wishbone rear 'U' clip bolt	4.5	32
C.V.J. to final drive (m8)	4.5	32
Hub securing bolts (drums)	6	43
Driveshaft nut (m18)	24	173
Camber adjustment nut	8	58

Steering

	Mkg	lbs ft
U.J. shaft lower clamp bolt (to steering gear) (m8)	2.5	18
U.J. shaft upper clamp bolt (to column) (m8)	2.5	18
Steering wheel nut (m18)	5	36
Steering column tube support bracket bolt	2	14
Tie-rod (trackrod) locknut	4	28
Tie-rod (trackrod) ball joint nut (m10)	3	21
Steering box securing bolts (m8)	2	14
Steering column switch housing	1	7

1 General description and steering geometry

1 The front suspension and steering gear is identical for all models covered by the manual but the driveshafts vary in length according to the model. A table is given in the Specification. The turning circle varies a little, mainly due to the offset of the wheels and body configuration, but may be safely fixed at 35 ft. Extra safety measures have been introduced to the steering column for some vehicles (Sections 18 and 19).

2 The suspension is simple and easily dismantled once the axle shaft nut is undone. This is tightened to 24 mkg (173 lb ft), and will present a problem for most owner drivers. The ways of overcoming this are discussed in Section 2, paragraph 5.

3 A straightforward MacPherson strut is housed in a bearing in the body and is located at the bottom by a ball joint attached to a wishbone bracket hinged to the frame. The roadwheel and brake are carried on a steering knuckle which is clamped to the bottom of the suspension strut and houses the wheel bearing. The top bolt of the clamp is eccentric and is used to adjust the camber angle. The steering knuckle is referred to throughout as the wheel bearing housing.

4 The drive to the roadwheel from the differential unit is supplied by a shaft with a constant velocity joint (C.V.J.) at each end. The inner end is flanged and secured by bolts to the final drive flange. The outer end is splined and passes into the splined inner part of the outer C.V.J.

The C.V.J. outer race is an integral part of the short wheel axle which is splined into the hub. The hub is carried in a ball bearing in the wheel bearing housing and the whole wheel hub is held in place by the axle nut.

5 An integral part of the wheel bearing housing is a lever extending to the rear of the suspension strut. To this is fastened, by means of a ball joint, the tie-rod which is connected at the inner end to the steering gear. Thus as the tie-rod moves the suspension strut rotates, and with it the wheel is turned in a vertical plane, so steering the vehicle. The dimensions of the tie-rods were altered in April 1975. (See Section 13).

6 The coil spring is mounted on a platform attached to the body of the shock absorber. The upper end of the spring is held by a cap and compressed slightly by a nut on the piston rod of the shock absorber. Thus as the spring is compressed the body of the piston moves up over the piston rod, and as the spring expands it pushes the body of the shock absorber down. In this way a controlled damping force is applied to the suspension.

7 The steering column is held in a tube which is fixed to the body-frame. The column runs in a spacer sleeve at the top and a ball bearing at the bottom. A safety feature of the system is the universal joint shaft which connects the bottom of the steering column to the steering gear. This is contained in a rubber cover. Besides catering for a change in direction of the drive, it ensures that should the steering gear be driven backwards in an accident such motion would not be transmitted to the steering column.

8 The lower end of the U.J. shaft is clamped to the pinion shaft of the rack and pinion mechanism. The casing of this is bolted to the frame and held rigid. As the pinion turns the rack is moved to the right or left. Attached to each end of the rack shaft, by means of ball joints, are the tie-rods which transmit the steering motion to the front wheels. The tie-rods are easily removable. On new vehicles only the right-hand rod is adjustable for length, and consequently 'toe-in', but should a replacement for the left-hand rod be required only the adjustable type is available. This is discussed in Section 13.

9 The steering gear may be removed without disturbing the column or front wheels. Adjustment is simple both for wear and correct track.

10 'Toe-in' and camber angles are easily adjusted but the measurement of these angles requires special equipment and is best left to the VW agent. The castor angle is fixed. If the geometry is incorrect the tyres will wear rapidly. If such wear is apparent the owner is advised to have the geometry checked forthwith.

11 The steering roll radius is negative. If a line is drawn through the top pivot point of the suspension strut and the ball joint connecting the wishbone to the wheel bearing housing (central point in each case) and the line extended to cut the ground surface, this will determine the steering roll radius. A second line through the vertical section of the tyre, such a line being the centre line of the tyre will give the middle of the area of contact of the tyre on the ground. The relationship of this point and the point determined by the roll radius line will measure the actual roll radius. If the centre point is inside the roll radius intersection point the radius is negative and any undue retardation of the forward motion of the tyre will tend to keep the wheels in the straight-ahead position. As the roll radius centre line is fixed the roll radius dimension will vary as the size of the tyre. This is shown in the table in the Specifications. It is not possible to measure the roll radius.

12 The diameter of the turning circle was reduced slightly in April 1975 by altering the dimensions of the tie-rods. This is discussed fully in the text of Section 13.

13 The text is written about LHD vehicles. Obviously the suspension does not differ for RHD but the steering gear differs, if only in the position of the pinion. Repair techniques are the same, and the photographs are of a RHD vehicle.

2 Maintenance and scope of repair

1 Apart from careful periodic inspection, maintenance is not necessary. All bearings and joints are prepacked and have no method of replenishment.

2 Check the state of wear of the tyre treads regularly and if there are signs of uneven wear action, as described later, is necessary right away.

3 Measure the free-play of the steering wheel as soon as you acquire the vehicle and if this measurement subsequently increases the reason must be located and corrected.

4 The rubber gaiters and covers must be checked for splits and age

hardening. They may be replaced as required.

5   The problem of undoing the axle nut may be solved by using a large lorry type spanner but it should only be done while the car is standing on its wheels. The force required could easily pull the vehicle off an axle stand. It **must** be tightened to the correct torque so this will probably mean going to the agent if the hub has been dismantled. At the same time the steering geometry may be checked.

6   We have deliberately omitted any discussion on the setting of the steering geometry. This operation requires special gauges and expensive experience in using them. For those who have that experience and access to the gauges the necessary angles are given in the Specifications. For the remainder our strong recommendation is to get this job done by the VW agent.

7   With the reservations given in paragraphs 5 and 6 there is no reason why the owner cannot dismantle the steering and suspension and replace worn parts as required. The method of doing these jobs is discussed in the rest of the Chapter.

3   Driveshafts - removal and replacement

1   The driveshafts differ in length and construction depending on the type of gearbox fitted. In all cases the longer shaft is 658 mm (25.9 in) long and is of hollow tubular construction to reduce vibration. Due to the offset of the final drive the other shaft is shorter, and is a solid shaft as vibration problems do not occur. The 020 gearbox (1.5 litre engine) and the automatic gearbox 010, have identical shafts 444.5 mm (17.5 in) long but the smaller gearbox 084, fitted to the 1.1 litre engine has a shaft 467.3 mm (18.4 in) long. In other respects the shorter shaft has identical measurements.

2   Removal of the shaft does not present many problems. While the vehicle is standing on its wheels, undo the axle nut and slacken the roadwheel studs. Jack-up the front wheels and support the vehicle on axle stands. Remove the roadwheel and turn the steering to full lock, left lock for the left shaft and right for the right shaft.

3   Using an 8 mm Allen key remove the socket head bolts holding the inner C.V.J. to the final drive flange (photo). Be careful to use a proper key for if the socket head is damaged the result will be time consuming to say the least. These bolts are quite tight (4.5 mkg/32 lbs ft) for the type of spanner used. Ideally a special hexagon 'screwdriver' bit should be used which will fit a torque wrench, but if one is not available then the bolts should be tightened as hard as possible on reassembly.

4   Once all the bolts are removed the C.V.J. may be pulled away from the final drive and the shaft removed from the hub (photo).

5   Replacement is the reverse of removal. Clean the splines carefully and smear a little molybdenum based grease on them. The problem of tightening the axle nut is again emphasised, and the nut fitted must be a new one.

4   Driveshaft - dismantling and reassembly

1   Having removed the shaft from the car it may be dismantled for the individual parts to be checked for wear.

2   The rubber boots, clips and thrust washers may be replaced if necessary but the CV joints may only be replaced as complete assemblies.

It is not possible to fit new hubs, outer cases, ball cages or balls separately for they are mated to a tolerance on manufacture; it is not possible to buy them either.

3   Start by removing the outer joint (refer to Fig. 12.1). Cut open the 34 mm clip and undo the 88 mm hose clamp. The boot may now be pulled away from the joint. Open the circlip with a pair of circlip pliers and tap the side of the joint. The circlip should spring out of its groove.

4   The outer CV joint may now be removed from the shaft and set aside for examination. The boot, clamp, dished washer and thrust washer may be pulled off the end of the shaft. See Fig. 12.2.

5   If the boot of the inner CV joint is damaged it should be removed and replaced from the outer end and the CV joint on the inner end left in place. If however, the inner joint is suspected then this too must be removed. The end of the shaft will look like the photo so a fair amount of cleaning is necessary before the job may proceed. Once the joint is clean, using circlip pliers remove the circlip from the end of the shaft and press off the CV joint. It will be necessary to ease the plastic cap away from the joint before pressing off the CV joint. The CV joint may now be set aside for inspection.

6   Assembly is the reverse of dismantling. Fit the inner CV joint first. It should be filled with 90 grams of Molybdenum-disulphide grease, filling in equal amounts from each side. The grease is obtainable in packets from official agents. Pump the grease in while pressing the CV joint onto the shaft. Pull the joint on until a new circlip may be fitted. The outer diameter of the dished washer should rest against the CV joint. Refit the plastic cover and the boot.

7   Push a new 34 mm diameter clip onto the shaft, then the boot for the outer CV joint and the boot clamp. Fit the dished washer so that the outer diameter rests against the spacer. Now fit the spacer with the convex side towards the joint.

8   Press a new circlip into the joint and drive the joint onto the shaft using a rubber hammer until the circlip seats in the groove. Pack the joint with 90 grams of MOS_2 grease and then refit the boot.

9   Re-install the shaft as in Section 3.

10   The CV joints should be washed clean and lightly oiled. Press the ball hub and cage out of the joint. Pivot the cage through 90° to extract it. Examine the balls and ball tracks for scoring and wear. There should be a bright ring where the ball track runs round the joint but no further scoring. If the joint does not seem satisfactory take it to the VW agent for advice and possible replacement.

5   Suspension strut - removal and replacement

1   Refer to Fig. 12.3. There are several ways in which the strut may be removed, depending upon the reason for removal and the tools available. If it is possible to remove the components without disturbing the axle nut or the camber, then so much the better.

2   It is quite simple to remove the whole assembly and then remove the damaged parts and replace them. If only the coil or shock absorber are to be removed then turn to paragraph 9.

3   Slacken the wheel nuts and support the front of the car on axle stands. Remove the wheel. Remove the socket-head bolts connecting the inner CVJ to the flange and encase the CVJ in a polythene bag. For vehicles with disc brakes remove the caliper and hang it to one side.

3.3 Remove the driveshaft from the inner flange

3.4 Pull the outer end of the driveshaft out of the hub

4.5 The driveshaft ready for dismantling

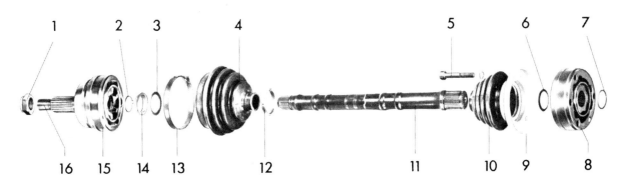

Fig. 12.1. Driveshaft and CV joints - exploded view (Sec. 4)

1	Axle nut	5	Socket head bolt	9	Cap	13	Clamp (88 mm)
2	Circlip	6	Dished washer	10	Boot	14	Thrust washer
3	Dished washer	7	Circlip	11	Shaft	15	CV joint outer
4	Boot	8	CV joint inner	12	Clip (34 mm)	16	Axleshaft

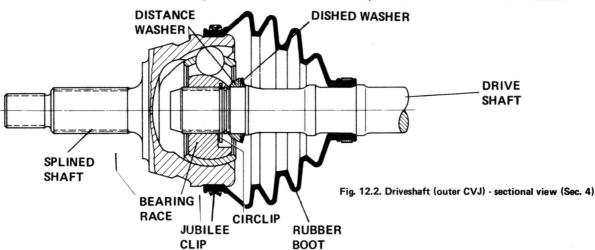

Fig. 12.2. Driveshaft (outer CVJ) - sectional view (Sec. 4)

For drum brakes disconnect the hydraulic line and plug the hose.

4   Remove the clamp bolt (photos) from the wheel bearing housing which holds the steering ball joint in place and separate the wishbone from the wheel bearing housing (photo). Undo the tie-rod securing nut and using a puller break the tie-rod ball joint (photo 13.6).

5   Remove the two nuts holding the top of the suspension strut to the bodyframe inside the engine compartment (photo). Lower the strut from the frame and take it away complete with driveshaft and disc.

6   The coil spring must be held in compression while the top nut on the rod is removed. There is a special tool VW340 and VW340/5 to do this but we managed by lashing the coils together with rope and easing

the pressure gently as the nut was removed. The piston rod must be held while undoing the nut. Fig. 12.4 shows details of the suspension strut. On early models use an Allen key in the hexagonal hole in the top of the rod. On later models the rod has flats to fit a spanner.

7   Remove the coil spring and test the shock absorber as in Section 7.

8   If the shock absorber is to be removed then the camber angle must be upset. To be able to reassemble the strut with the correct camber angle proceed as follows. Locate the top bolt holding the shock absorber clamp to the wheel bearing housing (photo). This is an eccentric bolt (photo). Mark the relative position of the bolt head to the clamp by two centre-punch marks. Undo the camber adjusting bolt and the lower

5.4a The steering ball joint is held to the wheel bearing housing by a clamp bolt ...

5.4b ... remove the bolt, pry the clamp open and ...

5.4c ...separate the ball joint from the bearing housing. The tie-rod joint has also been undone

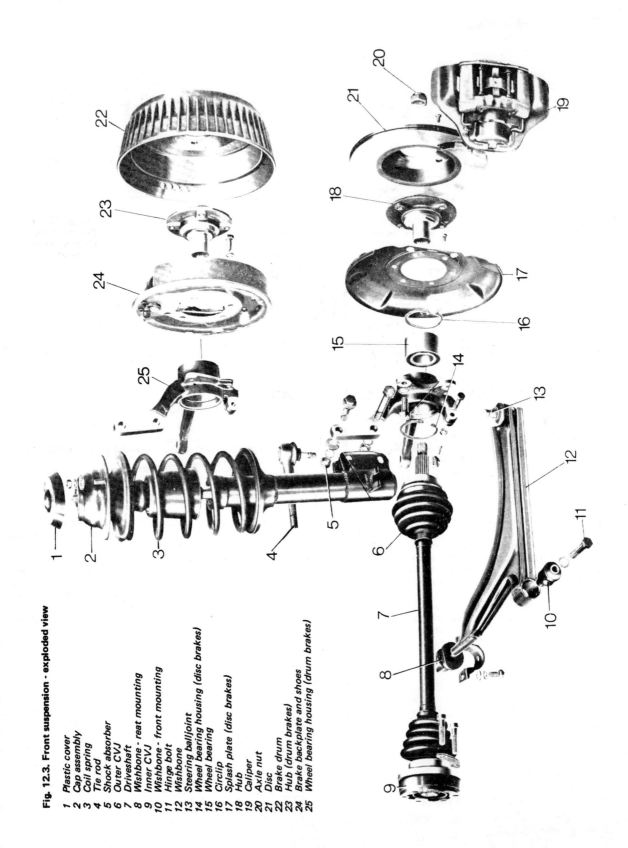

Fig. 12.3. Front suspension - exploded view

1 Plastic cover
2 Cap assembly
3 Coil spring
4 Tie rod
5 Shock absorber
6 Outer CVJ
7 Driveshaft
8 Wishbone - reat mounting
9 Inner CVJ
10 Wishbone - front mounting
11 Hinge bolt
12 Wishbone
13 Steering balljoint
14 Wheel bearing housing (disc brakes)
15 Wheel bearing
16 Circlip
17 Splash plate (disc brakes)
18 Hub
19 Caliper
20 Axle nut
21 Disc
22 Brake drum
23 Hub (drum brakes)
24 Brake backplate and shoes
25 Wheel bearing housing (drum brakes)

5.5 Remove the nuts holding the suspension strut to the wing inside the engine compartment. The nuts are arrowed 'A'

5.8a The camber adjusting bolt is arrowed 'A'. Mark the position with two centre-punch marks before moving it

5.8b The bolt and eccentric washer removed from the strut

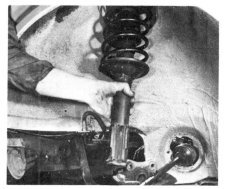

5.9a The wheel bearing housing has been removed and the top of the strut disconnected from the body. The strut may now be lowered away

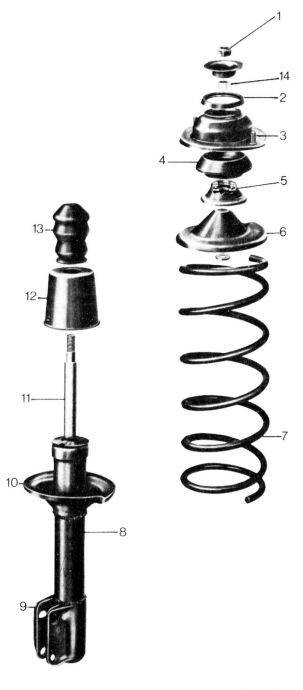

Fig. 12.4. Suspension strut front - exploded view (Sec. 5)

1 Compression nut
2 Stop ring
3 Cap with securing studs
4 Damper ring
5 Strut bearing
6 Cap
7 Spring
8 Shock absorber body
9 Camber adjustment hole
10 Spring platform
11 Piston rod
12 Cap
13 Bumper
14 Sealing bush

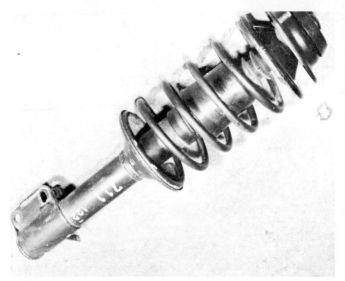

5.9b The strut removed from the body

8.1 The later type of steering ball joint is rivetted to the wishbone

8.3 Checking the wishbone with a straight edge

8.4 The 'U' clip mounting for the rear pivot of the wishbone

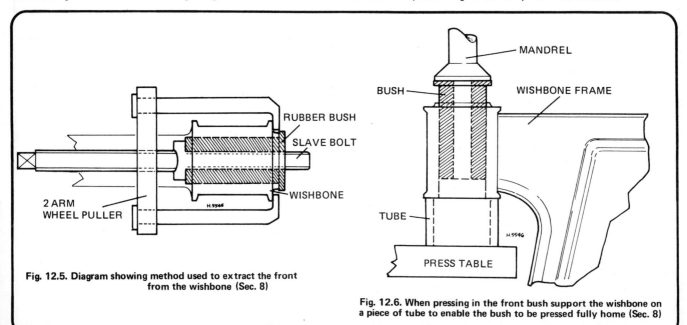

Fig. 12.5. Diagram showing method used to extract the front from the wishbone (Sec. 8)

RUBBER BUSH
SLAVE BOLT
WISHBONE
2 ARM WHEEL PULLER
H.5545

MANDREL
BUSH
WISHBONE FRAME
TUBE
PRESS TABLE
H.5546

Fig. 12.6. When pressing in the front bush support the wishbone on a piece of tube to enable the bush to be pressed fully home (Sec. 8)

bolt and remove them. Open the clamp with a lever and extract the shock absorber.

9 It is possible to extract the strut without undoing the driveshaft or wishbone. Remove the bolts from the clamp as in paragraph 8, disconnect the top of the strut from the body as in paragraph 5, prise the clamp apart and push the wheel bearing housing off the strut. Lower the strut and remove it (photos).

10 Assembly is the reverse of removal. Refit the shock absorber and coil spring to the wheel bearing housing. The spring must be compressed to start the securing nut. Torque the nut to the correct pressure. Adjust the camber eccentric correctly. Push the top of the piston rod through the wing into the engine compartment and secure it correctly.

11 Refit the steering ball joint and wishbone to the wheel bearing housing, refit the tie-rod ball joint and then refit the driveshaft to the final drive.

12 If you removed the caliper this must be replaced, or if the brake hose was removed from the drum brake the brake must be bled. Replace the wheel and lower to the ground.

13 This may seem a lot of work but it does avoid struggling with the axle nut. If you removed the camber eccentric bolt have the camber angle checked to make sure you assembled the bolt correctly.

6 Coil springs - inspection and renewal

1 There is not a lot to go wrong but even so the spring may require replacement. If it is broken read Chapter 8, Section 8, paragraphs 3 and 4 and examine the whole suspension very carefully.

2 If a banging noise is heard from the front suspension when travelling over rough ground then the end coils are bottoming on the next coils. Read Chapter 8, Section 8, paragraph 5 but this time fit the damping sleeve to the top and bottom coils.

3 There are six tolerance groups for the coil spring, each group denoted by paint spots. If a spring is faulty make sure it is replaced by one from the same tolerance group. Consult the VW storeman if in doubt about the marking.

4 The method of removal and refitting is given in Section 3.

7 Shock absorbers - inspection and replacement

1 A defective shock absorber will upset the steering and braking so it should be attended to right away. Apart from steering and braking difficulties it usually complains audibly as it operates.

2 A quick and reliable test is done by pushing the car down on the front corner and releasing the pressure suddenly. The car should return to its correct level without oscillation. Any oscillation indicates that the shock absorber is empty.

3 A small leak may be discounted for the assembly is overfilled to allow for this. Large leaks must be attended to at once.

4 The shock absorber removed from the suspension strut should be held by the cylinder body in a vice. Push the piston rod right down and then pull it right out. There should be a firm, even, resistance to movement throughout the stroke in both directions. If there is not then the unit is defective. If you are not sure take it to the VW agent and ask for it to be tested against a new one.

5 There is no repair, only renewal. It is not necessary to renew both shock absorbers if only one is faulty but it **must** be replaced by one of the same part number.

6 The method of removal and replacement is given in Section 8.

8 Wishbones (vehicles with manual transmission) - inspection, removal and replacement

1 Two patterns of wishbone have been fitted. Up to October 1974 the steering ball joint was fastened to the wishbone by two M8 bolts and nuts. After that date the bolts were replaced by three 7 mm rivets (photo). Replacement ball joints to the later types are fitted by drilling out the rivets with a 6 mm drill and fastening the new one in with three 7 mm bolts and nuts, tightened to 2.5 mkg (18 lb ft). If the old type needs a new ball joint then the outer holes of the new ball joint must be enlarged to 8.3 mm diameter and the joint fitted with two 8 mm bolts and nuts with spring washers. Torque to 2.5 mkg (18 lb ft).

2 Apart from fitting a new ball joint the pivot bushes may be replaced if worn. To do this properly the wishbone must be removed from the

vehicle. This is discussed below.

3 Accident damage to the wishbone may result in the camber angle being altered and rapid tyre wear. Check the underside for kinks and wrinkles and check that the front and profile sides are straight, using a straight-edge or an engineer's square (photo).

4 Although the wishbone may be removed with the roadwheel in-situ it is easier and safer to support the vehicle on axle stands and remove the front wheel. Support the wheel hub with a jack. Undo the clamp bolt holding the steering ball joint to the wheel bearing housing and lower the wishbone as far as possible (photo 5.2c). Remove the nuts holding the 'U' clip (photo) and rear pivot, hold the wishbone level and undo and extract the front hinge bolt. Remove the wishbone from the vehicle.

5 The rubber bush at the rear may be pressed off and after the pivot has been cleaned up a new one tapped into place with a hammer.

6 The front bush is a little more difficult. The simple way to press out the bush is to use a two arm puller. Fit a 10 mm bolt through the bush from the inside surface and push on the bolt with the puller centre bolt as shown in the diagram (Fig. 12.5), so that the bush is driven out from the wishbone. Smear the bore with a little brake grease and push a new bush in from the outside. When fully home, the bush protrudes past the bore of the wishbone so that the wishbone must be supported with a piece of tube large enough to allow the bush to slide inside it. A diagram shows this arrangement (Fig. 12.6).

7 With the older type of wishbone the steering ball joint may be removed, without disconnecting the wishbone from the vehicle, by unbolting it; the removal of the rivetted version presents difficulties. It is possible to remove the rivets without dismantling the wishbone from the vehicle but it is equally possible to let the drill run out and enlarge the hole as well as remove the rivets. We recommend the removal of the wishbone and the drilling out accurately under a pillar drill with the wishbone clamped in position on the drill table. Fit the new ball joint as described in paragraph 1. If you have an automatic gearbox read Section 9 and you may wish to drill the rivets out in position but be careful.

8 When refitting the wishbone to the vehicle great care must be taken not to destroy the thread of the nut which holds the front hinge bolt in position. The bolt must be tightened to 7 mkg (50 lbs ft). If this torque is not attainable then a new nut must be fitted and as the nut is welded **inside** the front crossmember the replacement of it is a major task only possible in a fully equipped workshop by professionals who have the right equipment. It involves opening up of the front crossmember — you have been warned! VW recommend the use of a new bolt the thread of which should be coated with D6 locking fluid (ask the VW storeman) and stress that lockwasher part no. 411 399 267 must be fitted under the head of the new bolt.

9 Before installing the wishbone try the new bolt in the nut. Make sure it screws in easily. Remove it and position the wishbone in the correct place. Install the 'U' clip for the back hinge but do not tighten it. Next try the front bolt and ease the wishbone until the bolt engages the thread in the nut easily. Keep the wishbone in that position, remove the bolt, fit the washer and coat the thread with D6 and install the bolt. Tighten to 1 mkg and then adjust the back bearing again. Check that the wishbone moves easily about the hinge bolts and then tighten the front one to the correct torque. Then tighten the rear hing clip securing bolts. Check that the wishbone moves easily about the hinge bolts with no tight spots. If it does not, readjust the rear clip.

10 Finally refit the steering ball joint to the wheel bearing housing. Remove the jack from under the housing, refit the wheel and lower the vehicle to the ground.

9 Wishbone (vehicles with automatic transmission) - removal and replacement

1 Vehicles fitted with automatic transmission present a little more work. Proceed generally as in Section 10 to isolate the wishbone from the suspension strut. It will be seen that the front hinge bolt is not accessible.

2 Support the engine, either with a hoist or beam from above, or with a jack below (use wooden packing) and remove the front left mounting, the securing nut for the rear mounting and the engine steadying strut (the front one). Now lift the engine until the front wishbone bolt may be removed.

3 Use the same careful procedure to remove and replace the wishbone and then lower the engine and reconnect the engine mountings.

10 Steering ball joints - inspection and renewal

1   A simple way to measure the vertical play of the ball joint is to fit a vernier caliper between the bottom of the wishbone and a convenient surface on the wheel bearing housing or brake caliper while the car is on its wheels (photo). Note the measurement. Jack-up the car so that the wheel is clear of the ground and recheck the measurement. Force the wheel down while measuring this distance. If the two measurements differ by more than 2.5 mm (0.010 in) then the joint requires renewal. However it will be best to have this rechecked by the agent with special tools before proceeding further.

2   The method of removal and replacement is described in Section 9, paragraphs 1 and 7.

11 Wheel bearing housing - removal and replacement

1   With the vehicle standing on all four wheels undo the axle nut and slacken the wheel studs. Jack-up the front wheels and support the vehicle on axle stands. Remove the front wheel.

2   Remove the nut from the tie-rod ball joint and break the joint using a wheel puller (photo 13.6).

3   Undo the clamp bolt and remove the steering ball joint from the wheel bearing housing. Push the wishbone down out of the way.

4   If the vehicle has disc brakes remove the caliper (Chapter 9) and hang it out of the way. **Do not** suspend it by the brake hose.

5   Undo the crosshead screw holding the disc to the hub and remove the disc. Now carry on as described in paragraph 7.

6   If the vehicle has front drum brakes refer to Chapter 9 and remove the drum brake and the shoes. Disconnect the hydraulic hose and plug it. Fasten the hydraulic cylinder pistons in place with wire to stop them coming out. It is not possible to remove the back plate or splash plate from the housing until the hub has been removed.

7   At this point there is a choice in procedure. Either remove the strut complete by undoing the nuts securing it to the frame in the engine compartment or remove the wheel bearing housing from the strut. The second method involves marking the camber adjustment bolt, so that it may be reassembled with the same camber adjustment, removing it and the lower bolt and then drawing the housing off the bottom of the strut and at the same time pulling it off the driveshaft splines. We found it easier to remove the wheel bearing housing from the strut. Whichever way you do it the bearing housing may now be removed from the car.

8   Assembly is the reverse of removal. If you have disturbed the camber angle set it as near as you can and have it checked when you go to the VW agent to have a **new** axle nut fitted to the correct torque. Do not forget to bleed the brakes if the hydraulic lines were disconnected.

12 Wheel bearings - removal and replacement

1   The removal of a wheel bearing is a lengthy job so it is as well to be sure that it is actually necessary before doing the job. A defective bearing will make a rumbling noise under load. Jack-up the suspect wheel and test the rim rock. Spin the wheel and listen for noise indicating wear. A good bearing will make little or no noise. If you are not sure consult someone with experience because a defective race could cause a lot of trouble and, if it collapses, a nasty accident.

2   Having decided that it is necessary, remove the wheel bearing housing as in Section 11. The next job is to press the hub out of the bearing race and for this job a press is necessary with the correct sized mandrels. **Do not** try to hammer it out. Using a feeler gauge measure the clearance between the hub and the wheel bearing housing to give you an idea of how much clearance to leave when replacing the hub in the housing. Once the hub is removed the brake backplate (drum brakes) or splash plate may be removed. The task will not present much difficulty if the wheel bearing housing has been separated from the strut (photo), but if it is still attached to the strut suitable provision must be made to support the strut during pressing operations.

3   The inner bearing race will come away on the hub and must be pulled off with a wheel puller. Hold the flange of the hub in soft jaws in a vice so that there is room for the inner race to be moved. Ideally a plug VW 431 which fits in the bore of the hub should be used on which the screw of the wheel puller can push. If such a plug is not available, then put a piece of plate behind the hub in the vice and, using a suitable piece of packing in the bore, push against that.

4   The outer bearing is held in the wheel bearing housing bore by two large circlips. Remove these and press the bearing out using a press and suitable mandrel. Again, do not use a hammer. Replace the outer circlip and press the new bearing into the housing from the inside pushing on the outer race only until it rests on the circlip. Now refit the inner circlip.

5   Install the splash plate or backplate (disc or drum) and then press the bearing housing on to the hub. This may sound the wrong way round but actually it is much easier to support the hub and press the housing on by pushing on the **inner** bearing race. **On no account** push on the outer race. If you measured the clearance between the hub and the housing before removing the hub then you know how much room to leave.

6   A word of caution. You will have gathered that the old race has been destroyed and a new one has to be bought. Unless you have a press and experience at this job we recommend you to ask the VW agent from whom you buy the race to install it. It is very easy to damage the race and possibly the bore of the hub if you do not have the correct tools. This will mean a new hub and another race.

10.1 Checking the vertical play in the steering ball joint

12.2 The hub and backplate ready for the hub to be pressed out of the wheel bearing housing

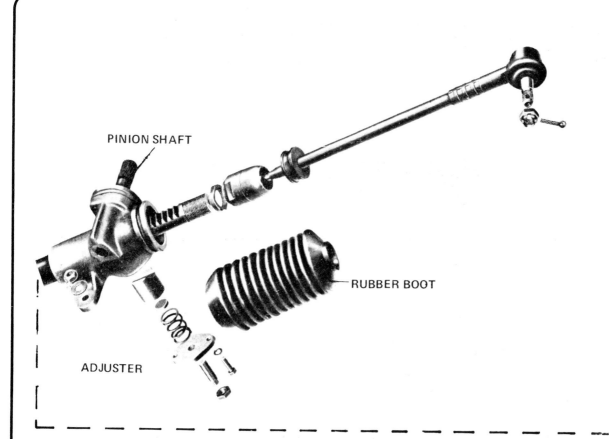

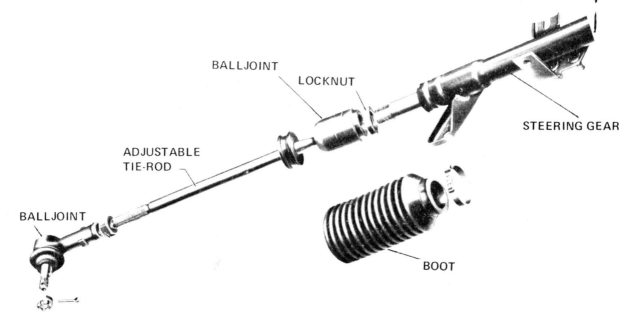

Fig. 12.7. Steering gear - layout of steering gear and tie-rods

7   When the hub is in position reassemble the wheel bearing housing, strut and wishbone. Refit the brakes and bleed them if necessary (Chapter 9). If the camber angle has been disturbed have it checked when you go to have the new axle nut tightened to the correct torque.

13 Tie-rods - removal and replacement

1   Refer to Fig. 12.7. On new vehicles the left-hand tie-rod is made in

Fig. 12.8. Diagrammatic arrangement of the steering gear. When assembling the tie-rods the rack rod must protrude equally (B) at each end (Sec. 13)

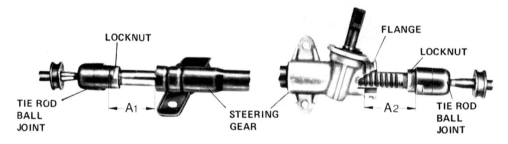

Fig. 12.9. Diagrammatic arrangement of tie-rods and steering box (See Section 13 for dimensions)

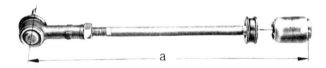

Fig. 12.10. Measuring the length of the tie-rods (See Section 13 for dimensions)

13.6a The tie-rod ball joint. Remove the split pin, slacken the nut and ...

13.6b ...using a wheel puller break the joint

one piece and is not adjustable. The right-hand one is made of two pieces which screw together so that its length may be altered to adjust 'toe-in'.

2 When a new tie-rod is required to replace the left-hand rod the solid type is not supplied, an adjustable one is provided which must be adjusted to suit the length of the original solid rod. This is just as well because the length of the solid rod was altered in cars produced after April 1975 to give a slightly smaller turning circle. The length of the new rod is 379 mm (14.7 in) as opposed to 381 mm (14.8 in) for the original rod as measured in Fig. 12.10.

This will mean that when refitting a tie-rod to a pre-April 1975 vehicle, the owner may set the tie-rods to the new dimensions and decrease the turning circle should he wish or stick to the old dimensions.

3 The matter is further complicated for vehicles with automatic transmission because the tie-rod must remain at 381 mm (14.8 in) to the right-hand side to clear the gearbox but the left-hand rod must be 379 mm (14.7 in)..

4 Refer to Fig. 12.8. When setting the tie-rods in position the steering rack must protrude equally from either side of the casing. Note the right-hand datum is the back (inside) of the flange.

5 When the rack is correctly set the tie-rods should be screwed on to the dimensions given in the table below as shown in Fig. 12.9. Once the rods are set the locknuts should be tightened and the rubber covers moved into place.

6 The outer ends of the rod are held to the steering arms by ball joints. Remove the split pin and castellated nut and break the joint with a wheel puller (photos). These joints are prepacked. If the rubber covering perishes and the ball joint becomes worn regrettably a new tie-rod must be fitted.

7 Toe-in must always be adjusted on the right-hand rod.

8 Dimensions are given in the table below. The variations may seem to be small but they are important and can have considerable effect on tyre wear and steering. If you are in doubt we suggest that expert help will cost less than new tyres. If the toe-in is adjusted it may result in the horizontal spoke of the steering wheel being other than horizontal at the straight-ahead position of the roadwheels. If this annoys you it may be corrected by removing the steering wheel and moving it round a spline.

	Up to April 1975		After April 1975	
	mm	in	mm	in
Fixed tie-rod length - LHS (manual and automatic)	381	15.00	379	14.92
Adjustable tie-rod length (see Fig. 12.10) - RHS:				
manual	381	15.00	379	14.92
automatic	381	15.00	381	15.00
Dimension 'B' (Fig. 12.8) - protrusion of rack shaft	Equal	Equal	Equal	Equal
Dimension 'A 1' (Fig. 12.9) - LHS:				
manual transmission	67	2.64	69	2.72
automatic transmission	67	2.64	69	2.72
Dimension 'A 2' (Fig. 12.9) - RHS:				
manual transmission	67	2.64	69	2.72
automatic transmission	67	2.64	67	2.64

14 Steering gear - removal and replacement

1 Refer to Fig. 12.7. The gear is in the engine compartment behind the engine. Push back the rubber cover from the universal joint shaft (photo) and remove the clamp bolt from the lower universal joint. Ease the universal joint up the pinion spindle as far as it will go. It will not come completely off at this stage.

2 Working underneath the car disconnect the bracket which holds the gearchange mechanism to the steering gear.

3 Refer to Section 13, and remove the trackrods. There is no need to undo the outer joints, slacken off the locknuts and unscrew the ball joints from each end of the gear (photo).

4 Remove the nuts holding the steering gear to the body and lift the gear from the studs pulling the U.J. off at the same time. The steering gear will now be removable through the right-hand wheel arch. It may be necessary to remove the roadwheel to pull the gear quite clear.

5 Replacement is the reverse of removal. When fitting the U.J. shaft take care that the flat on the pinion shaft lines up with the clamp bolt hole. Fit the bolt loosely, and then fasten the steering gear firmly in position over the studs. Tighten all the nuts to the correct torque.

6 Install the tie-rods (Section 13) and refit the gearchange. Adjust this correctly (Sections 25 and 26, Chapter 6). Check the toe-in and adjust if necessary, or better still have this done by the VW agent

7 From September 1975 only the steering assembly for vehicles with manual transmission is supplied as a spare. Before installing this type in a vehicle with automatic transmission the bracket on the body of the assembly which supports the manual transmission gearshift rod must be bent upwards at about 45 degrees. If this is not done the bracket may foul the exhaust pipe and cause banging noises of an alarming nature.

14.1 Pull back the rubber boot to get at the universal joint shaft from the steering gear to the steering column

14.3 The tie-rod is connected to the steering gear by a ball joint

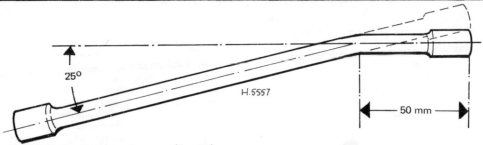

Fig. 12.11. Steering gear adjustment (Sec. 15)

A 17 mm ring spanner should be bent to the dimensions shown to make the adjustment more simple

15 Steering gear - adjustment

1   The steering gear may not be repaired; if it is damaged or worn beyond adjustment a complete assembly must be fitted.
2   The only adjustment is the pressure on the engagement between the rack and pinion. This is adjusted by a stud which is screwed in to increase the pressure and screwed out to release it.
3   This arrangement is located behind the assembly, and is so difficult to obtain access so that a 17 mm ring spanner must be bent, as shown in Fig. 12.11, before the locknut can be slackened sufficiently to enable the adjusting stud to be turned. The photograph shows the problem (photo).
4   If rattling noises are heard coming from the steering gear when the vehicle goes over rough surfaces then the pinion is loose in the rack and must be adjusted. To do this first jack up the front of the car and set it on axle stands. Undo the adjuster locknut and back off the adjuster a little. Now tighten it until it touches the thrust washer, you will note more resistance at this point. Hold the adjuster in this position and tighten the locknut.
5   A creaking sound from the rack and pinion denotes lack of lubrication. Move the steering to full lock and pull back the rubber rack cover on the extended side (eg; right for left lock on LHD), wipe the grease away and spray on Molykote 321 R. Allow this to dry for ten minutes and then apply a thin film of lithium based grease and replace the rubber cover.
6   When correctly adjusted there should be a natural self centring force when cornering: this will not be as strong as in cars with conventional steering geometry. If this is absent and the steering is stiff then the pinion is binding on the rack and should be adjusted.

16 Steering wheel - removal and replacement

1   Disconnect the battery earth lead to avoid accidental short circuits. The horn pad pulls off, after a struggle, to expose the steering column nut. Disconnect the lead (photo Chapter 6, Section 3), undo the nut and pull the wheel off the splines.
2   When replacing the wheel be careful to install the wheel in the central position (see Chapter 6, Section 16).
3   Do not forget to reconnect the battery earth lead.

17 Steering column - removal and replacement

1   Disconnect the battery earth strap and remove the steering wheel (Section 16). On some models a covering is fitted over the steering column under the dashboard. Remove this and the steering column is exposed.
2   Refer to Fig. 12.12. The procedure is the same for 1.5 litre and 1.1 litre models. Refer to Chapter 11, Sections 16 and 17, and remove the column switches. Now lever out the spacer sleeve.
3   At the bottom of the column tube there is a cross bracket which supports the pedals. Remove the pedal connections (for the clutch see Chapter 5, for the various arrangements for the brake pedal see Chapter 9).
4   Remove the nuts holding the bottom bracket to the body. Remove the screws holding the upper column bracket to the dashboard.
5   Undo the nut and bolt clamping the U.J. to the steering column and remove the column and tube from the vehicle. There have been several

15.3 The problem of adjusting the steering gear rack and pinion engagement

modifications to the pedal bracket. They do not affect this operation. They are discussed in Chapter 9.
6   In October 1974 a detachable steering column was fitted to all LH drive models. This is discussed in Section 18.
7   A further modification involving a telescopic steering column for vehicles fitted with an automatic gearbox and destined for France, Canada and Sweden was introduced. This is discussed in Section 19.
8   Returning to the standard column: Remove the column shaft from the tube. At the bottom of the tube there is a spring and spring seat which may get lost if you are not careful. Finally the bearing at the bottom of the column tube may be pushed out and a new one pressed in, if necessary.
9   Assembly is the reverse of removal. Fit the spring seat and spring, insert the column and reconnect the U.J. shaft at the bottom. Refit the nuts and bolts holding the steering column to the body and reconnect the brake pedal and clutch pedal. Refit the column switch and the multipin plugs and now press in the spacer sleeve until the distance from the top of the column to the top of the spacer sleeve is 41.5 mm (1.63 inches). This will set the gap between the steering wheel and the column switch at 2 to 4 mm (0.08 to 0.16 in). Fig. 12.13 shows the measurement. Now refit the steering wheel and the covers. Check the clutch and brake pedal movement.
10 While the column tube is being serviced it is as well to examine the welding of the bottom bracket. Cases have arisen where one of the welds has been omitted with the result that the tube can move and eventually cause fatigue damage to the welding on the upper bracket. With the brake and clutch pedals supported by this assembly there is a good deal of pressure on these welds and this particular fault caused up and down movement of steering wheel as the clutch was depressed and released. It is possible that a small batch of cars with this fault may have slipped through the inspection should you find this fault in your car report it to your VW agent.

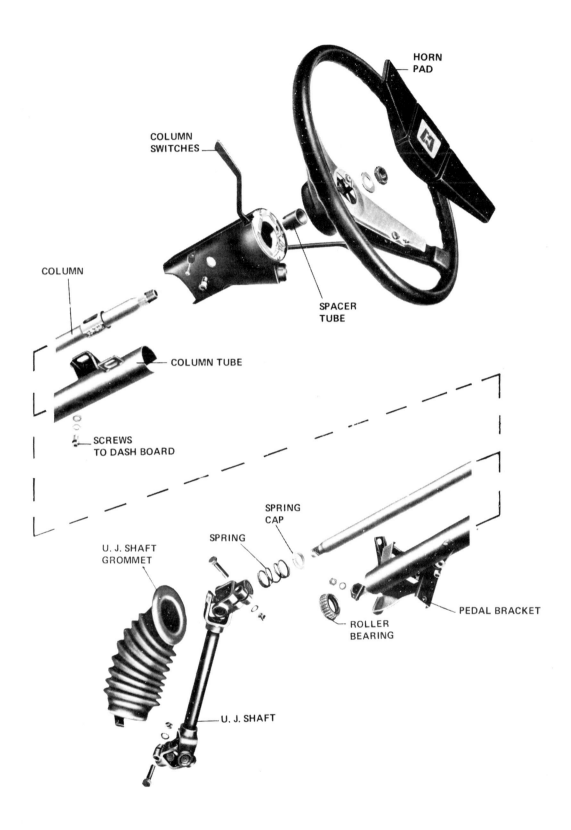

Fig. 12.12. Steering wheel and column - exploded view (Sec. 17)

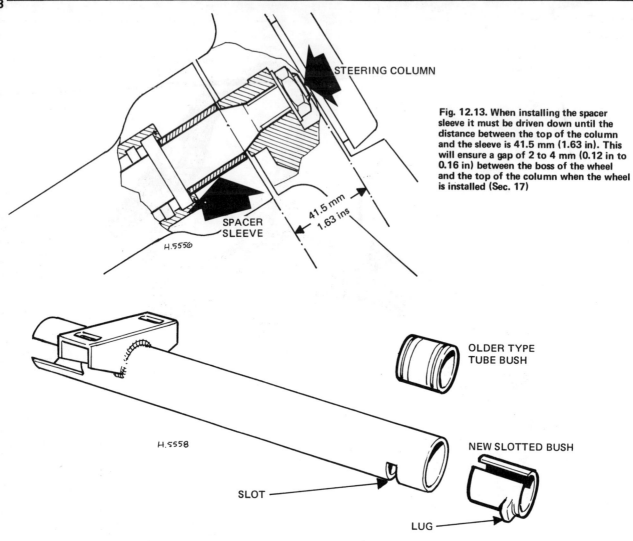

STEERING COLUMN

Fig. 12.13. When installing the spacer sleeve it must be driven down until the distance between the top of the column and the sleeve is 41.5 mm (1.63 in). This will ensure a gap of 2 to 4 mm (0.12 in to 0.16 in) between the boss of the wheel and the top of the column when the wheel is installed (Sec. 17)

41.5 mm
1.63 ins

SPACER
SLEEVE

H.5556

OLDER TYPE
TUBE BUSH

NEW SLOTTED BUSH

H.5558

SLOT

LUG

Fig. 12.14. Modified bush for the steering column (Sec. 17)

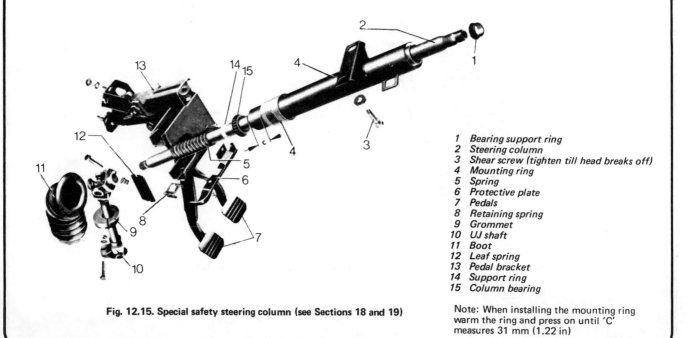

Fig. 12.15. Special safety steering column (see Sections 18 and 19)

1 Bearing support ring
2 Steering column
3 Shear screw (tighten till head breaks off)
4 Mounting ring
5 Spring
6 Protective plate
7 Pedals
8 Retaining spring
9 Grommet
10 UJ shaft
11 Boot
12 Leaf spring
13 Pedal bracket
14 Support ring
15 Column bearing

Note: When installing the mounting ring warm the ring and press on until 'C' measures 31 mm (1.22 in)

11 In August 1975 the steering column was lengthened 10 mm to give more room between the pedals and the wheel. The bush which is fitted to the end of the tube has been replaced by a slotted type (see Fig. 12.14). A lug on the bush fits into a slot in the column tube. It may be necessary to tap the lug into position.

12 Vibration in the steering at speeds of 70 to 100 miles per hour (110 to 160 km/hr) have been traced to unbalance of the wheels and tyres. Turning the tyres through 180° on the rims may produce some alleviation but the problem requires a careful check of the wheel balancing using a wheel centering adaptor, and the residual out of balance must not exceed 10 grams. This procedure is beyond the capacity of the owner but is known at the VW agents workshop.

18 Detachable steering column - general

1 With effect from October 1974 all left-hand drive models are fitted with a different type of steering column. As will be recalled the idea of the universal joint shaft between the steering gear and the column tube is to prevent the transmission of movement rearwards to the steering column by the steering gear in the event of an accident.

2 The modification improves on this idea. Instead of the column being fixed rigidly to the pedal bracket, which is bolted to the frame, the column is held to the bracket by a leaf spring. The bracket is reshaped so that the column may be inserted from the left-hand side and then a leaf spring inserted across the open 'U' of the brackets. See Fig. 12.15.

3 In the event of a collision the shaft will be pushed sideways removing the spring. After such happening the whole steering gear must be dismantled and inspected very thoroughly before using the car again.

19 Telescopic steering column - general

1 For vehicles bound for France, Canada and Sweden the arrangement described in Section 18 is also fitted and in addition an arrangement to prevent the tube moving axially. The bracket is fitted at the top of the tube and fixed to the bodyframe. The tube is cut at the lower end and the two pieces pressed into a plastic tube. In the event of axial movement the top of the tube stays in place and the movement is absorbed by crushing the plastic tube. Details are shown in Fig. 12.15.

20 Fault diagnosis - Front suspension, steering and driveshafts

Symptom	Probable cause	Remedy
1 Noise from front suspension	1 Coil springs bottoming	1 Fit plastic covers to springs (Section 6).
	2 Shock absorber defective	2 Test, replace if necessary (Section 7).
	3 Brake pads require renewal	3 Renew (Chapter 9).
	4 Front wheel bearing defective	4 Test and replace if necessary (Section 2).
2 Tyres wearing excessively on inner or outer edges of the tread	1 Steering geometry incorrect	1 Go to VW agent and have camber, toe-in and castor checked.
	2 Wishbone damaged or bushes worn	2 Inspect and replace if necessary (Section 8).
	3 Steering ball joint worn	3 Check and replace (Section 10).
	4 Tie-rod ball joints worn	4 Check and replace (Section 13).
3 Steering wanders and is unstable	1 Front tyres soft	1 Check pressure.
	2 Check all items from fault 2, (excessive tyre wear).	2 As for item 2.
	3 Shock absorbers defective	3 Replace shock absorber (Section 2).
	4 Wheel bearing defective	4 Replace bearing (Section 12).
	5 Steering gear loose	5 Tighten mounting bolts (Section 14).
	6 Steering column bracket welds defective	6 INspect and replace bracket (Section 17).
	7 U.J. shaft bolts not tight	7 Tighten.
4 Steering stiff and does not centre correctly	1 Steering wheel hard on spacer sleeve	1 Check and adjust (Section 17).
	2 Steering gear requires adjustment or lubrication	2 Check, adjust and lubricate (Section 15).
	3 Steering ball joints damaged	3 Check and replace (Section 10).
	4 Wishbones damaged	4 Check and replace (Section 8).
	5 Steering geometry incorrect (this will be a first sign before tyre wear occurs)	5 Check (by VW agent).
5 Wheel wobble or "shimmy"	1 Wheels or tyres out of balance	1 Have them rebalanced.
	2 Steering linkages worn or loose	2 Tighten or replace.
	3 Tyre pressures incorrect	3 Check and correct.
	4 Wear in suspension	4 Check and replace.

Chapter 13 Bodywork and fittings

Contents

1 General description

The Golf/Scirocco/Rabbit range is a new VW body design. It was styled by Guigiono and the *Italdesign* team and is based on the lessons learned from the VW Experimental Safety Vehicle (ESV) which produced so much new technology for the safety of the people riding in the car. Fore and aft there are 'crumple zones' which take the brunt of any accident leaving the passenger compartment with minimum distortion. In the front this takes the form of two corrugated box sections in the scuttle and firewall.

2 The floor pan, suspension and steering are the same for all models but the Golf/Rabbit body is slightly different in contour from that of the Scirocco. Thus, although the length and width are almost identical, the Scirocco is some four inches lower in height than the Golf/Rabbit.

3 All models have the large rear door hinged at the top. On the cheaper models this is propped open by a steel rod, but with a gas filled telescopic strut on the more expensive types. All models are available in two or four door options.

4 The types of bumper fitted vary. In USA and certain other countries shock absorbing bumpers are mandatory. Where this is not a legal requirement normal bolted-on types are fitted.

5 This Chapter does not go into the detail differences of the various models but confines itself to those jobs which can be done by the owner.

2 Maintenance - bodywork and underframe

1 The general condition of vehicle's bodywork is the one thing that significantly affects its value. Maintenance is easy but needs to be regular and particular. Neglect, particularly after minor damage, can lead quickly to further deterioration and costly repair bills. It is important also to keep watch on those parts of the car not immediately visible, for instance, the underside and inside all the wheel arches.

2 The basic maintenance routine for the bodywork is washing - preferably with a lot of water, from a hose. This will remove all the solids which may have stuck to the car. It is important to flush these off in such a way as to prevent grit from scratching the finish. The wheel arches and underbody need washing in the same way to remove any accumulated mud which will retain moisture and tend to encourage rust. Paradoxically enough, the best time to clean the underbody and wheel arches is in wet weather when the mud is thoroughly wet and soft. In very wet weather, the underbody is usually cleaned of large accumulations automatically and this is a good time for inspection.

3 Periodically it is a good idea to have the whole of the underside of the vehicle steam cleaned, so that a thorough inspection can be carried out to see what minor repairs and renovations are necessary. Steam cleaning is available at commercial vehicle garages but if not, there are one or two excellent grease solvents available which can be brush applied. The dirt can then be hosed off.

4 After washing paintwork, wipe it with a chamois leather to give an unspotted clear finish. A coat of clear protective wax polish will give added protection against chemical pollutants in the air. If the paintwork sheen has dulled or oxidised, this requires a little more effort, but is usually caused because regular washing has been neglected. Always check that drain holes are completely clear so that water can drain out. Brightwork should be treated the same way as paintwork. Windscreens and windows can be kept clear of the smeary film which often appears if a little ammonia is added to the water. If they are scratched, a good rub with a proprietary metal polish will often clear them. Do not use any form of wax or chromium polish on glass.

3 Maintenance - upholstery and floor coverings

1 Mats and carpets should be brushed or vacuum cleaned regularly to keep them free of grit. If they are badly stained remove them for scrubbing or sponging and make quite sure they are dry before replacement. Seats and interior trim panels can be kept clean by a wipe over with a damp cloth. If they do become stained (which can be more apparent on light coloured upholstery) use a little liquid detergent and a soft nailbrush to scour the grime out of the grain of the material. Do not forget to keep the head lining clean in the same way as the upholstery. When using liquid cleaners inside the car do not over wet the surfaces being cleaned. Excessive damp could get into the seams and padded interior causing stains, offensive odours or even rot. If the inside of the car gets wet accidentally, it is worthwhile taking some trouble to dry it out properly, particularly where carpets are involved. **Do not** leave heaters inside for this purpose.

4 Minor body damage - repair

See also the photo sequence on pages 231, 232, 233.

Repair of minor scratches in the bodywork

If the scratch is very superficial and does not penetrate to the metal of the bodywork, repair is very simple. Lightly rub the area of the scratch with a paintwork renovator (eg; T-Cut). or a very fine cutting paste, to remove loose paint from the scratch and to clear the surrounding bodywork of wax polish. Rinse the area with clean water.

Apply touch-up paint to the scratch using a thin paint brush, continue to apply thin layers of paint until the surface of the paint in the scratch is level with the surrounding paintwork. Allow the new paint at least two weeks to harden, then blend it into the surrounding paintwork by rubbing the paintwork in the scratch area with a paintwork renovator (eg; T-Cut), or a very fine cutting paste. Finally apply wax polish.

Typical example of rust damage to a body panel. Before starting ensure that you have all of the materials required to hand. The first task is to ...

... remove body fittings from effected area, except those which can act as a guide to the original shape of the damaged bodywork - the headlamp shell in this case.

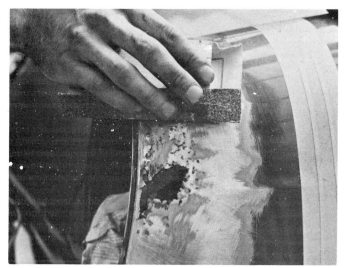

Remove all paint from the rusted area and from an inch or so of the adjoining 'sound' bodywork - use coarse abrasive paper or a power drill fitted with a wire brush or abrasive pad. Gently hammer in the edges of the hole to provide a hollow for the filler.

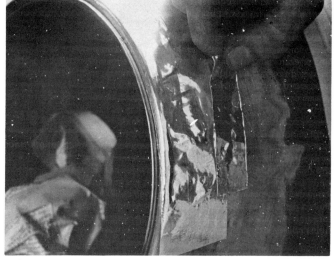

Before filling, the larger holes must be blocked off. Adhesive aluminium tape is one method; cut the tape to the required shape and size, peel off the backing strip (where used), position the tape over the hole and burnish to ensure adhesion.

Alternatively, zinc gauze can be used. Cut a piece of the gauze to the required shape and size; position it in the hole below the level of the surrounding bodywork; then ...

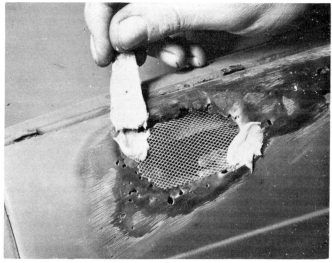

... secure in position by placing a few blobs of filler paste around its periphery. Alternatively, pop rivets or self-tapping screws can be used. Preparation for filling is now complete.

Mix filler and hardener according to manufacturer's instructions - avoid using too much hardener otherwise the filler will harden before you have a chance to work it.

Apply the filler to the affected area with a flexible applicator - this will ensure a smooth finish. Apply thin layers of filler at 20 minute intervals, until the surface of the filler is just 'proud' of the surrounding bodywork. Then ...

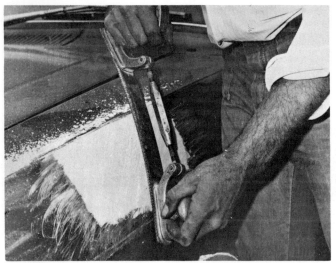

... remove excess filler and start shaping with a Surform plane or a dreadnought file. Once an approximate contour has been obtained and the surface is relatively smooth, start using ...

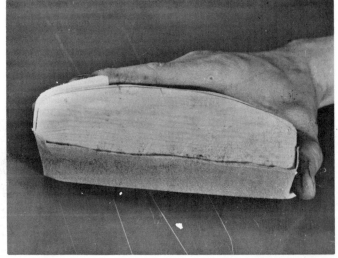

... abrasive paper. The paper should be wrapped around a flat wood, cork or rubber block - this will ensure that it imparts a smooth surface to the filler.

40 grit production paper is best to start with, then use progressively finer abrasive paper, finishing with 400 grade 'wet-and-dry'. When using 'wet-and-dry' paper, periodically rinse it in water ensuring also, that the work area is kept wet continuously.

Rubbing-down is complete when the surface of the filler is really smooth and flat, and the edges of the surrounding paintwork are finely 'feathered'. Wash the area thoroughly with clean water and allow to dry before commencing re-spray.

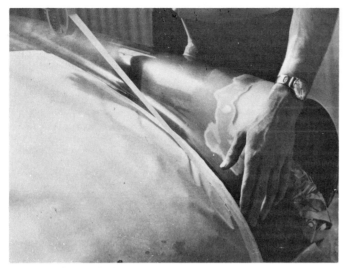

Firstly, mask off all adjoining panels and the fittings in the spray area. Ensure that the area to be sprayed is completely free of dust. Practice using an aerosol on a piece of waste metal sheet until the technique is mastered.

Spray the affected area with primer - apply several thin coats rather than one thick one. Start spraying in the centre of the repair area and then work outwards using a circular motion - in this way the paint will be evenly distributed.

When the primer has dried inspect its surface for imperfections. Holes can be filled with filler paste or body-stopper, and lumps can be sanded smooth. Apply a further coat of primer, then 'flat' its surface with 400 grade 'wet-and-dry' paper.

Spray on the top coat, again building up the thickness with several thin coats of paint. Overspray onto the surrounding original paintwork to a depth of about five inches, applying a very thin coat at the outer edges.

Allow the new paint two weeks, at least, to harden fully, then blend it into the surrounding original paintwork with a paint restorative compound or very fine cutting paste. Use wax polish to finish off.

The finished job should look like this. Remember, the quality of the completed work is directly proportional to the amount of time and effort expended at each stage of the preparation.

If the car is painted with a two-coat metallic finish an entirely different technique is required. The materials may be obtained from the official agent. Two types of repair are possible, the 80°C drying method and the Air-drying method. A 'wet-on-wet' procedure for the topcoat and clear varnish is used. The repair can be done satisfactorily only if the specified top coat and varnish are used with the specially developed synthetic thinner. After filling with Filler L145 if required sand down with the 400-500 wet and dry paper. Apply the first top coat using synthetic resin metallic paint LKL or spraying viscosity 15-17 seconds (DIN cup 4 mm). Let the paint flash off for 25 minutes, then apply the second layer of Air-drying L100 clear varnish with hardener L101 mixed in proportion 8:1. This becomes unusable after six hours. The repair is dust dry after 30 minutes but requires up to 8 days for complete drying. As can be seen it is a complicated process and you are advised to go to the official agent for advise if you have not done the job before. If you have other than a metallic finish then proceed as follows.

An alternative to painting over the scratch is to use Holts ' scratch patch'. Use the same preparation for the affected area; then simply pick a patch of a suitable size to cover the scratch completely. Hold the patch against the scratch and burnish its backing paper; the patch will adhere to the paintwork, freeing itself from the backing paper at the same time. Polish the affected area to blend the patch into the surrounding paintwork. Where a scratch has penetrated right through to the metal of the bodywork causing the metal to rust, a different repair technique is required. Remove any loose rust from the bottom of the scratch with a penknife, then apply rust inhibiting paint (eg; Kurust) to prevent the formation of rust in the future. Using a rubber or nylon applicator fill the scratch with bodystopper paste. If required, this paste can be mixed with cellulose thinners to provide a very thin paste which is ideal for filling narrow scratches. Before the stopperpaste in the scratch hardens, wrap a piece of smooth cotton rag around the tip of a finger. Dip the finger in cellulose thinners and then quickly sweep it across the surface of the stopperpaste in the scratch; this will ensure that the surface of the stopperpaste is slightly hollowed. The scratch can now be painted over as described earlier in this Section.

Repair of dents in the bodywork

When deep denting of the car's bodywork has taken place, the first task is to pull the dent out, until the affected bodywork almost attains its original shape. There is little point in trying to restore the original shape completely, as the metal in the damaged area will have stretched on impact and cannot be reshaped fully to its original contour. It is better to bring the level of the dent up to a point which is about 1/8 inch (3 mm) below the level of the surrounding bodywork. In cases where the dent is very shallow, it is not worth trying to pull it out at all.

If the underside of the dent is accessible, it can be hammered out gently from behind, using a mallet with a wooden or plastic head. Whilst doing this, hold a suitable block of wood firmly against the impact from the hammer blows and thus prevent a large area of bodywork from being 'belled-out'.

Should the dent be in a section of the bodywork which has a double skin or some other factor making it inaccessible from behind, a different technique is called for. Drill several small holes through the metal inside the dent area - particularly in the deeper sections. Then screw long self-tapping screws into the holes just sufficiently for them to gain a purchase in the metal. Now the dent can be pulled out by pulling on the protruding heads of the screws with a pair of pliers.

The next stage of the repair is the removal of the paint from the damaged area, and from an inch or so from the surrounding 'sound' bodywork. This is accomplished most easily by using a wire brush or abrasive pad on a power drill, although it can be done just as effectively by hand using sheets of abrasive paper. To complete the preparations for filling score the surface of the bare metal with a screwdriver or the tang of a file, or alternatively drill small holes in the affected areas. This will provide a really good key for the filler paste.

To complete the repair see the Section on filling and respraying.

Repair of rust holes or gashes in the bodywork

Remove all paint from the affected area and from an inch or so of the surrounding 'sound' bodywork, using an abrasive pad or wire brush on a power drill. If these are not available a few sheets of abrasive paper will do the job just as effectively. With the paint removed you will be able to gauge the severity of the corrosion and therefore decide whether to replace the whole panel (if this is possible) or to repair the affected area. Replacement body panels are not as expensive as most people think and it is often quicker and more satisfactory to fit a new panel than to attempt to repair large areas of corrosion.

Remove all fittings from the affected areas except those which will act as a guide to the original shape of the damaged bodywork (eg; headlamp shells etc.,). Then using tin snips or a hacksaw blade, remove all loose metal and any other metal badly affected by corrosion. Hammer the edges of the hole inwards in order to create a slight depression for the filler paste.

Wire brush the affected area to remove the powdery rust from the surface of the remaining metal. Paint the affected area with rust inhibiting paint (eg; Kurust). If the back of the rusted area is accessible treat this also.

Before filling can take place it will be necessary to block the hole in some way. This can be achieved by the use of one of the following materials: Zinc gauze, Aluminium tape or Polyurethane foam.

Zinc gauze is probably the best material to use for the large hole. Cut a piece to the approximate size and shape of the hole to be filled, then position it in the hole so that its edges are below the level of the surrounding bodywork. It can be retained in position by several blobs of filler paste around its periphery.

Aluminium tape should be used for small or very narrow holes. Pull a piece off the roll and trim it to the appropriate size and shape required, then pull off the backing paper (if used) and stick the tape over the hole; it can be overlapped if the thickness of one piece is insufficient. Burnish down the edges of the tape with the handle of a screwdriver or similar to ensure that the tape is securely attached to the metal underneath.

Polyurethane foam is best used where the hole is situated in a section of bodywork of complex shape, backed by a small box section (eg; where the sill panel meets the rear wheel arch - most cars). The unusual mixing procedure for this foam is as follows. Put equal amounts of fluid from each of the two cans provided into one container. Stir until the mixture begins to thicken, then quickly pour this mixture into the hole, and hold a piece of cardboard over the larger apertures. Almost immediately the polyurethane will begin to expand, squirting out of any holes left unblocked. When the foam hardens it can be cut back to just below the level of the surrounding bodywork with a hacksaw blade.

Bodywork repairs - filling and re-spraying

Before using this Section, see the Sections on dent, deep scratch, rust hole and gash repairs.

Many types of bodyfiller are available, but generally speaking those proprietary kits which contain a tin of filler paste and a tube of resin hardener (eg; Holts Cataloy) are best for this type of repair. A wide, flexible plastic or nylon applicator will be found invaluable for imparting a smooth and well contoured finish to the surface of the filler.

Mix up a little filler on a piece of card or board - use the hardener sparingly (follow the maker's instructions on the packet), otherwise the filler will set very rapidly.

Using the applicator, apply the filler paste to the prepared area; draw the applicator across the surface of the filler to achieve the correct contour and to level the filler surface. As soon as a contour that approximates the correct one is achieved, stop working the paste - if you carry on too long the paste will become sticky and begin to 'pick up' on the applicator. Continue to add thin layers of filler paste at twenty-minute intervals until the level of the filler is just 'proud' of the surrounding bodywork.

Once the filler has hardened, excess can be removed using a Surform plane or Dreadnought file. From then on, progressively finer grades of abrasive paper should be used, starting with a 40 grade production paper and finishing with 400 grade 'wet-and-dry' paper. Always wrap the abrasive paper around a flat rubber, cork or wooden block - otherwise the surface of the filler will not be completely flat. During the smoothing of the filler surface the 'wet-and-dry' paper should be periodically rinsed in water. This will ensure that a very smooth finish is imparted to the filler at the final stage.

At this stage the 'dent' should be surrounded by a ring of bare metal, which in turn should be encircled by the finely 'feathered' edge of the good paintwork. Rinse the repair area with clean water, until all of the dust produced by the rubbing-down operation is gone.

Spray the whole repair area with a light coat of grey primer - this will show up any imperfections in the surface of the filler. Repair these imperfections with fresh filler paste or bodystopper, and once more smooth the surface with abrasive paper. If bodystopper is used, it can be mixed with cellulose thinners to form a really thin paste which is ideal for filling small holes. Repeat this spray and repair procedure until you are satisfied that the surface of the filler, and the feathered edge of the paintwork are perfect. Clean the repair area with clean water and allow to dry fully.

The repair area is now ready for spraying. Paint spraying must be carried out in a warm, dry, windless and dust free atmosphere. This condition can be created artificially if you have access to a large indoor working area, but if you are forced to work in the open, you will have to pick your day very carefully. If you are working indoors, dousing the floor in the work area with water will 'lay' the dust which would otherwise be in the atmosphere. If the repair area is confined to one body panel, mask off the surrounding panels; this will help to minimise the effect of a slight mis-match in colours. Bodywork fittings (eg; chrome strips, door handles etc) will also need to be masked off. Use genuine masking tape and several thicknesses of newspaper for the masking operation.

Before commencing to spray, agitate the aerosol can thoroughly, then spray a test area (an old tin or similar) until the technique is mastered. Cover the repair area with a thick coat of primer; the thickness should be built up using several thin layers of paint rather than one thick one. Using 400 grade 'wet-and-dry' paper, rub down the surface of the primer until it is really smooth. While doing this, the work area should be thoroughly doused with water, and the 'wet-and-dry' paper periodically rinsed in water. Allow to dry before spraying on more paint.

Spray on the top coat, again building up the thickness by using several thin layers of paint. Start spraying in the centre of the repair area and then, using a circular motion, work outwards until the whole repair area and about 2 inches of the surrounding original paintwork is covered. Remove all masking material 10 to 15 minutes after spraying on the final coat of paint.

Allow the new paint at least 2 weeks to harden fully; then using a paintwork renovator (eg; T-Cut) or a very fine cutting paste, blend the edges of the new paint into the exising paintwork. Finally apply wax polish.

5 Major body damage - repair

1 Where serious damage has occurred or large areas need renewal due to neglect it means certainly that completely new sections or panels will need welding in and this is best left to professionals. If the damage is due to impact it will also be necessary to check the alignment of the body structure. In such instances the services of an agent with specialist checking jigs are essential. If a body is left misaligned it is first of all dangerous as the car will not handle properly - and secondly, uneven stresses will be imposed on the steering, engine and transmission, causing abnormal wear or complete failure. Tyre wear will also be excessive.

6 Front wings - removal and replacement

1 A badly damaged front wing may be removed complete and replaced by a new one. The wing is secured with 10 fixing screws. Refer to Fig. 13.1 in which the locations of the screws are shown. Those marked 'A1' are under the wing and not easily accessible.
2 It will be necessary to remove the side bumper before removing the wing. The screws fastening the wing are fitted very tightly and may not come out without considerable force. Do not use an impact screwdriver or you will distort the frame. It may be necessary to grind off the heads and drill out the shanks.
3 Once all the screws are out, the wing may be levered away pulling it out of the guides. If it does not come out easily it may be necessary to warm the line of the joint with a blow lamp to melt the adhesive under-seal. Be careful how you do this, for apart from the fire risk to the car the adhesive is also inflammable.
4 When removing, lever the wing away from the wheel housing and the door pillar, work it too-and-fro, pulling it forwards to the front of the car a little.
5 Clean up the frame and paint with inhibitor if any rust is present. Use a good sealing tape along the line of the bolts before installing the wing, and once the wing is securely in place treat the underside with underseal compound. Refer to Section 4 for respraying techniques, (the

last few paragraphs).

7 Radiator grille - removal and replacement

The grille is held in position by eight screws. There are four along the top, visible when the bonnet is opened. There are two more by each headlamp. Fig. 13.2 refers.

8 Rear door strut and lock - removal and replacement

1 Open the door and remove the straps which support the rear tray. Disconnect the door prop if a gas filled strut is fitted. Now it is necessary to ease the headlining cover from over the hinge bolts. Be careful not to tear it. Remove the hinge bolts. This will need an impact screwdriver with a special bit. Slacken all the bolts and then with a helper holding the lid remove the bolts and lift the rear door away. If a heated rear window is fitted the electrical circuit must be disconnected before the bolts are removed. In this case remove the battery earth strap before proceeding.
2 When reinstailing, fit the bolts and tighten them hand-tight. Close the door and check that there is an even gap around and that the lock works correctly. If it does not then adjust the hinges until it does. Tighten the hinge bolts firmly and install the headlining over them. Refit the door prop.
3 If the door prop is to be replaced, it is important to get the correct one. There are two kinds, type 'A' has one groove around the body of the strut just at the top. This type of strut has the tube attached to the door and the piston rod to the car body. The other type, 'B', has two grooves and the tube is attached to the body while the piston rod is attached to the door. Both struts have the same part number (171 827 550 A) but if you try to fit one in place of the other, the door will not function properly. Make sure you get the same type as the one taken off.
4 The lock is held to the bottom edge of the door by three crosshead screws. No repair to the lock is possible. If it is faulty remove it and fit a new one (photo).

9 Bumpers - removal and replacement

1 The front bumper of the Golf/Scirocco consists of a crossmember and two side pieces. The side pieces are secured to the cross piece by a stud and not to the wing by two studs and nuts. These are accessible from inside the wing. The side pieces must be removed before the brackets holding the cross piece may be removed. The parking light connections must be disconnected, then the bolts holding the brackets undone and the bumper taken away. It is best to replace a damaged bumper with a new one. The shape of the wing section where the side bumper is located on the Scirocco was altered in November 1974 but the change has not affected the fitting of the bumper.
2 The rear bumper is removed in the same way without the complication of the parking lights. The change in body contour presents a small problem. The older pattern of side bumper may not be available. If so the base of the studs on the new side bumpers must be filed away to give a chamfer of approximately 3 mm (1/8 in) to fit the side of the body. It will be necessary to drill two holes at the same level as the existing ones in the body but 12 mm (1/2 in) towards the rear. The holes should be made with a 6 mm drill (size A). The old holes must be plugged with rubber plugs, part number 111 857 145 A.
3 The Rabbit/Scirocco (USA) bumpers are a different business. To remove the front bumper remove the wires connecting the parking light and from underneath the car remove the bolts holding recuperators to the bodyframe. The bumper may then be removed and the recuperator taken off the bumper bar.
4 The bolts holding the rear bumper recuperators are accessible from inside the car on the wheelarch at floor level.

10 Bonnet - removal and replacement

1 The bonnet, or engine compartment cover, is hinged at the rear and held shut by a lock operated from inside the vehicle. It is held to the hinge by two bolts on each side. Remove these, and it may be lifted off and taken away. Two people are needed to lift it, not because it is

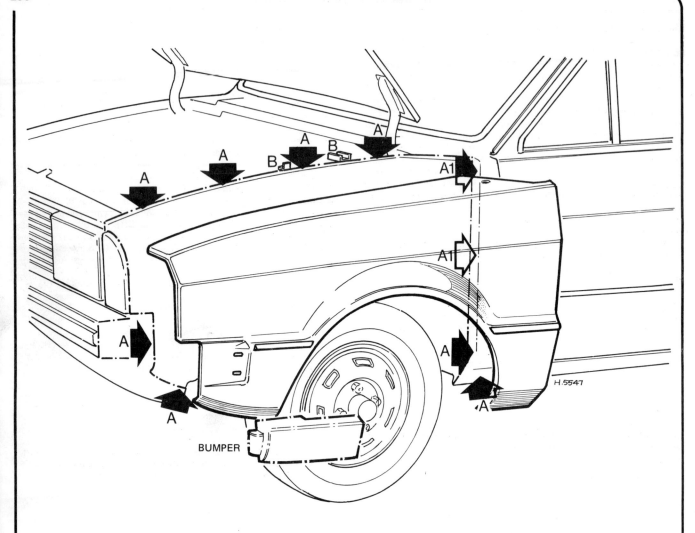

Fig. 13.1. Front wing - location of fixing screws (Sec. 6)

Note: Wing is shown in continuous line, car frame with broken line
A1   Two screws under the wing
A   Eight screws along the top and front of the wing
B   Guides
C   Bumper fixing location

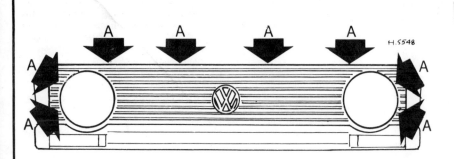

Fig. 13.2. Radiator grille - Golf/Rabbit (Sec. 7)

A = Position of fixing screws

8.4 The rear door lock is secured by three crosshead screws

heavy but to avoid scratching the paint.

11 Bonnet cable and lock - removal, refitting and adjustment

1 Inside the car remove the centre cover under the fascia, then the cover on the side of the bonnet lock handle and the glovebox. The cable now accessible at the inside end. Before it can be removed it must be released from the lock which is mounted in the centre of the cross-member just above the radiator grille.

2 Open the bonnet, remove the radiator grille and disconnect the cable.

3 Now back inside the car undo the crosshead screws which hold the bonnet catch release handle bracket to the side of the car and lift the bracket away from the trim. In the centre of the upper end of the operating handle is a small clamping plate. Bend this outwards and the handle may be released from the bracket. The cable may now be pulled out of the handle and out of the car. If you are wise you will tie a piece of thin wire or cord to the inside end and pull that into the place the cable occupied to make fitting a new cable more simple.

4 Replacement is the reverse of removal. Do not forget the water trap grommet. If a new cable is obtained from the official VW agent it will be the correct length, if you use other material the length must be determined by trial and error. Fasten the cable in the handle and assemble the handle to the car. Lead the cable through the correct run and measure the right amount to operate the lock correctly. The cable must be routed in such a way that there is no strain on it. Set the catch in the lock lower part without preload. Bend the cable over after securing it.

5 The top half of the lock may be removed by undoing two hexagon head bolts (photo).

12 Exterior mirror - fitting

1 If an extra mirror is to be fitted, to the rear side door look for a small rubber grommet on the top of the door moulding and lever it away (photo). Two holes are left and directly under them are the threaded holes in the support plate underneath. Line the mirror bracket with these holes and screw the bracket to the support plate.

2 If by chance these holes are not already drilled, as may happen on the Scirocco then holes may be drilled to gain access to the supporting plate which is installed underneath. Refer to Fig. 13.3. At the dimensions shown drill two 3mm holes (no. 31 drill). Put a small piece of sticky tape on the door where the holes are to go and mark the centres on the tape. This will help to prevent the drill wandering.

3 Locate th holes in the support plate and open the holes in the door panel to 10 mm (0.4 in) using a flat angle drill and taking care not to damage the threads in the plate underneath. Tidy the holes and paint any exposed metal then fit the mirror.

13 Seats - removal and replacement

1 Details of the methods of moving and adjusting the seats are given in the VW instruction handbook.

2 Removal of the front seat from the car is done in the following manner. At the back of the runners are small caps, lever these off the runners. Now look under the seat. There is an extra clip which must be removed and then the seat can be pushed onto the rear. When installing fit the spring clips in the upper slide, install the seat from the rear guiding the adjusting lever into the latch bolt mountings. Refit the covers on the runners.

3 The rear seat on the Scirocco may be removed after the backrest has been taken out. Press the backrest away from its guide on the driver's side of the car and pull the backrest forward onto the seat. Lift it out of the car. Now push the seat back and then lift up the front edge to unhook it from the securing clips. Installation is the reverse . When fitting the backrest guide it into the mounting on the right-hand side and then push the left-hand side in hard.

14 Doors (front) - removal and replacement

1 The hinges on the Golf/Rabbit are secured to the pillar with shallow socket headed bolts which are very difficult to undo unless the special tools are available. They are also in an awkward position. If the socket

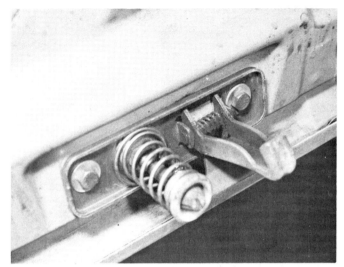

11.5 The top half of the bonnet catch

12.1 To fit the extra mirror remove the small rubber grommet from the top of the door

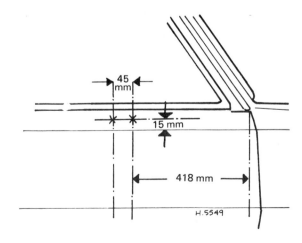

Fig. 13.3. Dimensions for drilling holes to fit extra mirror (Scirocco only) (Sec. 12)

45 mm = 1.77 in, 15 mm = 0.6 in, 418 mm = 16.45 in.

heads are damaged and the hexagon hole is converted into a round one then you are in serious trouble, as it will be necessary to drill the bolt and extract it with a special bolt extractor. For this reason we recommend that door hinges should be undone by professionals with the correct equipment. However, if you can undo these bolts the door is easily removed.

2 Take the pin out of the check strap, slacken the hinge bolts, have someone hold the door while you remove the bolts, and lift the door away. Check the weather strip and fit a new one, if necessary.

3 When installing the door first remove the door striker bolt from the frame. You cannot adjust the hinge while this is in place. Fit the door to the pillar and tighten the hinge bolts enough to hold the door in place. Close the door and check that the gap all round the edge is symmetrical. Adjust the hinge until it is correct then tighten the hinge bolts fully. Refit the striker bolt and adjust the lock if necessary (photo).

4 It is possible to remove the Scirocco door by driving the hinge pins out. Drive these downwards to extract and insert them from underneath. The hinges must be removed to adjust the hang of the door.

15 Door interior trim - removal and replacement

1 It is not necessary to remove the trim to remove the outside handle - see Section 16.

2 To remove the trim, first remove the window handle, door pull and the lock lever cover. The lock remains in place.

3 To remove the door pull, prise the covers from each end and slide them to the centre of the strap (photo). The four retaining screws may then be removed.

4 Pull the plastic cover off the window winder boss and turn it away from the boss, leaving it on the winder handle knob (photo). Remove the crosshead screw and the winder handle can be pulled away. It is best to close the window before doing this and note the angle of the handle when the window is shut.

5 Remove the screw from the centre of the lock lever cover plate and pull the cover off. The lock remains in place (photos).

6 Using a flat, smooth, piece of wood or plastic inserted between the

14.3 The door lock is secured by two screws

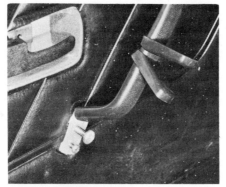

15.3 Pull the plastic tabs off the ends of the door pull and ease them into the centre, then remove the securing screws

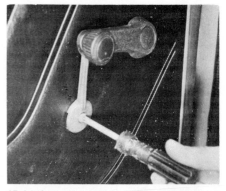

15.4 Lift the plastic cover off the winder handle, turn it out of the way and unscrew the screw in the centre

15.5a Remove the screw from the centre of the remote control lever plate and pull the cover off ...

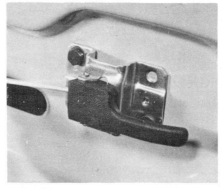

15.5b ...when the trim is removed the control remains in position

15.6 A stud in the corner on the back of the trim

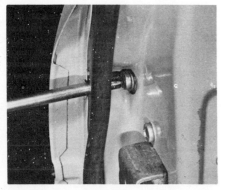

16.1 Move the rubber seal and undo the screw to remove the door handle

16.2a Door handle (exterior) removed

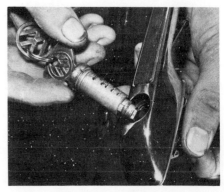

16.2b Withdraw the lock to the back

trim and the door ease the clips out of the door. The clips must remain in the trim (photo)so be careful, lever as near to the clip as possible.
7 Installation is the reverse of removal.

16 Door handle (exterior) - removal and replacement

1 Lift the rubber moulding away from the door just above the door lock and remove the screw situated in the recess (photo).
2 Push the door handle forward towards the hinge and extract the back of the handle first. The front end is held by a fork (photo). The lock barrel may now be removed (photo). If the lock is damaged take it to the VW agent to have the correct lock installed to fit your door key.
3 When replacing the handle make sure the handle lever engages with the door lock.
4 When removing the barrel lock always leave the key in the lock or the tumblers and springs will fall out.

17 Door lock mechanism - servicing

1 Remove the interior trim (Section 15). Remove the plastic cover from the face of the door. Refer to Fig. 13.4. Press the clip off the linkage inside the door (photo).
2 Remove the two screws, holding the remote control lever in the centre of the door, disengage the long link and then disconnect it from the lock.
3 Undo the two screws holding the lock to the door (photo 14.3) and remove the lock through the door opening.
4 When assembling make sure the door handle operating lever engages

17.1 The door lock inside the door, disconnect leakage 'A'

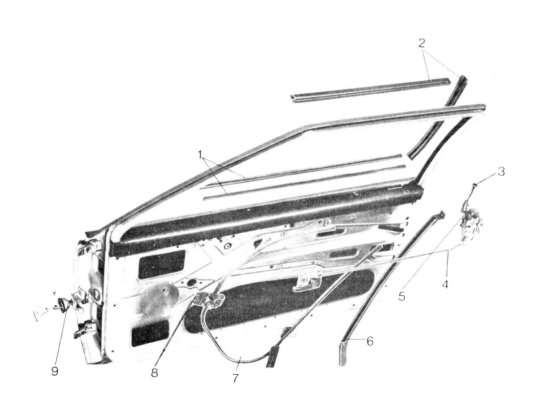

Fig. 13.4. Door assembly (Scirocco) - exploded view (glass not shown) (Sec. 17)

1 Window slot seals	4 Lock remote control rod	7 Winder assembly
2 Window guides	5 Door lock	8 Winder handle shaft
3 Interior lock control	6 Window channel rear	9 Door strap

with lock operating lever.

5   There is little that can be done to a faulty lock. The mechanism is
mostly made of pressed parts which can neither be repaired nor renewed.
The lock can be moved to the limits of the screws shown in photo 14.3
to engage the striker bolt more easily. The striker bolt may be rotated a
little if worn.

18 Window winder mechanism - servicing

1   Remove the door trim and plastic sheet.
2   The window glass may be disconnected from the window by undoing
the two bolts which secure the window support strip to the window
bracket (photo).
3   The winder mechanism is tubular and is secured at the bottom of the
door by a clip. It proceeds from there vertically through the winder
handle gear and then bends to the left inside the door along the top in
clips and then descebds vertically to the base of the door where it is
secured again. In this leg the stirrup which is bolted to the base of the
window glass operates.
4   By removing the screws which hold the winder handle mechanism
and then feeling inside for the various clips and brackets which retain
the winder cable it may be eventually be freed and withdrawn from the
door. It is a fiddling job and because the cable is covered with grease
you will get into a mess. The cable may be loose in the tube, which
causes an annoying rattle and may be cured by closing the opening in
the tube a little. When replacing the winder, or a new one, push and
pull it roughly into position, connect the wir.dow loosely and then fit
the winder handle to the door. Disconnect the window again and wind
the bracket up and down, adjusting the position of the window in its
clips until the bracket moves up and down freely. Now reconnect the
window to the bracket and test it again. It is a question of patience rather
than skill, and going softly for it is easy to damage a new winder when
fitting it to the door.

18.2 The bracket connecting the window glass to the window

19 Window glass - removal and replacement

The refitting of window glass is not difficult but it is fraught with
dangers. The trim and winder must be removed, and then the centre
channel which is bolted to the inside of the door frame. The slot seals
are secured with clips. The guides are removed top first and then rear,
and replaced rear first, top second. We do not recommend this job for
the D-I-Y owner. Unless it is done exactly right the window will rattle
and leak. The mouldings and clips have an exasperating way of cracking
and must then be replaced. Since you have to sit next to this part of the
car and suffer if it is not right we suggest that you leave it to the
expert.

Metric conversion tables

Inches	Decimals	Millimetres	Millimetres to Inches		Inches to Millimetres	
			mm	Inches	Inches	mm
1/64	0.015625	0.3969	0.01	0.00039	0.001	0.0254
1/32	0.03125	0.7937	0.02	0.00079	0.002	0.0508
3/64	0.046875	1.1906	0.03	0.00118	0.003	0.0762
1/16	0.0625	1.5875	0.04	0.00157	0.004	0.1016
5/64	0.078125	1.9844	0.05	0.00197	0.005	0.1270
3/32	0.09375	2.3812	0.06	0.00236	0.006	0.1524
7/64	0.109375	2.7781	0.07	0.00276	0.007	0.1778
1/8	0.125	3.1750	0.08	0.00315	0.008	0.2032
9/64	0.140625	3.5719	0.09	0.00354	0.009	0.2286
5/32	0.15625	3.9687	0.1	0.00394	0.01	0.254
11/64	0.171875	4.3656	0.2	0.00787	0.02	0.508
3/16	0.1875	4.7625	0.3	0.01181	0.03	0.762
13/64	0.203125	5.1594	0.4	0.01575	0.04	1.016
7/32	0.21875	5.5562	0.5	0.01969	0.05	1.270
15/64	0.234375	5.9531	0.6	0.02362	0.06	1.524
1/4	0.25	6.3500	0.7	0.02756	0.07	1.778
17/64	0.265625	6.7469	0.8	0.03150	0.08	2.032
9/32	0.28125	7.1437	0.9	0.03543	0.09	2.286
19/64	0.296875	7.5406	1	0.03947	0.1	2.54
5/16	0.3125	7.9375	2	0.07874	0.2	5.08
21/64	0.328125	8.3344	3	0.11811	0.3	7.62
11/32	0.34375	8.7312	4	0.15748	0.4	10.16
23/64	0.359375	9.1281	5	0.19685	0.5	12.70
3/8	0.375	9.5250	6	0.23622	0.6	15.24
25/64	0.390625	9.9219	7	0.27559	0.7	17.78
13/32	0.40625	10.3187	8	0.31496	0.8	20.32
27/64	0.421875	10.7156	9	0.35433	0.9	22.86
7/16	0.4375	11.1125	10	0.39370	1	25.4
29/64	0.453125	11.5094	11	0.43307	2	50.8
15/32	0.46875	11.9062	12	0.47244	3	76.2
31/64	0.484375	12.3031	13	0.51181	4	101.6
1/2	0.5	12.7000	14	0.55118	5	127.0
33/64	0.515625	13.0969	15	0.59055	6	152.4
17/32	0.53125	13.4937	16	0.62992	7	177.8
35/64	0.546875	13.8906	17	0.66929	8	203.2
9/16	0.5625	14.2875	18	0.70866	9	228.6
37/64	0.578125	14.6844	19	0.74803	10	254.0
19/32	0.59375	15.0812	20	0.78740	11	279.4
39/64	0.609375	15.4781	21	0.82677	12	304.8
5/8	0.625	15.8750	22	0.86614	13	330.2
41/64	0.640625	16.2719	23	0.90551	14	355.6
21/32	0.65625	16.6687	24	0.94488	15	381.0
43/64	0.671875	17.0656	25	0.98425	16	406.4
11/16	0.6875	17.4625	26	1.02362	17	431.8
45/64	0.703125	17.8594	27	1.06299	18	457.2
23/32	0.71875	18.2562	28	1.10236	19	482.6
47/64	0.734375	18.6531	29	1.14173	20	508.0
3/4	0.75	19.0500	30	1.18110	21	533.4
49/64	0.765625	19.4469	31	1.22047	22	558.8
25/32	0.78125	19.8437	32	1.25984	23	584.2
51/64	0.796875	20.2406	33	1.29921	24	609.6
13/16	0.8125	20.6375	34	1.33858	25	635.0
53/64	0.828125	21.0344	35	1.37795	26	660.4
27/32	0.84375	21.4312	36	1.41732	27	685.8
55/64	0.859375	21.8281	37	1.4567	28	711.2
7/8	0.875	22.2250	38	1.4961	29	736.6
57/64	0.890625	22.6219	39	1.5354	30	762.0
29/32	0.90625	23.0187	40	1.5748	31	787.4
59/64	0.921875	23.4156	41	1.6142	32	812.8
15/16	0.9375	23.8125	42	1.6535	33	838.2
61/64	0.953125	24.2094	43	1.6929	34	863.6
31/32	0.96875	24.6062	44	1.7323	35	889.0
63/64	0.984375	25.0031	45	1.7717	36	914.4

1   Imperial gallon = 8 Imp pints = 1.16 US gallons = 277.42 cu in = 4.5459 litres

1   US gallon = 4 US quarts = 0.862 Imp gallon = 231 cu in = 3.785 litres

1   Litre = 0.2199 Imp gallon = 0.2642 US gallon = 61.0253 cu in = 1000 cc

Miles to Kilometres		Kilometres to Miles	
1	1.61	1	0.62
2	3.22	2	1.24
3	4.83	3	1.86
4	6.44	4	2.49
5	8.05	5	3.11
6	9.66	6	3.73
7	11.27	7	4.35
8	12.88	8	4.97
9	14.48	9	5.59
10	16.09	10	6.21
20	32.19	20	12.43
30	48.28	30	18.64
40	64.37	40	24.85
50	80.47	50	31.07
60	96.56	60	37.28
70	112.65	70	43.50
80	128.75	80	49.71
90	144.84	90	55.92
100	160.93	100	62.14

lb f ft to Kg f m		Kg f m to lb f ft		lb f/in^2: Kg f/cm^2		Kg f/cm^2: lb f/in^2	
1	0.138	1	7.233	1	0.07	1	14.22
2	0.276	2	14.466	2	0.14	2	28.50
3	0.414	3	21.699	3	0.21	3	42.67
4	0.553	4	28.932	4	0.28	4	56.89
5	0.691	5	36.165	5	0.35	5	71.12
6	0.829	6	43.398	6	0.42	6	85.34
7	0.967	7	50.631	7	0.49	7	99.56
8	1.106	8	57.864	8	0.56	8	113.79
9	1.244	9	65.097	9	0.63	9	128.00
10	1.382	10	72.330	10	0.70	10	142.23
20	2.765	20	144.660	20	1.41	20	284.47
30	4.147	30	216.990	30	2.11	30	426.70

Index

Colour Code for all Current Flow Diagrams

BLUE:

Blue	Bl
Blue and White	Bl/W
Blue/Yellow	Bl/Y
Blue/Black	Bl/B
Blue/Grey	Bl/Gr
Blue/Light Green	Bl/LG
Blue/Brown	Bl/Br

BLACK:

Black	B
Black/White	B/W
Black/Yellow	B/Y
Black/Blue	B/Bl
Black/White/Light Green	B/W/LG
Black/Grey	B/Gr
Black/Dark Green	B/DG
Black/Red	B/R
Black/Mauve	B/M
Black/Light Green	B/LG

GREY:

Grey	Gr
Grey/Red	Gr/R
Grey/Black	Gr/B
Grey/Blue	Gr/Bl
Grey/Light Green	Gr/LG
Grey/Dark Green	Gr/DG

YELLOW:

Yellow	Y
Yellow/Blue	Y/Bl
Yellow/Black	Y/B
Yellow/Red	Y/R
Yellow/White	Y/W

DARK GREEN:

Dark Green	DG
Dark Green/Red	DG/R
Dark Green/Yellow	DG/Y
Dark Green/Black	DG/B

LIGHT GREEN:

Light Green	LG
Light Green/Black	LG/B
Light Green/Yellow	LG/Y
Light Green/Red	LG/R

RED:

Red	R
Red/Black	R/B
Red/Yellow	R/Y
Red/White	R/W

MAUVE:

Mauve	M
Mauve/Black	M/B

WHITE:

White	W
White/Black	W/B

BROWN:

Brown	Br
Brown/White	Br/W
Brown/Blue	Br/Bl